Neoliberalism and Contemporary Literary Culture

Neoliberalism and Contemporary Literary Culture

Edited by
MITCHUM HUEHLS
University of California, Los Angeles
and
RACHEL GREENWALD SMITH
Saint Louis University

Johns Hopkins University Press
Baltimore

Johns Hopkins University Press
2715 North Charles Street
Baltimore, Maryland 21218-4363
www.press.jhu.edu

Library of Congress Cataloging-in-Publication Data

Names: Huehls, Mitchum, 1976– editor. | Smith, Rachel Greenwald, editor.
Title: Neoliberalism and contemporary literary culture / edited by Mitchum Huehls and Rachel
    Greenwald Smith.
Description: Baltimore : Johns Hopkins University Press, 2017. | Includes bibliographical
    references and index.
Identifiers: LCCN 2016049251 | ISBN 9781421423104 (pbk. : alk. paper) | ISBN 9781421423111
    (electronic) | ISBN 1421423103 (pbk. : alk. paper) | ISBN 1421423111 (electronic)
Subjects: LCSH: Politics and literature—United States—History—20th century. | Literature
    and society—United States—History—20th century. | Neoliberalism—United States.
Classification: LCC PS228.P6 N37 2017 | DDC 810.9/3581—dc23
LC record available at https://lccn.loc.gov/2016049251

A catalog record for this book is available from the British Library.

*Special discounts are available for bulk purchases of this book. For more information,
please contact Special Sales at 410-516-6936 or specialsales@press.jhu.edu.*

Johns Hopkins University Press uses environmentally friendly book materials,
including recycled text paper that is composed of at least 30 percent
post-consumer waste, whenever possible.

CONTENTS

This project is, first and foremost, the product of the energy, intelligence, and commitment of its contributors. Thanks especially to Min Hyoung Song, Jennifer Ashton, and Matthew Wilkens for presenting their works in progress at the 2015 Association for the Study of the Arts of the Present conference. Many thanks also to Matt McAdam and Catherine Goldstead at Johns Hopkins University Press, Jeremy Horsefield for copyediting the volume, and the anonymous readers of the manuscript. We also thank the UCLA Friends of English for their financial support of the project. A condensed version of Walter Benn Michaels's "Fifty Shades of Neoliberal Love" appeared in the *Los Angeles Review of Books* as "Fifty Shades of Libertarian Love," and a version of Jennifer Ashton's "Totaling the Damage: Neoliberalism and Revolutionary Ambition in Recent American Poetry" appeared on *nonsite.org*. Jane Elliott's "The Microeconomic Mode" is forthcoming as "The Microeconomic Mode: Survival Games, Life-Interest and the Re-imagination of Sovereignty," in *Novel*, volume 51. Copyright, 2018, Novel, Inc. All rights reserved. It is republished by permission of the copyright holder and the present publisher, Duke University Press (www.dukeupress.edu). Thanks to *LARB*, *nonsite*, and Duke University Press for granting us permission to reprint that material here. Finally, thanks to our families for offering support, encouragement, and patience through the process of editing this volume.

Neoliberalism and Contemporary Literary Culture

Four Phases of Neoliberalism and Literature

An Introduction

MITCHUM HUEHLS

RACHEL GREENWALD SMITH

Protean, polymorphous, and frequently perverse, neoliberalism is everywhere but also, perhaps, nowhere. Depending on your critical viewpoint, the expansiveness of the term makes it either absolutely vital or totally useless for critical work on contemporary culture. Consequently, any investigation of the relationship between literature and neoliberalism must begin by proving the existence of something specific worthy of being called "neoliberalism" in the first place. We can't presuppose the coherence of our object of study. Or, as Mathias Nilges argues in his essay for this volume, when one writes about literature and neoliberalism in today's critical environment, it can feel as if one is trying to convincingly articulate the relationship between literature and the Sasquatch.

This Sasquatch-like quality has spurred some major critiques of the concept. A cadre of scholars—primarily anthropologists, geographers, and urban theorists—have pushed back against what they see as the overuse of *neoliberalism* as a critical term. Clive Barnett provides an apt example, as he views neoliberalism as a "consolation" for certain left-leaning academics: the term not only "supplies us with plentiful opportunities for unveiling the real workings of hegemonic ideologies in a characteristic gesture of revelation" but also "invites us to align our own professional roles" with real-world acts of "resistance or contestation."[1] Consequently, Barnett cautions us against reducing sociological complexity to economic structure, mistaking new "modalities of power" for older forms of hegemony and ideological interpellation, and imagining that so-called neoliberalism systematically opposes all things public, collective, and regulatory.[2] Without denying the economic inequality, social injustice, and corporate dominance plaguing contemporary life, thinkers like Barnett remain reluctant to blame a fuzzy concept like neoliberalism for our current condition.[3] In our own discipline, such critiques coalesced during the notorious "Kill This Keyword" panel at the 2014

American Studies Association meeting, which included *neoliberalism* as one of several critical terms that might be "so overused as to be evacuated of any specificity."[4]

Yet all the while neoliberalism has stubbornly refused to be killed. Whereas in 2012 only three sessions at the Modern Language Association's annual convention listed "neoliberalism" as one of their keywords, in 2016 there were eleven sessions that included the term in their description. The past three years have seen the publication of two special issues on neoliberalism and literature in major journals in the field, with at least one more in the works.[5] And the term *neoliberalism* has gone from appearing in 4 percent of ProQuest-archived dissertations in literature in 2010 to 9 percent in 2016. Neoliberalism may be an increasingly contentious term in literary studies, but its influence is still very much on the rise.

The controversial nature of the term stems, in part, from the fact that even the most widely accepted definitions of neoliberalism diverge sharply. David Harvey describes neoliberalism as an economic project, grounded in the free-market principles of Friedrich Hayek and Milton Friedman, initially designed to "restore the power of economic elites" after 1970s stagflation signaled the demise of postwar embedded liberalism.[6] More bluntly, Henry Giroux sees neoliberalism as "a more virulent and brutal form of market capitalism" justifying rapacious corporations' plunder of the earth's natural and human resources.[7] In distinction to such strictly materialist accounts, Lisa Duggan figures neoliberalism as a pro-business "secular faith" that manipulates our understanding of race, gender, sexuality, and religion in the interest of conservative politics and capital accumulation.[8] Taking an even broader approach, Wendy Brown conceives neoliberalism as a "political rationality" that "involves extending and disseminating market values to all institutions and social action."[9] For Brown, those market values change the very structure of neoliberal subjects who must transform themselves from *homo politicus* into *homo œconomicus*, an entrepreneurial form of subjectivity that refigures the human as human capital. While Brown still views *homo œconomicus* as a normatively constructed subject position, others describe *homo œconomicus* as uniquely removed from ideological and/or hegemonic modes of normative subject formation.[10] Distinct from Harvey's materialism, Duggan's politics, and Brown's "political rationality," this approach draws on Foucault's notion of governmentality, a neoliberal form of biopower that works on bodies from a distance, concerning itself more with the "*conduire des conduites*" (the conduct of conduct) than with belief and behavior.[11] As Aihwa Ong explains, neoliberalism as a "technology of government" establishes "a new relationship between government and knowledge through which governing activities are recast as nonpolitical and non-ideological problems that need technical solutions."[12] According to this model, neoliberalism sculpts environments but doesn't really worry about mystifying and manipulating the entrepreneurial subjects populating them.

Meanwhile, efforts to periodize contemporary literature have been similarly plural, internally contradictory, and fraught with disagreement. This is particularly true of recent efforts to define the literary period that follows postmodernism, efforts that have produced a dizzying proliferation of terms such as *late postmodernism, post-postmodernism, supermodernism, metamodernism, cosmodernism,* and *exomodernism*.[13] As Andrew Hoberek argues, the moment after postmodernism is characterized by "uneven transformations [in] a phase of as-yet uncategorized diversity similar to the one that prevailed following World War II."[14] And for Brian McHale, our moment is "another of those thresholds where cultural-historical and world-historical transitions coincide." McHale goes on to ask, "The question here is, the threshold of *what?* The transition to *what?*"[15] It would be reductive to suggest that "neoliberalism" could serve as a simple and universal answer to McHale's question. But, as the essays in this volume attest, the rise of neoliberalism does help to explain the coincidence of seemingly multiple and even internally contradictory aspects of contemporary literary culture. Moreover, literature can help us better understand some of the more confounding contradictions that appear to exist within theories of neoliberalism.

In what follows, we will contend that neoliberalism has advanced historically through four different phases or modes: the economic, the political-ideological, the sociocultural, and the ontological. The layering of these different phases explains much of the definitional complexity facing any contemporary attempt to deploy neoliberalism as a critical or analytic term. The story of these four phases' unfolding also maps onto the widely accepted story of post–Cold War literature. Neoliberalism's economic and political-ideological phases largely correspond to postmodernism's prominence in the 1970s and 1980s, a period that saw a handful of early literary attempts to represent and respond to neoliberal policies. Its sociocultural and ontological phases coincide with the period beginning in the 1990s when postmodernism started to lose purchase as both a theoretical and an aesthetic paradigm. As a result, texts from the 1970s and 1980s frequently represent neoliberal economic and political policies and their effects, but it isn't until the 1990s and 2000s—when neoliberalism expands more granularly into the sociocultural and ontological fabric of everyday life, and thus into the very structures and forms that writers use to make sense of the realities they represent, construct, and imagine—that we begin to see its effect on literary theory and form.

Guided by this idea that recent literary history broadly reflects the changing effects of neoliberalism on different registers of experience, this volume focuses in particular on the period stretching from the waning of postmodernism in the 1990s up through the present because that's when neoliberalism begins to inflect literary culture in much more profound ways.

Our aim in developing this four-phase approach to the historical emergence of neoliberalism is to provide a taxonomy that might allow us both to understand why theories of neoliberalism have been so contradictory and to see how the relationship between neoliberalism and literary culture has shifted over the past several decades. Our hope is that in offering such a mapping of theory, history, and literature, we can address the perceived incoherence of the field while maintaining a breadth of coverage, both here and in the chapters we have collected, that will be useful to students and scholars new to the field. We have, however, focused our geographical coverage, both in this introduction and in the volume as a whole, primarily on the United States and Great Britain. We focus on these two major sites of neoliberal policy, implementation, and cultural production not out of ignorance as to the significant effects neoliberalism has had on Latin America, Asia, and other parts of the globe, but out of a necessary narrowing of attention to literary institutions, forms, works, and approaches that have been in direct conversation with one another throughout the neoliberal period.

Origins

Neoliberalism doesn't emerge ex nihilo in the 1970s, but instead grows out of the various liberalisms implemented in the United States and select European nations after World War II. At Bretton Woods, the July 1944 gathering of delegates from all forty-five allied nations that birthed the International Monetary Fund (IMF), the World Bank, and the next three decades of international economic policy, classical liberalism's core philosophical principles—civil liberty and economic freedom—were emphasized but also reconciled with social liberalism's core values of equality and justice. This "Keynesian compromise" resulted in the embedded liberalism—a free-market economy "embedded" in a social safety net ensuring some semblance of justice and parity—that defined social and economic policy in the United States and England until the 1970s. Although its economists weren't invited to summer in New Hampshire in 1944, West Germany implemented similar economic reforms immediately after the war that facilitated its relatively speedy recovery. Balancing free-market economics with social welfare and government regulations designed to prevent monopolies, West German ordoliberalism aligned the country with the US-Anglo economic consensus, and West Germany officially joined the IMF in August 1952.[16]

Looked at differently, however, the balance that embedded liberalism achieved between liberty and equality, between freedom and justice, might just as easily be viewed as a tension or contradiction.[17] Doubly allergic to the New Deal social engineering of the 1930s and the postwar spread of communism, many economists, policy makers, and cultural leaders doubled down on classical liberalism, thereby laying the intellectual foundation for neoliberalism's emergence later in the twentieth century. In 1947, for example, Friedrich Hayek convened a group of economists, philosophers, and historians at a conference in Switzerland (Karl Popper and Milton Friedman were both there) to strategize a response to what they viewed as the ascendance of Keynesianism and Marxism around the globe. The group named themselves the Mont Pelerin Society; still in existence today, it has founded a number of think tanks committed to fighting all forms of collectivism. In 1950s New York, a weirder group of intellectuals, ironically calling themselves "the Collective," gathered around Ayn Rand to absorb and propagate the "philosophy" of selfishness she named "objectivism." Those ideas, first introduced in *The Fountainhead* in 1943, were crystallized in *Atlas Shrugged* in 1957, a text that Alan Greenspan, the chair of the US Federal Reserve between 1987 and 2006, read in draft form as an early disciple of the Collective. The contemporary influence of *Atlas Shrugged* extends far beyond Greenspan to the US Supreme Court, where Clarence Thomas cites it as a crucial text; the office of the US Speaker of the House, where it's required reading for Paul Ryan's interns; and everyday readers, who voted it the best book of the twentieth century in an online Modern Library poll.[18] Insofar as neoliberalism began as a form of theoretical utopianism, literature has been central to its development beginning in its earliest moments.

The Four Phases

In the decades immediately following World War II, then, we find the socioeconomic and cultural prehistory of the multifaceted neoliberalism that emerges in the concluding three decades of the twentieth century. That emergence begins with neoliberalism's *first, economic phase*, which can be traced back to 1971 when President Richard Nixon unpegged the dollar from its regulated gold equivalent, effectively undoing the Bretton Woods monetary agreement operative internationally since the end of World War II. Because the dollar was the international reserve currency, when the United States untethered the dollar from gold, other industrial nations followed suit, freeing capital to move more easily across inter-

national borders and creating conditions ripe for the accelerated rise of speculative financial capitalism. Although this deregulatory shock was actually followed
by a series of Keynesian regulations, the resulting stagflation of the mid-1970s
convinced economists that regulations should be further curtailed. As chairman
of the Federal Reserve in the late 1970s and early 1980s, Paul Volcker produced
the conditions necessary for free-market capital accumulation when he raised US
interest rates to over 20 percent, thereby stamping down inflation even as unemployment soared. In this period, economic stability increasingly became synonymous with labor deregulation, increased interest rates, privatized public services,
and local markets open to international competition.[19]

This was also true internationally, as the United States began exporting its
new economic rationality to Central and South America in an attempt to stem
communist influence in the region. In Chile, for example, US support for Au-
gusto Pinochet's 1973 overthrow of the Marxist president Salvador Allende was
accompanied by a cadre of Chicago School economists, trained by Milton Friedman, who brought the gospel of privatization and free trade to the newly dictatorial government. In the 1980s, the IMF imposed similarly neoliberal policies,
euphemistically referred to as "structural adjustments," on other Latin American
countries seeking relief from a widespread debt crisis. Although neoliberal economic policies emerge across the Americas in the 1970s and 1980s, the Latin
American nations ultimately follow a different path from the United States. There,
resistance to IMF austerity measures engendered numerous indigenous political
movements, and by the early twenty-first century many Latin American nations
(Uruguay, Brazil, Venezuela, Bolivia) recognized the failures of this grand neoliberal experiment and moved leftward to embrace a post-neoliberal socioeconomic
framework (the so-called pink tide turn to socialism).[20] Conversely, the United
States and Great Britain doubled down on neoliberal economics, expanding its
logic to the political, social, and cultural domains of everyday life.[21]

That expansion begins with the *second, political phase* of neoliberalization
when Ronald Reagan and Margaret Thatcher actively transform these economic
principles into the dominant political ideology of the 1980s. Of course, neoliberal
economic policies continued apace (the ten free-market principles governing domestic and international economic development are codified as the "Washington
Consensus" in 1989), but Reagan and Thatcher deftly integrated those economic
principles into their political and legislative agendas, further ensuring neoliberalism's ascendance. In both Britain and the United States, for example, the elevated unemployment produced by higher interest rates designed to fight inflation
became a means to weaken labor and privatize public institutions. Lower taxes,

deregulation, free and private markets: Reagan and Thatcher explicitly linked these economic concepts to a political conservatism motivated by anticommunism, Christian morality, and a generalized fear of minorities and immigrants. Sure, these free-market economic policies were always beliefs—Friedrich Hayek believed in them; Milton Friedman believed in them—but the 1980s saw those beliefs vigorously politicized and marshaled to establish conservative voting coalitions, enact regressive tax legislation, and erode the social safety net.[22]

In the 1980s, then, we also see the representational content of literature begin to address neoliberalism as both economic innovation and political policy. This is true for novels such as Jay McInerney's *Bright Lights, Big City* (1984), Bret Easton Ellis's *Less Than Zero* (1985), and Tom Wolfe's *The Bonfire of the Vanities* (1987), which describe the transformation of economic policy into lived political ideology through more conventional narrative forms. And it's also true of works that remain committed to the formal experimentation of the 1970s. Neoliberalism begins to inflect literary subject matter, for example, in postmodern works such as William Gibson's *Neuromancer* (1984), a science fiction novel about global privatization; Margaret Atwood's *The Handmaid's Tale* (1985), a speculative imagining of a religious right dystopia; Martin Amis's *Money* (1984) and *London Fields* (1989), two self-reflexive treatments of Thatcherite London, which complement Salman Rushdie's *The Satanic Verses* (1988) and Hanif Kureshi's *The Buddha of Suburbia* (1990), both of which explore the status of the postcolonial immigrant under similar conditions; and Thomas Pynchon's *Vineland* (1990), his postmodern take on 1980s Reaganomics. The 1980s also usher in an important moment in the literary history of neoliberalization as writers associated with 1960s and 1970s social, political, and avant-garde movements begin to find institutional and, at times, commercial success. We see this in phenomena ranging from the acceptance of Language Poetry into the academy to the widespread market success of antiracist and antisexist works such as Leslie Marmon Silko's *Ceremony* (1977), Alice Walker's *The Color Purple* (1982), Gloria Anzaldúa's *Borderlands / La Frontera* (1987), Toni Morrison's *Beloved* (1987), and Ana Castillo's *So Far from God* (1993). Finally, the 1980s saw the beginning of major changes in the publishing industry, with more publishing house mergers occurring in the four years between 1984 and 1988 than during the entire decade of the 1960s.[23]

If the 1980s saw a set of neoliberal economic policies explicitly politicized into a broader system of ideological belief, then the Clinton–Blair nineties mark a more granular extension of that ideology to previously noneconomic domains of human life. During the Cold War, neoliberal economic policy and its concomitant political ideology were historical tactics that the West deployed in its protracted geopolitical struggle with communism. Once the West emerged victorious, how-ever, neoliberalism lost that historical specificity. No longer an economic and ideo-logical weapon of the Cold War, neoliberalism gradually came to appear natural, universal, and true. Or as Francis Fukuyama famously declared, history ended and "the worldwide ideological struggle that called forth daring, courage, imagi-nation, and idealism, [was] replaced by economic calculation, the endless solving of technical problems, environmental concerns, and the satisfaction of sophisti-cated consumer demands."[24]

This is the moment in which neoliberalism enters its *third, sociocultural phase*, subjecting literature and other forms of art, alongside community, education, romance, entertainment, health, technology, law, and nature, to a rigorous eco-nomic calculus committed to efficient profit maximization. Culture absorbs and diffuses neoliberalism's bottom-line values, saturating our daily lives with for-profit rationalities of commerce and consumerism, eventually shifting neoliber-alism from political ideology to normative common sense. In turn, this phase of neoliberalism's rise initiates a more profound effect on literature as its entrepre-neurial spirit extends beyond representational content to begin influencing liter-ary form. David Foster Wallace, Jonathan Franzen, Dave Eggers, and other writ-ers who came to adulthood during the late postmodern period, for example, often articulated their formal innovations as responses to the literary marketplace, suggesting that reading and writing were activities that should be evaluated ac-cording to a market model. For these white male writers, this self-fashioning was often a direct response to the threat of other competing audiences and products. While Jonathan Franzen lamented the disappearance of his "tribe" of white male readers and saw a readership of women and people of color on the rise, David Foster Wallace worried about the effects of television on the readership for liter-ary fiction.[25] The would-be inheritors of high literary culture, then, saw their time as a moment of scarcity, leading them to treat formal literary innovation as a matter of competition, market assessment, and entrepreneurial risk-taking. Or as Wallace asserts, perhaps subconsciously channeling his inner Gordon Gekko, "The next real literary 'rebels' in this country . . . [must] risk things."[26] Emerging first and foremost in the context of neoliberalism's post–Cold War sociocultural phase, such writing—variously described as "post-postmodernism," "post-irony," and "The New Sincerity"[27]—doesn't just evince the neoliberal spirit on the level of these authors' formally "risky" choices. In addition, its so-called sincerity and commitment to "single-entendre values,"[28] whether manifest through Wallace's experimentalism, Franzen's realism, or Eggers's memoirism, reiterate neoliberal capital's expanding investment in consumer affect and sentiment.[29]

Meanwhile, with the 1996 debut of Oprah's Book Club, a new level of literary celebrity suddenly became possible, particularly for women writers and writers of color working in the genres of fiction and, increasingly as the decade progressed, memoir. This, in turn, gave greater prominence to what Walter Benn Michaels has dubbed "the novel of identity" or "the neoliberal novel," which, along with the memoir, he sees as "the neoliberal genre par excellence."[30] These forms, Michaels argues, place emphasis on individual and cultural identity to the exclusion of a larger structural understanding of the economy. For Michaels, neoliberalism allows, even encourages, diversity and the expression of individuality, because these forms of expression do not challenge the economic inequality at the root of neoliberal policy. Accordingly, the commodification of identity writing that occurred during the 1990s would come under critique by writers of color in the 2000s, beginning with Percival Everett's novel *Erasure* (2000), a blistering satire of literary prize culture and its dependence on notions of racial "authenticity" that are as often as not rooted in racist assumptions about what nonwhite voices, experiences, and expressions should look like.

The 1990s also saw a significant turn in poetry, with the emergence of a series of vehicles for the publication of work by poets who sought to avoid the polarizations of the 1970s and 1980s between the experimental tradition of Language Poetry on the one hand and the conservative, populist new formalism on the other.[31] For instance, Rebecca Woolf echoes both the anxieties and the entrepreneurial attitudes of Franzen, Wallace, and Eggers in her 1997 manifesto for the establishment of *Fence Magazine*: "There is nothing radical about this magazine," she writes. "*Fence* stands against . . . that which has been framed and sentenced to inaccessibility. We seek, above all, to increase the reader's pleasure."[32] This editorial policy of individualism, pluralism, and anticollectivism would make *Fence* among the most influential publications of the 1990s and 2000s, signaling the success of what Steve Evans argued was *Fence*'s participation in "the ideology of merge and market."[33]

Gradually, this extension of market rationality to otherwise noneconomic domains of life shifts from a way of thinking—quantitative, efficient, pragmatic, and profitable—to a way of being. No longer just a set of ideological beliefs or deployable rationalities, neoliberalism becomes what we are, a mode of existence defined by individual self-responsibility, entrepreneurial action, and the maximization of human capital. In this *fourth, ontological phase* of neoliberalism, neutral markets frame but do not determine the subjects acting within them. The market does not require specific economic pursuits, political commitments, or ideological beliefs; it only requires our presence, our being in and of it—which isn't hard, because after the expansion of neoliberalism in its third phase, the market and its bottom-line logic are everywhere. The market's neutral omnipresence in this fourth, ontological moment of neoliberalism also explains the increasing sense that the world has become post-ideological and post-political. What used to be matters of political belief and social justice—racial equality, gay marriage, transgender bathroom access—are now wholeheartedly endorsed by corporations committed to whatever proves best for business. PayPal's resistance to North Carolina's Public Facilities Privacy & Security Act, for example, provides the company the sheen of social justice activism even as it reduces political antagonism to economic calculation.

For many of the contributors to this volume, our contemporary moment requires an alternative to this form of biopolitical subjectivity that glides smoothly through a depoliticized world of networked relations and immaterial labor. These new modes of being are symptomatic of neoliberalism's immanence, and politics entails countering the neoliberal totality with forms of meaningful antagonism. This fourth phase of neoliberalism is also marked, however, by another set of scholars and theorists who accept neoliberalism's ontological transformations but explore alternative modes of being as potential forms of immanent resistance.[34] The emergence of this work explains why the much-discussed decline of High Theory that began in the 1990s finds its fulfillment here in neoliberalism's ontological phase: the critical power of poststructurally inflected Marxism, feminism, postcolonialism, and other politically committed theoretical approaches loses purchase on a reality fully subsumed by capital. Consequently, as many of the essays in this volume point out, the 2000s witnessed the full ascendance of a set of philosophical realisms—affect theory, biopolitics, ecocriticism, object-oriented ontology, embodiment theory, actor–network theory, and animal studies—all of which reformulate politics primarily as a way of being rather than as a way of thinking. Under the influence of this new body of theory after Theory, literary criticism begins a complementary shift in its methodological approach to literary inquiry. As the essays from Min Hyoung Song and Jason Baskin explain, with some skepticism, literary studies in the past decade have substantially embraced various forms of anti-symptomatic reading—surface reading, distant reading, reparative reading—which challenge what a critical politics can and should look like in our neoliberal age.

Authors of literary fiction have been wrestling with similar questions for at least two decades, producing texts that challenge readers to imagine what it would mean to mean differently, for meaning and value to derive not from referential acts of representation but from being's relation to other beings, as well as its relative position in space. For many writers of color this entails a move away from thinking about the representational "meaning" or "value" of racial and ethnic identity in favor of exploring its affective, bodily, networked way of being in the world. We can see this shift, for example, in contemporary work from Colson Whitehead, Karen Yamashita, Percival Everett, Chris Abani, Helena Viramontes, Teju Cole, Mat Johnson, Myriam Gurba, and Junot Díaz. Claudia Rankine's *Citizen* (2014), an extended meditation on the "feeling" of micro-aggressive racism, fits the post-representational bill as well. Equally invested in the value of being, independent of reference and representation, works like Tom McCarthy's *Remainder* (2005) and David Foster Wallace's *The Pale King* (2011), along with Ben Marcus's *Notable American Women* (2002) and *The Flame Alphabet* (2012), use language to construct alternative spaces where being can "mean" differently. Much of this work seems on its face to be post-racial and/or post-political. But that diagnosis misses the fact that these authors are also trying to think about politics immanently, biopolitically, and nondialectically. Although Michael Szalay's essay in this volume is skeptical of its ability to do so, Jennifer Egan's *A Visit from the Goon Squad* (2010) certainly attempts to imagine a politics immanent to neoliberal capital, as do an array of other contemporary novels deeply invested in revolutionary politics despite not being overtly revolutionary themselves: Dana Spiotta's *Eat the Document* (2006), Jonathan Lethem's *Dissident Gardens* (2013), Ben Lerner's *10:04* (2014), Viet Thanh Nguyen's *The Sympathizer* (2015), Susan Choi's *American Woman* (2003) and *A Person of Interest* (2008), and Rachel Kushner's *Telex from Cuba* (2008) and *The Flamethrowers* (2013). All of the texts and authors mentioned here, writing under this fourth, ontological phase of neoliberalism, recognize the potential obsolescence of earlier forms of representation and critique and struggle in various ways to develop new literary modes that acknowledge that condition without succumbing to the neoliberal totality that produced it in the first place.[35]

The unevenness of that struggle explains why some essays in this volume find qualified success (e.g., Jeffrey Nealon's reading of Robert Fitterman's "Directory," Jason Baskin's take on Lisa Robertson's *Occasional Work and Seven Walks from the Office for Soft Architecture*, and Jennifer Ashton's analysis of Lerner's *10:04*) while others see tendentious complicity (Jane Elliott's examination of Gillian Flynn's *Gone Girl*, Michael Szalay's evaluation of Egan, and Leigh Claire La Berge's treatment of Sam Lipsyte's campus novel *The Ask*) in contemporary literature's engagement with neoliberalism. And this lengthy historical trajectory—in which neoliberalism begins as a series of economic policies later deployed as a political ideology that eventually suffuses the sociocultural landscape until it becomes a post-ideological mode of existence—explains why contemporary scholarship is populated with so many competing takes on neoliberalism. Someone like David Harvey highlights neoliberalism's economic mode, while Lisa Duggan emphasizes its function as political ideology; Wendy Brown targets its sociocultural normativity, and Aihwa Ong focuses on its ontological effects.[36] Of course, as we noted before, just because neoliberalism's competing definitions can be historicized in terms of their moment of emergence doesn't mean that only one version operates exclusively at any given time. Instead, neoliberalism only becomes more complicated as the decades pass, accumulating economic, political, social, and cultural valences, while insinuating itself materially, ideologically, normatively, and ontologically.

The Chapters

Given this complexity, it shouldn't be surprising that our literary moment is one of dizzying plurality. The essays collected in this volume are evidence of the range of literary theories, forms, representations, and institutions that characterize our moment and offer insight into the mechanisms of neoliberalization.

The essays included in the book's opening section, "Neoliberalism and Literary Theory," highlight shifts in both theory's object and application. Walter Benn Michaels's theorization of masochism as a neoliberal contract that extends to the laboring body provocatively rethinks Giorgio Agamben's work on biopolitics. Jane Elliott continues Michaels's attention to the body in her own unique theorization of "the microeconomic mode," a specifically neoliberal mode of existence that induces agonizing choices with often brutal effects on bodies and lives. While both Michaels and Elliott register the aesthetic implications of this material shift in theory's object, those implications are further pursued in three other essays that more explicitly consider how this theoretical shift appears in the writing and reading of literature. Min Hyoung Song, wary of the potentially depoliticizing effect the new materialism might have on a commitment to racial politics, investigates both the limits and possibilities that a focus on material surfaces might have for scholarly work on race. Less circumspect, Jeffrey Nealon embraces theory's recent turn to objects and finds new political possibilities in the most thing-based of conceptual writing. Finally, Jason Baskin complicates the debate between surface and depth, advocating a synthesis of the two that he grounds in Merleau-Ponty's dialectical approach to modes of perception.

The second section of the volume, "Neoliberalism and Literary Form," finds that while contemporary developments in literary form—the return to realism, shifts in characterization and point of view, the rise of the memoir, innovations in the lyric—cannot be understood to have been solely determined by the widespread expansion of neoliberalism, we can nevertheless identify echoes of the neoliberal commitment to entrepreneurialism, individualism, and pragmatism in these formal shifts. It is therefore possible to read the major formal changes of the period as generally symptomatic of neoliberalism. As Mathias Nilges's contribution to this volume argues, the advent of neoliberalism can be understood to initiate a broad shift toward realist fiction in the early 1990s. For Nilges, postmodernism speculatively anticipates neoliberalism before its thoroughgoing emergence in the social domain. The turn to realism occurs, he argues, once neoliberalism no longer needs innovative or speculative forms to anticipate its implementation. While Nilges views developments in contemporary literature as symptomatic of neoliberalism, Jennifer Ashton sees many attempts to challenge neoliberalism in works of lyric poetry as ultimately advocating attitudinal change over material change, reflecting personal pain rather than structural exploitation. But turning to Ben Lerner's recent novel, *10:04*, she also highlights an opportunity for works of art to address their relationship to the structure of neoliberal exploitation more directly and, she argues, more fruitfully. And finally, Marcial González and Daniel Worden look at narrative and generic forms under neoliberalism. González investigates the role narrative omniscience plays in the oppression of farmworkers in Salvador Plascencia's *People of Paper*, suggesting that the forms of narrative resistance the farmworkers employ in the novel stand as a productively innovative critique of neoliberalism's totalizing grasp. And Worden turns to a phenomenon that tends to be seen as merely symptomatic of neoliberal individualism—the memoir boom—and argues that while the genre does formally reinforce many neoliberal assumptions, some works of memoir, when they affectively engage the immediate experience of material limitation, also challenge the premium neoliberalism puts on entrepreneurial individualism.

When neoliberalism's third phase begins impinging on social and cultural organization, and when its fourth ontological phase begins altering the way contemporary subjects think about themselves and their relation to the world, we can reasonably expect literature's representational content to shift accordingly as well. Matthew Wilkens opens this volume's third section, "Neoliberalism and Literary Representation," by asking whether or not that expectation is actually as reasonable as it might initially seem. Hypothesizing that the ascendance of neoliberalism as a global economic condition should manifest itself in the literary output of the same time period, Wilkens uses computational methods to track the prevalence of specific geographical place-names in an archive of thousands of texts. Wilkens suggests that the emergence of economic powers like India and China under global neoliberalism should be echoed in literary representation. Finding no such correlation, however, he speculates that contemporary scholars have perhaps overstated the dominance of market logic in the literary sphere. The other essays in this section take a narrower approach, indicating that even if neoliberalism itself hasn't emerged as a statistically measurable presence in contemporary fiction, neoliberalism has most certainly altered the way literature represents many of its dominant themes and concerns. Sheri-Marie Harrison, for instance, contends that neoliberalism's economic instrumentalization of immigrants, along with its potentially complicit intersection with theories of cosmopolitanism, requires a substantial rethinking of the conventional immigrant narrative. Unable to trace a linear trajectory from the ethnic margins to assimilated cosmopolitan nationalism, what she terms the neoliberal novel of migrancy instead represents immigrants as simultaneously resistant to and complicit with neoliberalism. Caren Irr identifies a similar shift in the way contemporary fiction treats children, particularly orphans. No longer objects of affection or sympathy, Irr suggests that the orphan becomes a crucial literary figure through which neoliberalism articulates and justifies its ideal of entrepreneurial individualism. Finally, Andrew Hoberek dives deep into Gillian Flynn's *Gone Girl*, reading it as the paradigmatic realist novel of our contemporary neoliberal moment to the extent that it manages to represent the neoliberal socioeconomic totality at the level of individual character and subject formation.

The final section of the volume, "Neoliberalism and Literary Institutions," traces neoliberalism's influence on the many institutions that have bearing on literary culture, from the corporatization of the university to the advent of publishing mergers, and from changes in the structure of public and nonprofit arts funding to the rise of media conglomerates. In fact, the relationship between neoliberal institutional shifts and literary production can be quite direct. Michael Szalay, for instance, chronicles the incorporation of contemporary writers into the world of multinational media conglomerates as cable networks like HBO recruit successful contemporary fiction writers to produce television. Authors therefore literally become producers—producers of successful media commodities. Expanding Szalay's observations on the growing intimacy between art and neoliberal institutions, Sarah Brouillette finds that the very notion of aesthetic autonomy is an untenable fantasy in the neoliberal present, entirely disconnected from the real economy, which, she maintains, largely structures the literary field today. Further, insofar as autonomy is itself a neoliberal value, the concept of the autonomous artwork paradoxically becomes ideological support for the continued dominance of neoliberalism. Finally, as Leigh Claire La Berge argues, the very study of literature itself as promulgated in English departments supports the neoliberalization of the university. For La Berge, differentiating universities from corporations has grown difficult, as universities look increasingly like corporations while corporations, with their sprawling "campuses," look increasingly like universities. But universities are able to retain their status as nonprofit entities, she argues, because they contain areas that fundamentally violate, even as they tacitly support, the economic logic of investment and return: English departments and other humanities divisions.

The essays in this collection trace the multifaceted and sometimes conflicting impulses in contemporary literature, both to understand how our literary culture responds to the neoliberal moment and to understand how neoliberalism has fundamentally altered the trajectory of contemporary literary production. As neoliberalism invades and suffuses the sociocultural sphere in the early 1990s, and as market rationalities extend to the daily human interactions that literature comprises, literary culture begins channeling, and challenging, neoliberalism's ascendance. As the essays collected here detail, contemporary literature often capitulates to neoliberalism, working complicitly with it. And it frequently tries to resist neoliberalism, struggling to innovate epistemologies that might escape it. But literature also sometimes capitalizes on neoliberalism, appropriating its forms in ways that may or may not reinforce its logic. The reciprocal relation between neoliberalism and literature is complex and multidirectional, but we believe that the analysis of that relation in the essays in this volume marks an initial step in determining the crucial role literary culture plays in the production and manipulation of neoliberal thought.

NOTES

1. Clive Barnett, "The Consolations of 'Neoliberalism,'" *Geoforum* 36 (2005): 10.

2. Clive Barnett, "Publics and Markets: What's Wrong with Neoliberalism?," in *The SAGE Handbook of Social Geographies*, ed. Susan Smith et al. (London: SAGE, 2010), 280.

3. Other versions of this argument can be found in Jamie Peck, *Constructions of Neoliberal Reason* (Oxford: Oxford University Press, 2010); and Jamie Peck, Nik Theodore, and Neil Brenner, "Postneoliberalism and Its Malcontents," *Antipode* 41 (2009): 94–116.

4. "ASA Program Committee: Kill This Keyword?," American Studies Association Annual Meeting, November 7, 2014.

5. See "Genres of Neoliberalism," *Social Text* 115 (Summer 2013); and "Neoliberalism and the Novel," *Textual Practice* 29, no. 2 (2015). *Novel*'s special issue is forthcoming.

6. David Harvey, *A Brief History of Neoliberalism* (Oxford: Oxford University Press, 2005), 19.

7. Henry Giroux, "The Terror of Neoliberalism: Rethinking the Significance of Cultural Politics," *College Literature* 32 (2005): 2.

8. Lisa Duggan, *The Twilight of Equality? Neoliberalism, Cultural Politics, and the Attack on Democracy* (Boston: Beacon, 2003), xiii. Other examples of this more political take on neoliberalism would include Walter Benn Michaels, "Plots against America: Neoliberalism and Antiracism," *American Literary History* 18 (2006): 288–302; David Theo Goldberg, *The Threat of Race: Reflections on Racial Neoliberalism* (Malden, MA: Wiley-Blackwell, 2009); and Costas Douzinas, *The End of Human Rights: Critical Legal Thought at the Turn of the Century* (Portland, OR: Hart, 2000).

9. Wendy Brown, "Neo-liberalism and the End of Liberal Democracy," *Theory and Event* 7, no. 1 (2003).

10. For Brown, "Political rationality could be said to signify the *becoming actual* of a specific normative form of reason; it designates such a form as both a historical force generating and relating specific kinds of subject, society, and state and as establishing an order of truth by which conduct is both governed and measured." Brown's account of neoliberalism therefore could be seen as a bridge between those who see neoliberalism as a cluster of beliefs and those who, like Aihwa Ong, see neoliberalism as a form of governmentality. See Wendy Brown, *Undoing the Demos: Neoliberalism's Stealth Revolution* (Brooklyn, NY: Zone Books, 2015), 118.

11. Michel Foucault, *Dits et écrits IV* (Paris: Gallimard, 1994), 237. The degree to which governmentality should be seen as continuous with or distinct from Foucault's earlier work on the power–knowledge nexus remains a matter of considerable debate. Expansive discussions can be found in Vanessa Lemm and Miguel Vatter, eds., *The Government of Life: Foucault, Biopolitics, and Neoliberalism* (New York: Fordham University Press, 2014); and Stephen Collier, "Topologies of Power: Foucault's Analysis of Political Government beyond 'Governmentality,'" *Theory, Culture and Society* 26 (2009): 78–108.

12. Aihwa Ong, *Neoliberalism as Exception: Mutations in Citizenship and Sovereignty* (Durham, NC: Duke University Press, 2006).

13. For each of these, see, respectively, Jeremy Green, *Late Postmodernism: American Fiction at the Millennium* (New York: Palgrave, 2005); Jeffrey Nealon, *Post-postmodernism; or, The Cultural Logic of Just-in-Time Capitalism* (Stanford: Stanford University Press, 2012); Hans Ibelings, *Supermodernism: Architecture in the Age of Globalization* (Rotterdam: NAi, 1998); David James and Urmila Seshagiri, "Metamodernism: Narratives of Continuity and Revolution," *PMLA* 129 (2014): 87–100; Christian Moraru, *Cosmodernism: American Narrative, Late Globalization, and the New Cultural Imaginary* (Ann Arbor: University of Michigan Press, 2011); and Mark McGurl, "The New Cultural Geology," *Twentieth Century Literature* 57 (2011): 380–90.

14. Andrew Hoberek, "Introduction: After Postmodernism," *Twentieth Century Literature* 53, no. 3 (2007): 240.

15. Brian McHale, "Break, Period, Interregnum," *Twentieth Century Literature* 57, nos. 3–4 (Fall/Winter 2011): 333.

16. Of course, IMF membership does not necessarily align a country with the founding liberalisms of Bretton Woods. China, for example, is a founding member, and other influential member nations such as France and Japan pursued more interventionist economic policies after the war.

17. Harvey, for instance, sees "the crisis of capital accumulation" that occurred in the

1970s as the result of the contradictions internal to embedded liberalism. Harvey, *Brief History of Neoliberalism*, 14.

18. Clarence Thomas, *My Grandfather's Son* (New York: HarperCollins, 2007), 62; Katherine Mangu-Ward, "Young, Wonky, and Proud of It," *Weekly Standard*, March 17, 2003; Bruce Headlam, "Forget Joyce; Bring on Ayn Rand," *New York Times*, July 30, 1998, G4.

19. As these economic policy shifts suggest, the question of regulation under neoliberalism is tricky. In general, neoliberals oppose government regulation and intervention, but only those regulations and interventions that impede or erode the free market. Most neoliberals would admit, however, that the free market still requires government actions that maximize and ensure the market's freedom. Accordingly, neoliberalism is perfectly comfortable with the Federal Reserve manipulating interest rates, or the federal government bailing out the banks, even as it resists labor, consumer safety, and environmental regulations that might subtract from its bottom line.

20. Clarifying work on neoliberalism in Latin America includes Mark Goodale and Nancy Postero, *Neoliberalism Interrupted* (Stanford: Stanford University Press, 2013); Gustavo Flores-Macias, *After Neoliberalism?* (Oxford: Oxford University Press, 2012); and Eduardo Silva, *Challenging Neoliberalism in Latin America* (Cambridge: Cambridge University Press, 2009).

21. We can also observe neoliberalism's uneven development in East Asia, where explicitly neoliberal economic policies don't emerge until after the 1997 Asian financial crisis, which, as with the 1980s debt crisis in Latin America, leads to IMF "bailouts" that impose laissez-faire neoliberal policies on still-developing economies that were unprepared to handle them. For a good social-science take on this, see Bae-Gyoon Park, Richard Child Hill, and Asato Saito, eds., *Locating Neoliberalism in East Asia* (West Sussex: Wiley-Blackwell, 2011).

22. Milton and Rose Friedman's *Free to Choose: A Personal Statement*, published in 1980 and broadcast as a ten-episode documentary on PBS that same year, stands as a crucial moment when culture facilitated neoliberalism's pivot from economics to political ideology. Presented as a set of values that guides the Friedmans' lives (and a picture of the happy couple appears on the cover of one of the book's many editions), the book and television program extend and apply Friedman's Chicago School economics to issues like education, FDA regulation, unionization, and welfare.

23. Albert N. Greco, *The Book Publishing Industry* (London: Lawrence Erlbaum Associates, 2005), 54.

24. Francis Fukuyama, "The End of History?," in *Globalization and the Challenges of a New Century: A Reader*, ed. Patrick O'Meara et al. (Bloomington: Indiana University Press, 2000), 178.

25. See Jonathan Franzen, "I'll Be Doing More of Same," *Review of Contemporary Fiction* 16, no. 1 (1996): 34–38; and David Foster Wallace, "E Unibus Pluram: Television and U.S. Fiction," *Review of Contemporary Fiction* 13, no. 2 (1993): 151–94. See also Dave Eggers's autobiographical account of his founding of *Might* magazine in *A Heartbreaking Work of Staggering Genius* (New York: Simon & Schuster, 2000).

26. Wallace, "E Unibus Pluram," 192–93.

27. For key works on these movements, see, respectively, Robert L. McLaughlin, "Post-postmodern Discontent: Contemporary Fiction and the Social World," *symplokē* 12, nos. 1–2 (2004): 53–68; Lee Konstantinou, *Cool Characters: Irony and American Fiction* (Cam-

bridge, MA: Harvard University Press, 2016); and Adam Kelly, "David Foster Wallace and the New Sincerity in American Fiction," in *Consider David Foster Wallace: Critical Essays*, ed. David Hering (Los Angeles: Sideshow Media Group, 2010): 131–46. On Wallace and neoliberalism, see Ryan Brooks, "Conflict before Compromise: A Response to Rachel Greenwald Smith," *Account* 4 (2015).

28. Wallace, "E Unibus Pluram," 192.

29. See Rachel Greenwald Smith, *Affect and American Literature in the Age of Neoliberalism* (Cambridge: Cambridge University Press, 2015), for a treatment of how literary affect functions as a form of complicity with and, in rarer instances, as a form of resistance to neoliberalism in its third, sociocultural phase.

30. Walter Benn Michaels, "Model Minorities and the Minority Model—the Neoliberal Model," in *The Cambridge History of the American Novel*, ed. Leonard Cassuto, Clare Virginia Eby, and Benjamin Reiss (Cambridge: Cambridge University Press, 2011), 1016–30; Walter Benn Michaels, "Going Boom," *Bookforum* (February/March 2009), www.bookforum.com.

31. For a longer examination of the relationship between this moment in poetry's self-understanding and the rise of neoliberalism, see Rachel Greenwald Smith, "Six Propositions on Compromise Aesthetics," *Account* 2 (2014), http://theaccountmagazine.com/?article=six-propositions-on-compromise-aesthetics.

32. Rebecca Woolf, "Fence Manifesto of 1997," republished in *Jacket2* 12 (2000), http://jacketmagazine.com/12/wolff-fence.html.

33. Steve Evans, "The Resistible Rise of Fence Enterprises," *Third Factory: Notes to Poetry* (2004), http://thirdfactory.net/resistible.html.

34. One of the most influential versions of this argument can be found in Michael Hardt and Antonio Negri's *Empire* (Cambridge, MA: Harvard University Press, 2000), which calls for "an ontological basis of antagonism" immanent to neoliberal capital (21).

35. See Mitchum Huehls, *After Critique: Twenty-First-Century Fiction in a Neoliberal Age*, (Oxford: Oxford University Press, 2016), for a thorough treatment of contemporary literature's parsing of the political possibilities available to us in neoliberalism's fourth, ontological phase.

36. For other treatments of neoliberalism as post-normative ontology, see Eva Cherniavsky, "Neocitizenship and Critique," *Social Text* 27 (2009): 1–23; and James Ferguson, "The Uses of Neoliberalism," *Antipode* 41 (2009): 166–84.

PART I

NEOLIBERALISM AND LITERARY THEORY

Fifty Shades of Neoliberal Love

WALTER BENN MICHAELS

"There is no man who does not want to be a despot when he has an erection," says Giorgio Agamben in *Homo Sacer*.[1] He is, of course, quoting the Marquis de Sade, and his point in doing so is to suggest the ways in which the "biopolitical" "meaning of sexuality and physiological life itself" is anticipated in what he calls "sadomasochism." The sadist, he thinks, confronts the masochist as "bare life," and it is the essence of his sadism that he can do with her (or him) anything he likes, unconstrained by law. Sade's Château de Silling is, on this reading, an early incarnation of the Nazi *lager*, where "human beings" were "so completely deprived of their rights and prerogatives that no act committed against them could appear any longer as a crime."[2] And the Nazis themselves are early adopters of that "modern totalitarianism" made possible by the "worldwide deployment" of the state of exception.[3] Thus, what Agamben calls "the growing importance of sado-masochism in modernity" is due to the way in which "the totalitarian character of the organization of life in Silling's castle" has modeled the threat—from Auschwitz to Guantanamo—of totalitarianism itself. And the moment of sado-masochism is the moment in which the state of exception proves the rule, the moment of "emergency" in which the sovereign's suspension of the laws reveals that the law is itself founded on a power that it cannot itself authorize. This is the moment in which the liberal state appears not as the alternative to totalitarianism but as its condition of possibility.

There is, however, another possible reading of what Agamben calls the modernity of sadomasochism. If sadism comes from Sade, masochism comes from the Austrian writer Leopold von Sacher-Masoch, whose *Venus in Furs* makes power matter equally but differently. And if in one sense this difference is just the reverse face of sadism—what the sadist wants is to be a despot, whereas what the masochist wants is to be, as the hero of *Venus in Furs* declares, a "slave"—in another sense, it undoes rather than fulfills the complementarity of the despot–slave relation. For the masochist doesn't *just* want to be a slave; he wants to be a slave by "contract," like the contract in which he agrees to become the "property" of his cruel mistress while she, "in exchange," agrees to "appear as often as possible in fur, especially when she's being cruel to her slave,"[4] as well as like the several contracts Sacher-Masoch actually entered into with his mistresses. Masochism is thus linked from the start not only to compulsion but to choice, and that "cruel mistress" has remained central to its libidinal economy, which identifies freedom with the right to sell not only one's labor but also, if one chooses, one's person, and which insists on the pleasure associated with the exercise of that right. If, in other words, the appeal of sadism is identified with the deprivation of a right (slavery), the attraction of masochism is as the assertion of a right (volunteer slavery).

Furthermore, inasmuch as the right asserted is the right to contract, to buy and sell, it's a right that is available only in a market economy and is as alien to the Château de Silling as it was to Auschwitz, where, as Agamben points out, "economic considerations" were sacrificed to the assertion of the "sovereign power" over "bare life."[5] The camps, in other words, may represent the utopia of the sadist, but—unlinked to economic considerations, indeed "put into effect at all costs" when, as Agamben suggests, by any economic logic, the war effort should have made those costs unacceptable—they are the masochist's nightmare. Or to put the point more positively, the economistic logic of masochism represents and has since their inception represented not just an alternative to but also a critique of the sadism of the camps. Thus, something like Agamben's remark about the refusal of economic considerations has been canonical in discussions of Nazi racism at least since the trials at Nuremberg, when Albert Speer insisted that the "problem of creating armaments to win the war for Germany was made much more difficult" by the "anti-Jewish campaign" "waged" by his codefendants. If the Jews sent to death camps "had been allowed to work for me," Speer said, "it would have been a considerable advantage" for the war effort.[6]

But modern masochism cannot be understood merely as a commitment to the primacy of economic considerations. Rather, it requires a commitment to a specific economic form. And although the cruel mistress of *Venus in Furs* says that in the ancient world "liberty and slavery went hand in hand," the idea that choice turns slavery into freedom is actually oriented more to the future of von Mises and Hayek than to the past; indeed, for them, "economic liberty" and competitive markets provided what Foucault called a "fondation légitimante" for the state, designed to replace the will of the race-based *volk*.[7] So where for Speer the problem with racism was just that it was bad for production, for neoliberalism, the problem is that it was bad for capitalism. Thus, the critique of racism appears in its decisive neoliberal form in Gary Becker's *The Economics of Discrimination* (1957), which argues that racism is harmful not so much to workers as to capitalists. Why? Because the capitalist who will only employ, say, whites arbitrarily limits the labor force available to him and thus drives up his labor costs. "There is a remarkable agreement in the literature," Becker wrote, "on the proposition that capitalists from the dominant group are the major beneficiaries of prejudice and discrimination in a competitive capitalistic economic system."[8] But, he says, "If W is considered to represent whites or some other dominant group, the fallacious nature of this proposition becomes clear, since discrimination *harms* W capitalists and benefits W workers." And if this conclusion seemed surprising when it was first announced, today, as the Library of Economics and History website puts it, the "idea that discrimination is costly to the discriminator is common sense among economists."[9]

Thus, for free-market economists (for whom all relations are essentially economic), the history of the past half century has represented a repudiation of the camps (where no relations were economic) and, in particular, a repudiation of the racism in which both the inefficient and immoral refusal of the market is embodied. For Agamben, however, the threat of the camps and of racism's power to, in Judith Butler's words, make some lives more "grievable" than others remains central.[10] Indeed, the Patriot Act, he says, produces "a legally unnameable and unclassifiable being" whose status "can only be compared . . . to the legal situation of the Jews in the Nazi *lager*," leading "inevitably to the establishment of a totalitarian regime."[11]

For Agamben, then, just as the sadism at the Château de Silling anticipates that of the camps, the "totalitarian character" of life in the chateau prefigures "modern totalitarianism."[12] And although this account of modernity is in certain respects very different from that of the neoliberals—what they see as the alternative to totalitarianism he sees as its gateway—it is in certain respects very similar: the great danger for both is the danger of the totalitarian. Hence, Agamben's and Butler's fear of the camps was characteristically shared by people with theoretical positions very different from theirs and with very different politics as well. For example, where Agamben criticized Bush for paving the way to totalitarianism, the American writer Paul Berman praised him for responding "to 9/11" by recognizing that the attack was "not just about terror" but was more fundamentally the expression of "a new kind of totalitarianism."[13] From this perspective, the war in Iraq counted as a continuation of the struggle against the Fascists, the Nazis, and the Communists, "totalitarian movements, each and all," as Berman put it.[14] And for Berman (as for Agamben), Hitler and the death camps were the gold standard of totalitarianism. Hence, the threat of a new Hitler looms as large in *Terror and Liberalism* as in *State of Exception*, with the difference, of course, being that in the former it was Saddam who posed that threat, whereas in the latter it was Bush. That's the point of identifying Guantanamo with Auschwitz.

Of course, during the Bush years, quarrels and comparisons like this were frequent. Joseph O'Neill's widely praised (not just by professional literary critics but by President Barack Obama, who called it "fascinating. . . . A wonderful book") *Netherland* (2008) captures their tone perfectly in an argument between a couple living in Manhattan whose marriage falls apart in the wake of the attacks on the World Trade Center and the beginning of the war in Iraq. Saddam is "horrible," the wife acknowledges, but the United States "has no moral or legal authority" to wage war against him; after all, we don't think that just because Stalin was a "monster" "we should have supported Hitler in his invasion of Russia."[15] To which the husband responds, "You're saying Bush is like Hitler." To which the wife replies, "I'm not comparing Bush to Hitler" (98). And so on. There obviously can be no winner in debates like this, and, in fact, their real function has nothing to do with producing a winner. That is, the relevant question is not whether Saddam or Bush is more like Hitler, and it's not about where the true totalitarian threat is coming from; it is instead about what it means to insist—with Agamben, Butler, Bush, and Berman—that totalitarianism is the threat.

And in *Netherland*, the identities—or rather, the job descriptions—of the arguers begin to suggest an answer to this question. Hans, the supposedly "conservative" husband, is an equities analyst, specializing in "large cap oil and gas stocks"; Rachel, the supposedly liberal wife, is a "corporate litigator," "radicalized," hitherto, "only in the service of her client," and "with not the slightest bone to pick about money and its doings" (96). When they begin a trial separation (in December 2001), they put the million dollars they make from the sale of their loft into "government bonds" and, "operating on a tip" from an economist they trust, into gold. The price of gold went from $280 per ounce in January 2002 to $350 in December of the same year, so they were right to trust that economist. And Hans was right to stay out of the market; although at the end of 2001 the Dow recovered briefly from its 9/11 crash, it wasn't until 2003 that it began seriously to rise. So our equities analyst and corporate litigator did exactly the right thing during the down years, and whatever they ended up feeling about the relative merits of Bush and Saddam, they ended up feeling it in a much higher tax bracket.

Or at least they would have if, at the end of the Bush years, there had still been a much higher tax bracket. But income tax rates have been in decline since the end of the 1970s, and tax cuts are, of course, only one aspect of the neoliberal agenda that has dominated American politics, in Democratic administrations as in Republican ones, over the past fifty years. Indeed, *Netherland*, as much as it's a novel of September 11th, is also a novel of the economic policies—the commitment to the mobility of both capital and labor—that helped make the World Trade Center a target for the attack in the first place. The mobility-of-capital part is, of course, suggested by its hero's job, but the mobility of labor—the obsession with immigration—is actually much more central, insisted on by its parallels with the novel on which it's modeled, *The Great Gatsby*. Thus, in *Netherland*, *Gatsby*'s Dutch sailors become the Dutch equities analyst and Jimmy Gatz becomes a Trinidadian entrepreneur with Indian roots, Chuck Ramkisson. And Fitzgerald's famous list of Gatsby's guests—"From East Egg . . . came the Chester Beckers" and "from farther out on the Island the Stonewall Jackson Abrams of Georgia" and "from West Egg came the Poles and . . . Don C. Schwartze"—gets reincarnated in descriptions of the people Chuck talks to on the phone: "From Bangalore, there came calls from a man named Nandavanam. . . . From Hillside, Queens, there was George el Faizy . . . and, from a private jet . . . there was Faruk Patel" (161).

But where *Gatsby* was dismayed by the multiracial America that immigration had produced, *Netherland* is exhilarated: its narrator is never happier than when he's finding himself "the only white man" on the cricket field. (Indeed, the repeated appearance of ethnic catalogs like the one above is *Netherland*'s outstanding formal feature.) A straightforward way to put the difference between the texts would be just to note that *Gatsby* was published in 1925, in the wake of the passage of the Johnson–Reed Act, which, if it closed the barn door a little too late on all the Abrams and Schwartzes, sought at least to keep their numbers from growing and to guarantee that no dark-skinned people from Asia would show up looking to play cricket. The immigration quota from India in 1925 was 100. In the year of *Netherland*, there were 66,644 Indian immigrants.

Thus, *Netherland*'s version of the American dream—featuring "black and brown and . . . a few white faces"—is not as white as *Gatsby*'s. And, more to the point, it's not as American either. For one thing, other countries have had the dream too. In the past half century, immigration worldwide has almost doubled. More crucially, it's not as American because it's not essentially national. Indeed, if what you want is to maximize the efficiency of labor markets, the insistence on the integrity of the nation and even of the state is essentially reactionary. That's why the current resistance to immigration in the United States can appeal only to a kind of shame-faced racism or to legality, which is to say, the state itself. We have nothing against immigration, the argument goes; we just believe everyone should follow the law. And, of course, neoliberal purists reject even this, arguing that illegal immigration is actually preferable to legal immigration because it "responds to market forces in ways that legal immigration does not."[16]

Thus, the neoliberal left (appealing to antiracism and the economy) and the neoliberal right (appealing to individual choice and the economy) both fight against closing the borders. And the nativist fantasy of ending immigration serves only as a symptom of the economic reality—the increasing gap between the rich and the poor—that the economic system embodied by the immigrant has produced.

For if increased immigration is a technology for fulfilling the commitment to competitive markets, increased income inequality is a characteristic outcome of that commitment. In 1982, the top 10 percent of the American population made about 35 percent of the money earned in the United States; by 2007, it had reached about 50 percent; today, it's over 50 percent. But this inequality represents an opportunity rather than a problem for a novel like *Netherland*, which enthusiastically registers the cultural differences neoliberalism makes available—that's the meaning of all its ethnic catalogs; that's the meaning, more generally, of the celebrations of diversity that characterize almost every institution of the American upper class—while at the same time redescribing neoliberalism's inequalities as opportunities for friendship, not just between the one white and the many black and brown faces but between the multimillionaire equities analyst and the fellow cricketer near the very bottom of the service sector. Thus, the "awkwardness" "beneath the slapping of the hands" that Hans experiences when he runs into one of his teammates working as a gas station attendant on 14th Street is attributed to the fact that they all respected each other's privacy off the field rather than to the fact that one of them is a multimillionaire and the other is behind a cash register (173). What the equities analyst wants above all from his black, brown, and broke teammates is their "respect," and although he wonders why it "matter[s] so much to him," anyone who's read Richard Sennett's encomiastic *Respect in a World of Inequality* or the political theorist William Connolly's paeans to what he calls "deep pluralism" and to transmuting "cultural antagonisms" into "debates marked by agonistic respect between the partisans" could give him the answer: respect is cheaper than redistribution.[17] The reason the equities analyst wants the respect of the gas station cashier is so he can imagine that what the gas station cashier wants is the respect—as opposed to the money—of the equities analyst.

Indeed, *Netherland* gives us a brilliant emblem of the transformations made available by the ambition to universalize the market and by political theory's redescription of class conflict as agonistic respect in its brief image of the one sexual encounter Hans has in the months after his marriage breaks up. The event does not advance the plot or illuminate much about Hans's character. But its sheer formal gratuitousness is part of its interest, highlighting the way it's made thematically relevant (indeed, almost indispensable) by the fact that Danielle, the woman Hans sleeps with, is of "Anglo-Jamaican" descent "with pale brown skin" and that what she wants in bed is for him to spank her with his belt (107). Racism and sadism have no place in a world imagined under the sign of the market, but antiracism and masochism are absolutely central to it. Thus, while the image of a "pale white" man whipping a "pale brown" woman might plausibly have come out of an earlier moment in the history of the neoliberal novel (say, *Beloved*?), here, as in *Venus in Furs*, that image is transformed by the fact that the slave is a volunteer, and the sex entirely conforms to the consensual erotic logic of anti-racist neoliberalism. Indeed, echoing the "word of honor" invoked in Sacher-Masoch's contracts, Danielle appeals to the fact that Hans is a "gentleman" and therefore she can "trust" him. Contracts outside the law cannot be enforced by the state, but, like illegal as opposed to legal immigration, they are that much more responsive to the desires of the market.

Of course, this sexual encounter would be even more gratifying if, instead of being a "visual creative" in an advertising agency, Danielle were, say, a cleaning lady at Goldman Sachs, which would make the assertion of her agency (of her desire) a perfect storm of race, gender, and class. Despite this shortcoming, however, in the sexual adventure of the equities analyst, *Netherland* produces a more plausible image of both the self-understanding of neoliberalism and its reality than does Agamben's fear of it as the way to totalitarianism or Berman's allegiance to it as the alternative to totalitarianism. And even if the novel's own allegiance is to a slightly less earnest version of Connolly's pluralism, at least the millionaire's belt puts some of the agony back into agonistic respect.

Furthermore, if we're looking for images of a labor force that's begging for it, the world has given us at least two—one from real neoliberal life, the other from the generic queen of neoliberal literature, the memoir—that are even better than my Goldman Sachs fantasy. Both involve Dominique Strauss-Kahn, who used to work at the IMF and, after his forced removal from public life, is now involved in several ventures, including the very successful DSK Global Investment Fund. The first image is DSK's outrageous claim that his relations with Nafissatou Diallo, the Sofitel housekeeper he was accused of raping, had, in fact, been "consensual," a claim that retroactively acquired a certain phantasmatic plausibility when he settled by paying her $6 million.[18] And the second is the supporting claim by a subsequent girlfriend/victim that it's essential to DSK that his partners do, in fact, consent—that he needs to be "sur que son partenaire consent."[19] These are the words of Marcela Iacub, who, during the period of the Diallo fiasco when he was being almost universally condemned, had an affair with DSK and who broke it off when, in what she describes as a fit of passion, he bit off part of her ear and ate it.

The violence of this assault notwithstanding, Iacub understands it too as a kind of free-market exchange. Earlier in *Belle et Bête*, before the affair has begun, she turns down an offer from DSK's then wife, Ann Sinclair, to work with her "for free" ("gratuitement à son journal") (26). Why does she turn it down? Because, she says, it seems to her wrong to "travailler" "sans être payé"; she is "par principe contre le travail gratuit." And the loss of her ear only confirms the principle that people should be paid for what they do and should pay for what they get since, in exchange for the ear, what she gets is "salut," which is, she says, more than worth it: "Ce n'est rien comme prix, une oreille." "To pay only an ear in exchange for understanding the true nature of my desires is a bargain" (113). So just as you don't write for free, you don't get to understand your desire to be "abused" for free, and once you do understand it, instead of writing for the French *Huffington Post* for nothing, you write your memoir for something.

In the event, however, the sales of *Belle et Bête* were disappointing, but not, of course, because female masochism doesn't sell. In fact, in the months just before and just after *Belle et Bête* appeared, *Cinquante Nuances de Grey* was doing almost as well in France as *Fifty Shades of Grey* did in the United States and the United Kingdom, and indeed, just as submission teaches Iacub about her desires, the opportunity for the "submissive" to learn about hers is described as the "fundamental purpose" of the contract that—laying out the dominant's right to "flog, spank or whip" the "submissive" and establishing her "consent" to being so spanked and whipped—looms even larger (ten full pages) in *Fifty Shades of Grey* than it does in *Venus in Furs*.[20]

Which, given the political role that contract and consent have been called upon to play in the past half century, makes some sense. Iacub has a series of what she calls "nightmares" in which she insists that she has the "right" to give herself to DSK, and, speaking in terms that any follower of Hayek or von Mises would immediately recognize, she complains that only in a "paternalist" or "tyrannical" society would "the State" insist on its power to "interfere" with the desire of one "consenting adult" to be eaten by another. Of course, von Mises's objections to "paternal government" involved the state's interfering with the consumption of "cigarettes" and "canned food," not ears; the state, he argued, had no right to compel producers to label the actual contents of their products and thus interfere with the ability of "individual citizens" to buy whatever they wanted. But the logic is the same.[21] *Human Action* makes a foundational distinction between "two kinds of social cooperation," preferring "contract," where "the logical relation between the cooperating individuals is symmetrical" ("John has the same relation to Tom as Tom has to John"), to "command" or "subordination," where "there is the man who commands and there are those who obey his orders," which is thus "asymmetrical" (196). And although the relation between a "Dominant" and a "Submissive" would seem like the exemplary instance of asymmetry (one commands, the other obeys), the reconfiguring of that relation as one that the Submissive desires and to which she consents renders them symmetrical. Like John and Tom, the submissive and the dominant are both getting what they want. If masochism in *Belle et Bête* is a kind of libertarian nightmare,[22] in *Fifty Shades of Grey*, it's a libertarian wet dream.[23]

At least it would be if the contract ever got signed. Or it is, but only because (while endlessly discussed) the contract never does get signed. Since Ana basically does everything Christian wants her to do right from the start and doesn't do anything she doesn't want to do, it becomes, Christian says, "moot" (498), and, of course, it always was, as they both know, "unenforceable" (216). One way to understand this rendering irrelevant of what is structurally at the center of the text's will-she-or-won't-she plot is as the expression of a certain ambivalence about understanding their relationship as contractual. After all, from page one, the novel is clearly headed toward marriage, and the attempt to avoid marriage being reduced to mere contract is a characteristic component of an older (late nineteenth and early twentieth century) domestic ideology, one that gets a fleeting reprise in James when Christian is outraged by his father's suggestion that he and Ana should sign a prenuptial agreement. The idea here is that what the two of them have is a freedom even purer than any that can be or needs to be embodied in a contract. But where the older resistance to seeing marriage as a contract involved the sense that contracts were too easy to dissolve (i.e., by divorce), this newer ambivalence involves just the opposite, the sense that contracts are too constraining, or, at least, constraining in the wrong way. For the scene in which Christian angrily repudiates the prenup is immediately followed by his telling her to propose a safe word (she chooses "popsicle"), smacking her bottom, and then (in traditional soft-core fashion) "thrusting" "deep" into her while her wrists and ankles are cuffed to the four corners of their bed.[24] The power of consent here—Ana experiences, as always, "the most intense climax" ever—not only doesn't require a contract but is, as the reminder about the safe word suggests, made possible by the contract's irrelevance. For once you have a safe word, you don't need a contract. As long as Ana doesn't say popsicle, she is getting exactly what she wants, and the second she does say it, she will also be getting exactly what she wants.

There's a sense, then, in which the sexual contract they didn't sign is both superseded and perfected by the sex they go on to have. Indeed, there's a sense in which the contract supersedes and perfects itself since it too contains a provision for safe words, while insisting (revealingly because tautologically) that "all that occurs under" its terms "will be consensual," including the Submissive's right to withdraw at any time and the Dominant's "right to dismiss the Submissive from his service at any time and for any reason" (166). In this refusal to countenance the paradox at the heart of contract (you choose to give up, in certain circumstances and for a certain amount of time, your right to choose), contemporary masochism (maybe we should call it neoliberal masochism) perfects what we might now call liberal masochism by replacing liberal freedom of contract—binding in a way that necessarily limits the will—with a fantasy of continuous consent, of a social bond, as one might put it (and as David Graeber *has* put it), based "solely on the free consent of (its) participants."[25]

What Graeber is imagining, of course, is an anarchist's utopia, one that might be contrasted to the reality in which the right to dismiss someone from your service at any time and for any reason (and, naturally, to quit at any time and for any reason) has assumed new prominence in the US labor market. Of course, at-will employment has been the default setting of the American workplace since the end of the nineteenth century, and instead of thinking of it as increasingly dominant, some commentators today worry about (or take satisfaction in) the fact that the state has carved out some exceptions to it. But the exceptions primarily (and predictably) involve only protected categories like race, sex, and age, and the primary bulwark against arbitrary dismissal—membership in a union, hence the protection of a union contract—has, in the neoliberal period, shrunk in tandem with the rise in inequality. The standard estimate is that three-quarters of the private sector workforce is composed of at-will employees.[26] In this world, as Andrew Hoberek convincingly argues (he's thinking mainly about repudiated pension plans, but the logic is the same), contract begins to look (but only for the worker) like "a site of nostalgia," since the union contract that binds you to a 1 percent raise and contains a no-strike clause is better than no contract and no raise.[27] From the boss's perspective, however, the handcuffs that bind Ana only as long as she wants to be bound and the image of her resistance ("Why do you defy me?" Christian asks) as the expression of her desire ("Because I love you," she replies) are the fantasy that makes the free market seem truly free—what workers really want is to be fucked.

This is what it means when Ana says, "Christian's idea of a relationship is more like a job offer" (232). This is also why the novel is unconcerned about the contract's unenforceability—the liberal bug (the state won't make you do what you promised) is the libertarian/anarchist feature (the state won't make you do anything at all). More importantly, perhaps, this is why—despite its unenforceability and despite its redundancy (the safe word really does all the work)—masochism can't quite let the contract go. For what is standardly described as *Fifty Shades'* contribution to the mainstreaming of the S&M lifestyle could almost as plausibly be described as its participation in what a writer in the *Harvard Business Review* calls the new "work style" that, as she enthusiastically observes, "more and more people are choosing," the "contingent work style."[28] The essence of the contingent work style is that contingent workers are understood not as employees but as "independent contracting parties"; indeed, the licensing agreement that Uber (perhaps the paradigmatic practitioner of the contingent work style) requires all its drivers to sign explicitly specifies that "no employment contract is created between [the Dominant and the Submissive, I mean between] Uber and the Drivers."[29] The point of this stipulation for contingent workers is that, as independent contractors, they have "the freedom to be their own boss."[30] The point for Uber is that because it's employing bosses rather than workers, it doesn't have to pay benefits like social security or workers' compensation (not to mention the fact that bosses can't form unions).

In other words, the reason neoliberal masochism won't just let contract go is because it's only employment contracts that it really wants to get rid of. After all, by making the neoliberal denial of the difference between employer and employee literal (i.e., by thinking of us all as investing our human capital), real capital saves itself a lot of money. Or, as the lead attorney in the class action suit recently filed against it says, "By not classifying its drivers as employees, Uber is shifting the expenses of running a business to its workers."[31] In *Fifty Shades of Grey*, it's not until Christian gives Ana the company she's been working for as a wedding present that she can fully experience the transcendence of the liberal relation between employer and employee by the neoliberal relationship between independent contractors.[32] But Uber drivers can get that same glow just by signing the licensing agreement. Which text—the novel or the agreement—is more influential is a hard question. But the easy answer is that we don't have to choose. There are lots of different ways to love freedom, all of them good.

NOTES

This is a longer, modified version of an essay originally published as "Fifty Shades of Libertarian Love," *LARB*, May 22, 2015, https://lareviewofbooks.org/article/50-shades-of -libertarian-love/.

1. Giorgio Agamben, *Homo Sacer: Sovereign Power and Bare Life*, trans. Daniel Heller (Stanford: Stanford University Press, 1988), 134–35.

2. Ibid., 171.

3. Giorgio Agamben, *State of Exception*, trans. Kevin Attell (Chicago: University of Chicago Press, 2005), 87.

4. Leopold von Sacher-Masoch, "La Vénus à la fourrure," in *Présentation de Sacher-Masoch*, ed. Gilles Deleuze (Paris: Les Editions de Minuit, 1967), 195. Translation mine.

5. Agamben, *Homo Sacer*, 141–42.

6. Albert Speer, *Nuremberg Trial Proceedings*, vol. 16, June 21, 1946.

7. Michael Foucault, *Naissance de la Biopolitique* (Paris: Gallimard, 2004), 85.

8. Gary Becker, *The Economics of Discrimination* (Chicago: University of Chicago Press, 1971), 21–22.

9. *Concise Encyclopedia of Economics*, s.v. "Gary Stanley Becker," accessed August 6, 2011, www.econlib.org/library/Enc/bios/Becker.html.

10. Judith Butler, *Frames of War* (London: Verso, 2009).

11. Agamben, *State of Exception*, 15.

12. Agamben, *Homo Sacer*, 2.

13. Paul Berman, *Terror and Liberalism* (New York: W. W. Norton, 2004), 191.

14. Ibid., xiii.

15. Joseph O'Neill, *Netherland* (New York: Vintage, 2009), 97. Hereafter cited in the text.

16. Gordon H. Hanson, *The Economic Logic of Illegal Immigration* (New York: Council on Foreign Relations, 2007), 4.

17. William E. Connolly, *Pluralism* (Durham, NC: Duke University Press, 2005), 47.

18. Russ Buetner, "Hotel Worker Settles Claim Strauss-Kahn Forced Sex," *New York Times*, December 10, 2012, www.nytimes.com/2012/12/11/nyregion/strauss-kahn-and -hotel-maid-settle-suit-over-alleged-attack.html.

19. Marcela Iacub, *Belle et Bête* (Paris: Stock, 2013), 13. Hereafter cited in the text. In general, the meaning of the French is very clear, even if you don't speak French. When it isn't, the translations I've included are mine.

20. E. L. James, *Fifty Shades of Grey* (New York: Vintage, 2012), 168. Hereafter cited in the text.

21. Ludwig von Mises, *Human Action: A Treatise on Economics* (Auburn, AL: Ludwig von Mises Institute, 1998), 377, 109–10. Hereafter cited in the text.

22. Iacub calls the aspect of DSK's character that interests (attracts and/or repels) her the "pig"—*cochon* or *porc*. And the essence of the pig is his love of freedom: "le propre du porc est la liberté" (48).

23. After writing this, I came across Heather Havrilesky's description of *Fifty Shades* as "the American (wet) dream on performance-enhancing drugs." Obviously, that's right too. Heather Havrilesky, "Fifty Shades of Late Capitalism," *Baffler* 22 (2013), www.thebaffler .com/salvos/fifty-shades-of-late-capitalism.

24. E. L. James, *Fifty Shades Freed* (New York: Vintage, 2012), 35, 40.

25. David Graeber, "Occupy Wall Street's Anarchist Roots," *Aljazeera*, November 30, 2011, www.aljazeera.com/indepth/opinion/2011/11/2011112872835904508.html.

26. "Three-fourths of the 80 million workers in the private-sector are employed 'at will' and can be fired for almost any reason, or for no reason at all." See www.workplacefairness .org/sc/sources.php.

27. Andrew Hoberek, "Adultery, Crisis, Contract," in *Capitalist Realism*, ed. Alison Shonkwiler and Leigh Clare La Berge (Iowa City: University of Iowa Press, 2014), 55.

28. Tammy Erickson, "The Rise of the New Contract Worker," *Harvard Business Review*, September 7, 2012, https://hbr.org/2012/09/the-rise-of-the-new-contract-worker/.

29. "Uber Software License and Online Services Agreement," https://docs.google.com /file/d/0B2UD4KpUZMvEczh2UVBxTURLN1k/edit.

30. Nicole Fallon, "Contract Workers vs. Employees: What Businesses Should Know," *Business News Daily*, October 21, 2014, www.businessnewsdaily.com/770-contract-vs-em ployees-what-you-need-to-know.html.

31. Michael B. Farrell, "New Lawsuit Claims Uber Exploits Its Drivers," *Boston Globe*, June 26, 2014, www.bostonglobe.com/business/2014/06/26/uber-hit-with-class-action-law suit/JFlTJLMuBoXuEmMU3elTAI/story.htmlU.

32. The company is "Seattle Independent Publishing"—in *Fifty Shades of Grey*, you can never get enough independence, just like you can never give enough consent.

The Microeconomic Mode

JANE ELLIOTT

Since the late 1990s in North America and Britain, the field of contemporary aesthetics has been marked by the appearance and growing prevalence of what I call *the microeconomic mode*. This mode has proliferated across media and genres, as well as the demarcations between high and low culture; it gives form to some of the most celebrated recent literary novels, as well as some of the most reviled products of popular culture. Texts in this mode are characterized by a combination of abstraction and extremity, a fusion that we can witness everywhere from the *Saw* horror-film series (2004–10) to Cormac McCarthy's *The Road* (2007), from the reality TV franchise *Survivor* (1997 to the present) to Steve McQueen's art-house film *Hunger* (2008). Abstraction results from a focus on delimited or capsule worlds in which option and decision, action and effect, have been extracted from everyday contexts and thus made unusually legible—for example, the life raft, the desert island, the medical experiment, the prison cell. Extremity registers in forms of painful, grotesque, or endangered embodiment, including deprivation, torture, mutilation, self-mutilation, and various threats to life itself. The combination of the two results in situations in which individuals make agonized choices among unwelcome options, options that present intense physical or life-threatening consequences for themselves or their loved ones. In its fullest manifestations, the aesthetic effect of this mode is brutal, in every sense of the word: crude, harsh, ruthless, unrelenting, and unpleasantly precise.

In order to suggest what this mode looks like in operation, I want to begin with a particularly stark and telling example: the film *127 Hours* (2011), based on the memoir titled *A Rock and a Hard Place* (2004) by rock climber Aron Ralston.[1] Aron, played by James Franco, becomes trapped in a slot canyon when his arm is wedged between a falling boulder and the canyon wall; eventually, after nearly dying from exposure and deprivation, he cuts off his arm in order to escape the canyon and find help. Some of Aron's personal history appears in flashbacks, but it isn't presented as qualifying or shaping the life-or-death choice that confronts him. The few elements with causal significance in the canyon—the trapped arm, the lack of food and water, the number of hours—concern Aron's sheer existence as a conscious mind that inhabits a body with certain essential needs and capacities. It is difficult to imagine any human being with this sort of body experiencing Aron's situation very differently, whatever the specifics of his or her personal psychology or place in the social order. Not only does Aron's decision to cut off his arm appear detached from any external processes that would render it something more than an expression of sheer individual choice, but the horrible nature of the act simultaneously throws into relief the fierce determination with which his choice is enacted. I refer to this experience of highly consequential, utterly willed, and fearsomely undesired action as *suffering agency*.

In animating interest in this way, I argue, works such as *127 Hours* offer a searing incarnation of the microeconomic model of human behavior. Often described via Lionel Robbins's now canonical description of economics as "the science which studies human behavior as a relationship between ends and scarce means which have alternative uses," this model combines methodological individualism, the foreclosure of interpersonal utility comparison, and the presumption that the choosing individual operates according to the parameters of allocative choice, weak rationality, and utility maximization.[2] There are significant disputes regarding the meaning and parameters of each of these terms even among contemporary orthodox economists, but these differences have not invalidated this definition so much as given shape to various schools and approaches within mainstream economics as a discipline. In practice, microeconomics relies on this axiomatic foundation to produce elaborate mathematic descriptions for the aggregate phenomena guided by consumer behavior—for example, demand curves and price points. My focus instead is on the designation of agential allocative choice as an absolute, which emerges most visibly via the granularity of microeconomics as a subdiscipline even as it functions as an unquestioned and unquestionable foundation for the mainstream of the discipline as a whole.

We can get a sense of the conceptual power of this model by turning to the work of Chicago school economist Gary Becker. Because of its movement into areas normally associated with sociology, his work represents a methodologically radical edge of microeconomics, but it is for this reason that his approach is especially revealing. When he applies the microeconomic view of choice "relentlessly and unflinchingly" to areas formerly consigned to other disciplines, Becker distills what he calls "the economic approach to human behaviour" from its usual content and makes its self-reinforcing nature apparent.[3] For Becker, what makes the economic understanding of human behavior unique is precisely its universality: not only is there no act of human choice to which the model cannot be said to apply, but also the model renders every choice by definition equally rational and allocative. Becker's overarching methodology depends on aggregate presumptions of market efficiency and equilibrium, but his description of the individual as a "decision unit" functions without reference to such aggregate factors. Instead, it emerges from the tautologies that make up the model alone.[4] Because allocative choice necessarily takes place in conditions of scarcity, resources distributed in one area are necessarily not available for distribution in another. In effect, that is, every benefit comes with a cost, and vice versa. Add to that closed system the definition of choice as the expression of individual preference, and any choice that at first glance appears irrationally costly can be understood to meet preferences that are not immediately apparent. If an individual choice does not yet appear to us to maximize utility, then that is only because we have not yet identified the evaluation of cost and benefit, means and end, that guided the choice in question.

When combined with methodological individualism, this tautological account transforms every human action into an expression of individual agency.[5] Not only does methodological individualism strip out contextual factors that might determine or mitigate individual choice, but also the factors that do remain in play become transposed into the closed system of costs and benefits. In this way, the very existence of constraints becomes the vehicle through which we enact our capacity to act in our own best interests. For example, in his analysis of life expectancy, Becker posits that every death must be considered in some sense a suicide, since it "could have been postponed if more resources had been invested [by the subject] in prolonging life."[6] Even seemingly self-destructive behavior becomes the logical result of the pursuit of some goal other than that of prolonging life. And once the existence of that goal is taken as proven by the presumption that it was chosen, the choice can retroactively be determined to be an expression of interest since it led to this end. By foreclosing the importance of any contextual factor that does not function as either a resource to be distributed or an end to be met, this model turns even the negotiation of profound constraints—for instance, the finitude of life itself—into the rational enactment of sheer individual will. In this model, taking action in one's own best interest is not a measure of true liberty or full personhood but rather an inescapable feature of human life itself.

In *127 Hours*, we witness a relentless, nearly unbearable literalization of this conviction that, for human beings, to be alive is to be interested. From the geographical reproduction of methodological individualism in the stark emptiness of the canyon to the binary nature of the decision Aron confronts, the film incarnates the microeconomic imagination of choice in near-algorithmic form. Through his serial and evolving enactment of the choice between life and limb, Aron endures a nightmare version of the comparison process that underlies the presumption of rational allocative choice: 127 hours of weighing the benefit of his life against the cost of cutting off his arm. Moreover, as his example demonstrates so viciously, the intrinsic quality of interest in life doesn't take away the subject's capacity for choice; instead, to borrow Becker's terminology, Aron postpones his death by choosing to put his every resource, including the determination required to amputate his arm, toward life. Aron's experience manifests at the forcible intersection of profoundly agential choice and his existence within a container of living flesh. Yet, as the film's title also suggests, Aron's fierce attachment to life registers not only in his final decision but also in his sheer endurance of his circumstances. With each hour that passes, the effects of exposure and deprivation on Aron increase, so that the progression of time itself becomes a measure of both his torment and his commitment to survival. As he nears death, Aron's every breath signals that he is still clinging to life, with all the grasping desperation that the phrase suggests. When being alive transforms from a largely background, involuntary function to a profoundly important feat of individual will, the unfolding of life becomes both the object of interest and the moment-by-moment demonstration of that interest. Aron's interest is in life, and his life expresses his interest.

As a manifestation of a shift in the imagination of political subjectivity that has thus far escaped cognition even if it has not escaped perception, the microeconomic mode both registers and fills a gap in our understanding of the present that has not yet been traversed by the important body of work on neoliberal governmentality. In Michel Foucault's reading of Becker, he famously defines the neoliberal form of governance as one in which "action is brought to bear on the rules of the game rather than on the players, and . . . there is an environmental type of intervention instead of the internal subjugation of individuals."[7] In the microeconomic mode, however, it is the perspective of the player rather than the view of the field as a whole that takes center stage, and that player is necessarily facing life-and-death choices. What emerges as a result is not adequately explained by either the microeconomic model of human behavior or the forms of governance associated with that model, and that is why I need recourse to an unfortunate number of neologisms to describe its central concerns. If apt terms were already in existence—if the transformation in question were either less radical or more established—then this mode would likely not exist in its same ubiquitous form. That my central terms here—suffering agency, life-interest, the microeconomic mode—seem to embody or unfold across seeming contradictions indicates something of the stress this shift places on our usual ways of comprehending political experience. By treating the microeconomic mode as a form of compressed knowledge about this ongoing transformation, I aim to uncover what it is that this mode seems to know about the transformations associated with neoliberalism that has otherwise remained unthought.

In this essay, I offer one segment of this analysis by interrogating the form most consistently associated with the microeconomic mode: the survival game. Although it has appeared intermittently throughout the twentieth century, the survival-game form has boomed since the late 1990s, giving shape to works as diverse in tone, ambition, and audience as Michael Haneke's *Funny Games* (1997), postapocalyptic video games such as *Left 4 Dead* (2008), and the Discovery Channel's reality TV show *Naked and Afraid* (2013), in which two contestants find themselves stranded in the wild and exposed, so to speak, to extreme weather conditions. Survival-game texts participate in the microeconomic mode almost by definition; not only is the survival game created from the intersection of the necessarily abstracted game form and extreme life-and-death consequences, but it also requires, propagates, and harnesses each contestant's seemingly ineradicable interest in life. I focus first here on Gillian Flynn's novel *Gone Girl* (2013) and unpack the arguments it makes about the situations in which survival games come to be constituted. Unlike the majority of survival-game texts, *Gone Girl* interrogates the utility of the survival game as a response to the circumstances evident in its created world; it attempts to identify not only how the survival game functions but what its function is. In its exploration of this question, *Gone Girl* offers an opportunity to evaluate the purposes served when life-interest is manifest, over and over, across the field of contemporary aesthetics.

One of these purposes, I will argue, is to model and test a set of transformed relationships among interest, sovereignty, and the biological status of human being. Although this model resonates in certain ways with contemporary theorizations of affective labor and the biopolitical, it cannot be mapped against our existing assumptions about these categories, which may explain why the microeconomic mode has unfolded in a critical blind spot. When we assume we will find the tide of the multitude, the dispersions of affect, or the inertia of bare life, it is difficult to know what to make of all these visions of a single subject's insistent, agential, agonized embodiment, which, despite deviating from theoretical accounts, still register as a defining feature of twenty-first-century aesthetics. In what follows, I document the way in which the microeconomic mode requires us to think very differently about what is meant by the political capture of life itself in the present. In order to track this thinking, I read the survival game not as an object of existing theoretical discourse, but rather as the theory that it is.

Survival Games and Sovereignty

The plot of *Gone Girl* centers on a young wife, Amy, who has gone missing, and her husband, Nick, who is suspected of having murdered her. Although the opening clearly designates the novel as a thriller, the account of what has led Nick and Amy to this pass is closer to social realism in tone, with a specific emphasis on the social effects of contemporary capital. We learn that Amy's character has been shaped by the fact that, since her early childhood, her parents have been cowriting and publishing books for children based on her life, called the *Amazing Amy* series. Rather than cherishing her for her own sake, they seem to have taken Becker's infamous microeconomic analysis of parental motivations as their instruction manual: they treat Amy's existence as an investment, and they reap the financial rewards accordingly.[8] When Amy uses her trust fund to bail out her parents after the 2008 stock market crash, she can no longer support Nick, who has lost his job as a writer owing to the casualization of journalism in the Internet age, and they move from Manhattan to Nick's hometown, North Carthage, Missouri. The town's status as postindustrial backwater is neatly signaled by the fate of the local mall: having gone bust, it now houses an encampment of men who became homeless after they lost their jobs when the local plant shut down. In sum, Amy and Nick's arrival in North Carthage is determined by a confluence of monetization, flexible employment, financialization, and Web 2.0—in other words, by the real subsumption of the most ephemeral, minute, and personal aspects of human behavior by capital.[9]

What makes *Gone Girl* revealing is that it turns this canny if familiar account of immaterial labor in America into fuel for a mystery-thriller potboiler, complete with bizarre twists, misplaced trust, and a killer on the loose. And that generic shift gives the novel an imaginative reach quite different from what we find in contemporary Marxist theory. Tellingly, the hinge between *Gone Girl*'s social-realist and thriller registers is another feature of the social landscape associated with the regime of immaterial labor: the gamification of dating.[10] By only slightly exaggerating the approach recommended by dating manuals such as *The Rules™: Time-Tested Secrets for Capturing the Heart of Mr. Right* (1995), *Gone Girl* skewers the expectation that women can find love provided they understand what men really want and have the discipline to play the game accordingly. After meeting

Nick at a party, Amy intuits that he is looking for what she calls "the Cool Girl." Self-confident but undemanding, a gorgeous Size 2 yet addicted to hot dogs and burgers, the Cool Girl can be easily identified by her professed love of football, poker, cheap beer, threesomes, and anal sex.[11] Winning Nick requires that Amy convince him that she is the Cool Girl of his dreams, who, of course, would never be so uncool as to modify her behavior to catch a man. Once Amy successfully embodies the Cool Girl and captures Nick's affections, however, she comes to the outraged realization that playing love like a game is an inherently self-canceling project. Transforming herself into someone to whom Nick will commit turns out to mean that Amy has foreclosed the possibility that she will be loved for herself, since it is not Amy that Nick has chosen but the Cool Girl she has been impersonating. Not only is winning in this scenario indistinguishable from losing, but it is specifically Amy's capacity to game the system that has caused her to wind up with the booby prize. Precisely because it creates such a clear and instrumental path to the goal of love, the power of Amy's will turns into a source of self-injury. When capturing Mr. Right is just another form of rational action in one's own best interest, as *Gone Girl* suggests, it becomes a form of suffering agency for the woman involved.

This realization sparks the novel's thriller plot because, as readers discover in the novel's central twist, Amy is actually a psychopath who cannot bear to have her will thwarted or her amazingness denied. In part 1 of the novel, we read a series of diary entries by Amy cataloguing her relationship with Nick from their first meeting in Manhattan to his gradual shift to selfish indifference and finally violent outbursts. At the start of part 2 of the novel, however, narrator-Amy gleefully informs the reader that "Diary Amy" is a fake, created to cast suspicion on Nick. Instead of being a victim of forces beyond her control, Amy turns out to be a monster whose villainy is directly tied to her creepy but not at all supernatural capacity for goal-directed action, from secretly crafting her faux diary over months to slicing into her own arm to leave her blood at a staged crime scene. As she advises readers, "You just have to decide to do it and then do it. . . . Discipline. Follow through. Like anything."[12] What infuriates her about the results of her Cool Girl initiative is not that she has missed out on real love, but rather that her feat of discipline and follow-through somehow failed to garner the results it should have. Amy's ultimate interest is in coming out on top, in having her will always and everywhere recognized as superior to everyone else's, and the prizes that accrue along the way are welcome but largely superfluous. As a villain, Amy embodies microeconomic interest taken to a ludicrous yet logical extreme, and that is why her capacity for evil emerges full-blown when she encounters the problem of suffering agency. Suffering agency belies the inherent benefit of successful action in one's own best interest, and Amy rightly understands herself as that principle incarnate. She figures the outraged, spiteful energy of a person betrayed by a system whose dictates she has followed with unimpeachable fidelity.

In order to reverse this defeat, Amy does something only a villain could do: she forces Nick to play a survival game that she designs. She fakes her own death in a fashion that will cast suspicion on Nick, and then leaves a series of clues for Nick to solve seemingly based on details of their relationship, which he can solve provided he has been paying attention to their interactions. Not only does Nick have no choice but to *"play the Missing Wife game,"* as he describes it, but he also reminds readers that, given that Missouri is a death penalty state, this game is life-or-death for him.[13] In order to humble Nick on the same ground where her victory turned to defeat, Amy designs her survival game to resemble the gamification of love as viewed from a heterosexual male perspective. Familiar from countless sit-coms and rom-coms, this is the narrative in which women baffle men by turning communication into guesswork and minor interactions into symbolic relationship landmarks. Amy's sly twist is that, in this case, the clues actually refer to Nick's affair with a much younger woman, and with each riddle he solves he digs himself in deeper with the police. When she gets Nick to play the survival game she has created, Amy successfully traps him in an all-consuming structure that threatens to be fatal for him but is a voluntary and delightful fabrication for her. She uses the survival game to materialize a division between those with the power to legislate a self-contained realm governed by rules of their own design and those who cannot help but treat these manufactured, artificially delimited worlds with all the seriousness reserved for matters of life and death.

This division is what makes the survival-game designation more than simply a category error. In the survival game, the game form's characteristic distance from necessity persists for the game's designers even as it is eradicated for the game players, who must inhabit the game whether they like it or not. As Amy's example suggests, survival-game designers demonstrate their power by ensuring that others must pursue tremendously important ends through inexpedient means—that contestants will play out their real lives in a fabricated world, like lab rats running a maze. Yet, because these contestants are playing for their lives, this form of power over others specifically requires that subordinated subjects also take agential action of the most consequential kind. Amy proves herself the ultimate microeconomic agent not only because of her supreme capacity to act in her own best interest but also because her revenge depends on Nick's lesser capacity to do the same. She doesn't take away Nick's ability to choose; she *captures* his capacity for choice, and that is how she performs her dominance over him. She relocates his will inside a set of life-and-death parameters whose very existence expresses her will, and, in so doing, she proves that hers is the meta-will. Or, to put it in more familiar terms, she proves that her will is sovereign. But what the survival-game designer decrees is not who lives or dies, but rather the terms by which players may either win or lose their lives. Sovereign is he—or she—who decides on the rules of the game.

Because it locates the survival game within a mystery-thriller plotline that centers on the real-world game of love, *Gone Girl* creates a through line from the ubiquity of gamification to the imposition of the survival game. As the title of *Gone Girl* suggests, Amy's successful disappearance from the field of play is what indicates her triumph—not only over Nick but over gamification at large; it is by decisively exiting the fray in favor of the game designer's spectator seat that she aims to prove her superiority. Of course, we might doubt Amy's assertion that being thwarted in the game of love is what drove her to create the Missing Wife Game, especially given that her critique of heterosexual romance appears in the second part of the novel, voiced by Amy as unmasked psychopath. Yet, even if it is clearly insufficient motivation for the specific action she takes, Amy's sneering dissection of contemporary dating mores in this section is too well observed and resonant for it to read as merely her insanity talking. Women readers may not go as far as Amy in attempting to capture the heart of Mr. Right, but there is a reason that "the Cool Girl" became a media buzzword after the novel's publication. In skewering a recognizable dating dynamic, Amy's assessment of the gamification of love still participates in the novel's social realism even as her insane response to her defeat becomes the primary engine of the novel's genre-fiction status, both authorized and pathologized by its mystery-thriller conventions. Amy's takedown of the Cool Girl provides the conceptual switching point between the novel's two generic and epistemological registers—the one that purports to represent the world as it is, and the one that features the shocking acts of individuals who interrupt everyday life with their evil machinations.

One result of this nexus is to undercut the reader's identification with the feminist ire in the novel's satire of heterosexual dating habits, by making it the motivation for an over-the-top form of revenge that readers cannot be expected to endorse. More importantly for my specific purposes here, however, this structure suggests that the survival game in *Gone Girl* is not a meditation on or metaphor for the process by which each human life becomes a locus of capital, but rather an example of the profound, outsized measures required to set oneself outside—

above—that process. The survival game is Amy's answer to the question, what does it take to achieve sovereignty over the countless games in which everyone acts in their own best interests? It can provide this answer because, as Nick learns to his peril, the survival game captures life in a very different way than gamification does. The assumption that underwrites gamification, the perception that everyday life activities operate and are best approached as games, emerges from a regime of immaterial labor that codifies and monetizes the sum total of human behaviors as constantly shifting flows of affect and action. The survival game works in the opposite direction. By activating each player's interest in life, it forcibly locates each individual agent inside the container of its single, irreplaceable human organism. Amy knows that Nick will play her game because, short of science fiction measures, even a man who subsists on his protean charm cannot charm his way to inhabiting a second living human body should his first be taken by lethal injection. The human organism is where the buck of exchangeability stops—not for capital, but for the individual who necessarily has one and only one body, and who can usually be expected to act to preserve it. If the survival game stages a form of sovereignty particular to the present, then this is a power that guarantees that the same aggregation of human being expressed as countless shifting streams of interfused data will also be spooled up into individual life-forms, piloted by conscious agents who have no choice but to keep making choices.

From one sort of Deleuzian perspective, this insistence on the individual agent as a unit of domination may seem out of keeping with contemporary forms of control, but *Gone Girl* also brings to mind Deleuze and Guattari's insistence that the molecular and the molar operate simultaneously.[14] Precisely through its crude distortions, the novel crystallizes a world in which the same subject who dissolves into various monetized flows of information can also be an individual whose one and only life is irreversibly blighted by a felony conviction or a bad credit score or the closing of the local plant—that is, by permanent consequences that attach to a single, identified human life. This, I want to suggest, is what life-interest is for: it constitutes the reterritorialization that accompanies the deterritoralization of the subject in contemporary capital. Although biopolitics and immaterial labor have been frequently understood as elements of the same process, the microeconomic mode thus represents their interaction quite differently. Instead of the mass populations we find in Michel Foucault's account of biopower, life-interest concerns the singularity of each living human body; instead of legislating a boundary between full persons and mere life as in Giorgio Agamben's theorization of biopolitics, sovereignty over life-interest fuses the capacity for agential action with human being itself, whether that human life has been recognized as possessing political personhood or not. Life-interest is a biopolitical category, but it is one that scrambles our usual ways of thinking about the term.

The Subject of Life-Interest

Before gesturing toward some of the implications of this shift, I want to step back for a moment and consider this conceptual gap between life-interest and contemporary theorizations of life itself. Although there are also important distinctions to be made between life-interest and the approach to the politics of life associated with biophilosophy, I will concentrate here on a theoretical trajectory that is more revealing in terms of locating life-interest: that emerging from Michel Foucault's argument regarding the relationship between the subject of right and the subject of interest. Foucault suggests that the development of the liberal subject of right has a parallel accompaniment in the subject of interest as envisioned by English empiricist philosophers. Whereas the subject of right accepts limits on his liberty in order to preserve a negotiated, continued access within the state to what were once original, nonmediated rights, the subject of interest "is never called upon to relinquish his interest."[15] Instead, this subject is expected to pursue interest to the utmost and must be allowed and encouraged to do so. Rather than a negotiation or dialectic with the powers of the commonwealth, interest unfolds as a form of immediately and absolutely subjective will. Because of their heterogeneous relationships to the application and reach of power, the subject of right and the subject of interest remain unassimilable to one another, with the latter operating as substrate and guarantee for the subject of right: "The subject of interest constantly overflows the subject of right. . . . He overflows him, surrounds him, and is the permanent condition of his functioning."[16] For Foucault, "liberalism acquire[s] its modern shape precisely with the formulation of this essential incompatibility between the non-totalizable multiplicity of . . . subjects of interest and the totalizing unity of juridical sovereignty."[17]

Although Foucault does not directly relate the subject of interest to the genealogy of biopolitics that occupies him elsewhere, a fundamental connection between self-interest and the preservation of life has been noted by another thinker whose work has become foundational to biopolitical critique: Hannah Arendt. In her excoriating account of what she calls "life philosophy," Arendt argues that the fixation on self-interest in the era of modern political theory arises from the presumed importance of preserving life. As she puts it,

Hidden behind . . . the sacredness of egoism and the all-pervasive power of self-
interest, which were current to the point of being commonplace in the eighteenth
and early nineteenth centuries, we find another point of reference which indeed
forms a much more potent principle than any pain-pleasure calculus could ever
offer, and that is the principle of life itself. What pain and pleasure, fear and desire,
are actually supposed to achieve in all these systems is not happiness at all but the
promotion of individual life or a guarantee of the survival of mankind. . . . In the last
resort, it is always life itself which is the supreme standard to which everything else
is referred, and the interests of the individual as well as the interests of mankind are
always equated with individual life or the life of the species as though it were a matter of course that life is the highest good.[18]

For Arendt, governance through interest of the kind associated with utilitarian-
ism rests on and aims for the reference point of life itself. We can see the defining
nature of this interest in the modern approach to suicide: "If modern egoism
were the ruthless search for pleasure (called happiness) it pretends to be, it would
not lack what in all truly hedonistic systems is an indispensable element of argu-
mentation—a radical justification of suicide."[19] When we render suicide illegal in
order to protect what we assume is any sane person's interest in life, we make
clear the conviction that individual interest can never truly be against survival.

With such life philosophy in place, Arendt argues, the protection and advance
of the life of the species become the unifying and authorizing aim of good government. We can recognize in this account something akin to Foucault's well-
known description of modern biopolitics as that which governs in relation to the
life of the species at large. In Foucault's account, biopolitical regimes treat human
life en masse as something to be actively either preserved or abandoned, as serves
ends regarding the national population. Yet, Arendt ties individual self-interest
to modern life philosophy in a fashion that cannot be explained in terms of the
sovereign power to foster or consign to death large-scale human populations. In
pinpointing the fundamental, necessary function that self-preservation serves in
doctrines of self-interest, Arendt's analysis indicates that the liberal individual
possesses a fundamental *interest* in life alongside its more famous right to life.[20]
If, as Foucault argues, the yoking together of rights and interests is characteristic
of liberalism, then this pairing includes the essential combination of the individual right to life and the individual interest in life. Individual self-preservation thus
occupies a specific intersection between governmental power and life itself that
arises alongside but is distinct from both the liberal right to life and sovereign
decision over life and death. Even when biopolitical regimes stimulate and rely

on the individual self-preservation to foster the health of mass populations, interest in life cannot be acted on directly by juridical will, since it unfolds within the radically subjective and inaccessible realm occupied by the subject of interest.

Tellingly, it is an expansion of the sphere of economic rationality that leads Foucault to explore the role of the empiricist subject of interest in grounding contemporary forms of governance. In Foucault's oft-cited description of the emergence of ordo- and neoliberalism, he argues that in the postwar period we witness a shift to the "use of the typical analysis of the market economy to decipher nonmarket relationships and phenomena which are not strictly and specifically economic but what we would call social phenomena."[21] When economics becomes a "principle of intelligibility and a principle of decipherment of social relationships and individual behavior," the result is the "application of the economic grid to a field which since . . . the end of the eighteenth century, was defined in opposition to the economy, or at any rate, as complementary to the economy."[22] Although this expansion means that governmentality must shift to accommodate the subject of interest, the result is an approach to politics that itself appears to be an instantiation of economic reason. In effect, the subject of interest swallows the liberal subject of right. Rights remain but are lodged within the comprehensive logic of interest as found in the microeconomic imagination, which treats every choice or action as an outcome of interest. Any actions undertaken in the sphere of rights become contingent on and activated by interests.

From one widely circulated Marxist perspective, this transformation appears as an aspect of capital's increasing incorporation and valorization of all of human life, understood here as the totality of human behavior. For example, Michael Hardt and Antonio Negri describe this process as one in which "capital has become a world. Use value and all the other references to values and processes of valorization that were conceived to be outside the capitalist mode of production have progressively vanished. Subjectivity is entirely immersed in exchange."[23] In this view, the application of what Foucault calls "the economic grid" of rationality to formerly "opposed or complementary" fields is part of this progressive disappearance of what were once values and modes exterior to capitalist valorization. However, another side to this process becomes visible when we attend to the role of self-preservation in constituting individual interest. From this perspective, the same expansion of capital that is seemingly poised to engulf all of life itself brings with it the apotheosis of individual interest as an explanatory regime, and that regime is based on self-preservation—on a relationship of individual self to individual life that is essentially immune to direct interference. And once rights, normative values, and even vulnerability to juridical will become mere data to be fed into this calculus of interest, the politics of life in each of these realms is re-imagined in terms of this individual interest in life. Rather than a liberal subject with a right to life, we find a subject with an interest in life; rather than a subject who is the object of a sovereign decision over life and death, we find a subject who actively pursues self-preservation, such that acts of juridical will become mere factors to be weighed in the course of this individual pursuit. Although this subject of life-interest does not appear to be recognizably political in the liberal sense of having rights and obligations as a citizen, it now occupies—with all the sense of forcible displacement that word can imply—the position formerly inhabited by the liberal individual. The result is a political category keyed to the expansion of capital it accompanies: the subject of life-interest.

The Ticking Time Bomb

I want to conclude by turning very briefly to a survival game that has an express connection to American geopolitics, in order to suggest something of the perme-ation of life-interest as a biopolitical category. Usually referred to as the "ticking-time-bomb scenario," this game has been the subject of political debate, as well as being famously and frequently incarnated in the television series 24. Its cen-tral features are a hidden bomb that will soon go off, a tortured terrorist who knows where the bomb is, and an American who must decide whether torture is justified in these extraordinary circumstances.[24] In its archetypal form, torture in general offers what might be the ultimate version of the abstraction and ex-tremity that characterize the microeconomic mode: through the stripped-down confrontation between the torturer and the tortured, it aims to produce interests in the torture victim so profound that they white out and render irrelevant every-thing else in the world.[25] In the ticking-time-bomb scenarios through which American torture has been most frequently fictionalized and debated, however, more attention has, if anything, been paid not to the painful interests of the tor-tured, but to those of the torturer, who must steel himself to withstand the moral agony of undertaking horrific actions in order to serve the greater good. Whereas in Elaine Scarry's famous account the eradication of agency via torture serves to turn the victim's pain into the torturer's power, torture in the ticking-time-bomb scenario instead transforms the victim's pain into the torturer's pain. That is, in facing an unbearable choice that requires subordinating one profound interest to another, the torturer manifests his or her own version of suffering agency.

Although there is an obvious political utility in imagining the torturer as an even greater victim than his victim, I think this depiction suggests that the ticking-time-bomb scenario also has a more specific function, which may explain some of its more puzzling features. Numerous commentators have noted a mismatch between the ticking-time-bomb scenario and the historical context in which it emerges. Not only does this scenario appear as a feature of public debate almost immediately after the destruction of the World Trade Center, well before there is any official acknowledgment of the United States as engaging or needing to engage in so-called enhanced interrogation techniques, but also the torture that was eventually revealed to be perpetrated by the United States in the War on Terror bears very little resemblance to the dynamic that drives the ticking-time-bomb scenario.[26] However, the early, repeated, and erroneous recourse to the ticking-time-bomb scenario makes a different kind of sense if we understand its purpose otherwise: not as a means of mediating the actual use of torture in the War on Terror, but instead as a way to negotiate the uncanny, powerful, and disturbing resemblance between the act of the suicide bomber and the form of individuality guaranteed by life-interest.

The dangers become evident if we consider the suicide bomber's decision in the light of the model of choice I have been examining here. Not only is microeconomic interest by definition nonfalsifiable and incontestable—it is unquestionably in my interest to blow myself up if I decide that it is—but the suicide bomber also pays for his or her choice in the very currency that underwrites agential action in the present, the embodiment of life-interest. Considered from this perspective, it is difficult to refute the logic that leads one individual to judge the benefit of making a fatal strike against one's enemies to be worth the cost of his or her life. In fact, once self-preservation operates as the clearest sign of interest, acting against self-preservation in order to achieve another objective becomes a profound expression of suffering agency, of the commitment to attain one interest at the expense of another held almost equally dear. And, unlike the self-sacrifice of the soldier who flings himself into the breach to save his comrades, the premeditated nature of suicidal terrorism puts the focus on the calculated trade-off that brings a person to see something else as more valuable than continuing to live. When the confluence of life and choice operates as the medium of individual will, deliberately and consciously turning suicide into a weapon may come to seem one of the most cogent and agential acts a subject can take.

To be clear: my point is not that this logic has any bearing on the actual motivations of those performing so-called enhanced interrogation or those labeled as terrorists within the context of twenty-first-century geopolitics. Rather, I am suggesting that the ticking-time-bomb trope is in part an attempt to engage and revalue a perceived resemblance between the deployment of life-interest by the figure of "the terrorist" and the experience of life-interest that guarantees political subjectivity within post-Fordist capital. If the suicidal terrorist appears to triumph through an ingenious renegotiation of this fusion of life and will, then it becomes imperative to imagine an American victory over this particular form of power. In order to both activate and overcome the life-interest of the terrorist, it is not sufficient in this version for the torturer to force the victim to subordinate one profound interest for another, since it is the terrorists' profound capacity to do exactly this that constitutes the threat to be eliminated. Rather, in order to prove his power, the torturer must demonstrate that he can best the victim on the same ground that the terrorist has gained the advantage: the enactment of suffering agency. That is why the reluctant torturer is not outside the game, a sovereign designing its rules, but inside of it, a player fighting to win; that is why he must be both torturer and self-torturer. In order to stage the defeat of an enemy who has found a way to weaponize life-interest, the ticking-time-bomb scenario proves that its American hero can withstand more suffering for his agency than the terrorist can.

Taken together, the texts and tropes I have examined begin to suggest the potent elasticity of life-interest as a biopolitical category. On the one hand, *Gone Girl* demonstrates that life-interest can function as a reterritorialization of the subject because of its presumed status as a feature of each human body. On the other hand, the ticking-time-bomb scenario clearly indicates an anxiety regarding this very universality, which means that there can be no necessary, categorical distinction between humans who do and do not master life-interest. Even in survival-game texts that insist on life-interest as a stable site of sovereign power, the very frenzy of representation that has given us so many texts in the microeconomic mode points to the unfinished and inconclusive nature of these imaginative experiments. What a regime based on life-interest can enable, contain, or set loose is a question currently subject to near-constant hypothetical extrapolation, in the innumerable forking paths of the narratives that make up the microeconomic mode. In its melding of the state of nature and sovereignty, living being with choosing subject, suffering with agency, the microeconomic mode registers a rethinking of contemporary political subjectivity whose reach and consequences are still being worked out around us.

NOTES

1. *127 Hours*, directed by Danny Boyle (Los Angeles: Fox Searchlight, 2011); Aron Ralston, *Between a Rock and a Hard Place* (New York: Atria, 2004).

2. Lionel Robbins, *An Essay on the Nature and Significance of Economic Science* (London: MacMillan, 1932), 15. On the gradual canonization of Robbins's definition as a measure of shifts in the topics and methods of postwar economics, see Roger E. Backhouse and Steven G. Medema, "Retrospectives: On the Definition of Economics," *Journal of Economic Perspectives* 23 (2009): 221–34.

3. Gary S. Becker, *The Economic Approach to Human Behavior* (Chicago: University of Chicago Press, 1976), 5, 1.

4. Ibid., 167, 7.

5. Becker describes his method as tautological but defends it on the grounds of its predictive power. Ibid., 4.

6. Ibid., 10.

7. Michel Foucault, *The Birth of Biopolitics: Lectures at the Collège de France, 1978–79*, trans. Graham Burchell (Basingstoke: Palgrave Macmillan, 2008), 260.

8. See, e.g., Gary S. Becker, Kevin M. Murphy, and Jörg L. Spenkuch, "The Manipulation of Children's Preferences, Old-Age Support, and Investment in Children's Human Capital," *Journal of Labor Economics* 34, no. S2 (2016): S3–S30.

9. For key arguments describing this shift, see Gilles Deleuze, "Postscript on the Societies of Control," *October* 59 (1992): 3–7; Michael Hardt and Antonio Negri, *Empire* (Cambridge, MA: Harvard University Press, 2000); Maurizzio Lazzarato, "Immaterial Labor," in *Radical Thought in Italy: A Potential Politics*, ed. Michael Hardt and Paolo Virno (Minneapolis: University of Minnesota Press, 2006); and Neferti X. M. Tadiar, "Life-Times of Disposability within Global Neoliberalism," *Social Text* 31 (2013): 19–48. Although there are significant disagreements among these theorists in terms of the way they describe the form, reach, and global dispersion of this shift in contemporary capital, I focus on their general areas of overlap in order to illuminate the particular, overarching distinction that concerns me here: that between the subject of immaterial labor and the subject of life-interest. I use the term *immaterial labor* and not *affective labor* in this essay, but both terms circulate as a means to describe this transformation, and both have been subject to arguments regarding their limitations.

10. In general, *gamification* refers to the creation or amplification of game-like features within a system that exists for reasons other than the experience of playing a game. See, e.g., Jane McGonigal, *Reality Is Broken: Why Games Make Us Better and How They Can Change the World* (New York: Penguin, 2011). For a critique of such arguments focused on the relationship between neoliberalism and gamification, see McKenzie Wark, *Gamer Theory* (Cambridge, MA: Harvard University Press, 2007).

11. Gillian Flynn, *Gone Girl: A Novel* (New York: Crown, 2012), 301.

12. Ibid., 369.

13. Ibid., 39; italics in the original.

14. See Deleuze, "Postscript"; Giles Deleuze and Felix Guattari, *A Thousand Plateaus: Capitalism and Schizophrenia*, trans. Brian Massumi (London: Bloomsbury, 2013), 157.

15. Foucault, *Birth of Biopolitics*, 275.

16. Ibid., 274.

17. Ibid., 272.

18. Hannah Arendt, *The Human Condition* (Chicago: University of Chicago Press, 1958), 284–85.

19. Ibid.

20. For John Locke, for example, self-preservation is both the first law of nature and the foundation for liberty within the commonwealth; only with liberty can Man be sure of fulfilling the duty of preserving himself and other humans. John Locke, *Two Treatises of Government* (Cambridge: Cambridge University Press, 1998), 270–71, 279.

21. Foucault, *Birth of Biopolitics*, 240.

22. Ibid.

23. Hardt and Negri, *Empire*, 386.

24. On the ubiquity of and political and ethical problems with the ticking-time-bomb scenario, see, e.g., David Luban, "Liberalism, Torture, and the Ticking Bomb," *Virginia Law Review* 91 (2005): 1425–61. I'm grateful to audience members at the ASAP/5 conference in October 2013 for questions regarding the relationship between the ticking-time-bomb trope and the microeconomic mode. At the time, I was unconvinced of the connection, but the discussion encouraged me to consider the issue further.

25. For the classic account of this type, see Elaine Scarry, *The Body in Pain: The Making and Unmaking of the World* (New York: Oxford University Press, 1985).

26. On the chasm between the scenarios through which we theorize torture and its current manifestations in the War on Terror, see Stephanie Athey, "The Torture Device: Debate and Archetype," in *Torture*, ed. Zalloua Zahi and Shampa Biswas (Seattle: University of Washington Press, 2011), 129–57; and Michael P. Vicaro, "A Liberal Use of 'Torture': Pain, Personhood, and Precedent in the U.S. Federal Definition of Torture," *Rhetoric and Public Affairs* 14 (2011): 401–26.

The New Materialism and Neoliberalism

MIN HYOUNG SONG

It's only a slight exaggeration to say that no intellectual development in the humanities in the past half century has been the cause of as much controversy as the culture turn, along with its closely allied philosophical movement often referred to as the linguistic turn. As Nancy Armstrong succinctly puts it, the former, in its purest form, is the argument that holds that "no form of cultural representation ever simply reproduces what it represents; it always produces that person, place, or thing, as such."[1] While this argument has always had its vocal critics, what is remarkable is that in the past decade or so many critical theorists who have been deeply immersed in the intellectual projects behind the culture turn have pushed against this founding premise. The new materialism, as Diana Coole and Samantha Frost explain, is actually a loose confederation of intellectual trends that have taken a renewed, and perhaps even a radical, interest in "fundamental questions about the nature of matter and the place of embodied humans within a material world." It involves "taking heed of developments in the natural sciences as well as attending to transformations in the ways we currently produce, reproduce, and consume our material environment."[2]

There are many schools of thought within this confederation that go by many different names—such as affect theory, posthumanism, cognitive theory, vibrant materialism, speculative realism, object-oriented ontology, thing theory, some versions of ecocriticism, some versions of digital humanities, and maybe medical humanities. Many practitioners of these schools may feel that theirs is a unique movement separate from the others, an activity that can't be so easily pigeonholed, or a task so inchoate that any attempt to name what they are doing is inappropriate and premature. My grouping them all under the category of new materialism is, I fear, likely to be controversial. Nevertheless, it seems worthwhile to take this risk if only to acknowledge that we are in the midst of a potentially profound transitional moment in the humanities. There is growing frustration, if not hostility, toward arguments about a reality that is merely a consequence of our linguistic and cultural mediations. The real seems once again more accessible, or at the very least knowable in ways that aren't hopelessly tainted by ideology. Phenomena that were once vehemently argued to belong to the realm of culture are being returned, at least in part, to biology and chemistry.

The new materialism is less about matter and things, then, than it is about our ability to make truth claims. The focus on matter and things is an assertion of a truth that exists regardless of whether we can make reasoned claims about this existing. Starting with the assumption that this truth exists, a kind of ontology, enables critics to recalibrate their methodologies and gear them toward ascertaining such a truth. As such, the new materialism can be understood as a form of realism, in that it seeks to represent what is real without the representing getting too much in the way. It might also be seen as actualizing a desire to reclaim an epistemological power that was given up in the culture turn, a move toward authority that might be attractive at a time when so much academic labor is becoming casualized and the humanities as a whole is left wondering about its place in the academy. Such a move is just as importantly about recognizing that we cannot reconfigure reality by calling greater attention to how it is constructed; we are constrained as much by the physical world as we are by our ideas about it.

In trying to make sense of this emergent body of scholarly work, I find myself struggling with the political ramifications of trying to think of a materiality that exists independently of our apprehension of it at a time when so much seems, simply, to be going wrong. What can the new materialism add to an understanding of the dominant economic and political belief of our present, which commentators have named neoliberalism? This belief may not be the cause for all that is wrong with our world, but it certainly does little to address our problems and in many cases exacerbates them. It assumes that discrete individuals engaged in rational market exchanges with the least amount of state interference enable the maximum amount of freedom possible. The market, in turn, becomes the very model for all social institutions and interpersonal relations. We are all asked to think of ourselves as rational individuals constantly seeking to maximize return on our investments, which we can best do when freed from the constraints of state control and bureaucracy. Lost is the sense that a representative democracy can actually represent the best interests of its subjects. Lost is the sense that the state could be a protection against, much less a shaper of, the forces of the market itself. Lost is the sense that collective interests can take precedence over individual ones, and that any form of living together requires a sharing of resources.

In the place of such ideals, greed, competition, efficiency, and moralism become our king.[3]

What marks the 1990s as an especially important decade in neoliberalism's ascendency is the formal end of the Cold War, which, among other things, enabled what Mark Fisher calls capitalist realism. This is the belief that, after all the disastrous experiments with alternative political and economic models, capitalism remains the only system of social organization possible. The end of capitalism has thus literally become equated in our minds with the end of the world. Its very flaws make it irresistible because capitalism is the only system of human organization that realistically treats humans, with all their innate and hardwired flaws, as they actually are rather than how some idealists would like them to be.[4] As literary scholars have pointed out, this notion of capitalist realism recalls the ways in which literary realism is the genre most intimately intertwined with capitalism. If the task before us is to question the idea that capitalism is as good as it gets, we might begin to undertake this task by challenging the way literary realism itself works. "Realism is repoliticized," Alison Shonkwiler and Leigh Claire La Berge write. "It was always political, of course, but now the stakes are raised again, calling attention to the ways in which capitalism impoverishes our imagination while simultaneously claiming that impoverishment cannot be imagined otherwise."[5]

Following on the heels of this analysis, I want to insist that a replenishing of our imagination must entail both breaking the illusions that the currently existing realism depends on for its reality effects and, in these illusions' stead, the creation of other reality effects. These other reality effects must, in turn, find ways of making sense of how neoliberalism fuels, and perhaps is fueled by, the disparate problems pressing violently on our present. These problems include anthropogenic global warming, extreme wealth and income inequality, mass demographic changes, disruptive advances in technology, and impressive advances in the natural sciences. For the new materialism to contribute to this kind of endeavor and not be, as some of its critics argue, simply complicit with neoliberal thinking, it needs to remember what we have already learned along the way about social construction and mediation. It should also include a less adversarial engagement with historical materialism (something that was also lacking during the heyday of the culture turn) than can currently be found in its growing archives. Such an engagement can help give the new materialism an account of history and of being in time that may be greater than the human but is nevertheless focused on the needs of actual human beings and their aspirations to lead dignified, meaningful lives. Finally, the new materialism should eschew the description of a materiality that simply exists in the same way that we should all contest the idea that what we have in the present is all the reality we can hope for. It should, to put this point in a slightly different way, try to imagine its realism as something creative rather than merely descriptive. If the most productive way to pursue viable alternative visions to capitalist realism continues to be through collective action and a search for what we can share in common, then one of the great insights the new materialism can offer is an unusually expansive idea of what the commons can be.

In Defense of Symptomatic Reading

The literary study of race and racism has been my primary research focus. From this perspective, the following is obvious but worth stating: those of us who study race and racism tend to view claims about nature as inescapably constructed. This is because when we talk about race, we are almost always talking about history, imperialism, power relations, and ideology. Our attention is focused on habits of thought, beliefs formed out of their service to ruling ideas, ways of seeing that only see what has already been given to sight. We are on the lookout for lacunae and contradictions that reveal the fundamental ways in which ideas of race cannot be trusted, states that maintain their legitimacy by erasing or at the very least obscuring the violence that helps found them and maintains them, and unequal economic relations that likewise must distract from the mechanisms that enable and exacerbate inequalities based on tendentious biological distinctions.[6] We are ever sensitive to biopolitical determinations about whose lives should be enhanced and whose lives either can be ignored or, in the necropolitical obverse of the biopolitical, must end.[7] Very much in the mainstream of this way of thinking about race and racism, Ruth Wilson Gilmore provides this especially memorable definition of racism: "the state-sanctioned or extralegal production and exploitation of group-differentiated vulnerability to premature death."[8] Building on Gilmore's definition, Lisa Marie Cacho offers her readers something pithier: "Racism is a killing abstraction."[9] Or consider the way Karen Fields and Barbara Fields understand racism as "a social practice, which means that it is an action and a rationale for action, or both at once. *Racism* always takes for granted the objective reality of *race*." But, as they proceed to explain, the "shorthand" that fails to make their distinctiveness clear enough "transforms *racism*, something an aggressor *does*, into *race*, something the target *is*."[10]

Note that in these recent examples (selected because they are recent and influential) and in the numerous other examples I could have quoted in their place, race never refers to human differences somehow found outside structures of meaning and social organization that are artifacts of human manipulation. Race is not an ontology. When we talk about race and racism, we are talking about ideas that are at once deeply anthropocentric and constantly in denial about this fact. Racism operates by refusing to disclose the constructedness of race. Its field of operations is the terrain of common sense, of objectivity, of the God-given, of biology and genetics, of what lies always outside the human and what is outside our control. Nature is another such terrain, maybe the epitome of such a terrain. Nature is an outside to the human that gives shape to the human and hence is easily available for rationalizations of our construction of human difference without any necessary lingering over how such constructions benefit some at the expense of the many. While we may be very good at pointing out how race is constructed, it's also the case that because race gains in power by operating as if it were natural, a way of seeing that, as Judith Butler has helpfully put it, "is itself a racial formation, an episteme, hegemonic and forceful,"[11] we cannot easily shake off its hold on our imagination. To suggest that there is a nature that exists beyond race and is a more accurate understanding of human difference would always be shadowed by concern that such an outside is never outside. "Defined in opposition to the subject," Joseph Jonghyun Jeon insists, "the *thing* in American literature and culture has stood for nothing short of dehumanization."[12] What we think we have somehow intuited as what exists exterior to the human remains simply another projection of the human.

This very well founded concern that nature naturalizes racism is one significant reason why an engagement with the new materialism is for me so daunting. Stephen Best and Sharon Marcus, for instance, are in a new material mode of thought when they argue against what they call "symptomatic reading," a term they trace to Fredric Jameson's *Political Unconscious*. Symptomatic reading denotes the literary scholar's efforts to plumb the hidden depths of a text that its surface conceals. Hence, the two write in the introduction to a special issue of *Representations* that offers us a critique of this reading practice, "When symptomatic readers focus on elements present in the text, they construe them as symbolic of something latent or concealed; for example, a queer symptomatic reading might interpret the closet, or ghosts, as surface signs of the deep truth of a homosexuality that cannot be overtly depicted."[13] As N. Katherine Hayles observes, reflecting on this argument and gesturing to its growing influence, "After more than two decades of symptomatic reading, however, many literary scholars are not finding it a productive practice, perhaps because (like many deconstructive readings) its results have begun to seem formulaic, leading to predictable conclusions rather than compelling insights."[14]

Both of these calls for experimenting with a different mode of reading, one that turns away from a sounding of depths, a rubbing against the grain, an almost paranoid search for hidden meanings (one that leads to what Best and Marcus call "surface reading" and is echoed in Franco Moretti's "distance reading" and Hayles's "machine reading" and "hyper reading"), were in some ways already anticipated by Eve Sedgwick.[15] In one of her last published works, she recalls Paul Ricoeur's notion of a "hermeneutics of suspicion" to lambast what she sees as a stultifying critical practice. Notably, she ends up finding fault most particularly with Jameson, who, while often critical of the culture turn, also shared many of its assumptions:

> In the context of recent U.S. critical theory, however, where Marx, Nietzsche, and Freud by themselves are taken as constituting a pretty sufficient genealogy for the mainstream of New Historicist, deconstructive, feminist, queer, and psychoanalytic criticism, to apply a hermeneutics of suspicion is, I believe, widely understood as a mandatory injunction rather than a possibility among other possibilities. The phrase has now something of the sacred status of Fredric Jameson's "Always Historicize"— and, like that one, it fits oddly into its new position in the tablets of the law. *Always* historicize? What could have less to do with historicizing than the commanding, atemporal adverb "always"? It reminds me of the bumper stickers that instruct people in other cars to "Question Authority."[16]

The same kind of dismissiveness of the apparent routinization of contemporary critical practice can also be found in José Esteban Muñoz's *Cruising Utopia: The Then and There of Queer Futurity*: "The moment in which I write this book the critical imagination is in peril. The dominant academic climate into which this book is attempting to intervene is dominated by a dismissal of political idealism. . . . The antiutopian critic of today has a well-worn war chest of post-structuralism pieties at her or his disposal to shut down lines of thought that delineate the concept of critical utopianism."[17]

It might not be surprising to find that Sedgwick and Muñoz share similar attitudes toward the critical establishment of their day, both having been prominent critics in the field of queer theory. What is at least interesting to note is that their sense of frustration with current dominant strains of academic thinking is also shared by Graham Harman, whose speculative philosophy is one of the keystones of what is now generally known as object-oriented ontology. In *Guerilla Metaphysics: Phenomenology and the Carpentry of Things*, he observes, "The so-called linguistic turn is still the dominant model for the philosophy of access, but there are plenty of others—phenomenology, hermeneutics, deconstruction, philosophy of mind, pragmatism. None of these philosophical schools tells us much of anything about objects themselves; indeed, they pride themselves on avoiding all naive contact with nonhuman entities."[18] Or, even more interesting is the fact that the same frustration has been echoed by the prominent feminist scholar Elizabeth Grosz: "We need to understand not only how culture inscribes bodies—a preoccupation of much social and cultural theory in the past decade or more—but, more urgently, what these bodies are such that inscription is possible, what it is in the *nature* of bodies."[19] Or, again still, in a way that we can begin to see is its own hard-and-fast critical convention (as formulaic as the arguments being critiqued), there is Bruno Latour worrying that "entire Ph.D. programs are still running to make sure that good American kids are learning the hard way that facts are made up, that there is no such thing as natural, unmediated, unbiased access to truth, that we are always prisoners of language, that we always speak from a particular standpoint, and so on, while dangerous extremists are using the very same argument of social construction to destroy hard-won evidence that could save our lives."[20]

All of these critiques of the culture turn seem to share the view that the humanities has been for too long caught up in its own inward-looking sleepy world. As a result, it has been left behind by surging advances in the natural sciences and a generally apathetic public. Inbred, it takes itself far too seriously, overestimates the impact of what it is trying to do, and repeats itself endlessly with variations of the same findings. Such dismissive antagonism to the culture turn makes manifest concern that a turn away would inevitably be a reactionary move toward an apolitical formalism that demands we pay attention to only what is there on the page, the text being, again, the only kind of materiality that matters. Or, alternatively, a post-culture turn could mean a relationship to the natural sciences where the humanities are tasked merely with finding cogent and lively demonstrations of scientific principles without the possibility of dialogue or opportunity to question the assumptions that have gone into the formulation of such principles. Or, another fear, a post-culture turn might reject arguments about social construction, ideological state apparatuses, and hegemony in favor of something more ethereal and abstracted, and as far away from what was once called materialism as possible.[21]

What in short might be most troubling about a move toward the new materialism is the potential that it might lead us to ignore how our very social order is propped up, maybe even driven, by a dizzying intersection of inequalities. Such a move would be especially troubling in the current global crises of governance defined by the wholesale rejection of the rigors of formal governing except in the areas of police action, military engagement, and bailouts of major financial firms in favor of simplistic market-based approaches to distributing resources, arranging social interactions, and determining value, all of which severely exacerbate current inequalities. If the new materialism is a challenge to symptomatic reading, it may not be well suited for discerning the truths of our present moment. We need symptomatic reading now more than ever because neoliberalism wants to claim itself as an improvement on the capitalism that came before even though it is just as bad or in some cases worse.[22] While lip service continues to be paid to the idea that capitalism can be a force that constantly breaks down old social barriers, frees individuals to make their own choices, and hence acts as a boon (even if it also has its destructive side) to the liberal vision of producing individuals engaged in rational behavior, all while operating at maximum efficiency, what the many scholars and commentators who have helped popularize the word *neoliberalism* seem to gesture toward is the idea that capitalism itself has changed form. It is no longer the industrial variety ever focused on discipline, regimentation, and hierarchy. Rather, it stresses flexibility, independence, and shifting social arrangements that either dispense with leaders or shift the leadership role among team members depending on the specific projects they are working on.

Neoliberalism gives a name to this variation of capitalism. It is perhaps for this reason that the word is so often invoked in scholarly work that refuses to shy away from questions of politics and economics. The frequency with which the word has been used has also led many academics I know, all of whom I deeply respect, to question whether the word itself is useful. The arguments I have heard insist that it has merely become a way to disparage any present-day phenomenon we dislike, as well as an impediment to a more precise description of the problems we wish to lay bare.[23] Such arguments formally mimic the arguments I quoted above, which express deep dissatisfaction with the culture turn and symptomatic reading, even if they often sharply depart from each other content-wise. It may well be true that the word *neoliberalism* is overused and that critics risk falling into overly familiar lines of reasoning. Still, we nevertheless need to endeavor to find ways to talk about these problems. Exhaustion with a word does not mean that what it seeks to uncover does not deserve our attention.

So what form, more precisely, has capitalism taken? If we look, as Thomas Piketty has most famously done, at the impressive concentration of wealth that is now occurring at a global scale and how this wealth is passed down across the generations, what we find is that class structures are becoming almost as rigid as they were in nineteenth-century Europe.[24] Against the promise of fluidity and the rejection of disciplinary rigidity, there is a firming up of class identities, a slowing down of socioeconomic mobility, a narrowing of social interactions determined by access to wealth. We might say that contemporary capitalism remains as dedicated as ever to hierarchy, and may in fact be even more dedicated than what came immediately before, despite whatever the evangelists of neoliberalism claim about the form capitalism has taken and the kind of values they espouse. Andrew Hoberek captures the dynamics at work here as an axiom: "*capitalism is no longer capitalistic, insofar as it increasingly reinforces economic and social hierarchies even as it celebrates idealized versions of its own opposition to such hierarchies.*"[25] Effusive encomiums to freedom, individuality, and choice can be seen from this perspective as yet another ideological bait and switch: promise one thing and deliver in its place impressive amounts of exploitation, misery, and boundless personal accumulation. For us to believe this argument requires that we engage precisely in the very kind of thinking that Best and Marcus, Hayles, Sedgwick, Muñoz, Harman, Grosz, Latour, and many others have faulted for its lack of imagination. We continue to turn to culture, perform symptomatic readings, and engage in a hermeneutics of suspicion because we refuse to believe what neoliberalism tells us about the world it says it is creating. We also try to remain thoughtful of our own place within its narratives and of how our own attempts to surpass its limitations might simply reinforce them. As Patricia Stuelke succinctly observes, "as we seek to remake the world, to reinvent relationality and reciprocity beyond the modes that neoliberalism and imperialism allow, we must remain critical of our own utopian imaginations."[26]

What Comes after the Cultural Turn?

My defense of symptomatic reading still leaves unaddressed questions raised by the new materialism. Have we who study race and racism (and class, gender, sexuality, disability, and so forth) become "formulaic" and "predictable," to borrow a couple of Hayles's adjectives? Are we too willing to shout down utopian possibilities, as Muñoz insists? Have we, as Sedgwick argues, merely become purveyors of ideas that can easily fit on a bumper sticker? And in being these things, have we somehow failed to appreciate as fully as possible what might follow after the contradictions of the present—with its worsening inequalities, its careening toward climate disaster, its constant state of numb anhedonia—become too bright for anyone to ignore? Have we, in other words, been caught up in our own use of a capitalist realism, such that our efforts through symptomatic reading to describe the world as it is have made it more difficult for us to imagine worlds that do not yet exist? To address these questions, I want to offer a brief reading of Thoreau's essay "Walking." My reading pays attention to the way this essay's idea of the wild is built on, and reinforces, long-circulating racial meanings, performing what I hope is a symptomatic reading that seeks to be informed by what the new materialism can offer.

I focus on "Walking" because it is probably one of the most well-known celebrations of the wild in American literature (and it is also an essay I very much admire). Indeed, the following might be one of the most quoted phrases from the large body of Thoreau's very quotable writings: "The West of which I speak is but another name for the Wild; and what I have been preparing to say is, that in Wildness is the preservation of the World."[27] What makes this passage so memorable is the way in which it imagines the wild as a zone of nature into which human activities have somehow not yet penetrated or altered to usefulness in any way. As such, the wild is also a source of human vigor, the place from which we draw inspiration, strength, and even power. Not long after this passage, Thoreau observes, "It was because the children of the Empire were not suckled by the wolf that they were conquered and displaced by the children of the northern forests who were" (225). While he is obviously thinking about the Roman Empire, and its foundational myth of Romulus and Remus being raised by wolves, he could just as easily be referring to the United States as an emerging imperial power expanding west across the continent, conquering and at the same time weakening as future generations become too used to the wealth of conquest.

As a rumination on nation building, "Walking" should stir skepticism, especially when it begins to take seriously the idea that history marches westward. Here is one example: "I must walk toward Oregon, and not toward Europe. And that way the nation is moving, and I may say that mankind progresses from east to west. . . . The eastern Tartars think there is nothing west beyond Tibet. 'The world ends there,' say they; 'beyond there is nothing but a shoreless sea.' It is unmitigated East where they live" (218). All sorts of racial assumptions abound in this passage. The east becomes the East, a remote place of mystery and stalled development against which the west as West knows itself to be rational and progressive. We hardly need to refer to Edward Said's *Orientalism* to know how much the thinking in this passage reflects geopolitical realities that reify asymmetrical relations of power as self-evident facts of nature.[28] The nature of the Orient is to be mysterious and set in its ways. The nature of the Occident is to be rational and always striving for improvement.

Just as important, we can see in the way progress is understood as always headed west how much Thoreau's thinking is a part of the very kind of expansionist thinking he resists in his writings. That is, the "walk toward Oregon" mirrors and reflects thinking that saw the United States' expansion as a settler colonial nation as inevitably destined to occupy the whole of the continent, all the way to the Pacific. We can see how Thoreau contributes toward making something profoundly ideological seem like something that isn't. In the section that begins his ruminations on the westward march of history, he writes, "What is it that makes it so hard sometimes to determine whither we will walk? I believe that there is a subtle magnetism in Nature, which, if we unconsciously yield to it, will direct us aright" (216). If so, the fact that we all seem somehow to be drawn to "walk toward Oregon" is to yield to a force so natural it reflects something intrinsic in the very spin of the planet and the energies this spin produces. Later, he elaborates: "I know not how significant it is, or how far it is an evidence of singularity, that an individual should thus consent in his pettiest walk with the general movement of the race; but I know that something akin to the migratory instinct in birds and quadrupeds . . . that something like the *furor* which affects the domestic cattle in the spring, and which is referred to a worm in their tails, affects both nations and individuals, either perennially or from time to time" (219). Everything seems to move westward, from the spin of the earth that leads the Sun to set in the west to the migratory patterns of animals to the solitary walker, so that it seems perfectly natural somehow that the motion of "nations" also always strives in this direction.

These thoughts should lead us to reflect on the ways in which his famous quotation "in Wildness is the preservation of the World" is preceded in the very same sentence by the conflation of the wild with the west: "The West of which I speak is but another name for the Wild." Such a conflation could only have meant for Thoreau and his peers the opening of the westward parts of North America to US nation-building ambitions. As history marched westward, it gobbled up the wild; transformed it into organized plots of land, interconnected tracks, and roadways; and fed the growth of suffocating social organizations, all of which led over time to an inevitable weakening of civilization. The latter is a kind of domestication that is equal to a feminine lack of vigor. Early in the essay, Thoreau makes the gendered nature of his thinking explicit in his celebration of sauntering: "If you are ready to leave father and mother, and brother and sister, and wife and child and friends, and never see them again . . . you are ready for a walk" (206). The antecedent of "you" in this sentence is obviously male.

If westward expansion is inevitable, all we could hope for is the preservation of the wild, the "wolf" from which we could feed and be nourished in a way that reinvigorates us. We might also then consider how odd it is that the west/wild conflation marginalizes the presence of Native Americans. While Thoreau does make mention of them early in the essay, they quickly become confused with the landscape they inhabit and an example of the very wild in all of its dangerous

vigor he wishes to preserve. They are thus like the "Hottentot," who "eagerly de-
vour the marrow of the koodoo and other antelopes raw, as a matter of course,"
in that they too "eat raw the marrow of the Arctic reindeer" (225). Thoreau's wild
is both gendered and racialized; there's nothing natural about it. At the same
time, it's clear that such an awareness of what informs his thinking is yet far on
the horizon—maybe beyond the horizon—for Thoreau, whose musings about
nature and the wild have no room for reflecting on these concepts as being socially
constructed in all sorts of suspect racial and gendered ways. To suggest such a
possibility is anachronistic. For Thoreau, nature and the wild simply seem to exist,
a part of the world that he observes and can reliably count on to be. His rhetorical
embellishments are attempts to give aesthetic shape to an experience, to communicate, in as lively and vivid a manner possible with the language and imagery
and allusions available to him, what he senses and marvels at.

From our contemporary perspective, this kind of thinking might seem almost childlike in its wonder at the world. This is also the feeling that many new
materialists prize overtly. In her earlier work, *The Enchantment of Modern Life:
Attachments, Crossings, and Ethics*, Jane Bennett states, "The depiction of nature
and culture as orders not capable of inspiring deep attachment inflects the self
as a creature of loss and thus discourages discernment of the marvelous vitality
of bodies human and nonhuman, natural and artifactual."[29] Such thinking leads
her in more recent writings to posit the existence of a material world beyond our
own, one that exists independent of us and may just as importantly shape our
own world in hard-to-discern but nevertheless significant ways. Bennett argues
in *Vibrant Matter: A Political Ecology of Things* that the prevailing understanding
of the physical world is that it is full of "passive stuff," which in turn encourages
the "habit of parsing the world into dull matter (it, things) and vibrant life (us,
beings)."[30] Recognizing the more active role that things play in the way action
occurs is for Bennett a way to upend this habit of thought, so that "matter" and
"life" are actually so confused that it is impossible to say where one begins and
the other ends. She concludes the book, "I believe that encounters with lively matter can chasten fantasies of human mastery, highlight the common materiality
of all that is, expose a wider distribution of agency, and reshape the self and its
interests."[31]

Likewise, our tendency to separate the world between us and not-us may have
made it more difficult for us to appreciate the significance of neurological research that has revealed a marvelous plasticity. This plasticity gives our brains
their capacity to produce thoughts, maintain them in usable shapes, and explode
these shapes when necessary. Catherine Malabou has reasoned that such advances

in neuroscience have failed to excite a more general public because they have not provided models for altering our relations to each other. Our improved understanding of the way the brain works has done little to stir the imagination about a different kind of life from the ones we are living, and as a result it has not helped us to access as-yet-unthought modes of enjoyment, or, as Malabou puts it, "new ways to be happy."[32] Our rutted habits of relating to the physical world may also prevent us from seeing how our habits themselves are shaped by unseen but pervasive forces that we might call affect, defined by Kathleen Stewart as "the commonplace, labor-intensive process of sensing modes of living as they come into being. . . . The lived spaces and temporalities of home, work, school, blame, adventure, illness, rumination, pleasure, downtime, and release are the rhythms of the present as a compositional event—one already weighted with the buzz of atmospheric fill."[33] Such an eclectic enjambment of phenomena and sensual experience insists that we pay close attention to relationality rather than separation, a kind of being-in-the-world that does not afford an easy prizing of individual autonomy and self-possession. As Jason Moore insists, "Everything that humans do is a flow of flows, in which the rest of nature is always moving through us."[34]

Such arguments seem to me to call for a tempering of the kind of critical move my reading of "Walking" makes. The wild is surely a social construct, but perhaps it also names something palpable and real? There is, in other words, an actual zone beyond human influence—a spin of the earth, a migration of birds, a magnetic force—that at the same time exerts an enormous influence on us. This zone is something we aspire to know, however inadequately and distorted by our beliefs, and something that exerts an influence we need desperately to find ways to account for. From such a perspective, we might say that symptomatic reading is an attempt to make sense of the distortions in the language available to us to describe this zone. Symptomatic reading does not posit that no such zone exists, but calls attention instead to the ways in which trying to make sense of what is beyond the human, or what Thoreau calls the wild, is flawed and requires forceful self-conscious critique. What the new materialism seeks to teach us, then, is to pay attention to what may always be an element of critique, its shadowy positing of what can be otherwise.

Ecologies

In the fast-growing scholarly literature of the new materialism, words such as *ecology* and *world* and *planet* are invoked with great frequency. Mainly, this seems to reflect the ways in which what motivates many of the authors of this literature is an abiding concern with environmental issues. The new materialism seeks to overcome divides formed during the culture turn, and to help rehabilitate ideas of nature that have been put into question. As I noted earlier, those of us who study race and racism have been devoted to unraveling the thoughtless claims made about race as reflecting something found in nature. As a result, this study has found itself facing off against ecocriticism as a field devoted to resuscitating interest in nature as inhuman but nevertheless worthy of our care. In a succinct review of the development of ecocriticism, Ursula Heise observes that both it and the fields of study that focus on identity had parallel developments in the 1960s and 1970s. During these tumultuous decades, there was fast-growing concern about pollution, environmental degradation, and ecological collapse. There was also growing concern about oppression based on race, gender, and sexual orientation. And yet, as the latter gained prominence in academic literary circles, the former lost ground "even though environmentalism succeeded in establishing a lasting presence in the political sphere."[35]

The reason why it was only in the mid-1990s and beyond that ecocriticism began to emerge as an important area of literary investigation is the culture turn. Heise argues, "Under the influence of mostly French philosophies of language, literary critics during this period took a fresh look at questions of representation, textuality, narrative, identity, subjectivity, and historical discourse from a fundamentally skeptical perspective that emphasized the multiple disjunctures between forms of representation and the realities they purported to refer to. In this intellectual context, the notion of nature tended to be approached as a sociocultural construct that had historically often served to legitimize the ideological claims of specific social groups."[36] In other words, as scholars began to investigate the ways in which injustices based on differences of race, gender, and sexual orientation relied on naturalizing human relationships, they began to grow suspect of any claims of the natural as a prior being to the human. The current emphasis on ecology, world, and planet among new material scholars, then, can be attributed to a desire to reinvigorate a more robust idea of nature, one that exceeds the culture turn's claims about its constructedness by returning nature to the human. We are not what stands apart and separate from nature, which our analyses can sometimes reinforce, but are a part of nature. Our very beings are constituted by our entanglements within ecological processes that continue inexorably around and through us, regardless of our willingness to acknowledge them.

It's these entanglements that the new materialism seems poised to explore with increasing sophistication and insightfulness. While I am skeptical of a lot of work that I have read in this field, I am also drawn to continue reading in it because it is often an attempt to find connections where we have tended to see only separation.[37] As Moore again puts it, "The Cartesian binary says, more or less automatically, that something like unemployment insurance is a social issue, and something like climate change is an environmental issue. But this is completely arbitrary. It distracts us from asking how configurations of power, wealth, and nature are inscribed in everything that humans do."[38] What's most compelling about new materialism, then, is its insistence that we turn our attention to a materiality that we too often think about as something removed, and removable, from who and what we are.

NOTES

The author would like to thank Joseph Jonghyun Jeon, Sarah Brouillette, and Sue Kim for discussing this topic with me as I began to engage it in earnest, Sarah Wald and Cathy Schlund-Vials for reading a much earlier version of this chapter, and Mitchum Huehls and Rachel Greenwald Smith for providing substantial editorial commentary that undoubtedly saved me from a lot of embarrassment. This chapter draws significantly from a PhD seminar I taught, entitled "New Materialism and American Literature." I thank the graduate students in the seminar for teaching me so much.

1. Nancy Armstrong, "Who's Afraid of the Culture Turn?," *differences* 12, no. 1 (Spring 2001): 18.

2. Diana Coole and Samantha Frost, "Introducing the New Materialisms," in *New Materialisms: Ontology, Agency, and Politics*, ed. Diana Coole and Samantha Frost (Durham, NC: Duke University Press, 2010), 3. Coole and Frost opt to use the term *materialisms* to emphasize a plurality of approaches. I use the singular *materialism* to emphasize the ways in which the movements I am classifying together seem motivated by a similar impulse. I think of these movements as moving toward a more or less common destination along widely divergent paths and not as movements spiraling off in their own independent directions.

3. See Wendy Brown, *Undoing the Demos: Neoliberalism's Stealth Revolution* (New York: Zone Books, 2015), and "Neo-Liberalism and the End of Liberal Democracy," *Theory and Event* 7, no. 1 (2003); David Harvey, *A Brief History of Neoliberalism* (Oxford: Oxford University Press, 2005); and Lisa Duggan, *The Twilight of Equality? Neoliberalism, Cultural Politics, and the Attack on Democracy* (Boston: Beacon, 2003). I also discuss these ideas in my book *Strange Future: Pessimism and the 1992 Los Angeles Riots* (Durham, NC: Duke University Press, 2005); see esp. 5–12. The four phases described in the introduction provide a useful way for thinking about how neoliberalism began as an economic concept and has bled into other aspects of social organization and experience. I am focused here primarily on the politico-ideological and sociocultural, and I am somewhat skeptical about claims that its reach has gone further into the ontological (which I believe Brown claims in her recent book).

4. Mark Fisher, *Capitalist Realism: Is There No Alternative?* (London: Zero Books, 2009), 2.

5. Alison Shonkwiler and Leigh Claire La Berge, "Introduction: A Theory of Capitalist

Realism," in *Reading Capitalist Realism*, ed. Alison Shonkwiler and Leigh Claire La Berge (Iowa City: University of Iowa Press, 2014), 16.

6. Some of the key works I have in mind here are Michael Omi and Howard Winant, *Racial Formation in the United States: From the 1960s to the 1990s*, 2nd ed. (New York: Routledge, 1994); Lisa Lowe, *Immigrant Acts: On Asian Americanist Cultural Politics* (Durham, NC: Duke University Press, 1996); George Lipsitz, *The Possessive Investment in Whiteness* (Philadelphia: Temple University Press, 1998); and Eduardo Bonilla-Silva, *Racism without Racists: Color-Blind Racism and the Persistence of Racial Inequality in America* (Lanham, MD: Rowman & Littlefield, 2003). All of these works have profoundly shaped my understanding of race and racism, and they no doubt (except for the last one) also say something about when I was trained as a scholar.

7. See, e.g., Achille Mbembe, "Necropolitics," trans. Libby Meintjes, *Public Culture* 15, no. 1 (2003), 11–40.

8. Ruth Wilson Gilmore, *Golden Gulag: Prisons, Surplus, Crisis, and Opposition in Globalizing California* (Berkeley: University of California Press, 2007), 28.

9. Lisa Marie Cacho, *Social Death: Racialized Rightlessness and the Criminalization of the Unprotected* (New York: New York University Press, 2012), 7.

10. Karen Fields and Barbara Fields, *Racecraft: The Soul of Inequality in American Life* (London: Verso, 2012), 17.

11. Judith Butler, "Endangered/Endangering: Schematic Racism and White Paranoia," in *Reading Rodney King, Reading Urban Uprising*, ed. Robert Gooding-Williams (New York: Routledge, 1991), 17.

12. Joseph Jonghyun Jeon, *Racial Things, Racial Forms: Objecthood in Avant-Garde Asian American Poetry* (Iowa City: University of Iowa Press, 2012), xviii.

13. Stephen Best and Sharon Marcus, "Surface Reading: An Introduction," *Representations* 101, no. 1 (Fall 2009): 3.

14. N. Katherine Hayles, *How We Think: Digital Media and Contemporary Technogenesis* (Chicago: University of Chicago Press, 2012), 59.

15. On surface reading, see Best and Marcus, "Surface Reading." On distance reading, see Franco Moretti, *Graphs, Trees, Maps: Abstract Models for Literary History* (London: Verso, 2007); and Matthew Wilkens, "Contemporary Fiction by the Numbers," *Post45 Contemporaries*, March 3, 2011, http://post45.research.yale.edu/2011/03/contemporary-fiction-by-the-numbers/. On "machine reading" and "hyper reading," see Hayles, *How We Think*.

16. Eve Sedgwick, *Touching Feeling: Affect, Pedagogy, Performativity* (Durham, NC: Duke University Press, 2003), 125.

17. José Esteban Muñoz, *Cruising Utopia: The Then and There of Queer Futurity* (New York: New York University Press, 2009), 10.

18. Graham Harman, *Guerilla Metaphysics: Phenomenology and the Carpentry of Things* (Chicago: Open Court, 2005), 1.

19. Elizabeth Grosz, *The Nick of Time: Politics, Evolution, and the Untimely* (Durham, NC: Duke University Press, 2004), 2.

20. Bruno Latour, "Why Has Critique Run Out of Steam? From Matters of Fact to Matters of Concern," *Critical Inquiry* 30 (Winter 2004): 227. Also, for an updated version of these arguments, see Rita Felski, *The Limits of Critique* (Chicago: University of Chicago Press, 2015); and Mitchum Huehls, *After Critique: Twenty-First Century Fiction in a Neoliberal Age* (New York: Oxford University Press, 2016).

21. The new materialism has often been met by a fierce critical response. See, e.g., Jordana Rothberg, "The Molecularization of Sexuality: On Some Primitivisms of the Present," *Theory and Event* 17, no. 2 (2014); Nathan Brown, "The Nadir of OOO: From Graham Harman's *Tool-Being* to Timothy Morton's *Realist Magic: Objects, Ontology, Causality*," *Parrhesia* 17 (2013): 62–71; and Svenja Bromberg, "The Anti-Political Aesthetics of Objects and Worlds Beyond," *Mute*, July 25, 2013, www.metamute.org/editorial/articles/anti-political-aesthetics-objects-and-worlds-beyond. The anti-critique or postcritical position has also drawn important responses. For an especially articulate example of these responses, see Lee Konstantinou, "The Hangman of Critique," *Los Angeles Review of Books*, July 17, 2016, https://lareviewofbooks.org/article/the-hangman-of-critique/.

22. I thank Mitchum Huehls for this observation.

23. Sara Ahmed offers an especially sharp version of this argument. Acknowledging the importance of the insights that critiques of neoliberalism enable, especially of the transformation of the contemporary university, she points out how "neoliberalism" can be used to criticize students for having the wrong desires. She writes, "The figure of the consuming subject who wants the wrong things, a student who is found wanting, is hard at work. She is how an idea of universal knowledge or universal culture can be so *thinly disguised* as a critique of neoliberalism and managerialism." Sara Ahmed, "Against Students," *New Inquiry*, June 29, 2015, http://thenewinquiry.com/essays/against-students/. It's worth noting here that Ahmed offers this argument less to steer her readers away from critique and more to insist on even more rigorous critique. She would, thus, be the very kind of suspicious reader that arguments in favor of surface reading want to dismiss as overly predictable.

24. Thomas Piketty, *Capital in the Twenty-First Century* (Cambridge, MA: Harvard University Press, 2013).

25. Andrew Hoberek, "Adultery, Crisis, Contract," in *Reading Capitalist Realism*, ed. Alison Shonkwiler and Leigh Claire La Berge (Iowa City: University of Iowa Press, 2014), 47; italics in the original.

26. Patricia Stuelke, "The Reparative Politics of Central America Solidarity Movement Culture," *American Quarterly* 66, no. 3 (September 2014): 787.

27. Henry David Thoreau, "Walking," in *The Writings of Henry David Thoreau*, vol. 5, *Excursions and Poems* (Boston: Houghton Mifflin, 1906), 224. Hereafter cited in the text.

28. Edward Said, *Orientalism* (New York: Vintage, 1978).

29. Jane Bennett, *The Enchantment of Modern Life: Attachments, Crossings, and Ethics* (Princeton, NJ: Princeton University Press, 2001), 4. It's probably no coincidence that Bennett is also the author of a book entitled *Thoreau's Nature: Ethics, Politics, and the Wild*, 2nd ed. (Lanham, MD: Rowman & Littlefield, 2002).

30. Jane Bennett, *Vibrant Matter: A Political Ecology of Things* (Durham, NC: Duke University Press, 2010), vi.

31. Ibid., 122.

32. Catherine Malabou, *What Should We Do with Our Brains?*, trans. Sebastian Rand (New York: Fordham University Press, 2008), 67.

33. Kathleen Stewart, "Afterword: Worldling Refrains," in *The Affective Reader*, ed. Melissa Greg and Gregory J. Seigworth (Durham, NC: Duke University Press, 2010), 340.

34. Jason Moore, *Capitalism in the Web of Life* (London: Verso, 2015), 7.

35. Ursula Heise, "Hitchhiker's Guide to Ecocriticism," *PMLA* 121 (2006): 505.

36. Ibid.

37. I have been most skeptical of arguments that posit a materiality completely alien from our own, one that exists in a retracted isolation from the static ontologies of other beings. This is an approach most saliently advocated by object-oriented ontology. I am also skeptical of accounts that try too rashly to return us to some prior state that we have apparently fallen away from, a rhetorical appeal to recover what we have lost by willfully blinding ourselves to what we are already seeing too plainly. If, as Best and Marcus argue, everything is on the surface now and there aren't many depths for symptomatic reading to uncover anymore, a big reason why is precisely because we are so good at making such depths visible and dredging to the surface what would contentedly linger in the shadows. What might be easy to forget is how difficult it can be to learn these techniques and to gain these insights (a point I borrow from Patricia Stuelke, personal communication). Personally, I had to struggle a long time to make sense of the culture turn and the insights it offered. And of course for many, what appears to Best and Marcus as surface—such as the "images of torture at Abu Ghraib" and "the state's abandonment of its African American citizens" in the wake of Hurricane Katrina—would seem an intensely paranoid and suspicious accusation to make. See Best and Marcus, "Surface Reading," 2.

38. Jason Moore, "Wall Street Is a Way of Organizing Nature: An Interview with Jason Moore," *Upping the Anti: A Journal of Theory and Action* 12 (May 2011): 41.

Realisms Redux; or, Against Affective Capitalism

JEFFREY T. NEALON

> So from age to age a new realism repeats its reaction against the
> reality that the previous age admired.
>
> —*Lyn Hejinian*, My Life

For me, the new realism definitively arrived on Wednesday, February 18, 2015, at or around 7:30 pm (EST). That evening I was guest-lecturing in a graduate theory seminar on posthumanism, filling in for a colleague who was out of town. The topic was Michel Foucault's *The Order of Things* (*Words and Things* in the original French, I dutifully begin by pointing out), and about an hour into talking about the dramatic epistemic changes at the beginning of the nineteenth century in Europe (with special emphasis on the discursive formations of life, labor, and language, and the distributions of objects they make available), seemingly out of nowhere comes the question, "So, Foucault's work is hostile to realism, then? He doesn't believe that things pre-exist their discursive articulation? Isn't that blatant, correlationist anthropomorphism?" There it was, the arrival of "realism" on the inland theory shores of my little college town. Just as someone of my generation had probably asked a similar Foucaultian "gotcha" question in the Marxism seminar several decades earlier ("So Marx believes that power is scarce and held by certain people or social groups? It doesn't circulate through the socius? There's a central conflict—the class struggle—that organizes all the others?"), here was a potential "passing of the torch" moment.

In response, I try to suggest that for Foucault, if you're asking after the "truth" or "essence" of things (or if you're asking for clarification of philosophical positions), you're already asking anthropomorphic, largely political questions—what does the bacterium, the napkin dispenser, or the tulip care for enforcing the "truth" of "things"? Similarly, I try to suggest that Foucault seems somewhat ill chosen as the fall guy (or cheerleader) for humanist anthropomorphism, what with his insistence that "man is an invention of recent date. And one perhaps nearing its end."[1] In fact, *The Order of Things* is largely given over to looking at the historical preconditions for the (very recent and precarious) emergence of something like "correlationism," the word coined by Quentin Meillassoux in *After Finitude* in his attempt to get back behind Kant's Copernican revolution of subjectivity. Meillassoux defines the term quite simply: "Correlationism consists in disqualifying the claim that it is possible to consider the realms of subjectivity and objectivity independently of one another."[2] For Meillassoux and a series of other "speculative realist" or "object-oriented" thinkers, it's the great "outside" of the real that was lost with Kant and then further mystified by Hegel, bracketed by Husserl, and ignored as "essentialist" or "totalizing" by virtually all continental existentialism, phenomenology, and deconstruction. These modern and post-modern discourses remain (on Meillassoux's account) hopelessly filtered through (and thereby openly centered on) human subjectivity, precisely insofar as these philosophies all follow Kant in resolutely refusing to say anything at all about the real, or at least not without saying something at the same time about the perceiving subject. To put it another way, at a certain point in Western thinking, the mediation between subject and object becomes the only way to think subject or object, and thereby the anthropomorphic question of signs or language becomes the necessary and irreducible detour in any theoretical work.

In *The Order of Things*, Foucault is in fact following out a version of this "anti-correlationist" argument—trying to show how "things" became inexorably entangled with human "words." (Foucault's earliest work was on Kant's anthropology, after all, and in fact he suggests that philosophy becomes anthropology with Kant.) Likewise, Foucault is certainly no fan of the linguistic turn, phenomenology, or subject-centered thought in general, and his analysis of "life, labor, language" and their emergence at the beginning of the nineteenth century concerns nothing less than the birth of biopower within the episteme of the human sciences, a knowledge–power regime primarily characterized by a misplaced confidence that nothing is "real" until and unless it passes through the mediation of the human and its sciences (biology, economics, linguistics).[3] Finally, Foucault shows that, like the representational regimes of the early modern period and the fabulation and magic practices dominant in the Renaissance, this myopic nineteenth-century centrality of "man" is doomed to historical eclipse and anachronism and was in fact already on the way out in 1966, when Foucault published *Les mots et les choses*. But all that didn't seem very convincing to the new realists on the block.

So I give it one more try on Foucault and realism, by suggesting that for Foucault, the question surrounding "realism" has nothing to do with the veracity of various realist philosophical positions. If you're a Foucaultian, you can forget tracking the seemingly endless Internet blog posts that attempt to mark out the nuanced differences in philosophical realism among Graham, Quentin, Ian, Levi, et al.—all of them arguing, quite vehemently and apparently in all sincerity, that we should stop focusing on what (individual) humans think. In his recent book *Onto-cartography*, Levi Bryant perhaps speaks for the group when he dismisses Foucaultian critique because "discussions of the role played by technology and non-humans in the formation of social ecologies is [sic] severely underdetermined."[4] (As a reviewer wryly notes, "To anyone who has read *Discipline and Punish* or any of the *History of Sexuality* series, this statement will come as a great surprise.")[5] In the end, though, the point perhaps is this: for Foucault the archaeologist or genealogist, the primary question about philosophical realism is not, "Is it true that things possess a kind of withdrawn essence, to which we have only specula- tive access?" (the "dogmatic" position that was bracketed by Kantian critique but had a prior life as medieval "equivocity," the foil to Duns Scotus's "univocity").[6] Rather, the Foucaultian question would be, "Why at a certain historical juncture (for example, this one) does realism become an attractive position to adopt or espouse? What composes the historical a priori that allows realism to re-emerge now—positioned as something new, against the hegemony of the present?"

Indeed, one could hesitate here and begin not just to think about recent phil- osophical movements but to wonder about the larger cultural or academic re- turn of what looks like several unrelated strands of realism (movements that only half a generation ago would have been branded naïve or, worse yet, essentialist). Take a look, for example, at recent fiction (which I guess means post–David Fos- ter Wallace fiction—from the anti-postmodern neorealism of the North American McSweeney's crowd, or the various rejections of semiotics by those trained in the literary theory of the 1980s and 1990s,[7] all the way through to Karl Ove Knaus- gaard's excruciating realism in *My Struggle*). In philosophy, I've already noted the vehement anti-linguistic turn in object-oriented philosophy and speculative real- ism, of course, as well as various forms of neo-Deleuzean vibrant or agential matter (in the work of Jane Bennett and Karen Barad, for example); gender stud- ies, which was ruled a generation ago by the sign- and language-based theories of performativity (Eve Sedgwick and Judith Butler), has gone in a series of other "new materialist" directions; in literature departments, think of the recent anti- hermeneutic methodological rise of data analysis, most convincingly thematized as distant reading (Franco Moretti), not to mention emergent methods of surface reading (Stephen Best and Sharon Marcus) or postcritical reading (Rita Felski);

or consider various kinds of scientific, neuroscientific, and new media approaches to literature—examining everything from the nonhuman networks in which we act (Bruno Latour) to the brain chemistry of reading or the evolutionary functions of storytelling (Lisa Zunshine); all the way to animal studies and posthumanism, with their stinging critiques of linguistic anthropomorphism (say, Cary Wolfe's work). Cinema studies, the home of so much foundational work in semiotics, must note with anxiety that Jean-Luc Godard named his final film *Farewell to Language*; or consider the MP3-fueled rise of ubiquitous listening and poptimism in music criticism (which doesn't critique or interpret individual songs, artists, or albums, but rather downloads them all and lets the iPod shuffle sort them out).[8] Or think about the artistic practice that will become my central focus here, conceptual writing in poetics (which deflects the uncertain depths of poetic expression altogether and merely copies preexisting documents—a quite severe brand of poetic realism). If we look closely at the signposts concerning the present, it begins to look like we are post-signs, on the other side of the postmodern linguistic turn.

But all this begs the question of the relations between these new realisms and neoliberal capitalism, the socioeconomic field in which they emerge. Alexander Galloway has suggested that *philosophical* realism has taken off in recent years because of its close imbrication with the dictates of multinational finance capitalism.[9] Galloway points especially to the total commodification of the earth and the concomitant reduction of everything (and everyone) to a "thing," and to speculative realism's homological relations with object-oriented computing (the language that makes finance capital tick). Likewise, new realism's very strong ontological caveat against a privileged human mediation necessarily commits it to weak or nonexistent political positions (indeed, continuance of the so-called Pottery Barn Doctrine seems crucial in the era of the Anthropocene: now that it's clear that humans broke the earth's ecosystems, it may not be the right time to give up on human agency's role in repairing those systems). And we might add in passing that object-oriented thinking's appeal is overwhelmingly among younger white males, who feel disenfranchised in a humanities "theory" world overtaken a generation ago by issues of race, class, gender, ethnicity, sexual orientation, disability, and politics more generally. In all this, Galloway suggests that the new philosophical realism arises and moves forward precisely because of its snug, uncritical fit within the neoconservative ideologies and practices of late capitalism.

While I leave it to the reader to decide about Galloway's indictment of object-oriented philosophy and speculative realism in terms of capitalist imperatives, I would like to ask a different question here and look at a different cultural form of "realism": in short, I'd like to wonder about the anticapitalist potentials of realisms across the board, and most specifically about the anticapitalist potential of so-called conceptual writing. I'd like to return, in other words, to a kind of Foucaultian genealogical question concerning the returns of realism: why realism, why now? Might these transversal returns of realism constitute less a series of ideologically unaware embraces of late-late, always-already, or just-in-time capitalism (as Galloway charges), and maybe constitute instead a kind of post-postmodern reinvigoration of realism and its mode of cultural critique? Of course, I don't want to suggest that conceptual poet Kenneth Goldsmith is the new Theodore Dreiser (because he's not), nor that the ubiquitous listening made possible by the iPod is the replacement for Woody Guthrie's guitar as the fascist-killing machine of our era (because it's not). Likewise, I'm fully aware that contemporary experimental poetry is probably not the best place to begin looking for widespread forms of opposition to capitalism (because it's both too easy and too hard—poets are almost axiomatically "anticapitalist" types, so that makes it too easy; but simultaneously, it's too hard to locate widespread versions of any practice by looking at a somewhat marginal social formation like conceptual poetry). My question is more modest and somewhat more focused: have mutations in finance or neoliberal capitalism over the past few decades refashioned an oddly utopian job for a certain kind of "realism" in popular culture today?

Conceptual Writing and/as Realism

For those unfamiliar with "conceptual writing," here's a quick primer: conceptual writing wants poetics to follow in the utopian footsteps of the 1960s conceptual artists (who, given the increasing commodification of art, eschewed the production of ever-more art *objects* and took up instead the task of producing art *concepts*—which is primarily to say, they looked to produce communal discussions, performative provocations, or sociopolitical impacts rather than saleable, privatizable works of art). As capitalism found an increasingly central place for art objects and processes (which is to say, as innovation, affect, and creativity became integral to capitalist profit making), artists felt the need to migrate their practice elsewhere. Starting from the similar premise that affective capitalism has turned its advertising and branding sights on the cash value of expressing authentic feeling, conceptual writing takes an aggressively anti-expressivist tack and takes as its primary practice a very severe form of realism, which consists of selectively transcribing existing texts—some of them literary (say, Caroline Bergvall's "The Not Tale," a transcription of all the negative phrases in Chaucer's "Knight's Tale"), but most of them much more mundane (much of Vanessa Place's work, for example, consists of recopying legal documents). The most infamous conceptual poet, Kenneth Goldsmith, stirred up a great deal of controversy in 2015 by reading from the autopsy of Michael Brown (the unarmed African American teenager killed by Missouri police) at a poetry event.[10] So conceptual poetry is literally a kind of "realism redux"—offering a little piece of the real more in the Lacanian sense (as the kernel that resists enjoyment, signification, or meaning) than in the nineteenth- and twentieth-century senses of literary realism (the imaginatively heightened re-presentation of actual social conditions under capitalism).

With that as a kind of background to conceptual writing, we might go on to point out that contemporary American poetry, especially contemporary experimental poetry, has long hung its critique of capitalism on a transversal connection to the critique of meaning. Think, for example, of Charlie Altieri's sense, in his 1970s essays on postmodern poetry, that an emphasis on the local, the idiomatic, and the affective was taken up by poets as a kind of critique of capitalism, which by extension wants to flatten out complexity and thereby standardize, rationalize, and commodify our lives. Altieri's argument that the "contemporary aesthetic calls for participation far more than for interpretation" was intensified further in much of the theoretical work of the language school,[11] which (especially in the essays of Lyn Hejinian and Bruce Andrews)[12] found its critique of capitalism in a kind of participatory democracy of meaning making. The poem would no longer mirror "the blank stare of the commodity,"[13] in Charles Bernstein's words, but would constitute a field wherein the reader could be an affectively charged participatory cocreator through the act of reading. In short, meaning making (in Hejinian's important phrasing, "the rejection of closure") could become a kind of cottage industry of endlessly remaking subjectivity, in opposition to the Fordist dictates of capitalism and its demands for a standardized, normative brand of rational choice subjectivity. If the slogan of poetry in the twentieth century was "make it new," that's at least in part because the slogan of twentieth-century industrial capitalism—of Fordist factory mass production—was "make it the same." The turn away from meaning and toward affective relations, in poetry as much as in fiction or drama or architecture, was dedicated to the unleashing of multiple meanings that was so much a piece with the linguistic turn in critical theory: if signs are the terrain of contestation, then overflowing meaning is (at least the beginnings of) a mode of social critique.

The primary thing that will interest me in this "postmodern" drama is less the portrait of poetry than the portrait of capitalism it assumes. Certainly, one of conceptual writing's major questions in the present is whether one can really "make it newer" in the twenty-first century, or whether the whole affective economy of poetic "originality" needs to be rethought, at least in part because of the structural position of an artistic notion of "innovation" within post-postmodern capitalism, where everything has to be made new, made individual, niche marketed. (Welcome to amazon.com, Jeffrey, we have some suggestions for you.) As Fredric Jameson showed us more than three decades ago in "Postmodernism, or The Cultural Logic of Late Capitalism," "Make it new!" has become the mantra and dominant practice of capitalism, rather than the assured formula by which one could recognize its critics. As Jameson puts it in his 1984 "Postmodernism" essay, "What has happened is that aesthetic production today has become integrated into commodity production generally: the frantic economic urgency of producing fresh waves of ever more novel-seeming goods (from clothing to airplanes), at ever greater rates of turnover, now assigns an increasingly essential structural function and position to aesthetic innovation and experimentation."[14]

So there's question #1 posed by much conceptual writing and its anti-expressivist reliance on found, "real" materials: if late-late capitalism has wholly swallowed the slogan "make it new," does poetry have to expend its energies elsewhere? The second question concerning conceptual writing's "realism redux," related but a bit thornier, concerns conceptual writing's critique of "affective meaning" and its relation to poetry. Because whatever else you might say about them, poems that consist of retyping every word in a daily newspaper (Goldsmith's *Day*) or retyping brand names, twitter feeds, and blog posts (as Robert Fitterman does in much of his work, like his excellent *Metropolis* series) seem not to be directed exactly at producing "new meaning" through the act of affective interpretation—or at least not in the same way as the "make it new" strand of modernism and postmodernism located its primary warrant (and, as I suggested, its primary critique of capitalism at the same time). It's the largely affectless banality of language usage, a little piece of the real, that someone like Goldsmith is looking to foreground in his texts and readings: what he wants you to hear is the ubiquitous functioning of language as a set of material practices, not the redemptive meaning or innovative epiphany that poetry is famous for adding to the banal experience of the everyday. As Goldsmith puts it in an interview, "The moment we shake our addiction to narrative and give up our strong-headed intent that language must say something 'meaningful,' we open ourselves up to different types of linguistic experience, which . . . could include sorting and structuring words in unconventional ways: by constraint, by sound, by the way words look, and so forth, rather than always feeling the need to coerce them toward meaning."[15]

Of course, meaning itself (understood by Hejinian, Andrews, and others as multiple, rich, conflicted, open-ended, maybe even impossible) was never the

thing to be avoided in most modern and postmodern critiques of artistic interpretation; rather, it's an instrumental, totalizing, or univocal notion of meaning
that's the bad guy for virtually all of contemporary poetry. The instrumental rationality of everyday objects is the reified "real" that must be resisted by the imaginative poetic transformation: the red wheelbarrow's not there to haul firewood,
but to reveal the redemptive "ideas" hidden among mere utilitarian things. And
here's the punchline: that "bad" instrumental rationality is consistently understood as linked to (if not birthed by) capitalism itself—from the banality of clock
time (versus lived time) to the rationally choosing consumerist individual (versus
the open, deconstructed self). In short, it's the critique of instrumental rationality that takes the meaning overflow generated by the refusal of closure and specifically connects it to a critique of capitalism (which presumably requires the
instrumental univocity of meaning to do its affectless, sinister, standardizing
work). Even people with very different positions within the twentieth century's
theoretical or political spectrum—say, Heidegger and Adorno, or Derrida and
Habermas, or Hejinian and more traditional lyric poets—would, it seems to me,
agree on this critique of instrumental rationality as the wages of capitalism. Since
what we find in everyday objects is this impoverished capitalist "real" of instrumental rationality, such rampant commodification must be combated by an affective, poetic re-enchantment of everyday life and everyday objects.[16]

As I said, though, here I'm less interested in the discourses of poetics in all
this than I am in the discourse surrounding capitalism. I suppose the question
becomes something like this: while the reduction of everything to a kind of instrumental rationality was almost certainly the primary problem with twentieth-
century Fordist capitalism, does it remain so under the apparatus of what has
been called post-postmodern capitalism? Hasn't such super-late or just-in-time
capitalism also abandoned the instrumentalist dictates of Fordism and mass production (Marx's formal subsumption of the socius) and moved on to a "real subsumption" of even greater parts of our lives? As Michael Hardt and Antonio Negri
argue, post-Fordist capitalism finds its home terrain in the biopolitical registers
of our entire lives—not just our jobs, but even our identities and sexualities, precisely those everyday, local, idiomatic, and meaning-making affective processes
that had previously been the bulwark against capitalism's reach: "The great industrial and financial powers thus produce not only commodities but subjectivities. . . . They produce needs, social relations, bodies, and minds—which is to say,
they produce producers."[17] In short, insisting on the excessive, affective mean-
ingfulness of everyday life is no longer foreign or resistant to affective, biopolitical
capitalism, but constitutes its bleeding edge. Take, for example, Apple's 2014 ad-

vertising campaign for the iPad Air, "What Will Your Verse Be?," featuring Robin Williams's monologue from the 1989 film *Dead Poet's Society*:

> We don't read and write poetry because it's cute. We read and write poetry because we are members of the human race. And the human race is filled with passion. And medicine, law, business, engineering, these are noble pursuits and necessary to sustain life. But poetry, beauty, romance, love, these are what we stay alive for. To quote from Whitman, "O me! O life! . . . of the questions of these recurring; of the endless trains of the faithless—of cities filled with the foolish; what good amid these, O me, O life?" Answer. That you are here—that life exists, and identity; that the powerful play goes on and you may contribute a verse. That the powerful play *goes on* and you may contribute a verse. What will your verse be?[18]

In the face of an affective capitalism that invites you to produce your life, to "contribute a verse," a capitalism that feeds on the supposed excessive re-enchantment of virtually every moment of our commodified lives, maybe what you need to do is shift ground from the project of excessive signification, overflowing meaning, and affective re-enchantment altogether. And maybe that's at least some of what's going on in conceptual writing at the moment.

Indeed, to my eyes, an affective re-enchantment of the artwork—gesturing always toward the multiplicity of its meanings, against any single interpretation—seems quite foreign to conceptual writing. As the most intense version of this anti-meaning tendency, I'd reference Goldsmith's practice of retyping radio broadcasts, in his great American trilogy—*Sports* (a transcription of every word of a Yankees–Red Sox radio broadcast), *Traffic* (a full day of traffic reports, on the 1s), and *The Weather* (a year of nightly reports). And the ethos of overflowing signification or re-enchantment is even more foreign to the somatic encounter of actually reading Goldsmith's work—which he will often suggest you shouldn't bother doing, as it's finally the idea or the concept that's interesting, rather than the text itself. In other words, Goldsmith's anti-hermeneutic gesture seems radically different from the mainstream modernist or postmodernist critique of meaning: rather than trying to re-enchant, enliven, or reinvent artistic hermeneutics, Goldsmith's work seems to want to abandon it altogether—which is, of course, easier said than done, and thereby remains a certain kind of utopian project. But I'm suggesting that it may be one strategy for dealing with the colonization of everyday life by the increasing saturation of affective capitalism—which no longer just wants you to produce for it from nine to five; it wants you to prosume (produce through consumption), and it wants you to do it 24/7.[19] Which is maybe to say again that symbolic production or affective overproduction (the excessive or open-ended text) is no longer the dependable bulwark against the dictates of capitalism that it was even twenty or thirty years ago. Insisting on the open-endedness of "new" meaning, the endless deconstruction of subjectivity, and the constant re-negotiation of value may at present constitute pushing against an open door. If the reality of capitalism (or what Mark Fisher calls "capitalist realism") today thrives on "excess" and the endless production of new meanings and possibilities (if the cutting edge of financial and affective capitalism is the excessive, unfet-tered, or immaterial itself), then there may be good reason to try to abandon that turf of meaning altogether, even if it remains a kind of (anti)utopian gesture.

Finally, if you still rightly remain skeptical of any kind of oppositional or polit-ical potential for conceptual writing's realism redux (just copying or categorizing existing texts would seem to doom one to confirmation of the status quo—there would have to be some critical judgment offered or implied in poetry for it to have social effectivity), I offer the following concrete example—Rob Fitterman's "Directory":[20]

Macy's	Hickory Farms
Circuit City	GNC
Payless ShoeSource	The Body Shop
Sears	Eddie Bauer
Kay Jewelers	Payless ShoeSource
GNC	Circuit City
LensCrafters	Kay Jewelers
Coach	Gymboree
H&M	
RadioShack	
Gymboree	The Body Shop
	Hickory Farms
	Coach
The Body Shop	Macy's
Eddie Bauer	GNC
Crabtree & Evelyn	Circuit City
Gymboree	Sears
Foot Locker	
Land's End	
GNC	H&M
LensCrafters	Kay Jewelers
Coach	Land's End

Famous Footwear	LensCrafters
H&M	Eddie Bauer
	Cinnabon
	LensCrafters
Foot Locker	RadioShack
GNC	GNC
Macy's	Sears
Crabtree & Evelyn	Crabtree & Evelyn
H&M	
Cinnabon	
Kay Jewelers	
Land's End	

This poem is, of course, "about" going to the mall, that paradigmatic experience of everyday consumerist life in the United States—in short, it's about capitalism. Aesthetically, there's a lot you could say about this poem as an object—Goldsmith, who edited the *Poetry* magazine cluster where Fitterman's poem appears, examines this poem paired with a poem by Tony Hoagland about how shopping at the mall is bad for the soul, and Goldsmith shows convincingly that Fitterman's is a far better poem qua poem: Hoagland's finger wagging breaks the first rule of the workshop—"show don't tell!"—while Fitterman delivers that "showing" in relentless fashion.

In any case, I'm primarily interested in offering Fitterman's "Directory" as a concrete example of realism's critical function or potential in the present—precisely through a kind of refusal of meaning or poetic depth or expression, it manages to open a discussion about capitalism. (One could also wonder here about Goldsmith's recent—and, most people would agree, misguided—reading from Michael Brown's autopsy report, or Vanessa Place tweeting out lines from *Gone with the Wind* in an attempt to critique ongoing racism: whatever you think of white poets calling attention to racism in this way, however dubious or appropriative it is as an artistic strategy, it certainly has opened a series of vehement discussions about race and its relations to poetry in the present.) The draining of affective textual *jouissance* that one sees in various forms of realism gains a new critical life at this historical moment, when capitalism has become almost completely territorialized on the production and consumption of affective experience. Of course, that's not to say that conceptual writing—or any other kind of realism—is inherently uncommodifiable or anticapitalist. If you can invite Goldsmith to read poems at the White House,[21] you no doubt could put Fitterman in an iPad commercial, reading off the names of big-box stores where Apple products are available; but I doubt that his iPhone is ringing off the hook.

Back to the Present

Turning toward a conclusion, I would like to end by circling back to where I began, with Foucault, and the importance of describing the current episteme or *dispositif*—in short, the project of diagnosing contemporary capitalism. The axiomatics of the new realisms—the sense that there's always something affective, rhizomatic, or excessive that comes before human reason or decision—might in the end be connected with a slogan that Deleuze associates with Foucault's work on power: "Resistance comes first." But for better or worse, resistance within this "realist" mesh doesn't guarantee anything politically, or maybe even ontologically. It's just a fact of life. In a very late capitalist territory made up of lines of flight, strategies of deterritorialization remain as available to anarchists and union organizers as they are to Army counterinsurgency experts and neoliberal finance executives.

In this context, it seems important to recall the specific political note on which Deleuze insists in his "Societies of Control" essay: "There is no need to fear or hope, but only to look for *new weapons.*"[22] In other words, for Deleuze, the political upshot of a certain kind of realism does not rest in some ideological unmasking or knowledge about the state of things in the world (our territory is liberating us, or our territory is constraining us; we should be either hopeful or fearful), but in suggesting that the primary usefulness of a kind of realist, rhizomatic politics accrues to its *diagnostic* functions.

Rhizomatics is a certain kind of realism insofar as it diagnoses, rather than interprets, the territory—which is to say, the striating functions of our historical territory need to be named and explained, limned, if we are to have any hope of looking for new concepts to combat those striations or to activate them otherwise. Analysis of contemporary capitalism remains trained on a precise political diagnosis of the current configuration of this territory (how striation takes place within contemporary capitalism, what lines of flight might be available—where escape is possible, what lines are closed off). And this is likewise important because practices that freed people within the disciplinary human territory fifty years ago (maybe identity politics, maybe transgressive sexuality, maybe a commitment to indeterminacy and openness) will not be able to free them quite so unproblematically in the present.

The skeptic will counter that Walmart takes territory from mom-and-pop stores in precisely the rhizomatic way that switchgrass overtakes a meadow—which is, to some degree, correct; but as a diagnosis, it doesn't seem to follow that rhizo-matics is then an inherently dangerous political notion, a naturalizing front for advanced capitalism. As a diagnostic discourse, a kind of realist discourse like rhizomatics is neither good nor bad. Rhizomatic *effects* most certainly can be judged according to that ethical yardstick (cancer spreads rhizomatically—and that's very dangerous indeed for human life), but the transversal field in which those effects happen is beyond good and evil. (To continue the example, you don't combat cancer because cancer is "bad," but because its effects are devastating for a particular life. No matter how you feel or what you know about cancer, in order to fight it, you need to be able to diagnose it and to map how it spreads; knowing that it's bad is of very limited use in combating its effects.)[23] This is perhaps the primary cultural lesson of the control society in Deleuze's sense: however omi-nous the cage, it's still built from lines of flight. Far from composing the nihilist night in which all cows are black (power is everywhere, so resistance is futile), Deleuze's primary "realist" lesson in "Postscript on the Societies of Control" is that hope or despair is ultimately beside the point in the search for effective new weapons.

This diagnostic imperative seems to me especially important if we are search-ing for new modes of critical and artistic practice, insofar as that search will in-evitably involve recycling older ways of enacting the relations among economic and artistic production—like various forms of realism. For example, certainly something like affect theory—with its "new materialist" sense that something blurring and buzzing always comes before the deployment of human reason or decision—is nothing quite so "new": I can't think of a single philosopher (not even Plato) who doesn't already subscribe to that general sense that something non- or inhuman comes inexorably before human decision (the "good beyond being," anyone?). If that's too contentious, we'd at least have to admit that the "affective turn" got a very strong hearing with Hume's work, some 250 years ago, and in Spinoza's work a century before that. And of course within poetics, the practice of listing or the insistence on found materials is likewise nothing new and has been crucially important to various modernists and postmodernists, from Louis Zukofsky and Muriel Rukeyser through John Ashbery, whose 1975 *Vermont Notebooks* begins with a thirty-page list of stuff. Of course, realism will play in different ways in different historical moments and discursive formations— Ashbery's list works to enact a strong sense of place, rural Vermont, whereas Fit-terman's list works to evoke a quite literal no-place, the mall. Likewise, in the present context, I hold out considerably less hope for realism in philosophy than I do for realism in poetics, because the speculative realist project of being transhistorically "correct" about ontology seems to offer very few tools to understand or interrupt the workings of neoliberal capitalism. (Object-oriented ontology doesn't seem to me to be a diagnostic political discourse at all, seeking lines of flight within a territory, but a strictly ontological or even epistemological one: it's about being right concerning the way things really are and always have been.) Likewise, the recent "affective turn" in the humanities and social sciences seems more like a symptom of late, later, or just-in-time capitalism (all excess all the time) than it does an idea or practice that offers much friction against this form of capitalism. But I'm sure others have different assessments of this contemporary terrain, and in the end it's less some kind of consensus *answer* than it is the common *questions* that I'd urge us to hang onto in the present, like the question that names the primary territory of Foucault's thought: "What difference does today introduce with respect to yesterday?"[24] And at the end of the day, whether it's yesterday or today, this question of diagnosis has everything to do with charting changes within (and potential resistances to) capitalism itself. As capitalism over the past decades has become increasingly virtual, feeding on multiplicity and undecidability, so have various realisms reemerged as utopian reactions to the superfast flows of neoliberal capitalism.

NOTES

1. Michel Foucault, *The Order of Things: An Archaeology of the Human Sciences* (New York: Vintage, 1994), 386.

2. Quentin Meillassoux, *After Finitude*, trans. Ray Brassier (London: Bloomsbury, 2010), 5.

3. For an extended rehearsal of this argument, see Jeffrey Nealon, "The Archaeology of Biopower: From Plant to Animal Life in *The Order of Things*," in *Biopower: Foucault and Beyond*, ed. Vernon W. Cisney and Nicolae Morar (Chicago: University of Chicago Press, 2016), 138–57.

4. Levi Bryant, *Onto-cartography: An Ontology of Machines and Media* (Edinburgh: Edinburgh University Press, 2014), 285.

5. See Bryan E. Bannon, review of *Onto-cartography: An Ontology of Machines and Media*, by Levi R. Bryant, *Notre Dame Philosophical Reviews*, February 19, 2015, http://ndpr.nd.edu /news/55820-onto-cartography-an-ontology-of-machines-and-media/.

6. As Eugene Thacker puts it in *After Life* (Chicago: University of Chicago Press, 2010), medieval "equivocity posits no common terms between Creator and creature, Life and the living. Equivocity is blank thought, the thought of the neutral. Being is said in several senses, each in its own way, indifferent to each other instance" (154). Compare this sense of equivocity to Graham Harman's argument (in *The Quadruple Object* [Winchester, UK: Zero Books, 2011]) that things consistently withdraw into their own (largely unknowable)

essence, or Ian Bogost's seemingly endless lists of random things—turns out everything's different from everything else!—in *Alien Phenomenology; or, What It's Like to Be a Thing* (Minneapolis: University of Minnesota Press, 2012).

7. See Robert L. McLaughlin, "Post-postmodernism," in *The Routledge Companion to Experimental Literature*, ed. Joe Bray, Alison Gibbons, and Brian McHale (New York: Routledge, 2012): "Where postmodern authors often used self-reference to expose their own fiction's artificiality, . . . post-postmodern authors tend to offer an idiosyncratic respect for the suspension of disbelief, spending less time reflecting on their narratives as narrative . . . and more on exploring the protean and fractious nature of what their characters consider to be reality. This change of focus is the main reason why many critics have noted a sea change in fiction, a transition from postmodernism to something that seems to be different. It is also the reason that some critics and reviewers define this sea change as a return to some kind of realism" (218–19).

8. Just to scratch the surface of these various "new realist" or "new materialist" movements, see Jane Bennett, *Vibrant Matter: A Political Ecology of Things* (Durham, NC: Duke University Press, 2010); Karen Barad, *Meeting the Universe Halfway* (Durham, NC: Duke University Press, 2007); Iris van der Tuin, *Generational Feminism: A New Materialist Introduction to a Generative Approach* (Lanham, MD: Lexington Books, 2014); Franco Moretti, *Distant Reading* (London: Verso, 2013); Stephen Best and Sharon Marcus, "Surface Reading: An Introduction," *Representations* 108, no. 1 (2009): 1–21, Rita Felski, *The Limits of Critique* (Chicago: University of Chicago Press, 2015); Bruno Latour, "Why Has Critique Run Out of Steam?," *Critical Inquiry* 30, no. 2 (2004); Lisa Zunshine, *Oxford Handbook of Cognitive Literary Studies* (Oxford: Oxford University Press, 2015); and Anahid Kassabian, *Ubiquitous Listening: Affect, Attention, and Distributed Subjectivity* (Berkeley: University of California Press, 2013).

9. Alexander Galloway, "The Poverty of Philosophy: Realism and Post-Fordism," *Critical Inquiry* 39, no. 2 (2013): 347–66.

10. See https://www.theguardian.com/books/2015/mar/17/michael-brown-autopsy-report-poem-kenneth-goldsmith.

11. Charles Altieri, "From Symbolist Thought to Immanence: The Ground of Postmodern American Poetics," in *Early Postmodernism: Foundational Essays*, ed. Paul Bové (Durham, NC: Duke University Press, 1995), 100.

12. See Lyn Hejinian, "The Rejection of Closure," www.poetryfoundation.org/learning/essay/237870; and Bruce Andrews, *Paradise and Method: Poetics and Praxis* (Evanston, IL: Northwestern University Press, 1996).

13. Charles Bernstein, *Content's Dream* (Evanston, IL: Northwestern University Press, 2001), 59.

14. Fredric Jameson, "Postmodernism, or The Cultural Logic of Late Capitalism," *New Left Review* 1, no. 146 (1984): 5.

15. Kenneth Goldsmith, interview by Dave Mandl, *Believer*, October 2011, www.believermag.com/issues/201110/?read=interview_goldsmith.

16. Of course, while all agree that reification is a central problem, the source, target, and character of this aesthetic re-enchantment would differ greatly among various philosophical and poetic movements. The "expressivist" mode of poetic re-enchantment suggests, for example, that it's the subjective voice of the poet that can do the work of disrupting reification, while for Hejinian or Andrews it's the community of responding readers who

keep open the reifying structures of language and society. Likewise, Habermas and Derrida locate that interruption and reinscription of reification in very different places—Habermas in the communicative rationality of subjects, Derrida in the structure of the trace. All these folks share a diagnosis of reification brought about by Fordist leveling of the socius, but they propose vastly different solutions.

17. Michael Hardt and Antonio Negri, *Empire* (Cambridge, MA: Harvard University Press, 2000), 32.

18. See www.adweek.com/news/advertising-branding/ad-day-apple-borrows-dead-poets-society-evocative-ad-ipad-air-154937.

19. See Jonathan Crary, *24/7: Late Capitalism and the Ends of Sleep* (London: Verso, 2014).

20. The poem can be found at www.poetryfoundation.org/poetrymagazine/poems/detail/52691. See also Kenneth Goldsmith's treatment of Fitterman in his *Uncreative Writing* (Evanston, IL: Northwestern University Press, 2012), 94–99.

21. Watch it here: www.youtube.com/watch?v=nqHaKniXkF8.

22. Gilles Deleuze, "Postscript on the Societies of Control," *October* 59 (Winter 1992): 4.

23. Think of Deleuze's work on stupidity in *Nietzsche and Philosophy*, trans. Hugh Tomlinson (New York: Columbia University Press, 1982): stupidity is not the binary opposite of knowledge, but knowledge is simply that which injures stupidity, keeps it from taking over the entire territory of thought and action. "Great as they are, stupidity and baseness would be greater still if there did not remain some philosophy which always prevents them from going as far as they would wish" (106).

24. Michel Foucault, "What Is Enlightenment?," trans. Catherine Porter, in *The Essential Foucault*, ed. Paul Rabinow and Nikolas Rose (New York: New Press, 2003), 45.

The Surfaces of Contemporary Capitalism

JASON M. BASKIN

Surface Now

Stephen Best and Sharon Marcus's call to attend to the "surface" of texts has become one of the most influential and controversial critical statements of the twenty-first century thus far.[1] "Surface reading" stands at the vanguard of a broader movement away from suspicion and critique as underpinning scholarly engagement with literary texts. Pointing to Fredric Jameson's "symptomatic reading" as paradigmatic of a long-dominant critical focus on depth, Best and Marcus argue that at least since the 1970s, readers have been trained to see meaning as "hidden, repressed, deep and in need of detection and disclosure." Yet they note a generational shift in scholars who came of age in the 1990s: through a variety of means, these readers instead "attend to the surfaces of texts." Rather than "looking past the surface" to "plumb hidden depths," surface readers aim for an "accurate" or "neutral" description of "what is evident, perceptible, apprehensible in texts; what is neither hidden nor hiding."[2] Best and Marcus claim that surface reading is not antithetical to critique, but rather is animated by a "political realism" that remains skeptical about finding any "liberatory potential in the artwork itself or in the valiant labor of the critic." Instead of treating literature or criticism heroically, as if it can "explain our oppression or provide keys to our liberation," surface readers seek a "freedom in attentiveness."[3]

Surface reading has reinvigorated debates about the goals and methods of literary studies. Its supporters generally present the turn to surface as an alternative to traditional structures of meaning. Its detractors see it as a retreat from social and political engagement into either the immediacy of sensual experience or the objective neutrality of empirical data. The debate over surface reading thus recalls Jameson's identification of postmodernism with "depthlessness," an idea that Best and Marcus echo—even though they do not refer to it directly—when they define surface as "having length and breadth but no thickness . . . cover[ing] no depth."[4] In Jameson's account, the rejection of depth is symptomatic of an inability to cognize the structuring totality of contemporary capitalism. Best and Marcus, of course, distance themselves from symptomatic reading, but their appeal to surface celebrates the same attenuation of sociohistorical totality that Jameson diagnoses. They simply present surface reading as a conscious refusal to privilege that category, rather than a historical inability to grasp it.

Despite—or perhaps because of—the obvious echo with Jameson's account of postmodernism, few have asked why surface reading itself has gained prominence in this particular moment of austerity-induced crisis in the academy.[5] Jed Esty and Colleen Lye class surface reading within a more general resurgence of realist modes in literary study, including distant reading, cognitivist approaches, the new materialisms, and actor–network theory, all of which attempt to address the humanities' perceived failure to produce verifiable knowledge about the world.[6] This is a persuasive categorization. But more importantly, it raises the possibility that, rather than merely engage the turn to surface within scholarly debates over critical method, or "how we read now," we might consider surface itself to be a historical problem specific to the present. In this neoliberal era, where the extension of market values has infiltrated all aspects of society and daily life, it would be easy to equate Best and Marcus's critical appeal to surface with a general "triumph of superficiality."[7] But I want to suggest that debates over surface reading call out for a more dialectical and historically grounded reading: they reveal "surface" as a privileged site to engage the possibilities of critique at a contemporary moment when culture no longer enjoys a critical distance from economic production.

It helps to recognize that Best and Marcus are not the only ones who have appealed recently to the concept of surface. Surface reading is part of a broader, complex engagement with surface in recent aesthetic and theoretical activity over the past decade or so. This includes, for instance, the ineradicable "surplus matter" of Tom McCarthy's fiction, the "flattening" of the social in Bruno Latour's actor–network theory, and the shallow, technologically saturated social worlds of Tao Lin's writing.[8] Yet these contemporary writers and thinkers do not all presume the surface's utter "lack of depth" critiqued by Jameson and embraced by Best and Marcus.[9] Beyond the ongoing scholarly debates between depth and surface, hermeneutics and description, critical and postcritical reading, various writers and thinkers deploy the concept of surface to reveal, and in some cases critique, the seemingly fluid and immaterial world of neoliberal global capitalism.

It has been more than thirty years since Jameson posited that the general

"integration" of aesthetic production into commodity production was the underlying condition of postmodernism's "depthless" aesthetic, famously equating the
glimmering flatness of Warhol's silkscreen paintings with the late capitalist commodity fetish itself.[10] In the decades since Jameson's intervention, as the reigning
periodizing term has shifted from postmodernism to neoliberalism, critics have
marked an even deeper intertwining of creative and economic production. Not
only has the market intruded decisively on the autonomy of the aesthetic realm—a
separation still relevant enough to be debunked by Warhol and memorialized by
Jameson—but the notions of innovation, originality, and creative self-expression
once reserved for artistic production now characterize important portions of the
economic sphere itself.[11]

It is significant that, in literary studies, the concept of neoliberalism has really
taken hold since the global financial crisis of 2007–8. Neoliberalism emerged in
the early to mid-1970s as a political formation that sought to manage (to the interests of Western capital) the crisis of profitability that hit the global capitalist
system in the late 1960s, particularly through financialization and the globalization of production.[12] As David Harvey and Neil Smith have argued, urbanization
also has played a crucial role in this neoliberal project. Particularly in the Western
core of the capitalist world-system, the "entrepreneurial" city has served as a "spatial fix" that temporarily resolves one crisis while at the same time planting the
seeds of the next.[13] The realities of neoliberal urbanization suggest the need for
a dialectical account of surface as expression of both capitalist accumulation and
its unraveling. In such an account, surface cannot simply give way to depth; but
at the same time, surface cannot be imagined without it. Surface and depth are
mutually constitutive, each immanent to the other. However, this requires something that is not currently on offer from recent proponents of either surface or
depth: it necessitates, as the contemporary poet Lisa Robertson has put it, "re-
compiling the metaphysics of surface" in a materialist vein.[14]

In this essay, I turn to Robertson's 2003 volume, *Occasional Work and Seven
Walks from the Office for Soft Architecture*. In this book of essays, Robertson is concerned specifically with the "soft," pleasurable surfaces of a late capitalist Vancouver that has been remade through two decades of corporate urban restructuring.
Rather than undertaking a symptomatic approach that "plumbs hidden depths,"
Robertson fixes her attention throughout on the city's "florescence of surface"
(15). Yet Robertson offers a very different conception of surface from that of Best
and Marcus. Rather than describing a hard surface, completely lacking sociohistorical depth, she conceptualizes surface as "soft" in order to critically engage the
specific neoliberal restructuring of urban space that transformed the city of Van-

couver in the 1980s and 1990s. Foregrounding the economic conditions that produced the sleek glass surfaces of Vancouver's new downtown, Robertson takes on the corporate persona of the "Office for Soft Architecture." From this perspective, she uncovers the "negative ontologies" that expose the "hairline cracks" in capital's seemingly hard, flat surfaces (27, 231). Thus, even as she acknowledges her own "complicity" within a neoliberal capitalism fully invested in the aesthetic pleasures of surface, Robertson's soft architecture offers the possibility of a critique that, attuned to capitalism's immanent contradictions, depends not on distance, but on proximity and entanglement (79).

Surfaces Thick and Thin

Amid the ongoing debates over surface reading, few have considered precisely what a surface is, how it is conceived or perceived. A seemingly natural assumption, which Best and Marcus share with Jameson, pervades debates: that surfaces are completely flat ("length and breadth but no thickness"; "depthlessness"). Of course, one says that objects have "surfaces." But no object that can be perceived —rather than merely imagined—completely lacks thickness, and surfaces cannot be perceived separately from depth. This is because, as the phenomenologist Maurice Merleau-Ponty has argued, depth is a not a property of objects, but a property—a *dimension*, to be precise—of space itself.[15] One can only encounter objects in a whole, three-dimensional world—a sociohistorical totality—that at once exceeds and constitutes subjects and objects of perception. Depth is not a location in space, beyond or behind the surface. It is a fundamental condition of space and perception, of lived experience itself. Depth in this *dimensional* sense is perhaps most easily grasped with reference to the back side of an object. The back side is not "covered" by the object's "surface." It is the part of the object that cannot be seen by a living, embodied viewer "situated" in a whole, three-dimensional world.[16] This three-dimensional totality provides the depth that already, immanently constitutes the "surface." Thus, even the thinnest surface is never completely (ideally) flat but "thick."[17]

Best and Marcus build their model of reading on an idealization of the material object and the space it inhabits, reducing both to "geometrical" abstractions.[18] In so doing, they flatten out the dialectical nature of surface by ignoring the interrelation between surface perception and sociohistorical depth that constitutes any object that can be perceived. Merleau-Ponty shows that for embodied viewers there are neither "surfaces" nor "depths," but only a dialectically intertwined *surface-in-depth*.[19] Thus, inasmuch as perception is not the act of an isolated, individual mind or consciousness but actual, social and historical, embodied subjects,

"surface" remains to some, even if only to a minimal extent, elusive and mysterious, "thick" with "gaps" and "folds."[20] The irreducible complexity and ambiguity
of this materialist surface are a consequence of the fact that both viewer and object inhabit a greater totality—sociohistorical depth—that makes the act of perception possible in the first place. Only by ignoring the constitutive opacity and
provisionality of lived experience—consequences of the fact that our bodies inhabit a lived, three-dimensional space that cannot be seen from outside—can one
imagine anything like a pure, flat surface.

The problem with "surface reading," then, is not necessarily the turn to surface itself, or the attendant emphasis on perception and attention over objective
historical processes.[21] It is, rather, the *idealization* of surface as *hard*, an immediate self-present object, separated from sociohistorical depth and fully available to
an "attentive" "neutral description." If so, then those committed to critique might
respond not by privileging depth over surface, but instead by drawing out their
interrelation and mutual constitution. Robertson's work thus offers an example
of just such a materialist surface. Her essays on Vancouver proceed phenomenologically. Surface is elusive and ambiguous because it is intertwined with depth—
"soft," as she puts it, rather than hard.

Robertson's *Office for Soft Architecture* consists of "occasional" works, mostly
essays, lectures, and gallery notes, and a series of seven "walks" around Vancouver. Focusing on the inessential, ornamental, banal, and transient aspects of the
city—fountains, parks, local vegetation, color, the suburb, a used clothing store
chain, scaffolding—Robertson melds site-specific description with archival research (specific to Vancouver's colonial history) and the history of architecture
and architectural theory. As Robertson repeatedly reminds us, the book has been
written by her corporate alter ego, the "Office for Soft Architecture," a name that
recalls contemporary Dutch architect Rem Koolhaas's Office for Metropolitan
Architecture. Yet she endows this impersonal entity with an embodied presence,
emphasizing immediate bodily feeling, touch, physical movement, and the fleeting affects and whims of bodily desire, from hunger to consumption. These phenomenological descriptions are layered with discursive explorations of nineteenth-
century real estate transactions, a kitschy tour of Vancouver's fountains (postcards
included), the colonial settlement of the recently redeveloped New Brighton Beach,
and the transnational history of the *Rubus armeniacus* (the Himalayan black-
berry). "Our method," the office states, "will compile the synthesis of bodily intu-
itions, historical research, friendship and chance" (59). Yet bodily experience and
historical research (surface and depth) are never separated out. Robertson's plural narrative voice constantly fluctuates somewhere between subjective immedi-

acy and impersonal distance, offering a "supple" treatment of urban space as a "blurred texture" that is direct, immediate, and corporeal while also being historical, fleeting, and ambiguous (16, 13).

Robertson has said that her goal in this volume was to explore the possibilities for critique offered by an embodied, gendered version of the Benjaminian flaneur: "I wanted to bring historical materiality to the level of the flesh. . . . These terms can remain very abstract in left critiques. . . . I wanted [to see them] rooted in bodily pleasure."[22] Indexing the physicality of the body—"words are fleshy ducts," Robertson tells us—the structures of Vancouver presented in this volume are not made of the steel and concrete familiar to the modernist metropolis (67). Those triumphant constructions appear here in a state of ruin and decay. Instead, the contemporary city is composed of fraying textiles and pliant fabrics: "the holy modernism of the white room is draped and lined in its newness by labile counter-structures of moving silk, fur, leather, onyx, velvet" (14–15). Softness marks the transformation of urban space into an extension of the body: "place softens to become a lining of the mouth. . . . We must get into this soft lining."[23]

Robertson's attention to this "florescence of surface" (15) might seem to offer a surface reading of the contemporary city. Her soft, embodied aesthetic certainly abjures the critical detachment and ironic distance associated with suspicious reading and depth hermeneutics. In the volume's opening piece, "Soft Architecture: A Manifesto," Robertson's narrators declare that the goal of the volume is to "reverse the wrongheaded story of structural deepness" (16–17). "Structure or fundament itself, in its inert eternity," the Office later notes, "has already been adequately documented—the same skeleton repeating itself continuously. We are grateful for these memorial documents. But the chaos of surfaces compels us towards new states of happiness" (128). In this way, Robertson's emphasis on surface in *Office for Soft Architecture* extends her earlier interest in the pastoral. In "How Pastoral: A Manifesto" (1999), Robertson argues that there is political value in the seemingly inessential or banal aspects of contemporary experience.[24] Best and Marcus would see the overlooked surfaces of the pastoral as a basis for "objectivity, validity, truth," which is missed by symptomatic readers who ignore them in search of a "heroic" political agency.[25] Robertson, by contrast, argues that the value of pastoral is fundamentally political. Because the seemingly inessential or decorative, feminine mode of pastoral remains immanent to the fundamental structures of capitalism—as depth is immanent to surface—it is a site of contestation and critique.

Throughout *Office for Soft Architecture*, Robertson insists that the opposition between surface and depth is entirely mistaken. She turns, for instance, to the nineteenth-century architect Gottfried Semper, for whom "surface effects were not subordinated to deeper structural ideals; rather, structure partially extroverted to itself became a component in the ornamental grammar of surface" (148). Rather than covering up history (depth, structure), the surface (ornament) communicates it, specifically at the level of the bodily experience. By contrast with John Ruskin, who "preferred to govern ornament," Robertson privileges Semper's recognition that "the transience and non-essential quality of the surface did not lessen its topological value" (129). The recuperation of surface does not take place at the expense of depth. Rather, surface emerges through its imbrication in depth.

Thus, even as she embraces the city's surfaces, Robertson also "recompiles the metaphysics of surface" itself (17).[26] She brings out the ambiguity and opacity of an embodied, materialist surface, some aspect of which always escapes the perceiver's attention. Robertson's surfaces are never fully present, hard and immediate but "frail," "vulnerable," "transient": they "crack," "split," "leak," "fray," and "unravel" (17, 164, 184, 144, 17, 215). However hard they appear, they are always soft to the touch. The book opens with a scene of awakening to a world of sensual surfaces—to a bed of "worn cotton sheets" whose "thinning cloth" has been so frayed that "our feet would be tangled in the fretted gap" (13). This image presents us with a surface that is neither a hard object nor a covering for something else, but an "indiscreet threshold where our bodies exchange information with an environment" (13, 143).

Likewise, for Robertson, perception does not merely register empirical data; it is the site of social exchange and is conditioned by a "historicity" that exceeds the individual subject: "I'm looking at the structure of perception, the historicity of perception, how any act of perceiving—looking, describing—is shot through with agencies that are not 'mine,' that are not proper to any single subject."[27] These impersonal, nonsubjective agencies that "shoot through" any perceivable surface index the sociohistorical dimension of depth that is not separate from but immanently constitutes surface. As we will see shortly, the specific element of the "historicity of perception" that Robertson engages in *Office for Soft Architecture* is the shifting economic structure of the city itself in the last decades of the twentieth century. Thus, unlike surface readers, who turn to surface in order to achieve an ideal of "accuracy," Robertson's engagement with surface is fundamentally oriented toward the "utopian act" of critique. She seeks to "manifest current conditions" by directly implicating surface in depth, dialectically revealing surface itself to be constitutive of the economic realities of late capitalist urban life (16).

Thus, as Robertson's narrators state, the "negative ontologies" of Vancouver's surfaces are "an elegance specific to our economy" (28).

The Soft City

The economics of contemporary urban development—from the specific vantage point of the turn of the millennium—are crucial to Robertson's emphasis on the softness of the urban surface, the intertwinement of (even the most apparently thin and hard) surface with sociohistorical depth. In the acknowledgments to her volume, Robertson frames her investigation of Vancouver's surfaces within a specific historical moment of "accelerated growth and increasingly globalized economies" that remade the city's "urban texture" between the late 1980s and the early 2000s. Robertson refers here to a period in which Vancouver, like many other cities in these decades, successfully decoupled from its regional economy (based around shipping and the lumber industry) and became inextricably intertwined with a global economy increasingly oriented around international finance and, especially in the western core, service work and creative labor. In Vancouver, this involved significant job growth in real estate, tourism, retail, finance, technology, entertainment, film production, advanced education, and health care. When architectural transformation and economic dynamism are utterly intertwined, Robertson states, "it was efficient to become an architect."

Like many other observers of Vancouver, Robertson mentions two events—the 1986 World Transportation Exposition (known locally as Expo '86) and the 2010 Winter Olympics, which were acquired in 2003, the year *Office for Soft Architecture* was published—as bookends to Vancouver's shift from provincial colonial outpost to global city.[28] Expo '86, whose theme was "A World in Motion," was situated on land reclaimed by the government, previously used by the declining lumber and shipping industries. In 1988, the site was sold to the Concord Pacific development company, whose owner, Li Ka Shing, was one of Hong Kong's wealthiest businessmen. His investment helped pave the way for the huge influx of Asian investment, and immigration, into the city. Vancouver in general, and downtown real estate in particular, was seen as a safe and accessible location for Asian capital amid uncertainty over impending Chinese takeover in 1997. This investment fueled a significant real estate boom throughout the 1990s, which thoroughly remade Vancouver's downtown. At the same time, the influx of Asian immigrants, despite a significant nativist backlash, helped transform Vancouver into a diverse, multicultural city. The first construction on the Expo site began in 1991 with a cluster of "mixed-use" high-rise towers (residential, office, and public) and has continued in that vein, in the downtown area and beyond, to this day.

The second event Robertson mentions, the 2003 acquisition of the 2010 Winter Olympics, marked the city's successful management of this neoliberal transition and solidified Vancouver's arrival as a global city.[29]

Vancouver's downtown stands as a shining example of what Neil Smith has called the "generalization" of gentrification as a "global urban strategy" of neoliberal capitalism. In the 1950s and 1960s, gentrification referred to a "marginal process" based on the idiosyncratic preferences of private, individual consumers for preserving run-down but historically unique local buildings. However, Smith argues that by the 1980s, gentrification had become a fundamental technique of neoliberal urban management, a "subsidized private-market transformation of the city" and a major component of contemporary capital accumulation.[30] Of course, gentrification is often accompanied by progressive nostrums about urban livability, including public access and environmental responsibility. These ideals are a major source of the urban center's new appeal to elite workers, and many have become synonymous with Vancouver itself, as cities all over the world implement their own "Vancouverism": the production of mixed-use buildings designed with an emphasis on open and public access, walking and biking (rather than driving, since Vancouver has few freeways)—in short, a dense urban space in which people can live, work, and play simultaneously.[31] Of course, one has to be able to afford the rents, which have continued to skyrocket across Vancouver, and accept economic inequality and the anger of long-standing working-class and ethnic minority residents displaced by the "revanchist" city's attack on established social welfare policies and institutions.[32] It is no surprise that, as of this writing, many observers believe that Vancouver's real estate bubble is about to burst.[33]

In his earlier, seminal book on gentrification, focusing in particular on New York's Lower East Side, Smith pointed out that creative workers—artists, art dealers, gallery owners, designers—serve as the "shock troops of neighborhood reinvestment."[34] Robertson's narrators identify these creative denizens of the soft city as "the lyric class," a phrase that echoes contemporary urban redevelopment guru Richard Florida's influential concept of the "creative class." In a recent series of immensely popular books, Florida has argued that creative workers will form the economic basis of future urban growth.[35] His proposals have come to function as blueprints followed by policy makers looking to transform economically failing postindustrial cities in much the same manner as Vancouver. Florida's work converges with, and indeed depends on, a variety of currents within neoliberalism, including what Nigel Thrift has called the movement toward "soft capitalism." Thrift uses this term to refer to a shift in corporate ideology that he argues took place in the 1980s, when corporate elites began to define themselves and their practices in creative, artistic terms. "Soft capitalism" describes the ideology that pervades the businesses now occupying much of the revitalized downtown cores of the world's global cities, like Vancouver.[36]

To be sure, this neoliberal restructuring of urban space is not documented directly in Robertson's text, nor are the effects of segregation, displacement, and protest that have accompanied it. Yet I want to suggest that Robertson's recognition of the political and economic processes that have transformed Vancouver's "urban texture" explains not only her decision "to become an architect" but also why her depiction of the city's surfaces has to be soft. Since 2000, one of Vancouver's nicknames has been "city of glass," a phrase coined by hometown author Douglas Coupland as the title to his book of essays on the city, published that year. The phrase refers to the high-rise towers of Vancouver's revitalized downtown. Yet glass is also the closest an actual, perceivable surface can come to the idealized surface that Best and Marcus put forward as the basis for surface reading. Indeed, we might consider glass the neoliberal surface par excellence: it appears to be fully available to attentive description, but its self-sufficient transparency in fact obscures its historical conditions, its dependence on (and expression of) the shifting whims of capital. For Robertson, who aims instead to "manifest current conditions," to evoke the neoliberal city, whose architectural surface has been transformed to take full advantage of the fluid movements of global capitalism, a hard surface simply will not do. Surface has to be something softer, more ambiguous, more porous than glass: a "permeable boundary," "border," or "indiscrete threshold" (13, 141, 143). By contrast to the transparency of glass, Robertson brings out the opacity of a colored surface: "We always dream in colour. That is part of the history of surfaces" (139). No mere ornamental phenomenon, color reveals the processes of "exchange"—including "contamination," "accident," and "mix[ing]"—that constitute a soft surface "marbled by its historical medium" (139, 145).

By attending only to the hard transparency of the city's glass and steel structures, Robertson suggests, one fails to grasp the constitutive ephemerality of even the city's most apparently obdurate and triumphant surfaces. Yet Robertson doesn't look through the glass exterior to focus on the interior structure beneath it. She transforms both exterior and interior, "surface" and "fundament," into a soft, ambiguous surface. Robertson therefore devotes an essay to scaffolding, the "negative space of the building" that "impedes the transparency of vision" (165). By showing that "deep structure is intricate," her narrators tell us, scaffolding "disprove[s] the wrongheaded and habitual opposition of ornament and concept."

It "subtract[s] solidity from form" to reiterate the "vulnerability" of the city's soft surfaces. This offers a lesson crucial to contemporary urban life: "how to inhabit a surface as that surface fluctuates" (164). However much the neoliberal "city of glass" may look like a pure surface, Robertson's city is "persistently soft." She recasts Vancouver's imposing high-rise towers as provisional structures, "raw encampments at the edge of the rocks." Glass, steel, and cement become the soft fabrics of "tents rising and falling." The sight of this "permanent transience" may be "glittering," but this aesthetic pleasure also comes with a recognition of the hollow sameness of money, the "null rhythm which is the flux of modern careers" (15).

Instead of replacing aesthetic effect with economic cause, Robertson emphasizes the intertwining of surface and depth that constitutes both the city's surfaces and its economic structure. This is the neoliberal city seen from the perspective of capital itself. As Robertson explains in a prefatory note, "The Office for Soft Architecture came into being as I watched the city of Vancouver dissolve in the fluid called money. Buildings disappeared into newness. I tried to recall spaces, and what I remembered was surfaces. Here and there money had tarried. The result seemed emotional. I wanted to document this process. I began to research the history of surfaces. I included my own desires in the research. In this way, I became multiple. I became money" (1). As Vancouver's real estate investors know, money must "tarry" somewhere, for some amount of time. The unevenness of these "fluctuations" continually recomposes the urban surface. In *Office for Soft Architecture*, surface becomes the provisional residue of a city transfigured by the fluid movement of capital. But this movement is not simply located elsewhere, below or beyond the surface. It shapes the very contours—that is, the depth—of surface. Robertson "include[es] [her] own desires in the research" because surface is the site where capital engages—exploits, transforms, but ultimately fails to sustain—the needs (bodily, erotic, social) of living subjects on a collective scale. Surface is never completely thin or flat but always thick, layered. As Robertson states, "Under the pavement, pavement" (15).

This is one of two moments in which Robertson détourns the famous, situationist-inspired slogan ("under the paving stones, the beach!") displayed amid the barricades in Paris, May 1968. Robertson's other phrase—"*sous le plage, le pave* [under the beach, the paving stones]"—even more directly suggests that her reference is driven by a historical reversal (37). Unlike the Paris of the 1960s, in Robertson's Vancouver the utopian desire of revolutionary play has become the "new spirit" of a neoliberal capitalism in which aesthetic production plays an essential, rather than merely ornamental, role.[37] Thus, "complicity with the administration of shortage" is perhaps the final, overarching valence implied by Robertson's evocation of soft architecture's warm embrace (226). Her soft city offers a dialectical treatment of surface and depth in the specific context of a form of capitalism dependent on the structural value of the surface—on aesthetic or-nament, pleasure, desire: a neoliberal urbanism dedicated to the construction of "a zone of leisured flows" (41).

Conclusion: Cracks in the Surface

Rather than privilege either surface description or causal structure, Robertson's surface phenomenology grasps their constitutive, dialectical interrelation. Her work thus reorients the critical debates that have emerged in the wake of surface reading. The dialectical method of symptomatic reading, as it was developed from Althusser's work in the late 1960s to Jameson's reformulation a little over a decade later, did not involve unveiling the cause hidden underneath the surface. Symptomatic reading has always been about the *relation between* surface and depth, text and social totality.[38] The aim is not to look past the textual surface, but to read that surface more attentively by engaging the social totality both text and reader inhabit. Yet those calling for new, postcritical approaches are right to note that symptomatic reading has become a kind of mechanical reflex toward easy demystification. Indeed, Raymond Williams pointed out in the late 1970s that emphasis on depth can be as stifling to dialectical inquiry as an emphasis on the surface.[39]

If the dialectical tension that once animated symptomatic reading has gone slack—resulting in the current standoff between surface and depth—the re-sponse cannot be to embrace the "political realism" of the surface, nor to insist on the agency of a critique predicated on distance. In this sense much of the current debate has missed the importance of surface now. Surface reading hits on the right question but poses it the wrong way. Robertson's identification of aesthetic surface as a structural problem of contemporary capitalism shows that the intertwining of economic and creative production under neoliberalism has made it necessary to reimagine, rather than abandon, art's critical role in contem-porary life.

Robertson reminds us that surfaces are made, not given. It is no accident that her materialist surface emerges through an attempt to engage the recent dynam-ics of capitalist urban restructuring, because the neoliberal city is the privileged site of the creative labor that enables so much corporate profit today. As Robert-son points out, even in an age of "soft capitalism" the drive toward profit, along with its "instituted shortages," still holds (226). To grasp the neoliberal city's spatial contours therefore requires a dialectical concept of surface as intertwined with depth, thick with folds, gaps, and layers. The contradictions of capitalist accumulation—between profit and shortage, excess of goods and increasing immiseration—will inevitably manifest themselves as crises, the "hairline cracks" (231) in the city's surfaces. Obscured by the flat, hard surfaces of the "city of glass," these cracks emerge in the seams in the fabric of the soft city, the trace of the material processes by which urban space is being remade—and by which it can be made once again, differently.

Attentive to this possibility, Robertson does not thereby "ignore," "look past," or "see through" the surface (to recall the oversight that surface reading aims to correct). Rather, she *looks into* the surface by "open[ing] up a space" in it (145). These openings become a "potent space between substance and politics" (145). Robertson recognizes the artist's (or critic's) entanglement in these spaces. "Happiness," she writes, "is the consolidation of complicities" (257). Yet art can still bring out the conditions and processes that constitute that solidity, by unraveling, wearing through, or softening it. Robertson's soft architecture, however complicit itself, brings out the constitutive, historical dimensionality of surface in order to understand and critique the neoliberal city.

NOTES

1. Stephen Best and Sharon Marcus, "Surface Reading: An Introduction," *Representations* 108, no. 1 (Fall 2009): 1–21. In addition to responses from "prominent critics," Best and Marcus's essay has, according to Google Scholar, received 175 citations in just under six years, a time period in which most scholars are lucky to receive six or eight citations. See Jeffrey Williams, "The New Modesty in Literary Criticism," *Chronicle of Higher Education*, January 5, 2015.

2. "Surface" here can refer to a variety of things, including the materiality of the text, its verbal or linguistic density, or even the reader's affective or ethical responsiveness. Surface reading thus embraces a large variety of reading practices, including formalism (new and old), cognitive science, affective approaches, history of the book, and "distant reading" and other data-driven approaches. Best and Marcus, "Surface Reading," 1–2, 18, 16, 18, 9.

3. Ibid., 15, 13, 2, 13.

4. See Fredric Jameson, *Postmodernism; or, The Cultural Logic of Late Capitalism* (Durham, NC: Duke University Press, 1992), 9; Best and Marcus, "Surface Reading," 8.

5. One exception is Crystal Bartolovich, "Humanities of Scale: Marxism, Surface Reading—and Milton," *PMLA* 127, no. 1 (2012): 116.

6. Jed Esty and Colleen Lye, "Peripheral Realisms Now," *Modern Language Quarterly* 73, no. 3 (2012): 269–88.

7. Richard Sennett, *The Culture of the New Capitalism* (New Haven, CT: Yale University Press, 2006), 197. On the totalizing nature of contemporary capitalism, see Alison Shonkwiler and Leigh Claire La Berge, eds., *Reading Capitalist Realism* (Iowa City: University of Iowa Press, 2014).

8. See Tom McCarthy, *Remainder* (New York: Vintage, 2007), and *C* (London: Random House, 2010); Bruno Latour, *Reassembling the Social: An Introduction to Actor-Network-Theory* (Oxford: Oxford University Press, 2007); and Tao Lin, *Taipei* (New York: Vintage, 2013).

9. This turn to surface that does not "lack depth" but is intertwined with it indicates that Jameson's postmodernist paradigm is no longer adequate to map the literary and cultural forms of the present.

10. Jameson, *Postmodernism*, 4. See also Fredric Jameson, *The Cultural Turn: Selected Writings on the Postmodern* (London: Verso, 1998), 143–44. For an update and extension of Jameson's argument, see Nicholas Brown, "The Work of Art in the Age of Its Real Subsumption under Capital," *nonsite.org*, March 13, 2012, http://nonsite.org/editorial/the-work-of-art-in-the-age-of-its-real-subsumption-under-capital.

11. In *Literature and the Creative Economy* (Palo Alto, CA: Stanford University Press, 2014), Sarah Brouillette offers a comprehensive analysis of the consequences of this shift for contemporary literature. For a broader look at how contemporary capitalism redeploys earlier "artistic critique," see Luc Boltanski and Eve Schiapello, *New Spirit of Capitalism* (London: Verso, 2005).

12. See, e.g., David Harvey, *A Brief History of Neoliberalism* (Oxford: Oxford University Press, 2005). As Joshua Clover points out, the crises of 2008 and 1973 have to be thought together: "crisis is always plural, always *crises*, as one contradiction is displaced and returns as another." Joshua Clover, "Value|Theory|Crisis," *PMLA* 127, no. 1 (2012): 113.

13. Harvey and Smith address these issues throughout their writing, but in particular see David Harvey, "From Managerialism to Entrepreneurialism: The Transformation in Urban Governance in Late Capitalism," *Geografiska Annaler Series B, Human Geography* 71, no. 1 (1989): 3–17; "Globalization and the Spatial Fix," *Geographische Revue* 2 (2001): 23–30; "Right to the City" and "The Urban Roots of Capitalist Crises," in *Rebel Cities: From the Right to the City to the Urban Revolution* (London: Verso, 2012), 3–67; and Neil Smith, "New Globalism, New Urbanism: Gentrification as Global Urban Strategy," *Antipode* 34, no. 3 (2002): 427–50.

14. Lisa Robertson, *Occasional Work and Seven Walks from the Office for Soft Architecture* (Astoria, OR: Clear Cut, 2003), 17. Hereafter cited in the text.

15. Maurice Merleau-Ponty, *Phenomenology of Perception* (1965; repr., London: Routledge, 2002), esp. 308–10.

16. Merleau-Ponty chooses the word "situation" over the more natural word "position" because the former expresses the sense of being in a whole, three-dimensional and sociohistorical world, whereas the latter presumes a geometrical objectivity alien to lived experience. See ibid., 114–15.

17. See ibid., 309.

18. Best and Marcus, "Surface Reading," 9. While surface reading consistently appeals to the materiality of the text, it is only as a material object immediately available for subjective experience (e.g., affective or ethical responses) or objective (e.g., empirical, data-driven) research. In this respect, surface reading resonates with some of the new materialisms. See Diana Coole and Samantha Frost, eds., *New Materialisms: Ontology, Agency,*

Politics (Durham, NC: Duke University Press, 2010). A similar geometrical abstraction undermines Jameson's overarching goal of relating surface and depth dialectically. He collapses the two incommensurate notions of depth (objective and phenomenological) when he presents depth as both a separate "level" of an objective structure and the "underside" of a phenomenological object. This enables the kinds of appeals to surface we are seeing today. See Fredric Jameson, *The Political Unconscious: Narrative as a Socially Symbolic Act* (Ithaca, NY: Cornell University Press, 1981), 49. As I have argued elsewhere, Merleau-Ponty's phenomenology of perception provides an alternative model of reading to both surface and symptom that engages the Marxist concept of totality more effectively. See Jason M. Baskin, "Soft Eyes: Marxism, Surface, and Depth," *Mediations* 28, no. 2 (Spring 2015): 5–18.

19. We often forget that Merleau-Ponty understood his philosophical project as a contribution to the dialectical tradition initiated by Hegel. See Diana Coole, *Merleau-Ponty and Modern Politics after Anti-humanism* (Lanham, MD: Rowan & Littlefield, 2007). This dialectical emphasis counters the recent neo-phenomenology of postcritical readers such as Rita Felski and new materialists such as William Connolly, both of whom invoke Merleau-Ponty but ignore the dialectical basis of his philosophy. See Rita Felski, "Everyday Aesthetics," *minnesota review* 71 (2009): 175–76; and William Connolly, "Materialities of Experience," in *New Materialisms: Ontology, Agency, Politics*, ed. Diana Coole and Samantha Frost (Durham, NC: Duke University Press, 2010), 178–201.

20. Merleau-Ponty, *Phenomenology*, 308, 13, 250. In his later work, Merleau-Ponty emphasizes the concept of the fold as the site of an ambiguous form of absent presence. See Maurice Merleau-Ponty, "The Intertwining—the Chiasm," in *The Visible and the Invisible* (Evanston, IL: Northwestern University Press, 1968), 130–56.

21. See, e.g., Bartolovich, "Humanities of Scale"; and Suvir Kaul, "Reading, Constraint and Freedom," *Eighteenth Century* 54, no. 1 (Spring 2013): 129–32.

22. Lisa Robertson in conversation with Leonard Schwartz on *Cross Cultural Poetics*, https://media.sas.upenn.edu/Pennsound/groups/XCP/XCP_204_Robertson_12-10-09 .mp3. Robertson specifically references Merleau-Ponty's work in her most recent book *Nilling* (Toronto: Bookthug, 2012).

23. Quoted on the cover of the book.

24. Lisa Robertson, "How Pastoral: A Manifesto," in *Telling It Slant: Avant-Garde Poetics of the 1990s*, ed. Mark Wallace and Steve Marks (Tuscaloosa: University of Alabama Press, 2002), 21–26.

25. Best and Marcus, "Surface Reading," 17.

26. Jennifer Scappettone thus identifies Robertson's Vancouver as made of "sociohistorical substance." See Jennifer Scappettone, "Site Surfeit: Office for Soft Architecture Makes the City Confess," *Chicago Review* 51, no. 4 / 52, no. 1 (Spring 2006): 70–76.

27. Quoted in Sina Queyras, "About Surface: Lisa Robertson's Poetics of Elegance," in *Eleven More American Women Poets in the 21st Century: Poetics across North America*, ed. Claudia Rankine and Lisa Sewell (Middleton, CT: Wesleyan University Press), 383.

28. Vancouver exemplifies David Harvey's notion of the "entrepreneurial city," an increasingly important part of the shift to neoliberalism. Regarding Vancouver's successful hosting of Expo '86, Harvey argues, "They [cities/urban investors] increasingly focus on the quality of life. Gentrification, cultural innovation, and physical up-grading of the urban environment (including the turn to postmodernist styles of architecture and urban design),

consumer attractions (sports stadia, convention and shopping centres, marinas, exotic eating places) and entertainment (the organization of urban spectacles on a temporary or permanent basis), have all become much more prominent facets of strategies for urban regeneration. Above all, the city has to appear as an innovative, exciting, creative, and safe place to live or to visit, to play and consume in" ("From Managerialism to Entrepreneurialism," 9).

29. For detailed accounts of this transformation, see Kris Olds, "Liquid Assets: Producing the Pacific Rim Consumptionscape in Vancouver, Canada," in *Globalization and Urban Change* (New York: Oxford University Press, 2001), 57–140. Hong Kong financiers developed productive networks with local business and government elites to make Vancouver into a "Pacific Rim metropolis," no longer an "old colonial outpost of Europe" but "a functioning way-station for global flows," geographically and culturally positioned to connect Europe, Asia, and North America (92). Michael Davidson has read Robertson's writing about Vancouver in the context of NAFTA; see Michael Davidson, "On the Outskirts of Form: Cosmopoetics in the Shadow of NAFTA," *Textual Practice* 22, no. 4 (2008): 733–56.

30. See Neil Smith, "New Globalism, New Urbanism: Gentrification as Global Urban Strategy," *Antipode* 34, no. 3 (2002): 439–40.

31. On the importance of the "livable city" ideology in the remaking of Vancouver, see Olds, "Liquid Assets," 97.

32. See Neil Smith, *The New Urban Frontier: Gentrification and the Revanchist City* (New York: Routledge, 1996). For an account of the neoliberal political realignment that enabled Vancouver's transformation and the social disruption it entailed, see Katharyne Mitchell, *Crossing the Neoliberal Line* (Philadelphia: Temple University Press, 2004), esp. ch. 2. Since Robertson's volume appeared, gentrification has spread to Vancouver's traditionally poorer Downtown Eastside, whose residents have staged bitter protests. On rising inequality in Vancouver over the period Robertson documents, see David Ley and Nicholas Lynch, "Divisions and Disparities in Lotus Land: Socio-spatial Income Polarisation in Greater Vancouver, 1970–2005," Research Report 223 (University of Toronto Cities Centre, August 2012).

33. See, e.g., Jesse Ferreras, "Vancouver Real Estate May Already Be Crashing," *Huffington Post Canada*, July 8, 2016, www.huffingtonpost.ca/2016/07/08/vancouver-real-estate -crash_n_10869538.html.

34. Smith, *New Urban Frontier*, 198. For a more focused study of the role of artists and the art market in the process of gentrification, see Sharon Zukin, *Loft Living: Culture and Capital and Urban Change* (Baltimore: Johns Hopkins University Press, 1982). David Ley also discusses this topic, with particular attention to Vancouver, in "Artists, Aestheticization and the Field of Gentrification," *Urban Studies* 40, no. 12 (November 2003): 2527–44.

35. Richard Florida, *The Rise of the Creative Class* (New York: Basic Books, 2002), *The Flight of the Creative Class* (New York: Basic Books, 2005), and *Cities and the Creative Class* (New York: Basic Books, 2005). For incisive discussion of Florida's work, see Jamie Peck, "The Creativity Fix," *Eurozine*, www.eurozine.com/articles/2007-06-28-peck-en.html#foot NoteNUM42; and Sarah Brouillette, "Creative Labor," *Mediations* 24, no. 2 (Spring 2009): 140–49.

36. Lance Berkowitz's celebratory recent assessment is typical: Vancouver boasts an "energetic small-business sector, thriving 'green' research and development, and a growing creative class. . . . Vancouver's focus on quality of place and quality of life is increasingly attracting the knowledge workers, the global citizens and the 'cultural creative' whom

the new city states are targeting." See Lance Berkowitz, *Dream City: Vancouver and the Global Imagination* (Vancouver: Douglas & McIntyre, 2005), 265–66.

37. Luc Boltanksi and Eve Schiappello, *The New Spirit of Capitalism* (London: Verso, 2005).

38. See Ellen Rooney, "Live Free or Describe: The Reading Effect and the Persistence of Form," *differences* 21, no. 3 (2010): 112–39.

39. See Raymond Williams, "Base and Superstructure in Marxist Cultural Theory," in *Problems in Materialism and Culture* (London: Verso, 1980), 31–49.

PART II

NEOLIBERALISM AND LITERARY FORM

Fictions of Neoliberalism

Contemporary Realism and the Temporality of Postmodernism's Ends

MATHIAS NILGES

In his essay "What Kind of Thing Is 'Neoliberalism'?," which introduces a 2013 special double issue of *new formations* dedicated to the study of the relation between neoliberalism and culture, Jeremy Gilbert dedicates significant space to tracing the diachronic and synchronic complexity of the term *neoliberalism* itself. That Gilbert's essay and indeed the special issue itself require a significant amount of conceptual framing before being able to address itself to its topic—"Neoliberal Culture"—is on the face of it not unexpected. In fact, this is how literary and cultural criticism works. Before carrying out a particular analysis that brings a cultural or literary artifact into relation with a problem of material reality, a sociopolitical field, or any given concept, it is usual to map the field of inquiry and to articulate one's particular contribution in relation to existing conceptual definitions and approaches. A literary critical project that examines the relation between the contemporary American novel and employment, for instance, would have to trace the changing history and the contemporary complexity of the term with which it seeks to bring the novel into conversation. It would seem natural in such a situation to ask what employment is, how it has been understood in different moments in American history, and how the novel bears out the history of this changing understanding of the term, as well as situates itself in relation to the particular complexity of the term in the present context. However, as Gilbert's introduction and the essays that make up the special issue illustrate, the term *neoliberalism* requires something different. Gilbert's introduction serves a very specific and rather unusual purpose: "it situates the eleven other contributions to the volume in the context of the wider field of debate over the existence and nature of 'neoliberalism' as a specifiable and analyzable phenomenon."[1] The difference between a project dedicated to "neoliberal culture" and one that addresses itself to "fictions of employment" is, in other words, that the latter project may have to map its field of inquiry, but it does not have to begin by proving the existence of employment as a specifiable and analyzable phenomenon. The engagement with neoliberal culture, therefore, is a bit less like a project such as "fictions of employment" and a bit more like a project such as "American literature and the Sasquatch."

What this suggests, as Gérard Duménil and Dominique Lévy similarly argue in *The Crisis of Neoliberalism*, is that neoliberalism is best understood not as a term that designates a socioeconomic or political given that exists for us to understand, but instead as a term that describes a strategy.[2] It is this particular logic of the term *neoliberalism* that, as I attempt to show in what follows, carries with it a specific set of challenges and opportunities for literary criticism. Specifically, I will argue, if we conceive of neoliberalism as a strategy, then we are able to see that the origin and implementation of this strategy are directly bound up with the history of postmodernism. This essay then departs from the assumption that it is this particular conceptual peculiarity of the term *neoliberalism* itself that allows us to generate some insights into how precisely the term may be of use for literary criticism. To begin unfolding this argument, I will first turn to a little-discussed essay that Pierre Bourdieu published in 1996, in which he provides us with an alternative way of understanding neoliberalism that allows us to connect neoliberalism directly to literature and recent literary history: neoliberalism, Bourdieu suggests, is a fiction tending toward reality. It is in this way, then, that we can understand neoliberalism as a strategy that moves from the status of fiction to the point of its structural implementation, which profoundly reshapes material and social reality.

"What is neoliberalism?" asks Bourdieu at the beginning of his essay "The Essence of Neoliberalism." In the essay's subtitle, he provides a clear, direct answer: "a programme for destroying collective structures which may impede the pure market logic."[3] But Bourdieu immediately undercuts his initial suggestion and wonders whether we can really consider this program and the new economic order it brings with it our new material and social reality: "What if, in reality, this economic order were no more than the implementation of a utopia—the utopia of neoliberalism—thus converted into a *political problem*? One that, with the aid of the economic theory that it proclaims, succeeds in conceiving of itself as the scientific description of reality?" Neoliberalism can thus be understood as a matter of "*making itself true* and empirically verifiable," Bourdieu suggests. There lies at the heart of neoliberalism, in other words, a dialectic of form and content, since not only is neoliberalism itself formally a matter of a fiction tending toward reality, of a utopian fiction that confirms itself in reality, but also, Bourdieu argues, neoliberalism's realities lead back toward abstraction, since it "tends on the whole to favour severing the economy from social realities and thereby constructing, in reality, an economic system conforming to its description in pure theory." What Bourdieu diagnoses here is the specific logic of neoliberalism that, in economic form and lived content, is a matter of the dialectical tension between abstraction and reality (say, the relation of finance and value to real capital, or the relation of production and exchange to labor and even consumption), between fiction and realism, which creates the logical problems with the term's critical circumscription we saw above, which seem to locate it somewhere between Sasquatch and employment.

If we understand neoliberalism in this way, as the historical development of a strategy that is driven forward by the dialectical relationship between fiction and reality, it becomes clear that literary criticism has a clear disciplinary stake in the general effort to study the history of neoliberalism and the particular sets of conceptual and logical problems that its move from fiction to reality creates in our present. Furthermore, if we examine the rise to dominance of neoliberalism in the United States as a transition from theoretical fiction to reality as a process that gathered momentum in the general effort to manage the structural crises of capitalism of the 1960s and 1970s and that began to transition into an economic order that since the 1980s and 1990s can be described as dominant neoliberalism and our new economic reality, then it becomes clear that it is possible to locate important elements of the recent history of the novel in relation to this context. This centrally includes, I argue, the transition away from the experimental forms of high postmodernism and toward the forms of realism that have come to define our moment in literary history. This is admittedly a very large project, one that far transcends the limits of this brief essay. But the great value of collections such as this one is that they provide a space for broad strokes, for experimentation, for sketching out conceptual and critical blueprints, and for proposing alternative points of departure that aim to generate further debate. As a consequence, this essay is largely programmatic in nature and aims to forward a range of basic provocations that, unless completely mistaken, will hopefully lead to further discussion. This initial approach to the particular way of bringing neoliberalism and literature into conversation also expresses my conviction that there is an important place for literature in general and the novel in particular in discussions of the particular epistemological impasses of neoliberal capitalism. And in particular from a perspective that examines neoliberalism as constitutively connected to the tension between fiction and realism and reality, the place of the novel is more than a matter of reflection and representation or even of the full subsumption of literature and the novel under neoliberalism.

Tracing the relation between the recent formal history of the novel and the rise of neoliberalism provides us with one way of understanding the novel's ability to make legible the epistemological horizons of that which neoliberalism establishes as our new reality. What is more, such attention to the formal relation between neoliberalism and the novel allows us to understand crises of neoliberalism as crises of neoliberalism's enabling fictions. In the remainder of this essay, I will propose that neoliberalism's transition from utopian fiction to reality is mediated by the rise and exhaustion of postmodernism, suggesting that the conceptual instability that Bourdieu locates as a formal basis of neoliberalism echoes the struggle of recent literary criticism to articulate that which may succeed postmodernism. Here the term "neoliberal novel" becomes one possible way of expressing the novel's literary historical move away from forms we associate with the postmodernism of the 1960s and 1970s, registering that move not as postmodernism's disappearance, but as a consequence of the structural implementation of postmodernism's constitutive wishes in neoliberalism. Once both neoliberalism and postmodernism have completed their historically parallel journey from fiction to reality, those forms of the novel we traditionally associate with high postmodernism disappear and we witness the emergence of a range of forms that are connected to the novel's attempt to register the moment at which neoliberalism and postmodernism coincide to form our present structural reality. Central to this formal change, I will argue, is the novel's recent turn back to matters of time and history as a way of addressing the crisis of temporality and futurity that is bound up with the structural standardization of postmodernism (and its trademark effacement of time by space) and neoliberalism's move from utopian fiction to structural reality.

In *Post-postmodernism*, Jeffrey Nealon proposes that the addition of a second "post-" should be understood as marking the distinction between contemporary culture and that of the sixties and seventies, the decades we traditionally associate with high postmodernism. Nealon's reasoning is utterly persuasive: if we compare today's cultural forms with those of the sixties and seventies, then there is little doubt that things have changed significantly and that we need to develop an adequate account of the historical change that is expressed in this formal difference. Yet while Nealon insists on the significant differences between postmodernism and today's culture, throughout the book he also stresses that the second "post-" carries with it a substantial conceptual and temporal awkwardness connected to postmodernism's apparent simultaneous exhaustion and persistence in different implementations. Nealon ascribes this to the fact that postmodernism has not actually fully disappeared. Instead, he argues, it is now expressed in the structures of our neoliberal present, and, since the 1980s, we have been witnessing an intensification of postmodernism. At the same time, Nealon argues, this intensification is also the reason that we must no longer hold on to postmodernism, because "the ethos of liberation that surrounds cultural postmodernism (the transgressions of hybridity, the individual ethics of self-fashioning, Dionysiac celebrations of multiplicity, endlessly making it new) can't simply be walled off from the substantially more sinister work that these very same notions index within the economic realm—they're the watchwords of neoliberal capitalism as well."[4] Similarly, Mark C. Taylor describes "today's globally wired financial markets" as "postmodernism on steroids,"[5] echoing Nealon's logic and understanding neoliberalism as both the structural implementation and the intensification of postmodernism.

But what if we understood the phenomenon highlighted by Nealon and Taylor as logically and indeed historically congruent with Bourdieu's account of neoliberalism—as also a matter of the transition of a fiction to the status of realism? If neoliberalism is in fact a matter of the structural implementation of a utopia, of speculative theory, ought we not commit fully to the historical connection between neoliberalism and postmodernism and suggest that postmodernism does not simply coincide with neoliberalism in the present but was in fact instrumental to the process of resolving the capitalist crises of the 1960s and 1970s, providing important aspects of those cultural and theoretical forms that contributed to forming the bases of the new capitalist system? From such a perspective, postmodernism does not simply lose its original edge or become co-opted and structurally intensified by neoliberalism. Rather, postmodernism emerges as a central part of precisely that set of fictions that gave rise to neoliberalism and that began to be structurally implemented as the new dominant system in the late 1980s and early 1990s, the point at which we witness the novel's departure from postmodernism's characteristic forms. "When one dialectically overcodes the liberated cultural effects of postmodernism with the substantially more dire economic realities that rely on the same concepts," Nealon suggests, "one can no longer assess the cultural effects in quite the same way."[6] And while this is no doubt the case, this insight indicates more than postmodernism's exhaustion. It raises the question of the degree of the structural relation between postmodernism and realism (here in strategically hyperbolic form): would the rise of neoliberalism as we know it have been possible without the cultural and theoretical fictions provided by postmodernism?

Conceiving of the relationship between neoliberalism and postmodernism in such a way also raises important questions about our understanding of literary history itself. Articulating the exhaustion of postmodernism in relation to neoliberalism's transition from fiction to reality indicates that our continued struggle with the temporality of the second "post-" indicates first and foremost the need to historicize and temporalize the way we think literary history itself. "The formal possibilities of literary history," Hans Ulrich Gumbrecht argues, emerged under very specific historical conditions "in the mid-nineteenth century alongside nineteenth-century historicism."[7] What emerged was "a complex structure of imagining time and, through it, of experiencing change" that "was so universally accepted that people soon tended to confuse it with 'historical consciousness' in the sense of a metahistorical condition."[8] "Its most basic feature," Gumbrecht claims, "was the asymmetry between an open future lived as the horizon of expectations and a past that the ongoing time, at each moment, seemed to leave behind as a closed space of experience."[9] In the present moment, however, as Gumbrecht argues, this notion of the open future has given way to an increasingly broadening present, a commonly made assertion about the time of our present that is by now well known and has found its way into the work of a wide range of philosophers and literary critics, including Lauren Berlant's account of our "broad, stretched-out present" in *Cruel Optimism* and Mark Fisher's association of neoliberalism with the "eternal now" in *Capitalist Realism*.[10] In this context, neoliberalism's transition from fiction to reality also binds itself to the gradual erosion of the future and its contraction into a timeless present, thereby undercutting those forms of temporality that define literary history as we know it. Similarly, such a perspective would allow us to understand the turn to realism in times of neoliberalism not only as an expression of dominant neoliberalism but also as a way of formally registering the transformation of both neoliberalism itself and postmodernism's quintessential forms from experimental fiction into realism. Consequently, it seems possible to suggest that the "neo-" in neoliberalism is structurally and historically congruent with the "post-" in postmodernism.

Likewise, one might therefore suspect that this is the source of the unease that Nealon senses when he wishes to point out the complicity between neoliberalism and postmodernism while also sensing that the second "post-" rubs uncomfortably against the temporal logic of this relation. Put differently, one way of explaining the current struggle in criticism to come to terms with that which may succeed postmodernism is to understand it as a temporal consequence of the fact that postmodernism did not disappear but instead actualized itself in neoliberalism, which, in its structural implementation of a broad present of instantaneous exchange and communication, is in turn connected to a cultural and social logic that is defined by the very impossibility of generating another "post-." The contemporary novel registers this transition from fiction to reality by turning to realism and to matters of time and temporality. One of the central and most belabored aspects of postmodernism is the effacement of time by space. To be sure, one must even read the literature of the 1960s and 1970s somewhat selectively in order to maintain the validity of this by now almost stereotypical description of postmodernism. What may hold for some aspects of white American literature, for example, is not quite as true for African American literature of the period, which relates quite differently to the pressures on temporality that characterized aspects of material and cultural life in those decades. Still, the aspects of postmodernism that have since been standardized in neoliberalism are in many ways the most stereotypical aspects of postmodernism, such as the focus on a politics of identity and difference and the central tenets of the linguistic turn. In fact, as Nealon indicates throughout his book (but does not directly state), Jameson's account of postmodernism (and to a similar degree that of Jean-François Lyotard, irrespective of the profound political differences between the versions of postmodernism Jameson and Lyotard forward) can serve as a guidebook for tracing some of neoliberalism's fundamental aspects. The reappearance of the attention to time in the contemporary novel, which, together with realism, aims to examine our present as a matter of actually existing postmodernism, accordingly articulates itself in opposition to these—in many ways necessarily most mainstream—characteristics of postmodernism.

But as soon as we attempt to discuss the contemporary novel's departure from and its opposition to the postmodern novel beginning at the moment at which postmodernism becomes standardized as neoliberalism, our established temporal and periodizing vocabulary becomes troubled. Postmodernism disappears from literature once it becomes the new structural reality of our present. The logic of chronology that underlies the predominant models of periodization, however, is wedded to a temporality that measures life cycles. It traces births, lives, and deaths. But postmodernism did not exactly die. It transitioned from a fictional life to a real existence. Likewise, postmodernism did not really end. And we are not in a period that has moved beyond postmodernism. More accurately, the fictions of postmodernism of the sixties and seventies have become the reality of the neoliberal present, and what becomes visible in this process is not postmodernism's end but its ends. This is also to say that the conceptual awkwardness that tends to arise from attempts to speak about this transition can be understood as a result of the fact that literature turns away from postmodernism once it realizes postmodernism's actual function and ontology. It is no longer possible to write postmodern literature not because history has moved past postmodernism and rendered it unable to speak to the present. Postmodernism is no longer a vehicle for current literature, especially literature that seeks to politically engage with the present, because postmodernism's fictions have become the dominant language of the neoliberal present. We haven't moved beyond postmodernism as much as we are finding ourselves in a situation comparable to that of Goethe's sorcerer's apprentice. We have lost control over the spirits that we have conjured up, who have taken on a life of their own. But we do not need to await the return of our master to solve this problem. The contemporary realist novel has tasked itself with this project.

This is, ultimately, why we struggle to talk about that which may succeed postmodernism, as well as its own potential afterlives. The additional "post-" does not help us make sense of this development because we are not confronted with a transition from life to death but from fiction to reality. The impression that the end of postmodernism is somehow related to its ubiquity in fact underwrites some of the earliest accounts of postmodernism's exhaustion, which begin to emerge in the early 1990s, at the moment in which neoliberalism reaches dominance. Already in 1993, Raymond Federman proclaimed that "postmodernism changed tense when Samuel Beckett changed tense."[11] "Postmodern fiction experimented with death, or rather with its own death," argues Federman, adding, "It won" (107). Invoking the famous opening passage of Thomas Pynchon's *Gravity's Rainbow*, which is often associated with the beginning of postmodernism, Federman's understanding of postmodernism as a period limits it quite helpfully for our purposes to a short moment in time, since notions of a long postmodernism, which we still encounter quite frequently, disallow for the kind of historicization that, I believe, helps us better understand not only the relation between postmodernism, neoliberalism, and contemporary literature but also, retroactively, postmodernism itself. For Federman, postmodernism was a short flash: "like a screaming . . . no, better yet, like a ghost it passed across the sky." The death of postmodernism is for Federman a direct, inevitable result of its constitutive contradictions: "postmodernism was an exercise in discontinuity, rupture, break, mutation, transformation, therefore doomed from the beginning" (110).

But Federman's analysis also contains a second logical strand that notably differs from the account of postmodernism outlined above. This account of postmodernism's demise begins with the suggestion that "Postmodern fiction was ... both an escape and a transcendence" (111). The end of postmodernism, then, is marked also by the successful completion of one of its constitutive projects, but the end itself is qualitatively different, since it is brought about not by postmodernism's disappearance and shift into the past tense, but instead by its shift into the status of omnipresence. Consequently, Federman argues, "now that the entire world, the entire universe for that matter has become Postmodern, these [postmodern] writers can now stand back and watch, with some degree of amusement, the consequences of what they set in motion some years ago" (107–8). Postmodernism did not fail because of its immanent contradictions or because it was an avant-garde movement that became too popular and spread across the globe. It brought about and was actualized in the current stage of capitalism. Once the gap between avant-garde and the quotidian closes, we see a turn to realism and matters of time and temporality to register precisely this transition from fiction to present reality. To periodize the exhaustion of postmodernism and with it contemporary literature therefore requires us to think time otherwise. This includes, as the contemporary realist novel shows, the concept of the contemporary itself, which carries a muddled temporality that results in part from postmodernism's tense switch.

Consequently, it appears that we should orient ourselves terminologically in relation to other systems that imagine their existence speculatively, as a process, and as the temporality arising from the transition from utopia to realism. The term *Realsozialismus*, actually existing socialism, famously seeks to highlight the differences between socialism as a utopian project and socialism as a matter of real or actual politics and material structures in the present. Might we not likewise benefit from expressing the difference between postmodernism and its exhaustion by way of its structural implementation in our present neoliberal reality as the difference between postmodernism and *Realpostmodernismus*, actually existing postmodernism? The move of neoliberalism from fiction to reality is, after all, congruent with the move of postmodernism to actually existing postmodernism. This terminological and conceptual change appears particularly necessary since the novel itself is well aware of this historical development, seeing as the turn to realism in the contemporary novel is a matter not only of the inescapability of neoliberalism but also of the formal commitment to registering precisely the temporality and logic of neoliberalism's presence—something that we can trace in the novel since the late 1980s and early 1990s.

In this situation, literary history certainly experiences a moment of crisis. But this should not be taken as a sign of the need to abandon projects of periodization altogether. In her essay "On the Period Formerly Known as the Contemporary," for instance, Amy Hungerford questions the usefulness of the practice of periodizing in our time: "how interesting are the arguments about how to choose beginnings and ends?"[12] For the relation between neoliberalism and literature as conceived in this essay, Hungerford's essay also contains a second important line of inquiry: does the dominant way we talk about recent literary history limit the things we can say about literature? Hungerford appears to believe that it does—and I share this conviction. To be sure, I do not take Hungerford's initial question to be a matter of simple opposition to the project of periodization. Rather, I understand it as a provocation challenging critics to develop fully historicized accounts of the methodological bases underlying periodizing projects, a challenge that is particularly important at a moment in which the crisis of temporality that results from the intertwined history of postmodernism and neoliberalism appears to trouble the temporal foundation of literary history as a critical practice. Consequently, when Hungerford suggests that it may be more productive to stop worrying about "the hieroglyphics we have nominated for the header of this period" and simply produce scholarship on contemporary literature,[13] it becomes clear that this in itself is a matter of historicization and periodization in the context of postmodernism's exhaustion into the neoliberal contemporary. The way we talk about the contemporary itself, in other words, is a problem that is wedded to the temporal relation between neoliberalism, postmodernism, and the contemporary. The contemporary, which was in postmodernism rife with a plurality of temporalities, acquires a status of omnipresence and becomes stretched out into a timeless monad in full neoliberalism. Confronted with the broadened present and eternal now of neoliberalism, the logic of periodization inevitably emerges and suggests that our now ought to be distinguished from postmodernism. As a consequence, the concept of the contemporary raises a question that, as we saw at the beginning of this essay, the term *neoliberalism* raises about itself, a question that becomes one of the defining points of departure for projects that aim to trace the history of literature and the novel after postmodernism: what exactly is the concept's referent?

What, then, might such a project look like? A beginning sketch of the ways in which the purported end of time is bound up with forms of thinking time in the novel's endings helps illustrate the logic, the stakes, and the basic aims of such a focus on the recent novel's engagement with time and contemporaneity. In one of the classic essays on the time of the novel, John Henry Raleigh illustrates that the time that underlies the form of the novel emerges in part in connection to a specific form of temporal thought that arose in the context of eighteenth-century liberalism. Given that we are here concerned with the ways in which the contemporary novel may be brought into relation with neoliberalism, it seems helpful to revisit the ways in which this connection presented itself at the time of the historical emergence of both the novel and neoliberalism. In fact, Raleigh argues, it was not until modern liberalism was well established and had reached a dominant historical status that the novel addressed itself to this new situation by way of a formal transition. The novel did so, Raleigh illustrates, by addressing itself to the temporal logic of liberalism itself, in much the same way that the contemporary novel's turn to time and realism constitutes an effort to work through the temporal logic of neoliberal omnipresence. While the famous turn of the nineteenth-century (realist) novel toward time and history sets it apart clearly from the novel of the eighteenth century, Raleigh suggests that the nineteenth-century novel inherits its form of thinking time from eighteenth-century liberalism. "Dickens and Trollope," for example, Raleigh writes, "were committed . . . to historical time, or time as a straight line, from the past into the future. In their case the idea of time was tied up with the idea of progress . . . with the result that one looked forward to a pleasant but indefinite future and shunned a definite but unpleasant past. This attitude—rationalistic, progressive, secular— . . . is known as liberalism."[14] "But what is noteworthy about the liberal attitude toward time-history," Raleigh adds, "is that, while it is generally confident about the future, it is vague about the concrete content of the future" (248). Liberalism's thinking of time and futurity, Raleigh suggests, is crystallized in the time of the novel and in particular in its endings. The ending of a novel, Raleigh argues, "is a specific and concrete manifestation of the general sense of time-history underlying the novel as a whole" (248). From this perspective, the changing valences of liberalism throughout history register in different ways of conceiving of the future in the novel's endings. Raleigh further argues that while Victorian society is still marked by a more direct relation to the heritage of liberalism that is bound up with the Victorian novel's trademark happy endings, liberalism takes on a more complicated function for "the moderns," who, beginning with Thomas Hardy and culminating in William Faulkner, are "the rationalists, the dependents on a liberalist future," for whom "there is only tragedy, or misery, waiting in the future" (249).

Insofar as liberalism is bound up with a particular form of thinking time that then expresses itself in the novel in general and in the novel's endings and their relation to the future in particular, one might wonder how the neoliberal novel's endings express the temporal logic of this stage of liberalism, which experiences the collapse of its trademark notion of time, progress, and futurity at the moment at which it pushes this logic of time to its full implementation and thus to its immanent boundaries. Once neoliberalism's omnipresent contemporaneity and absorption of the future into the present not only become the structural logic of capitalism but also are woven into the sociocultural fabric, how do novels' endings engage with the problem of the end of time? As we have seen, the end of time is a less severe problem for postmodernism. After all, postmodernism itself commits itself to an anti-teleological and anti-temporal project that resolves modernism's struggle with the future as both progress and tragedy by way of the contraction of teleological futures into a perpetual present. Of course, as Daniel Grausam shows, there are a range of important ways of understanding postmodernism's relationship to a nonexisting future and the threat of endings that highlight a direct commitment to history and historicization, including postmodernism's engagement with the geopolitical consequences of the nuclear arms race.[15] However, it is also important to foreground the ways in which postmodern thought, in spite of its famous opposition to the tradition of humanism and liberalism, remains logically wedded to liberalism's trademark temporal imagination.

Postmodernism's perpetual present is anticipatory inasmuch as it is formulated in relation to the refusal of a damaging and damaged past, as well as the refusal of the predetermined futures of modernity's emancipatory narratives. The disavowal of teleological futures therefore is not a matter of the utter absence of futurity, which would fail to account for both the frenzied forms of futurism that determined the 1960s and 1970s and the anticipatory openness of the postmodern novel's endings. This is the temporal logic of the ending of Kurt Vonnegut's *Slaughterhouse Five* (1969), which oscillated between the departure from the past ("Poo-tee-weet?," whose interrogative mood itself is a gesture toward openings)[16] and the desire for a new form of thinking temporality, of a future without old futures and linearities, which Billy Pilgrim finds in the Trafalmadorians's idea of time—and, of course, the place of the ending of the novel itself, as both an ending and a middle, complicates the association of the refusal of modernity's futurity with the absolute end of time. Similarly, while Kilgore Trout cries out "*Make me young!*" to the narrator of *Breakfast of Champions* (1973) (notably in the narrator's father's voice), this refusal of the renewal of modernity's paternalism and its time is balanced against the novel's final word (or, rather, two words): "ETC."[17] And just as the moment of suspended waiting for the calling of lot 49 is bound up with both anticipation and the departure from modernity's time of Oedipalism in Thomas Pynchon's *The Crying of Lot 49* (1966), Donald Barthelme's *The Dead Father* (1975) ends with the Dead Father's desperate plea for more time, for just one more moment, which the group of young people who have accompanied him to his grave deny him in order to make way for their own post-Oedipal future. Barthelme's novel ends with one word: "Bulldozers."[18] But just because one may have chosen to depart from the temporal logic of modernism's architecture and spatial configurations does not mean, of course, that the act of bulldozing cannot also be understood as another way of clearing the present to make room for possibility.

In novels such as Bret Easton Ellis's *American Psycho* (1991), which mediate the emergence of a historical situation that we can begin to associate with full neoliberalism in the late 1980s and early 1990s (as opposed to neoliberalism as an incipient structural logic in the 1970s that takes on a particular function in relation to the crisis of the previous stage of capitalism), the relation to the present changes decidedly. Instead of postmodernism's celebration of a present that is defined by the anticipation of the large-scale move beyond modernity's old limiting futures, the logic of the present in *American Psycho* is one of confinement and of the exhaustion of difference into ultimate sameness. In a neoliberal world in which all aspects of life are routed through the logic of the market, finance, and consumerism, the novel's protagonist, Patrick Bateman, struggles with the inability to register as an individual precisely at the moment at which neoliberalism dissolves all former forms of social relationships and community into the universal commitment to individualism and identity. Trapped between his desire to "fit in," which he reiterates throughout the novel, and his quest to set himself apart as an individual, Bateman ultimately cannot accomplish either and is constantly mistaken for someone else in a society in which now "*everybody's* rich, . . . *everybody's* good looking, . . . *everybody* has a good body."[19] Consequently, throughout the novel Bateman is always mistaken for someone else. The terrifying murders committed by Bateman can be understood as desperate attempts at wresting individual recognition from a society that is defined by the functional standardization of difference, culminating in the horror of ultimate sameness. But Bateman is never able to escape the condition that is anticipated by the novel's second epigraph borrowed from the Talking Heads: "And as things fell apart / Nobody paid much attention." The true horror of the novel therefore lies not in Patrick's actual murders, but in his inability to get the people around him to care about the murders.

However, it is precisely in the attempt to understand the end of difference in relation to the new neoliberal dominant that emerges in the late 1980s, which Ellis's 1991 novel is able to retrospectively historicize, that we can locate both an index of the novel's move beyond postmodernism and the recent novel's aim to interrogate neoliberalism's logical limits. The novel's constant play with the tension between fiction and reality—does Bateman actually commit the murders, or does he only imagine them?—mediates the transition from fiction to reality of a range of neoliberalism's enabling narratives. Bateman is confined to a situation in which a range of wishes, such as the liberal narrative of individualism and postmodernism's politics of difference, which assign such great value to the subject, are structurally fulfilled. However, since neoliberalism fulfills these wishes on capitalism's terms and assigns them a central function in the new dominant, these wishes, Bateman finds, have been robbed of their satisfying content. Reeling from his inability to register as an individual because he can only signal his identity via the same channels that all those around him use—the reservation lists of restaurants and clubs, business cards, expensively modified bodies, clothing, and so on—Bateman seeks to turn the new reality, which robbed the dream of individuality of its gratifying core through its complete structural implementation, back into fiction. The climax of this occurs in a memorable scene toward the end of the novel in which Bateman finds himself in a police chase. However, at the beginning of the scene, first-person narration gives way to a third-person point of view that is additionally accompanied by the overuse of his first name, Patrick. Bateman imagines himself in the car chase as seen and narrated through the lens of a camera eye, as the protagonist of an action movie whose actions and dialogue in the chase scene are the sole motor of plot and the sole, exaggerated focus of the audience's attention. Yet, as it becomes clear, such turns back to fiction constitute nothing more than forms of escapism from the reality of the present, and the novel's final words seemingly solidify the foreclosure of all future possibility: "THIS IS NOT AN EXIT."[20]

From such a perspective, it is possible to read *American Psycho* not merely as the confirmation of the suspicion that neoliberalism marks an ultimate limit and horizon of time and thought but also as a novel that places itself in relation to a history of novels that address precisely such moments of perceived stasis and timelessness. Additionally, we can read Ellis's novel as an argument for the importance of locating the critical engagement with the neoliberal present in the realm of reality and realism, since it is precisely Bateman's escape into a variety of established forms of fiction that leaves him unable to come to terms with the experience of the limits of his time. In fact, it is possible to argue that novels such as *American Psycho* do for us in the time of neoliberalism what Marcel Proust did for the temporal crises that plagued the modernist imagination, suggesting at the same time that the notion of the end of time is, of course, not new and ought to be historicized in itself. Erich Auerbach's famous reading of Proust's *Remembrance of Things Past / In Search of Lost Time* may help illustrate this point. "Even the souls of the damned know that there is a life other than theirs," writes

Auerbach. But in Proust, he continues, "there is nothing of this sort": "Permanently and hermetically sealed off in a rotten social structure (that is nevertheless the prevailing one) and in the domain of hypersensitive powers of observation that are so logical as to drive one both mad and into atrociously digressive trivialities, the gargantuan novel paces back and forth, as if in a cage, between a very small number of motifs and events."[21] Life and the experience of time in Proust's novel, Auerbach argues, are trivialized to the degree that its time becomes a matter of confinement and is utterly severed from history itself and, ultimately, rendered timeless, a situation that, even more than the above sketch of Proust's novel, describes Bateman's experience of his own world. But it is precisely through the novel's own foreclosures, limits, and confinement, Auerbach argues, that Proust is able to make legible the logical foundations of the temporal problem and its connection to thought and social form that the novel examines. Here, Proust succeeds in fully committing himself to the limit itself, making it visible as precisely that, a limit, based on which he is able to make it visible not as a categorical limit but rather as a historically specific end. It is in this way, Auerbach argues, that "Proust's narrator can achieve what the entire generation of his author could not."[22] And it is in this way, therefore, that we can understand the ways in which *American Psycho* importantly addresses itself to neoliberalism. In other words, it is precisely through Bateman's tragic failures that Ellis's novel uncovers the logic of that which imposes on the contemporary the semblance of impossibility and at the same time historicizes the end of time and the neoliberal contemporary. The history of the realist novel and in particular modernist realism offers us an important vocabulary and archive of temporality through which it is possible to read the horizons of the neoliberal contemporary. It is possible to understand the conversations with modernism in the contemporary novel as an expression of precisely such a historical project that aims to engage with the time and fictions of neoliberalism.

In this way, *American Psycho* can be read as an important event in American literary history, marking the departure from postmodernism through the engagement with neoliberalism, as well as exemplifying one of the key characteristics of the novel after postmodernism: the novel's commitment to the project of developing forms of reading the seemingly empty time of neoliberalism's omnipresence as history, with its own built-in, historically specific limits and aporias. A focus on this aspect of the recent American novel outlines the contours of a rich archive of novels that follow in Ellis's path, including works such as Jonathan Lethem's *Amnesia Moon*, in which the tension between speculative fiction and realism mediates the structural congruency between postmodernism and neoliberalism. Similarly, Percival Everett's *Glyph* asks how we may write novels about the standardization of post-structuralism and postmodernism, about which it seems to be impossible to speak. Jess Walters's *The Financial Lives of Poets* and Jennifer Egan's *The Keep* explore how fictions and reality, old and new, crash into each other and transform the way in which these concepts relate to our present and how we are able to think and narrate them. And in addition to recent work from Don DeLillo, Richard Powers, and William Gibson, along with that of a new generation of authors including Lauren Groff, Colson Whitehead, and Ben Marcus, novels such as Ben Lerner's *10:04* deliver striking examinations of the forms of time that define our present. Lerner's novel in particular presents a powerful commitment to the utopian project of inhabiting collectively the multiple temporalities of our present that neoliberal singularity flattens out into a timeless contemporary—and to do this, Lerner is well aware, he must write his novel "at the limit of fiction," as it is precisely this limit that makes visible the limits of neoliberalism's constitutive fictions. In engaging with the seeming end of time and fiction in the omnipresent realism of neoliberalism, the novel after postmodernism provides us, therefore, not only with new ways of thinking time but also with new ways of thinking the time, future, and possibilities of the novel, which is expressed deeply movingly in the letter that concludes Peter Dimock's *George Anderson: Notes for a Love Song in Imperial Time* (2012): "I have found no counternarrative that is not complicit in the history we are living of absolute possession and perfect loss. Still, in your singing there is time itself and the grace of unformed reciprocity. No event has been completed. History creates an unformed future out of love's immediacy: I'm valuable because she came back. Make reading this into love's requited listening."[23]

NOTES

1. Jeremy Gilbert, "What Kind of Thing Is Neoliberalism?," *new formations* 80–81 (2013): 7.

2. Gérard Duménil and Dominique Lévy, *The Crisis of Neoliberalism* (Cambridge, MA: Harvard University Press, 2013).

3. Pierre Bourdieu, "The Essence of Neoliberalism," *Le Monde Diplomatique*, December 1998, http://mondediplo.com/1998/12/08bourdieu.

4. Jeffrey T. Nealon, *Post-postmodernism; or, The Cultural Logic of Just-in-Time Capitalism* (Stanford, CA: Stanford University Press, 2012), 23.

5. Mark C. Taylor, *Speed Limits: Where Time Went and Why We Have So Little Left* (New Haven, CT: Yale University Press, 2014), 236.

6. Nealon, *Post-postmodernism*, 23.

7. Hans Ulrich Gumbrecht, "Shall We Continue to Write Histories of Literature?," *New Literary History* 39, no. (2008): 522.

8. Ibid.

9. Ibid.

10. See Lauren Berlant, *Cruel Optimism* (Durham, NC: Duke University Press, 2011); and Mark Fisher, *Capitalism Realism: Is There No Alternative?* (Hants, UK: Zero Books, 2009).

11. Raymond Federman, *Critifiction: Postmodern Essays* (Albany, NY: SUNY Press, 1993), 105. Hereafter cited in the text. The death of Samuel Beckett on December 22, 1989, marks for Federman the death of postmodernism, and Beckett's *Stirrings Still* marks the "last gasp of postmodern fiction" (105), an argument that also directly finds its way into Federman's 2001 novel *Aunt Rachel's Fur*.

12. Amy Hungerford, "On the Period Formerly Known as Contemporary," *American Literary History* 20 (2008): 418.

13. Ibid.

14. John Henry Raleigh, "The English Novel and the Three Kinds of Time," in *The Novel: Modern Essays in Criticism*, ed. Robert Murray Davis (Englewood Cliffs, NJ: Prentice Hall, 1969), 248. Hereafter cited in the text.

15. See Daniel Grausam, *On Endings: American Postmodern Fiction and the Cold War* (Charlottesville: University of Virginia Press, 2011).

16. Kurt Vonnegut, *Slaughterhouse Five* (New York: Dell, 1991), 221.

17. Kurt Vonnegut, *Breakfast of Champions* (New York: Dial, 2011), 302.

18. Donald Barthelme, *The Dead Father* (New York: Farrar, Straus & Giroux, 2004), 177.

19. Bret Easton Ellis, *American Psycho* (New York: Vintage, 1991), 23; italics in the original.

20. Ibid., 399.

21. Erich Auerbach, "Marcel Proust and the Novel of Lost Time (1927)," in *Time, History, and Literature: Selected Essays of Erich Auerbach*, ed. James I. Porter, trans. Jane O. Newman (Princeton, NC: Princeton University Press, 2014), 158.

22. Ibid., 161.

23. Peter Dimock, *George Anderson: Notes for a Love Song in Imperial Time* (London: Dalkey Archive, 2012), 157.

Totaling the Damage

Neoliberalism and Revolutionary Ambition in Recent American Poetry

JENNIFER ASHTON

"All around us the bodies rose out of the stone, crowded into groups, intertwined, or shattered into fragments, hinting at their shapes with a torso, a propped up arm, a burst hip, a scabbed shard, always in warlike gestures, dodging, rebounding, attacking, shielding themselves, stretched high or crooked, some of them snuffed out, but with a freestanding, forward-pressing foot, a twisted back, the contour of a calf harnessed into a single common motion. A gigantic wrestling, emerging from the gray wall, recalling a perfection, sinking back into formlessness."[1] Some readers will recognize this passage as the opening of the first volume of Peter Weiss's novel trilogy *The Aesthetics of Resistance*, published in German in 1975. We'll return to it below. Now here is a different description of the same bodies rising out of stone, this passage focused on a single group of figures; in this case, they are also explicitly named, starting with "the giant Alkyoneus whose head . . . is seen to be wrenched back by the hand of the Olympian paragon, Athene, who is about to destroy him. Alkyoneus's right hand grasps the fatal right hand of Athene. His left arm is stretched out in hopeless appeal to his gigantic but only partially realized (eidetically incomplete) Mother Earth. Nike has appeared to crown the Olympian."[2] These stone figures, belonging to the war between the Olympian gods and the Titans and giants, form the great frieze of the Pergamon Altar, housed at the Pergamon Museum in Berlin. The second description, published roughly three decades after Weiss's novel, in 2002, is from the poet Allen Grossman's essay "The Passion of Laocoön: Warfare of the Religious against the Poetic Institution," in which Grossman argues that the face of the giant Alkyoneus is a model for that of the central figure in the famous (and two centuries later) statue of the Trojan priest Laocoön, punished for prophesying the fall of Troy. In the sculpture, we find him in agony as he is destroyed, along with his younger son, by a giant serpent, while the elder son looks on. At the same time, Grossman argues, the faces of both Alkyoneus and Laocoön represent a type that we see in multiple depictions, spanning many centuries, of the face of the poet Homer. For Grossman, the giant in the frieze is an archetype, moreover, not just of Homer but of the poet in general. What this means for poetry is that the face—more precisely, the practice of recognizing the face and giving it form— is at the center of the work the poet is called upon to do: "The practice of poetry makes faces manifest and is constituted of the faces it manifests."[3] What, then, is it that makes the giant Alkyoneus, the priest Laocoön, and the poet Homer alike in what their faces manifest?

One answer, Grossman argues (and we see this particularly in the case of Laocoön), is pain (hence the "passion" of the essay's title). The pain on both figures' faces, moreover, refers us to something else, something that we know about Laocoön even though we don't see it in the statue itself, and something that we do see—that we see depicted—in the Pergamon Altar, not only in the Alkyoneus panel, but in every panel of the frieze: the overturning of one "institution" (as Grossman terms it) by another. In both cases, whether it's the giants who stand for unassimilable chaos under the Olympian order and must therefore be killed or forced underground, or else the Trojans who are predestined by the Gods' internecine rivalry to be defeated by the Greeks, "the Laocoön narrative," by which Grossman means the *type* that the Laocoön represents, "specifies the crisis that gives rise to new representation. Pain locates that moment: the moment of the superseding of one institution that grounds representation by another."[4]

The un-grounding of representation in the violent overturning of one institutional order by another—in other words, the un-grounding of representation through what surely qualifies, at least in Grossman's account, as a form of domination—also leads him to argue that the beings who suffer defeat become the archetype of another crisis, conceived in different terms, in terms, that is, of "scarcity": what Grossman calls the "exclusionary difference that effects recognition" also "produces the archetype of economic scarcity. . . scarcity of what constitutes the human interest, the image."[5] What does it mean for our contemporary *poetic* practice, and for what we might take to be its politics, to see "eidetic" scarcity as "the archetype of economic scarcity"? Is conflict over the latter—what we might also call class conflict—at bottom a conflict over representation? Could something like eidetic justice bring about economic justice?

The struggles through which some (the giants in the Theogony, for instance) are excluded from civilization, and thereby from representation, extend, according to Grossman, from moments in which differences in kind (gods versus giants, divine versus human) are, as he puts it, "unfixed." These are imagined, as we've already begun to see, as struggles over a resource that is precisely eidetic—that of image making. And the struggle over image making very quickly becomes synonymous for Grossman with a struggle over identity as such. It is, he argues, the source of our terminologies of difference—not just of differences like the human versus the divine, but one kind of human versus another kind: "After the first unrepresented moment (the beginning of the world), which unfixed the difference of divinity, there follows the cosmic (i.e., general) conflict—Olympian against chthonian—which, in order to restore that difference or its effect, supplies the (unstable) terms—race, class, and gender—by which the recognizability of the face (its value, acknowledged, its intelligibility determined) is narrated."[6] Part of the point that Grossman means to make about the poetic imperative to acknowledge—to manifest, to name, to recognize, and above all to value and give form—is that it's not confined to the representation of giants or Trojans, but extends across the entire history of poetry as a "civilizational" undertaking.[7] It must extend, in other words, to all subjects, both beloved and abject, and so it must extend to poets in all times. Indeed, at the time in which Grossman was writing "The Passion of Laocoön," the "unstable" terms of identity ("race, class, gender" in his terms) that he understands to be supplied by an ongoing crisis of recognition were—and they obviously continue to be—at the center of our contemporary institutional struggles, including those within the much narrower precincts of contemporary American poetry. Here I want to try to trace out what it might mean to think one step further and ask what exactly the economic meaning of scarcity would be in the context of our contemporary institutional concerns. To put my earlier question somewhat differently, if we could imagine something like a just redistribution of the image, what would be economically different? Can utopian ends be achieved by what Grossman thinks of as eidetic means?

If we return now to *The Aesthetics of Resistance*, we can begin to see where the limits of this form of poetic justice might reside, and precisely in terms of economic scarcity. When Weiss's novel opens with the same figures in the Pergamon frieze that Grossman connects to Laocoön and Homer, its depiction of the Olympians destroying the giants also provokes a recognition. The first-person narrator stands in the museum with his two comrades—the three are young communists from the working class living in Berlin—and the scene takes place "on September twenty-second, nineteen thirty-seven," as he is "about to leave for Spain," where fascism is about to win out, as it already has in Germany since the Nazi takeover in 1933.[8] What the narrator sees, just as what Grossman sees (and for that matter, what Alkyoneus sees, what Laocoön sees, and what Homer sees), is one group of beings overpowering another group. And in seeing the figures in this way, the narrator also sees the beings overthrown as fundamentally different—that is, different in kind—from the beings who overthrow them. This recognition occurs, moreover, precisely at a moment when the narrator looks closely at a face—not the face of one of the stone figures, but the face of his friend and comrade: "Heilmann's bright face, with its regular features, bushy eyebrows, and high forehead, had turned to the demoness of the earth. . . . She had given birth to the Giants, the Titans, the Cyclopes, and the Furies. This was our race."[9] To look at the features of Heilmann's face in this physiognomic way, where, I should add, we also cannot help but see the phrenological mind-set that helped to shape Nazi racial taxonomy, is, in other words, to see Heilmann's "race" in his face. At this moment the kinship between the young revolutionaries in the novel and the brutalized giants in the frieze appears to be a form of racial solidarity. But as the three comrades continue to discuss the work before them, we quickly find that what is meant in saying "This was our race" entails for them a very different kinship, a brotherhood of another kind.

The conversation unfolds around what this stone frieze, in whose "silence," the narrator tells us, "the paralysis of those fated to be trampled to the ground continued to be palpable," might mean to those viewing it in the novel's present (that is, in Berlin in 1937): "And has this mass of stone," one of the friends asks, "which served the cult of princely and religious masters of ceremony, who glorified the victory of the aristocrats over an earthbound mix of nations—has this mass of stone now become a value in its own right, belonging to anyone who steps in front of it."[10] The logic whereby the stone of the Pergamon Altar can be said to "belong" to anyone becomes clearer as Heilmann begins to elaborate on the social order of the ancient city of Pergamum itself and to imagine the altar viewed not only by the ruling class for whom it was made, but by the workers who did the making:

> They, the real bearers of the Ionian state, unable to read or write, excluded from artistic activity, were only good enough to create wealth for a small privileged stratum and the necessary leisure for the elite of the mind. The existence of the celestials was unattainable for them, but they could recognize themselves in the kneeling imbruted creatures. The latter, in crudeness, degradation, and maltreatment, bore their features. The portrayal of the gods in flight and of the annihilation of urgent danger expressed not the struggle of good against evil, but the struggle between the classes, and this was recognized not only in our present-day viewing but perhaps also back then in secret glimpses by serfs.[11]

Whether we imagine the viewer of the "imbruted creatures" in the frieze to be a serf in Pergamum or a worker in Nazi Germany, the idea that one might see in them one's *Geschlect* ("*Dies war unser Geschlecht*") means recognizing them not so much as members of one's race or even of one's family (or house, or lineage, to call upon some of the related connotations of the term), but as members of one's class.[12] Or perhaps a better way to put it would be to say that the young communists in the novel see themselves as belonging to the same *Geschlecht* as the ancient serfs *only* because they see themselves as members of the same class. It's important that the reference to the stone figures' "features," the same word as appears in the earlier description of Heilmann's face, is also repeated in both passages in the German text (*Züge*). It's also important that here the "features" that the young men recognize themselves to share are not eyebrows and bone structure, but "degradation" and "maltreatment." The ties that bind the ancient generation of serfs to the present generation of workers are those of exploitation. For the narrator's friend, Heilmann, it's this recognition—that the extraction of value from the labor of serfs in the second century is in some fundamental way the same as the extraction of value from the worker in 1937—that the work of art itself makes legible. But if, for the young communists, this recognition is a precondition of their politics, and the task the novel puts to them is to discover its aesthetics, what then does an aesthetics of resistance look like in our own time?

We can begin to answer that question by noting the high and still growing level of interest in the very question of finding political value in art in American poetic discourse, especially in the wake of the financial crisis of 2008 and the increasing attention we've seen paid to one of the most vivid effects of the neoliberal policies of the preceding three decades, namely, the rapid rise of economic inequality, which, as anyone reading this is no doubt aware, continues to be at its highest since the Gilded Age. The conjunction of poetry with crisis in the title of Christopher Nealon's 2011 book, *The Matter of Capital: Poetry and Crisis in the American Century*, indexes what I take to be a general state of affairs in contemporary American poetry in the neoliberal era, particularly for poets in the generation born roughly between 1960 and 1980 who think of themselves as both aesthetically ambitious and ambitiously anticapitalist.[13] For them this state of affairs has presented a problem that we can put in the form of a question: What should the revolutionary poet be doing, when crisis—whether it be economic, social, environmental, or, for that matter, aesthetic—appears increasingly frequent, inevitable, and irreversible? Or to ask the question in a slightly different form: What poetic *forms* do these conditions of crisis seem to require?

As it turns out, when looking at the work produced by poets with such ambitions in our current century, it's almost easier to describe what forms they think their poems cannot take. Ruling out the previous generation's hallmark techniques is, of course, one way to do this. The body of work that has served as the point of departure and resistance for so much of the politically ambitious poetry of our current moment has been what many to consider to be among the most politically ambitious avant-gardes in American poetry in the latter part of the twentieth century, namely, that which acquired the moniker of "Language" writing starting in the mid- to late 1970s and achieved a certain prominence from the mid-1980s through most of the 1990s. The movement's avant-garde credentials (along with the very idea of the avant-garde) were called into question in the late 1990s, however, as central figures like Lyn Hejinian and Charles Bernstein began to acquire the same stamps of legitimation—major national and international literary prizes, named professorships at elite universities, large press and wide-circulation magazine publication—as the poets of "official verse culture" from whom they had spent their careers differentiating themselves. The now defunct academic journal *Lingua Franca* helped to ring the death knell when it ran a cover story with the title "Verse vs. Verse: The Language Poets are Taking over the Academy, but Will Success Destroy Their Integrity" and pointed, among other evidence, to Charles Bernstein's appearance in a Yellow Pages ad that ran during the 1999 Super Bowl.[14] Even the Language poets themselves called attention to the perceived obsolescence. As one of the voices in the title poem of Bob Perelman's 2006 volume *IFLIFE* proclaims, "The gestures that Language poetry triumphantly said were still radical are super codified now."[15]

But after the fall of Language Poetry came the fall of the World Trade Center and then of Lehman Brothers, and the problems with the poetry of the previous generation started to look like a matter of political and economic as well as aesthetic collapse. If Language Poetry could appear to some as if it had simply run its course—as the poet Kenneth Goldsmith asks in an interview, explicitly in reference to Language writing, "Should we continue to pound language into ever smaller bits, or should we take some other approach?"—it had also begun to appear more reactionary than radical.[16] Indeed, for critics like Brian Reed, new techniques like Goldsmith's particular brand of conceptualism appeared necessary precisely because the old techniques looked indistinguishable from the opposition, both as a style and as a politics. The disjunctive syntax and semantic ruptures that had typified the experiments of the Language writers in the 1970s and 1980s could now be found in the pages of *Poetry* as well as, Reed argues, the speeches of then president Bush: "After 9/11 many assumptions and practices that defined the late twentieth-century American, British, and Canadian poetic avant-gardes . . . began to appear outmoded, even defanged. With grammar-mangling, fragment-spouting George W. Bush on television every night arguing for war, how could a leftist poet in good conscience continue to advocate anacoluthon, solecism, and other varieties of non-normative English usage as tools to achieve utopian ends?"[17] Of course, outmoded is one thing; defanged is another. If your dress is so five minutes ago, you can look for a new design. Maybe it shouldn't be surprising that, following the proliferation of free-market ideology that so notoriously characterized the decades following the advent of the Language movement and has only intensified in the years since their demise, one of the striking features of the first decade and a half of poetic production in our millennium has been its emphasis on innovation. On the one hand, we've seen a rapid succession of movements, collectives, and manifestos (conceptualism, Flarf, Mainstream poetry, the Black Took Collective, Gnoetry, Gurlesque, necropastoral), and on the other, the renewal and rebranding of older forms: the pantoum is the new villanelle, the cross-out is the new erasure, the concrete poem is the new collage. But if innovation as such is hardly a means to achieve left utopian ends—that is, if innovation is hardly the means to resist capitalism—where then, in the age of what Nicholas Brown has identified as the work of art's "real subsumption under capital," can a young poet find a sharp set of teeth?[18]

Timothy Donnelly, in his 2010 volume *The Cloud Corporation*, presents us with a vision of the poet as one who, in order to sing proper songs of resistance in a world of underwater mortgages, corporate personhood, and state-sponsored terrorism, seems to require the aid of a sharp object. While the volume is composed of ostensibly discrete lyrics, together they also form an epic narrative, in which the recurring first-person speaker appears in most of the poems in various states of inactivity, much like Achilles sulking in his tent. Only instead of refusing to enter battle, he finds his throat constricted, and instead of seething with anger, varying states of numbness are the only feelings available to him: "I have been held down / by the throat and terrified / numb enough to know. / The temperature at which no bird can thrive—."[19] The story told across the epic arc of the volume is the story of Walt Whitman's "Out of the Cradle, Endlessly Rocking," the paradigmatic tale of the lyric poet discovering his vocation. Following the many variant states of inactivity and anesthesia, including, at the end of one poem, "discovering me asleep on my own weapon, a threat to no one but myself," it is only in the very last lines of the last poem of the volume that the speaker not only awakens to his calling but appears capable of fulfilling it.[20] He imagines three different doors opening onto three different "opportunity rooms":

. . . it's the third I like best, the one

behind which opens a meadow, vast, and in it, grazing
    on buttercups, an errant heifer with a wounded foot,

its bloody hoofprints followed by a curious shepherd back
    to something sharp in the grass, the point of a long

sword which, unearthed, the shepherd now polishes with
    his rodent-skin tunic . . .

. . . a gift for me, a task, an instrument to lay
    waste to the empire now placed before me at my feet.[21]

It matters, here, that the "task" of the vocation comes by way of a shepherd, for in one of the foundational texts of the Western poetic tradition—the one to which I've already alluded through the images depicted in the Pergamon Altar and to which Donnelly's volume insistently pays homage, the tradition that gives us both epic and lyric—it's famously a shepherd, Hesiod, who finds himself one day in receipt of a staff handed to him by the muses and commanded thereby to sing. Here, in Donnelly's version, we have Hesiod transformed into Attila the Hun, delivered a sword, not a staff. Of course, the song Hesiod sings is the Theogony, in which the Olympian gods seize power over the cosmos by overthrowing the chthonians. In this latter-day cosmic allegory, it's the "Cloud Corporation"— capitalism itself—that stands in for the Olympian gods, and the poet, as Attila, awake and no longer a pathetic threat to himself, stands poised with his "instrument" to "lay waste to the[ir] empire." But what's also striking about this moment is that despite the fact that our man has been given arms and a mandate to sing, this epic lyric leaves us on a threshold, with only a prospect and, seemingly, no final achievement. We end in suspension, awaiting both the battle and the song that will sing of it.

In this respect Donnelly's poem shares in what Christopher Nealon identifies in his 2004 essay "Camp Messianism, or, the Hopes of Poetry in Late, Late Capitalism" as a tendency among poets writing in response to "the 'damaged' material life" of "late capitalism."[22] It's a tendency that Nealon calls a "posture."[23] And while I would not include Donnelly in what Nealon terms more precisely the "camp posture" that he locates, for example, in the work of Lisa Robertson, Kevin Davies, and Rod Smith—which is to say, I wouldn't describe Donnelly's work as "camp"—I think Nealon describes quite accurately what Donnelly does share of this posture, and inadvertently points to the fundamental problem with it. For as

Nealon puts it, these poets "expend their considerable talents on making articulate the ways which, as they look around, they see *waiting*."[24] Indeed, in all of these instances, the waiting counts as a poetic success because what matters is not what we are waiting for but the attitude we adopt in our waiting. Camp is an especially popular one, but melancholy and sadness have their attractions, and so does anger. Indeed, Donnelly's Attila completes the poem not when he takes up the sword (he's had it in his possession all along), but when, as the poem insists, through repeated iterations of the phrase "I feel," the speaker becomes capable of an attitude, in this case anger, for which expression the sword potentially has some use. But it's the attitude itself and, as the speaker says, the "gift for me" of the means to express it that matters in the end. Political resistance, under this dispensation, requires no action, only attitude. Poetry is a way to have an attitude, and the "task" of the poet is to express it.

Whether this is a good thing for either poetry or politics can for the moment remain an open question, although by the end of this essay I hope it will be clear that it's not, and why it's not. One way to pose the problem is to return it to Allen Grossman's terms and ask whether the kind of expression imagined in Donnelly counts as (in Grossman's terms) a kind of eidetic justice and to ask further what relation eidetic justice might have to redistributive justice—how, in other words, it might address the problem of scarcity. But it's important to see that whether good or bad, the way Donnelly and Nealon—and I would add poets like Juliana Spahr, Joshua Clover, and Dana Ward—understand what counts as an aesthetics of resistance is not the only way we have to understand it.[25] But to begin to see the alternative, I want to look at the work of a poet with four volumes to his credit, but whose most immediate relevance to this discussion may seem at first invisible, because the work I want to discuss is the most recent of his two novels.

Everywhere in Ben Lerner's *10:04: A Novel* we find what we could easily call, borrowing from Nealon's deployment (borrowing from Theodor Adorno) of the phrase, "damaged material life." The novel is set in New York, beginning in August of 2011, just before the Occupy protests would gain momentum, at the time when emergency preparations were underway in anticipation of another landfall for Hurricane Irene.[26] In its opening pages, the narrator is about to attend an auction of his as-yet-unwritten novel in hopes of a six-figure advance (which he will get), and by the end the reader has realized that the novel she has just finished (*10:04*) is the novel for which he received the advance. The plot of *10:04* is thus predicated on the fate of *10:04* itself, which, throughout its pages—that is, even as we are reading it—looms as a potential crisis. And the potential crisis is both aesthetic (will the novel be bad?) and financial (will the press reject it, leaving the author to be sued for the advance which he will have spent?). Furthermore, throughout the story, even as we confront the looming economic and ecological crises represented by two hurricanes (first Irene and later Sandy), the narrator himself is suffering from a vascular condition in which his aorta could explode at any moment and kill him instantaneously. In another story within the story, the narrator of the novel the narrator is writing faces a different but equally looming bodily threat, a sinus growth that could become malignant and destroy his brain function. Along the way, lesser and greater crises of scarcity arise—in the novel's present time one of the characters is unemployed and her health insurance is running out just as she faces an expensive and medically necessary wisdom tooth extraction; and as the narrator points out, the conditions that threaten to submerge Manhattan when the hurricane makes landfall are the same climate changes that with respect to the future mean that "almost half of humanity will face water scarcity by 2030."[27] More generally, the novel tends to understand every crisis happening to the narrator as part of something larger, or, as he himself puts it, "to figure the global apocalyptically."[28]

For our purposes, what matters is that the apocalyptic itself is being figured globally, that the crises and damages the characters envision and worry over are catastrophic to the point of being—as Lerner repeatedly insists—"total." And it's with respect to the idea of "total damage" (which is something quite different from, indeed almost exactly the opposite of, "material damage")—that *10:04: A Novel* is able to conjoin crisis with literature (and more specifically, as we'll see, with poetry) and to articulate an aesthetics of resistance very different from, and from my standpoint more convincing than, the postures adopted by Donnelly, Nealon, and many others in our current field of poetic production.

"Totaled" is, in fact, the term the novel uses, and it occurs most strikingly in an episode that takes place with the narrator's artist friend / sometimes girlfriend. The friends are in the process of creating what they will call "The Institute for Totaled Art":

> Along with an artist friend of hers, Peter, who also had a law degree, Alena had been working on a project—not an art project, she kept insisting—that she'd often described to me, but which I'd always largely dismissed as fantasy: she and Peter were in the process of trying to convince the largest insurer of art in the country to give them some of its "totaled" art. When a valuable painting is damaged in transit or a fire or flood, vandalized, etc., and an appraiser agrees with the owner of a work that the work cannot be satisfactorily restored, or that the cost of restoration would exceed the value of the claim, then the insurance company pays out the total value of

the damaged work, which is then legally declared to have "zero value." When Alena asked me what I thought happened to the totaled art, I told her I assumed that the damaged work was destroyed, but, as it turned out, the insurer had a giant warehouse on Long Island full of these indeterminate objects: works by artists, many of them famous, that, after suffering one kind of damage or another, were formally demoted from art to mere objecthood and banned from circulation, removed from the market, relegated to this strange limbo.[29]

What the novel gives us if we read closely here—and if we miss it, by the time we reach the final sentence of *10:04* we've been carefully instructed to see it—is a lesson in the difference between art and objecthood by way of what it means for something to be "totaled," on the one hand, and for it to be "total" on the other: in short, a lesson in totality. Lerner has obviously read his Michael Fried, and he seems to have gotten the point.[30] The first evidence we see comes from the very first object the narrator encounters in his visit to the soon-to-be Institute for Totaled Art: "Put out your hands, she said, and I did. She dropped what felt like a series of porcelain balls or figurines into them. Now open them, she said: what I was holding were the pieces of a shattered Jeff Koons balloon dog sculpture, an early red one. It was wonderful to see an icon of art world commercialism and valorized stupidity shattered."[31] It isn't just that Lerner is so disparaging about Jeff Koons that suggests he might have some grasp of the Friedian argument to which his narrator alludes. What is also important here is that the narrator recognizes the work—I don't mean by this that he sees it as a Koons (it's not a matter of brand recognition), but that he recognizes the porcelain balls in his hand as *parts of a work*. In other words, by understanding that the balls are parts, he understands the work as something whole.[32] Without the concept of the work as a whole, without the concept of the *total* work, in other words, there can be no "totaled work." This is a claim about the ontology of the work of art, about the conditions under which something counts as a work of art. Here what makes something a work of art, what makes it not merely an object, is that *any* damage to it renders it "totaled."

But the particular formulation Lerner uses in giving us the Friedian version of this claim also points, by way of a qualification, to another crucial distinction. For when the narrator says that works in this damaged condition are "formally demoted from art to mere objecthood," he informs us that the damage that demotes them is *formal*.[33] This is why Lerner makes certain that the Institute for Totaled Art also contains objects whose damage is barely or not perceptible at all: "But it was not the slashed or burnt or stained artworks that moved me the most, that

made me feel that Peter and Alena were doing something profound by unearth-
ing the living dead of art. To my surprise, many of the objects were not, at least
not to my admittedly inexpert eye, damaged at all. Here was an unframed Cartier-
Bresson print. I held it up to the pale light streaming in through the studio win-
dow but perceived no tears, scratches, fading, stains. I asked Peter and Alena to
show me the damage, but they were equally baffled."[34] The implication here is
that the damage by which the Cartier-Bresson print counts as "totaled" needs to be
understood as present in the work, even if the narrator and his friends never discover it. In other words, to total the work is to damage it in a way that violates the
principles of its integrity. The novel insists that these principles exist (this is the
point of the Cartier-Bresson) even if the narrator and his friends fail to grasp
them. And it insists also that this is the basis on which they might be able to look
together at the work and see in it the same thing. This is part of what it means
for the ontology of the work of art to be a matter of *form* (rather than, say, mere
shape).[35]

Why this ontology of the work of art might count as an aesthetics of resistance
becomes clearer when the narrator returns to look again at the print by Cartier-
Bresson: "It had transitioned from being a repository of immense financial value
to being declared of zero value without undergoing what was to me any perceptible material transformation—it was the same, only totally different. . . . I held a
work from which the exchange value had been extracted, an object that was otherwise unchanged. It was as if I could register in my hands a subtle but momentous transfer of weight: the twenty-one grams of the market's soul had fled; it was
no longer a commodity fetish; it was art before or after capital."[36] We might be
tempted to read this little encomium to the autonomy of the work of art as an
anachronism, a belated attempt to embrace modernism, as if in 2014, a world in
which everything belongs to capital, the work of art could somehow be undam-
aged. As if, in other words, the subsumption of the work under capital were somehow not complete. But the autonomy that the novel actually ends up imagining
for itself as a work of art and as a form of aesthetic resistance now is not quite the
same as what is being envisioned for the Cartier-Bresson. In the scene with the
dismembered Koons, the narrator describes Alena, enthusiastically hurling one
of the porcelain balls at the floor and watching it shatter, as a "chthonic deity of
vengeance," and then goes on to say, "Not for the first time, I wondered if she was
a genius."[37] The critical indication of her genius for the novel's purposes comes
near its conclusion, when, after Hurricane Sandy has wrecked Lower Manhattan,
the narrator observes that "scores of Chelsea galleries had been inundated and
soon the insurers would be welcoming the newly totaled art into their vast ware-

houses. Alena's work wasn't on a ground floor, I remembered; besides, she strategically damaged her paintings in advance; they were storm-proof."[38] The ingenious form of aesthetic resistance that the novel imagines for itself is based on Alena's ingenious form of risk management. *10:04* imagines, in short, that instead of the work of art being subsumed within the inevitable damages of capital, the damages of capital are subsumed within it. *10:04* presents itself as the achievement of this work.

The first paragraph of the novel begins with a description of a meeting between the narrator and his agent over "an outrageously expensive celebratory meal in Chelsea that included baby octopuses the chef had literally massaged to death."[39] What they are celebrating, of course, is the successful auction of his novel. The narrative then simultaneously loops back in time and into the future: "A few months before, the agent had e-mailed me that she believed I could get a 'strong six-figure' advance based on a story of mine that had appeared in *The New Yorker*; all I had to do was promise to turn it into a novel. I managed to draft an earnest if indefinite proposal and soon there was a competitive auction among the major New York houses and we were eating cephalopods in what would become the opening scene."[40] Later we learn that the *New Yorker* story, which is published with changes that the narrator has been forced to make in order to sell the story to the magazine, has also been incorporated in its entirety as one of the chapters of the novel, marked by a shift from first-person to third-person narrator, referred to only as "the author." In it one of the key situations attributed in the main frame story of the novel to the narrator's friend—her need for an expensive dental extraction—is transposed onto "the author." We might describe the various signs of alteration that emerge within and between the stories as evidence of a kind of damage, of outside forces affecting the work, and thereby as evidence not of its autonomy but its heteronomy. But this is exactly what the novel means for us to see and to think, and insofar as it's part of the meaning of the work, part of what the artist intends for it as a whole, it also becomes integral to the form of the work.

If the novel allows (even requires) its characters to become interchangeable (and doubles down on this fungibility by refusing to describe its characters' faces, suggesting that friends requested this as a guarantee of anonymity), it is explicit about the idea that artworks are not.[41] In the chapter in which "the author" undergoes the wisdom tooth extraction that the narrator's girlfriend is supposed to have in the frame narrative, he sits in a doctor's office (it's his dental X-rays that have revealed his perilous sinus growth) and fantasizes a conversation in which he trashes the pictures hanging on the wall: " 'Who chooses this art?' the author wanted to ask. . . . They are images of art, not art. . . . The problem, one of the problems . . . is that these images of art only address the sick, the patients. It would be absurd to imagine a doctor lingering over one of these images between appointments, being interested in it or somehow attached to it, having his day inflected by it or whatever. Apart from their depressing flatness, their interchangeability, what I'm saying is: we can't look at them together."[42] We are reminded here of the point of the invisible damage to the Cartier-Bresson—damage to the whole of the work turns the work into something else, an object rather than art, even if we can't see it. We see or fail to see the same thing. But Lerner goes further here to suggest that the force of the work's wholeness, the thing it loses if it's damaged, is also what renders it impossible to exchange for anything else.

"I am looking back at the totaled city in the second person plural," the narrator says at the end of the novel.[43] But while the speaker addresses that second person plural in the final sentence of the novel, the sentence itself is framed in the first person singular: "I know it's hard to understand / I am with you, and I know how it is."[44] In describing the perspective of the first-person narrator as happening "in the second person plural," Lerner renders this final statement an acknowledgement of the plural second person by the singular first person, at the same time that he renders both persons interchangeable—literally and grammatically. The statement can be understood to be in the second person plural even if the speaker is first person singular, because the difference between you and me (the difference recognition recognizes) no longer matters. The sentence that we're looking at, we're looking at together.

As the narrator looks at the "totaled city," we are looking at a work that has been totaled in advance. Its damage—the fact of it being totaled—is no longer understood as something that has happened *to* it but as something that is, in the form of the novel, subsumed *by* it. We can think about what we're looking at when we finish Lerner's "totaled" novel, when we understand ourselves to be looking at a damaged work of art, by thinking about the difference between what Grossman and Weiss see when they look at the damaged Pergamon Altar. At the same time, we can think about it in terms of the difference between the unwilled damage to the work (whether it's visible damage like that in the frieze or the hidden damage to the *New Yorker* version of the story or the Cartier-Bresson photograph) and the willing subsumption of damage within the completed, "total" novel that is *10:04*: the difference, in other words, between the literal shape of the work (including what we can't see) and its intended form. Lerner removes any possibility of understanding the damage to the work as damage to the reader's experience of it; unlike the pain of a bad tooth in need of extraction, it's not about your pain or my pain—it isn't about anyone's pain. But precisely because the subsumed damage is a matter of the intended form of the work and not a matter of your experience or mine, it has become something we can look at together. This is what I meant by suggesting earlier that *10:04* gives us a better aesthetics of resistance. What Grossman sees in the disfigured Alkyoneus is Laocoön, and what he sees in Laocoön, in Laocoön's face, is pain. What Weiss's communists see in the figures of the Pergamon Altar is the effects of exploitation and of the economic structure that causes it. If what we see is pain, it can only be yours or mine or someone else's. We can't see, much less feel, the same thing. If what we see is exploitation, we are looking together at the same thing. What Lerner wants us to see in the totaled work that is *10:04*, what the work is designed to help us imagine, is not the end of pain but the end of exploitation.[45]

NOTES

An earlier version of "Totaling the Damage" appeared at *nonsite.org* (October 8, 2015, http://nonsite.org/feature/totaling-the-damage), along with a response by Theodore Martin, "The Dialectics of Damage: Art, Form, Formlessness" (October 9, 2016, http://nonsite.org/feature/9500). I would like to express my gratitude to the board of *nonsite.org* for granting permission to republish the essay in this volume.

1. Peter Weiss, *The Aesthetics of Resistance*, vol. 1, trans. Joachim Neugroschell (Durham, NC: Duke University Press, 2005), 3.

2. Allen Grossman, "The Passion of Laocoön: Warfare of the Religious against the Poetic Institution," in *True-Love: Essays on Poetry and Valuing* (Chicago: University of Chicago Press, 2009), 98.

3. Ibid., 82.

4. Ibid., 74.

5. Ibid., 85.

6. Ibid., 76.

7. Ibid.

8. Weiss, *Aesthetics of Resistance*, 7.

9. Ibid., 6.

10. Ibid., 8.

11. Ibid., 9.

12. Peter Weiss, *Ästhetik des Widerstands: Band 1* (Frankfurt am Main: Suhrkamp, 1975), 10.

13. Christopher Nealon, *The Matter of Capital: Poetry and Crisis in the American Century* (Cambridge, MA: Harvard University Press, 2011).

14. Andrew Epstein, "Verse vs. Verse: The Language Poets Are Taking over the Academy, but Will Success Destroy Their Integrity?," *Lingua Franca*, September 2000, 45–54. PennSound houses an archive of the Yellow Pages advertisements: PennSound, "Charles Bernstein and Jeff Preiss: The Yellow Pages Ads, Filmed in Hollywood, November 14,

1998: conceived and directed by Jeff Preiss," http://writing.upenn.edu/pennsound/x/Yellow
-Pages.php.

15. Bob Perelman, *IFLIFE* (New York: Roof Books, 2006), 52.

16. Sarah Posman, "Transitzone: An Interview with Kenneth Goldsmith," *nY*, June 2,
2010, www.ny-web.be/transitzone/interview-kenneth-goldsmith.html?view=none&cp=4261.

17. Brian M. Reed, "Textbook Uncreative Writing," *American Book Review* 32, no. 4
(May/June 2011): 5.

18. Nicholas Brown, "The Work of Art in the Age of Its Real Subsumption under Capital," *nonsite.org*, March 13, 2012, http://nonsite.org/editorial/the-work-of-art-in-the-age-of
-its-real-subsumption-under-capital.

19. Timothy Donnelly, *The Cloud Corporation* (Seattle: Wave Books, 2010), 10.

20. Ibid., 113.

21. Ibid., 147.

22. Christopher Nealon, "Camp Messianism, or, the Hopes of Poetry in Late-Late Capitalism," *American Literature* 76, no. 3 (September 2004): 579.

23. Ibid.

24. Ibid., 588.

25. A few works I have in mind include Jasper Bernes, *We Are Nothing and So Can You*
(Oakland, CA: Commune Editions, 2015); Joshua Clover, *The Totality for Kids* (Berkeley:
University of California Press, 2005); Juliana Spahr, *this connection of everyone with lungs*
(Berkeley: University of California Press, 2005); and Dana Ward, *The Crisis of Infinite
Worlds* (New York: Futurepoem Books, 2013).

26. Ben Lerner, *10:04: A Novel* (New York: Faber & Faber, 2014), Kindle edition.

27. Ibid., 222.

28. Ibid., 14.

29. Ibid., 129–30.

30. Michael Fried, "Art and Objecthood" (1967), in *Art and Objecthood: Essays and Reviews* (Chicago: University of Chicago Press, 1998), 148–72.

31. Lerner, *10:04*, 131.

32. It's not clear, of course, that Fried would view a Koons in the same way that the
narrator of *10:04* does. For Fried in "Art and Objecthood," what distinguished the work of
sculptors like Anthony Caro and David Smith as modernist and as art from the "literalist"
"non-art" of minimalists like Carl Andre, Donald Judd, and Tony Smith is the extent to
which the parts that form the whole of the work (indeed the very reason for their forming
a whole) involve "the mutual inflection of one element by another" so that "the identity of
each element matters . . . the same way . . . as the fact that it is this word or this note and
not another that occurs in a particular place in a sentence or melody . . . it is in this sense,
a sense inextricably involved with the concept of meaning, that everything in Caro's art that
is worth looking at is in its syntax" (Fried, "Art and Objecthood," 161–62). The way that a
Koons balloon dog is put together is not quite a "syntax" of the kind a Caro sculpture possesses because what one might see in the former as "inflection of one element by another"
is simply that of a typical balloon dog, not a matter of artistic intention. Or to put this in
Fried's terms, the articulation of the Koons sculpture's parts is not "involved with the concept of meaning." My claim about *10:04*, however, is that Lerner understands the form of
the work of art—both its capacity to be "total" and its risk of being "totaled"—to require the

kind of syntax that Fried aligns with Caro, with modernism, with meaning/intention, and with art as such. Fried recently recalled *nonsite.org* readers' attention to precisely this aspect of Caro's work, pointing to the form of the work as a "naked" assertion of "will," in "Anthony Caro's *Park Avenue Series*," September 13, 2013, http://nonsite.org/feature/anthony -caros-park-avenue-series.

33. Lerner, *10:04*, 130.

34. Ibid., 132–33.

35. As Fried famously argues in "Shape as Form: Frank Stella's Irregular Polygons," shape and form are not mutually exclusive. In the developments Fried charts beginning in the mid-1960s in the work of Stella along with Kenneth Noland and Jules Olitski, shape becomes "a medium with which choices about both literal and depicted shapes are made, and made mutually responsive" (Fried, "Art and Objecthood," 77). In opposing shape to form here, I simply mean to foreground the difference between something like literal shape (for example, the rusted surfaces, I-shaped beams, and hexagonal bolts we can see in a Caro sculpture) and what we might call intended shape (what form those things take when we understand them as contoured, painted, welded, and otherwise assembled in the ways that are intended by the artist).

36. Lerner, *10:04*, 133.

37. Ibid., 132.

38. Ibid., 231.

39. Ibid., 3.

40. Ibid., 4.

41. Lerner suggests, in the course of a 2014 review of the third volume of Karl Ove Knausgaard's six-volume and notoriously hyperdescriptive novel *My Struggle*, that the application of description is related to the recognition of value. In the case of Knausgaard, Lerner argues, the decision to create a world where it appears that no detail is neglected has a leveling effect: "If your attention as a writer is so egalitarian that your memoir describes a bowl of cornflakes and, say, your brother's face with the same level of detail, how do we determine a hierarchy of value?" ("Each Cornflake," *London Review of Books*, May 22, 2014, www.lrb.co.uk/v36/n10/ben-lerner/each-cornflake). If giving everything description in Knausgaard eliminates the possibility of assigning value to any one thing, then we might say that *10:04*'s narrator's refusal to describe faces is a way of doing something like the same thing with respect to individual characters in the novel—it makes them impossible to differentiate or hierarchize in terms of value. Art works, by contrast both to characters and to non-art, receive the most detailed description in the novel and do not receive it uniformly.

42. Lerner, *10:04*, 72–73.

43. Ibid., 240.

44. Ibid.

45. It should be clear by now that insofar as the idea of the totality of the work of art (and our ability to see it as totaled) is inextricable from understanding the work's form as intentional, I understand my analysis of *10:04* to be consistent with Nicholas Brown's in "Art after Art after Art." I'm indebted in this essay not only to several previous exchanges with Nicholas Brown about the novel but also to conversations with Todd Cronan, Michael Fried, Rachel Greenwald Smith, Mitchum Huehls, Günter Leypoldt, Ruth Leys, Philipp Löffler, Walter Benn Michaels, Charles Palermo (whom I want to thank explicitly for giving

me the idea of the bad tooth analogy in the last paragraph), and Clemens Spahr, as well as with audience members in the Humanities Center at Johns Hopkins University and at the symposium on "Contemporary Literature and the Culture of the School" sponsored by the Heidelberg Center for American Studies, where I presented earlier versions of this essay.

Against Omniscient Narration

A Farmworker Critique of Neoliberalism

MARCIAL GONZÁLEZ

In his 2005 novel *The People of Paper*, Salvador Plascencia begins with a dedication to his wife that states, "to Liz, who taught me that we are all people of paper." In the novel, Plascencia employs fantasy and metafiction to dramatize exactly what he means by "people of paper." To do so, he allegorizes the lives of Mexican farmworkers who are constantly being watched by Saturn, a god-like figure later revealed to be Plascencia himself. The author becomes an omniscient, oppressive character in his own novel, dictating the workers' narratives, but most of the working-class characters resist his authority and declare war on him in an effort to determine their own stories. Retaliating against the workers' struggle, the author-based Saturn employs various techniques to monitor and subdue the other characters and to punish those who challenge his seemingly insurmountable power. Thus, the farmworker characters find themselves in a formal predicament that bears a striking resemblance to the social contradictions of neoliberal capitalism, in which people who work for a living must constantly look for ways to challenge a system that is politically ubiquitous, ideologically dominant, and structurally determining. The farmworker characters, however, cannot fight a traditional war with guns and bullets against their abstract creator—for how can a character kill an author? They strive nevertheless to subvert Saturn's power by refusing to adhere to a conventional author–character relationship and by attempting to change the structural and visual aspects of the novel itself. In this way, *The People of Paper* stages a battle over the novel's textual features, emphasized in the fact that characters are literally textual constructs—that is, people made of paper—which alludes to the social construction of political subjectivity that we all share. In this essay, I argue that the farmworkers' war against Saturn in *The People of Paper* can be read symbolically as a critique of neoliberal capitalism; that the fight against neoliberalism is essentially a fight between competing

narratives; that Saturn as an allegorical construct of neoliberal power is both omniscient and fallible; that the workers' struggle is fought on two fronts—against
Saturn and against their own ideologies; and that even though the farmworkers
fail to overcome the power of an omniscient narrator, they nevertheless employ
strategies of resistance that hold promise for the future.

Before proceeding, I want to clarify two points. First, the fact that the novel's
main characters are immigrant farmworkers is significant because historically
farm labor has been one of the most exploited sectors of the US working class,
and because immigrant farmworkers, the vast majority of whom are people of
color, have a long history of fighting back against an overpowering international
agricultural industry and the capitalist state. Second, I hold closely to the premise
that literary works—especially those that focus on subaltern struggles for justice—
have much to teach us about the social and political structures of our time. This
is certainly the case in *The People of Paper*, which imagines a world where working-
class characters understand that they have been created by a tyrannical, omniscient author who attempts to dictate every aspect of their lives, and yet the workers decide that they have no choice but to wage a war against these conditions
despite the odds against them. To comprehend the symbolic significance of this
imagined world, the critic would do well to pose and attempt to answer a fundamental question: What must the existential reality of society be like to necessitate
and provide the raw social substance for the creation of such a novel? To answer
this question is to theorize society. I am not proposing that literature can or
should take the place of theory; each obviously performs distinct functions. But I
do believe that literature and theory help us to grasp similar kinds of knowledge
from different perspectives—one aesthetic, the other critical. Thus, methodologically I draw on both the novel and critical works to analyze the critique of neoliberalism in *The People of Paper*.

The novel begins in the mid-twentieth century and centers on the life of Federico de la Fe. Originally from Jalisco, Mexico, he crosses the border illegally
into Southern California with his young daughter, Little Merced. They settle in
El Monte, a rural town at the outskirts of Los Angeles, where Federico finds work
as a farm laborer in the flower industry. He comes to discover that an unseen
power in the sky named Saturn—whose name aptly alludes to the "Roman god of
agriculture and harvest,"[1] or to a mythical god who devours his own children—
has written the script of his life and has determined the conditions under which
he and other workers live. So Federico decides to organize the workers to fight in
a war against Saturn, concentrating on a group called the El Monte Flores gang
(EMF). Little Merced explains that "EMF was not like city gangs. . . . They did not

loot fruit stores or steal car parts; they just drank mescal and worked in the fur-rows harvesting flowers next to my father."[2] Because of his profound commitment to overthrowing Saturn's deterministic powers, Federico eventually becomes the leader and war commander of the EMF.

Even though the EMF workers are locked in a war against Saturn throughout most of the novel—a war they ultimately lose by the novel's end—their struggle does not take shape as a "class struggle" in the traditional sense. These workers are not fighting against their employers, nor are they demanding higher wages, better benefits, or other economic reforms. They are fighting against a nearly omniscient, seemingly indestructible power that controls every aspect of their lives, a force that created them and therefore has access to all their thoughts and knows in advance how their roles in the novel will end. The workers become aware that they are in fact characters in a novel constructed to serve the imagina-tive and ideological needs of the author, and they feel both perplexed and angered by their paradoxical condition. How can they ever overcome the very agent that created them? To destroy Saturn and the novel he is narrating would result in their self-annihilation. And it is in this sense that, even though the workers are not fighting for economic reforms, the EMF's war against Saturn can neverthe-less be considered a class struggle because, from a Marxist point of view, workers can only truly achieve liberation when they defeat and ultimately destroy the structural and systemic apparatuses of inequality, exploitation, and oppression *totally*—which is to say, they need not only to defeat the capitalist class but also to abolish all classes that are part of the capitalist system, including the working class. In such a scenario, workers would cease to exist as working-class subjects, but they would become something else, something entirely new, a new kind of subject. Even though *The People of Paper* does not develop this theme to its logical conclusion, the allusions to a liberated working class are nevertheless clear, mak-ing Saturn roughly equivalent to the phenomenon that Guy Debord calls "the society of the spectacle" or the self-consciousness of capital. Debord theorizes a project, similar to that of the EMF, that "in its negative form has as its goal the abolition of classes and the direct possession by the workers of every aspect of their activity. The opposite of this project is the society of the spectacle, where the commodity contemplates itself in a world of its own making."[3] For Debord, cap-ital comes to exist exclusively for itself, and it projects itself as the center of the universe—as humanity's *raison d'etre*. "The spectacle is *capital* accumulated to the point where it becomes an image,"[4] particularly, an image that is worshiped or fetishized. From this perspective, Saturn can be conceptualized as a socially sym-bolic representation of accumulated capital, and thus the workers' enemy in the novel is not a particular employer, company, or corporation, nor is it even the state that represents the interests of the capitalist class; it is their systemic condition of subservience and the fact of their near total domination by a spectacular structure of power.

The structure of power that dominates the lives of the EMF workers, however, is not a static, automated, agentless structure. It is not a machine without machine operators. It is rather a structure marked by contradiction—at once intentional and chaotic, omnipotent and fallible, unified and fractured, structural and agential. The structure of power in the novel, much like the structures of neoliberalism in society generally, operates within a social sphere within which competing groups struggle against one another in defense of their class interests. Laurence Cox and Alf Gunvald Nilsen argue that neoliberalism seeks "to extend the hegemony of already-dominant social groups. . . . It's prime achievement has been *restoring the class power* of capital by fundamentally undermining the social restrictions and regulations imposed on capitalist accumulation as a result of the struggles of working classes and colonized peoples in the first half of the twentieth century."[5] But they also claim that neoliberalism encompasses more than merely the market-oriented economic reforms instituted by the capitalist class that are aimed at undermining regulations for the purpose of maximizing profits. It is that, but it is more too. They argue that neoliberalism is a "collective agency,"[6] conscientious and purposive in its actions, and capable of orchestrating "social movements from above" in the same way that subaltern groups organize "social movements from below."[7] To claim that neoliberalism is a "collective agency" is to say that its actions are deliberate and calculated, and that they are motivated by class interests. Stated differently, neoliberalism represents a renewed confidence on the part of capital that the level of economic crisis experienced during the Great Depression of the 1930s will not reoccur—that capitalism need not be regulated because it is no longer vulnerable to an economic crisis of such magnitude or to the possibility of popular rebellion and revolution. Hence, capital has become daringly more arrogant in its disregard for the well-being of the working classes, disbanding policies previously associated with what used to be called the Fordist contract and the New Deal.

If we were to conceptualize the history of capitalism as a narrative with chapters, characters, conflicts, plots, and subplots, then we might be tempted to think of neoliberalism (the latest chapter in the long history of capitalism) as attempting to perform a function similar to that of an omniscient narrator—a narrator that assumes to know everything about the characters, including their thoughts and feelings; a narrator that controls the characters' actions and makes decisions concerning their abilities, limits, and outcomes; a narrator that creates opportunities and destroys them in the same breath; or, in a word, a narrator that becomes a God-like figure, omniscient, omnipotent, and infallible. But this analogy between neoliberalism and the omniscient narrator is problematic for at least two reasons. First, the idea that a narrator can know absolutely everything there is to know about all of the characters in a novel is illogical and impossible, not to mention presumptuous and oppressive. Omniscience is a quality that exceeds human experience; it is a fantasy that exists only in the imagination. Second, the idea that neoliberalism is omnipotent is more fiction than fact because it fails to account for the narratives of resistance that tell the stories of people who demand justice and look for ways to challenge the system. That is to say, the narrative of neoliberal capitalism is not omniscient, nor is it omnipotent; it is full of internal contradictions and marked by endless forms of opposition from below. Like neoliberalism, the agent of power in the novel as personified by Saturn seeks to subdue the rebellious workers by demolishing the modest gains they have made in placing restrictions on the narrator's omniscience, and it seeks also to reestablish Saturn's absolute authority over the characters—even though some of the characters, as I discuss below, come to discover Saturn's weaknesses and internal contradictions.

Saturn's most effective strategic weapon against the characters is his power of determination: he alone created the characters, gave them names, fashioned their personalities, and narrated the specificities of their lives; and he alone determined their outcomes. What the EMF workers fight for is "their right to be unseen," to be uncontrolled and undetermined by the author. Froggy, the EMF's second-in-command, explains that to be truly free they must be given a "choice" about how to live, and that it is an injustice to "force us to . . . submit to the commands of a dictator" (232). Essentially, the EMF workers contest the fact that they are constructed as characters confined to a text—i.e., people of paper—in the same way that real workers are ideologically and materialistically constructed as subjects within the confined social parameters of capitalism. In delivering a recruitment speech to the EMF, Federico de la Fe describes their struggle as "a war for volition and against the commodification of sadness. . . . It is a war against the fate that has been decided for us" (53). The commodification of sadness refers to making profit from writing a novel about the suffering of people—or interchangeably, to the construction of ideological narratives that benefit those in society who profit at the expense of those who are exploited. In this way, the EMF's "war against the commodification of sadness" is also a "war on omniscient narration" (218)—a war against the fact that a "collective agency" at the top gets to write the narrative from an omniscient point of view and decide the specifics of the story, while those at the bottom are given little or no voice.

Ideology as a Weapon of War

The "war on omniscient narration" proves to be more difficult than the workers count on because it must be fought on two fronts: against Saturn and against the workers' own ideologies. To elaborate on this point, I first address the problem of ideology before analyzing the omniscient narrator and the workers' strategies of resistance. In the novel, ideology sometimes undermines the workers' efforts in the fight against Saturn, similar to the way the ideological contradictions of workers in the current neoliberal period sometimes prevent them from acting in their own class interests. These ideological contradictions in many ways have become sharper in recent decades because—despite the relative systemic weaknesses of capitalism as evidenced by, among other things, the 2008 financial crash—neoliberalism has become more aggressive in its endeavors to win the hearts and minds of workers, or to scare them into submission. But the fight to persuade people ideologically works both ways, influenced by movements from below as well as movements from above. For example, since September 2011 the Occupy movement, despite its political weaknesses and organizational unsustainability as a movement, has been highly successful in countering neoliberal ideology in three significant ways: (1) it heightened an awareness that capitalism is vulnerable, having suffered severe blows to its economic and political integrity resulting from its own internal contradictions; (2) it forcefully reminded millions of people that society is divided into socioeconomic classes, and that a small minority owns most of the wealth and makes most of the decisions that govern our lives;[8] and (3) it drove a huge wedge into the misconception that capitalism is ahistorical, or that it will exist forever, and it nurtured confidence in the belief that a postcapitalist society can and indeed should be conceptualized.

Perhaps a more appropriate example of a social movement for understanding the critique of neoliberal ideology in *The People of Paper* would be that of the Zapatista Army of National Liberation. In the Zapatista's "First Declaration of La Realidad for Humanity and against Neoliberalism" published in 1996, the Zapatistas denounce neoliberalism's ideological narratives of history and class power as attempts to mislead workers into believing that they are powerless and should abandon any expectation of challenging the system. The Zapatistas, of course, pay no heed to those defeatist narratives. On the contrary, in the declaration, they state, "A new lie is sold to us as history. The lie about the defeat of hope, the lie about the defeat of dignity, the lie about the defeat of humanity. The mirror of power offers us an equilibrium in the balance scale: the lie about the victory of cynicism, the lie about the victory of servitude, the lie about the victory of neoliberalism."[9] The characters in the *People of Paper*, some referred to with the Zapatista-like designation "subcomandante," assume a similarly defiant attitude toward the ideological deception of Saturn, who has constructed a narrative that represents the workers as defenseless and politically inept. Nevertheless, despite the gains made by the Occupy movement, the Zapatistas, and other "social movements from below" in recent years, the persuasiveness of neoliberal ideology remains powerful and relentless, and its effects are evident in the actions and narratives of common folks throughout the world, as well as on the pages of Plascencia's *The People of Paper*.

Our current period is marked ideologically by two significant gains made by neoliberal capital over the past several decades. First, neoliberalism has succeeded to a greater degree than earlier periods of capitalism in undermining the belief that a postcapitalist society is possible and achievable. Today a general (but not totalizing) pessimism exists toward the idea that people can overcome the structural domination of neoliberal capitalism—a kind of pessimism that Mark Fisher characterizes with the term "capitalist realism," by which he means that "it is now impossible to even *imagine* a coherent alternative" to capitalism.[10] Second, and more problematically, neoliberalism has consolidated the belief among large sectors of the working and middle classes that capitalism is on their side—that the system serves the interests of workers no more or no less than it does the interests of, say, the banking, oil, or arms industries. These two gains by neoliberalism expose two of the most effective forms of ideology in our contemporary moment—cynicism and consent, which I now address in short order.

The EMF characters in *The People of Paper* represent various shades of ideological conflict among workers, and political cynicism is certainly one of them. Federico de la Fe, whose last name literally means "of the faith," represents the novel's bulwark against cynicism, but not all characters hold as steadfastly to a belief that their struggle is winnable. Years after the war against Saturn has ended, Froggy tries to convince some young workers that it is in their interests once again to take up the baton left by their elders and wage a war against Saturn, and he attempts to instill in them confidence that both victory against the omniscient narrator and the formation of a post-Saturn world are possible. But the cynical youth bluntly respond, "The veteranos couldn't win it, we can't either" (49), and they refuse to renew a political campaign. Here the novel pointedly puts on display an example of how the ideology of cynicism has led workers to give up the fight and lose the war before it has even started.

No doubt the failure of revolutionary movements of the past and the absence of mass anticapitalist movements in this country and around the globe at this particular historical moment have produced widespread political cynicism toward the possibility of a postcapitalist future. But political cynicism can itself be considered an objective condition that functions as an obstacle to social change, while political optimism should be considered an objective necessity for any theory of practice aimed at overcoming the historical impasse in which we now find ourselves. We might recall here the following passage from Antonio Gramsci: "It is necessary to direct one's attention violently towards the present as it is, if one wishes to transform it," a statement that he qualifies with his now famous line, "Pessimism of the intellect, optimism of the will."[11] Pessimism of the intellect because every rational thought in our mind convinces us of the impossibility of overcoming a system as powerful as neoliberal capitalism—and of the even greater impossibility of establishing a society based on the abolition of social classes and money. Optimism of the will because revolutionary practice requires a subjective element—not an individual will, but a collective will, a collective praxis. Gramsci asserts that what appears as impossible to the intellect becomes possible only through the collective will and concerted actions of people acting jointly to destroy one world and replace it with another.

Peter Hallward expands on Gramsci's concept of "optimism of the will" and the critique of ideological cynicism by asking his readers to consider the possibility of a utopian society such as communism, generally considered an impossible social system or an unfeasible political strategy.[12] In an essay entitled "Communism of the Intellect, Communism of the Will," Hallward criticizes our contemporary "lack of political imagination" and urges us to learn from the wisdom of leaders who have paid no heed to the supposed impossibility of their struggles. He writes, "We would do better . . . to follow the example given by people like Robespierre, L'Ouverture or John Brown," who were confronted with the "indefensible institution of slavery" and eventually defeated it. He continues, "Che Guevara and Paulo Freire would do the same in the face of imperialism and oppression. . . . In each case the basic logic is as simple as could be: an idea, like the idea of communism, or equality, or justice, commands that we should strive to realize it without compromises or delay, before the means of such realization have been recognized as feasible or legitimate, or even 'possible.' It is the deliberate striving towards realization itself that will convert the impossible into the possible, and explode the parameters of the feasible."[13] The act of imagining and fighting for a future society based on social and economic equality and the abolition of classes, or what Carlos Gallego calls "the radical universality of truth,"[14] whether that society turns out to be communism or some social form that we have not yet even imagined, is "no facile optimism," according to Carl Freedman and Neil Lazarus, but we would still do well to recognize that the "very process of Utopian speculation participates in the production of Utopian possibility."[15]

To be politically cynical—like the young EMF workers who refuse to follow Froggy's leadership—about the possibility of overcoming neoliberalism's structures of power is strategically self-defeating for working- and middle-class people, but the political cynic at least still potentially recognizes the exploitative class character of neoliberalism. She or he recognizes the inherent faults of the system but just does not believe that the system can be changed. By contrast, the person who willingly and loyally grants his or her consent to be governed—or who has been persuaded that the system serves the best interests of everyone equally—has forfeited any critical consciousness in exchange for passive convenience and possibly for the hope of a slightly larger piece of the social pie.

The critical interpretation of consent, of course, has been most cogently formulated by Gramsci in his theory of hegemony. For Gramsci, the modern state maintains social control over the masses through a combination of force and ideological persuasion, or coercion and consent. The use of coercive force by the state—the military, police, prisons, judicial system, penalties, fines, and so on—is frequently employed by those in power to "enforce discipline on those groups who do not 'consent' either actively or passively" to the rule of class power. Coercion is especially effective during moments of political instability or when "spontaneous consent has failed."[16] But coercion alone is insufficient because it tends to provoke discontent and rebellion, and it unmasks the true repressive character of the neoliberal state. A so-called democratic society operates much more effectively if it is able to persuade members of exploited classes that it is in their best interests to follow the leadership of the ruling class, to adopt its world outlook, and to believe in its political and moral judgments.

In the novel, the minor character Smiley best demonstrates the actions of a worker who has embraced the ideology of consent. He has been persuaded that living under Saturn's rule is a good thing. Unlike the other members of the EMF, he has consented to Saturn's hegemonic order, and he wonders, "Was Saturn really so ominous and threatening? Could he not be protecting us?" (95). Smiley, conscious of his status as a fictional character, does not agree with other members of the EMF in waging war against Saturn. He fears that destroying Saturn "would bring our own end" as characters because then the novel would cease to exist. In a literal sense he's correct, but his views are also allusions to his profound cynicism about the possibility of winning the war against Saturn. Representing a skeptical possessive individualism in which he's more concerned about saving his own skin than the well-being of the collective, Smiley aspires to be recognized by Saturn and rewarded for his loyalty. He confesses as much in stating, "I was not worried about the galaxy and the fall of its satellites. I thought of my own existence, of my own place in this novel" (101).

Despite Smiley's blind devotion to Saturn and his willingness to consent to the author's dictatorial role in the novel, his relationship with the author becomes fractured and nearly unravels when Saturn's weaknesses are exposed. Upon learning that Saturn and Plascencia are one and the same and that he lives just on the other side of the sky, which is made of out of newspaper and glue, he figures out how to tear a hole in the sky large enough to crawl through, where he finds himself in Saturn's home. But Saturn is not nearly as divine as Smiley had imagined: he's unkempt, dirty, forgetful, unsightly, and flawed—flawed because he cannot always see everything, he is unknowing rather than omniscient, and he sometimes allows the narrative to slip away from his control. Smiley's ideological outlook is jolted in witnessing the author's weaknesses and faults as this experience disrupts his impression of Saturn (and by implication, political power generally) as infallible and omniscient. "When I came to Saturn he was no longer in control. He did not have the foresight to see that I was coming, nor did he care. He had surrendered the story and his powers as narrator" (103). Finding the author in this condition, Smiley considers slitting Saturn's throat with the knife he uses to harvest flowers at work, but he fails to execute what would have been a historic act—a character killing the author. Instead, he merely steals Saturn's book manuscript and leaves only the title page behind after writing on it, "You are not so powerful" (105). Yet despite his moment of anger and disillusionment toward Saturn, Smiley nevertheless is not able to overcome the consent he has granted to Saturn to be governed and led ideologically, and after a while he begins to dream regularly that he is sitting at a table with Saturn playing dominoes, and in his dreams he smiles whenever Saturn calls him "Comandante Smiley" (154). In the end, Smiley's loyalty to Saturn is not repaid in kind, and he experiences the most pathetic outcome among the EMF workers when Saturn forgets his name and overlooks him in summarizing the lives of the main characters in the novel's final pages.

Smiley is not the only farmworker character in the novel who fails to overcome the ideological influence of Saturn. Little Oso, for example, believes that "whatever happens beyond our borders is not my worry. . . . [I]t is only Monte and its sky that I care about" (215). Similarly, Pelon becomes politically sterile (a de facto form of consent) as a result of the conditioning associated with alienated labor. While at work during the war, Pelon stops thinking about worldly matters and important ideas, concentrating instead on the minutiae of harvesting and soil cultivation. He performs these routine acts for so long during the war that he becomes ideologically nearsighted, no longer able to think beyond the immediacy of his life as a worker. "This is what I see," he says. "There is no world beyond the till of the land and the planting of seeds" (213).

Pelon's tragic outcome recalls the scandalous claims of Frederick Winslow Taylor in his 1911 monograph *The Principles of Scientific Management*. Taylor proposed a strategy to give capital the power to overcome the economic problems associated with the falling rate of profit in the early periods of industrial capitalism. With Taylorism, the worker-subject did not merely operate a machine in the factory but, measured by stopwatches and slide rules, was made an appendage to the machine. The worker ceased to be a *relation* of production and became a *means* of production. For Taylor, the now dehumanized, machine-like, mindless workers were incapable of understanding "scientific" production and "too stupid" to understand how they were being exploited.[17] More significantly, the workers' minds would become even more intellectually disabled because of the constant meticulous attention they were required to pay to the monotonous, brain-consuming details of production. While Taylor's theories were based partly in actuality in that certain work environments did (and still do) deaden the imaginative faculties of workers, Taylor grossly underestimated the capacity of working-class consciousness and the potential for insurgency. As Gramsci reminds us in "Fordism and Taylorism," workers' minds do not become "mummified" merely because their work has become mechanized.[18] Nevertheless, Pelon, along with countless other workers like him, falls prey to the mind-deadening effects of alienated labor, and he serves as an example of the novel's critique of consent manufactured through Tayloristic working and living conditions.

In the world of the novel, ideology is an effective strategic weapon that aids Saturn in his war with the EMF. It is both intentional and structural, and it can be described as what Cox and Nilsen call a "social movement from above." The novel alludes to the way ideology is perpetuated among workers via the metaphor of a crop duster. Once a day, a crop duster would fly over El Monte, "leaving behind a mist that ate away the larvae of medflies and also the paint coats of unprotected cars," (38) not to mention the physical health of workers and their families. Here the novel offers a not-so-subtle condemnation of the harm that pesticides cause to farmworkers and others, but the scene should also be read as an allusion to the manner in which neoliberalism pervades every aspect in the lives of workers, reinforced with unhealthy doses of ideology regularly "sprayed" on them by a "collective agency" from above.

The Fallibility of an Omniscient Narrator

As mentioned earlier, the "collective agency" that the workers are up against is marked by contradiction; it is simultaneously powerful and fallible, omniscient and at times unknowing. As the representative incarnate of this "collective agency," Saturn adds a profound complexity to the novel's already complex narrative structure. At first glance, the narration appears democratic and inclusive because of its multiple points of view; numerous characters are given a voice in telling their own stories. The twenty-six chapters are divided into sections, and almost all sections bear a header with the name of a character. The sections are narrated from the perspective of that character either in the first person or from a third-person limited point of view, and occasional sections are told from the first-person-plural perspective of particular groups. There is also an omniscient narrator in the prologue and in the sections labeled "Saturn," but Saturn is not the narrator in any of these sections. Nor does he ever speak for himself as a first-person narrator, except in chapter 10, where he has a brief conversation with his estranged lover, Liz. But even though he is not the literal narrator, he nevertheless performs a function that is similar to but also calls into question what Wayne Booth refers to as the "implied author." For Booth, the "implied author" is not the real or actual author, but an imaginary substitute for the author. The real author "creates not simply an ideal, impersonal 'man in general' but an implied version of 'himself'" to assume the responsibility of calling the narrative shots.[19] The implied author might best be understood as what H. Porter Abbott calls the "sensibility" of the narrative, or its most reliable conscious subject, given that both the real author and the narrator proper can easily be considered unreliable either because of their personal biases and ideological values or because the truth of the narrative exceeds the limitations of their consciousness. In this case, the implied author represents something akin to the "intentionality" of the narrative.[20] As a character in the novel, Saturn takes form as a parody of Booth's implied author in that he is a fictive construct with the authority to write the story, create narrative voices, give stage directions, construct characters and storylines, decide both the conflict and the outcome of the narrative, and, as in the present case, give minority characters their own sections to narrate in the first person as a sign of his benevolent multiculturalism. Stated differently, Saturn/Plascencia—not the real author but the fictive construct, the amalgamation of assumed author and mastermind character, the narrative's consciousness—is the behind-the-scenes omniscient narrator. Saturn, however, differs from Booth's implied author in a fundamental way: he loses his imperviousness and unbridled authority when the farmworker characters, Smiley in particular, dismantle his facade and expose both his arbitrariness and his despotic value system, ripping away his veil of omniscience and, in the process, weakening (but not overcoming) the power he has over them.[21] In effect, not only does Saturn's fallibility in his role as the novel's intentionality create a sense of deep instability in the logic that holds the novel together, but it also threatens to tear that logic asunder. Thus, the novel stands as, among other things, a sharp critique of the supposed neutrality or objectivity of the implied author in realist fiction, and perhaps as an indictment of the assumed stability of the novel form itself.

Saturn's role in the novel as implied author/omniscient narrator generates a series of paradoxes. A war between characters and the novel's author challenges the conventional contract between author, text, and audience that we expect when we read a fictional work. We don't normally expect characters to be conscious of the fact that they are indeed characters. Nor do we expect them to challenge the authority and intentions of the author who created them. Saturn is correct to recognize, and perhaps even to be concerned about, the fact that novels often take on a life of their own beyond the intentions of the author, and he tries to stunt the characters' efforts to make this happen. Yet even though Saturn ultimately wins the political war in the novel, he is not successful in reigning in the extratextual signification that occurs beyond the pages of *The People of Paper*. Despite Saturn's obsessive desire to maintain strict control of the production of meaning in the novel, the novel's signification nevertheless exceeds the author's intentions. This is to say that within the logic of the novel's status as an art object, Saturn has lost the war of aesthetics insofar as the characters' thoughts, words, and actions have assumed a dynamic social significance that surpasses the author's individual consciousness. The irony of Saturn's situation is that as much as he tries to control every aspect of his characters' lives as he strives to complete the narrative, his failure to do so is actually the mark of a successful novel, for it is precisely the meanings in the novel that surpass authorial intentionality that give it critical depth, aesthetic complexity, and historical relevance. In this case, when the farmworker characters expose Saturn's fallibility, they have also brought to light the unequal relations between author and characters, or relatedly, between the power of capital and the needs of the working class. More pointedly, and in a symbolic sense, the near dismantling of the novel form caused by the breakdown of the conventional author–character–reader relation strongly parallels the unraveling

of neoliberalism's structure of power brought on by its own internal contradictions and the struggles of the working class.

EMF Strategies of Resistance

Now that I have established that the EMF's war is fought on two fronts—against
ideology and a fallible omniscient narrator—I shall discuss the strategies the
workers deploy to fight the war. To wage an effective campaign against Saturn,
the EMF workers rely on various plans and tactical maneuvers with varying degrees of success and failure, but given the particular kind of enemy that the EMF
is fighting against, and given the characters' condition as discursive constructs,
the workers come to recognize that they must engage in a nontraditional kind
of warfare. Thinking back to his youth years later, Froggy remembers, "What we
fought against didn't use guns or shanks . . . didn't use stones or weapons of
steel, nor could it be defeated by such" (46). When they try shooting guns up into
the air, attempting to penetrate the sky and injure Saturn, the bullets fall harm-
lessly to the ground. So they decide to launch a "full assault" on Saturn, but "it [is]
an attack without gunfire or mortar explosions" (87). They host cock fights, start
a dairy farm, and collect donations to produce income that will sustain the war
financially, even though their financial limitations are not the primary impediment to victory. They burn lumber and tires to create smoke in an effort to block
Saturn's vision, but this strategy backfires as it eventually causes health problems
for the group. They line the walls and roofs of their homes with sheets of lead,
which Saturn's vision cannot penetrate, but the lead eventually leaks into the air
and water and makes them sick, so they are forced to abandon that strategy. Late
in the novel, the EMF launches an offensive by attempting to crowd Saturn off
the page, forcing him into a corner. They attempt to out-populate his power on
the page and to speak so loudly and forcefully that they will be able to "drown the
voice of Saturn." In so doing, their plan is to seize control of the novel's pages, a
textual coup d'état. For a while, the strategy is successful in forcing Saturn to retreat, and the EMF characters believe that they have finally caused his downfall
from the sky. "Saturn heard them approaching, crowding into the page, pushing
and trying to press Saturn further and further to the margin" (208).

Notwithstanding their weaknesses, the farmworker characters seize control of
page space and narrative structure as part of their war strategy. The layout and
appearance of the chapters in the novel coincide with the story of the war between
the EMF and Saturn as it unfolds. Of the twenty-six chapters, sixteen are typeset
in a standard single column of text that spans the page from the left to the right
margin. Six chapters (1, 4, 7, 15, 20, and 24), however, are typeset with two narrow

vertical columns on each page. In the first four of these two-column chapters, the left-hand pages are always devoted to Saturn's point of view, who occupies just one column, while the other is left blank. His columns are noticeably wider than those of other characters partly owing to the fact that he does not have to share the page with any other characters. The right-hand pages are reserved for all other characters. At one point (in chapter 4), Saturn reflects on the EMF's two battalions, one led by Froggy and the other by Subcomandante Sandra.[22] As if to emphasize the age-old strategy of divide and conquer, Saturn splits the narrative into two sub-columns, one for each of the battalions (56). Saturn's vulnerability begins to appear in chapter 15, where he is missing entirely from his dedicated page. Only the header with his name remains, as his columns are empty. Saturn has gone AWOL as he attempts to escape his own internal weaknesses. Then in chapter 24, at the height of EMF's most successful military campaign against Saturn, and with Saturn retreating, some of the vertical columns are now turned sideways, or horizontally aligned, and for the first time in the novel other characters begin to appear on the left side of the book to share Saturn's space. More significantly, Saturn's columns have now become narrower, shorter, and noticeably pushed into a corner. But Saturn eventually returns with a vengeance, ultimately seizing total control of the narration in the final pages of the novel and reassuming his role as the novel's narrator, effectively ending the EMF's offensive to bring him down.

Of all the plans implemented by the EMF against Saturn, Little Merced employs what is perhaps the most effective strategy, even if at first it might seem individualist, escapist, and not fully developed in the novel. Through the power of mental concentration and the redirection of her emotions, she learns how to block her thoughts from both Saturn and the reader, and the blockage appears as a black patch on the page, covering some of the text. At first the black patches are small, obscuring a few lines of text at most. But Little Merced develops her skill to the point that she is able to blacken entire columns with varying degrees of success. While her obfuscation skills provide temporary relief for the young girl and her father, they are still severely limited and fall far short of neutralizing Saturn's power over the EMF workers.

Little Merced's blackout skills, however, can be read as an emergent structure that, when developed to its full potential, will be able to overcome Saturn and the power he represents. She learns her skills from Baby Nostradamus, whom she meets on the bus during her migration from Mexico to Southern California. At first Baby Nostradamus, a slobbering child, appears to be brain dead or severely challenged mentally, but the girl soon learns that he possesses the gift of clairvoyance, allowing him to see, among other things, the book's last sentence before it is written. The extraordinary Baby Nostradamus knows the exact temperatures of halos, he can cryptically predict the future, and he is able to communicate with his sense of touch and through his emotions. Most importantly, he is able to hide his thoughts from Saturn and the readers.[23] As such, his columns are filled not with words but with black ink. In an interview with Matthew Baker, Plascencia (the real author) reveals that "Baby Nostradamus is a prolific mind but masquerades as a retarded baby," and Plascencia draws a distinction between the "white space" readers occasionally find on literary pages and the blackened spaces that fill Baby Nostradamus's columns. "The way I understand the page . . . white space is silence and any inscription equals sound. Yet when I see the black rectangle in *Tristram Shandy*, I read a quiet sadness—death. . . . I wasn't satisfied with the Baby Nostradamus signifying silence. As the novel progressed, I tried to turn the darkness from a limp muteness into an active form of resistance."[24] While Baby Nostradamus does not pose any significant threat to Saturn as a "form of resistance" in the novel proper, he represents symbolically, together with Little Merced, the emergence of a structure that at some point will enable workers to challenge Saturn's claim to power. I make this assertion because of Baby Nostradamus's characteristics: he is a child, not fully developed and still emerging; he has the ability to see the future, which implies that to some extent he is already in the future, or from the future; his thoughts are closed off to Saturn, or he is immune to Saturn's panoptic gaze; and he has the ability to communicate without language through his emotions. Because of these characteristics, I want to suggest a strong correlation between Baby Nostradamus's alternative form of consciousness and Raymond Williams's concept of "structure of feeling."

In *Marxism and Literature*, Williams rethinks the concept of "structure" through a critical examination of the base–superstructure model of orthodox Marxism, arguing that Marx's conception of determination has been misunderstood by most Marxists who came after Marx. He shows that Marx himself stood against the separation of thought from material production and criticized definitions of "structure" and "superstructure" that treat these abstractions as if they were separable concrete entities.[25] Williams states, "It is the reduction of the social to fixed forms that remains the basic error," and he adds that the "mistake . . . is in taking terms of analysis as terms of substance."[26] For him, Marx did not argue for a study of "base" and "superstructure" as fixed forms, the former as a timeless synchronic structure determining the latter, but for an analysis of the "processes" that inform the ever-changing relationships between the material and nonmaterial aspects of social and cultural life. Thus, for Williams the concept of "structure" as a shaping social force should not be limited to the economic, but must include social institutions, cultural traditions, and ideological formations. He further categorizes these institutions, traditions, and formations as either "residual, dominant or emergent," depending on whether they originally sprung from a now archaic mode of production, serve the interests of the contemporary status quo, or represent the aspirations of some futuristic society, respectively.[27] Of these categories, the emergent alone possesses the potential for creating revolutionary change. It is not surprising then that Williams attempts to answer the question of where emergent structures come from. In order to be genuinely emergent, a structure must already exist as a knowable system, that is, as an already contemplated and articulated set of ideas, a method of explanation, or an ideology that can be named and categorized. But *before* the emergent structure ever becomes articulated, *before* it is understood intellectually or analytically, *before* it is ever explained in written form, it exists in a "pre-emergent" stage where it is *felt* in the lived experiences, desires, attitudes, and emotions of individuals—in their "practical consciousness." This pre-emergent stage of emergent structures is what Williams refers to as "structures of feeling."[28]

The skill that Little Merced learns from Baby Nostradamus and that she begins to develop on her own toward the end of the novel can be understood, within the logic of the argument I have been making, as a "structure of feeling"—an emergent formation of revolutionary consciousness still in its embryonic state, an "optimism of the will," that with time will allow the EMF workers to develop a revolutionary practice not dependent on the structures of dominance and in this way shut out Saturn entirely from their stories and from their lives. As the novel ends, Little Merced shades her father with a parasol, sheltering them both from Saturn's view as they walk off the page together, successfully escaping the deterministic world of Saturn's novel and, more importantly, directing our attention to the possibility of a futuristic, truly democratic world not based on the commodification of sadness.

Conclusion

In *Zombie Capitalism: Global Crisis and the Relevance of Marx* (2009), Chris Harman argues against the idea of a bad capitalism (neoliberalism, financialization, trickle-down economics, etc.) versus a good capitalism (regulation, Keynesianism, demand-side economics, etc.). In Harman's view, one with which I concur, capitalist ideology must always "pin the blame on something other than capitalism, as such," even if this means vilifying one aspect of capitalism rather than placing blame on the entire system of accumulation itself.[29] Similarly, as we come to discover in *The People of Paper*, the problems faced by the EMF workers do not lie exclusively in the motives and actions of the fallible Saturn, as omniscient narrator, implied author, and the figurative embodiment of neoliberalism, but also, and principally, in the entire structure of power that he represents, a structure that determines the unequal relations between author and characters, or between class power and subservience, consolidated or challenged by narratives from both above and below. The main conflict in the novel then comes down to who will control the writing of the workers' narratives (both literary and ideological) and who will decide what lies in store for them in the future. This battle over narrative control takes shape partly in the formal structures of the novel and its typography, but it is also a fight over the narrative's content. Ralph and Elisa Landin, the characters who provide financial support for Saturn/Plascencia's novel, state this point most emphatically: "If we had learned anything from this story it was to be cautious of paper—to be mindful of its fragile construction and sharp edges, but mostly to be cautious of what is written on it" (219). Plascencia's fictive benefactors fear the subversive content of literature, but the farmworker characters by contrast come to embrace its revolutionary potential. Initially the farmworkers attempt to prevent Saturn from hearing them by keeping silent or whispering, by hiding their words and thoughts, but they later come to realize that to challenge their domination successfully they need to be vocal. They need to write their stories, and they need to rewrite history. In a speech to the EMF workers, Froggy explains, "We are fighting a war against a story, against the history that is being written by Saturn. We believed that silence was our best weapon against the intrusion of Saturn [but] learned that history cannot be fought with sealed lips" (209).

The People of Paper dramatizes a conflict that exposes the correlation between literature and society, between narratives and ideology—that is, between the structures of the novel and the social structures of dominance in the current period of neoliberal capitalism. And the novel makes us wonder as well about the similarities between the lives of the characters and our own lives. In a sense, we are all indeed people of paper, textualized within neoliberalism's ideological narratives of history and class power, and faced with a choice either to grant our consent passively to be dictated by those narratives or to wage a war against their claims of omniscience.

NOTES

Thanks to Marcelle Maese-Cohen, John Alba Cutler, Dennis López, and Emma Appel for their comments on an early draft of this essay.

1. Ramón Saldívar, "Historical Fantasy, Speculative Realism, and Postrace Aesthetics in Contemporary American Fiction," *American Literary History* 23, no. 3 (Fall 2011): 596n4.

2. Salvador Plascencia, *The People of Paper* (New York: Harcourt, 2005), 34. Hereafter cited in the text.

3. Guy Debord, *The Society of the Spectacle*, trans. Donald Nicholson-Smith (New York: Zone Books, 1995), 34.

4. Ibid., 24.

5. Laurence Cox and Alf Gunvald Nilsen, *We Make Our Own History: Marxism and Social Movements in the Twilight of Neoliberalism* (London: Pluto, 2014), vi. I added emphasis to the phrase "restoring the class power" because it implies misleadingly that capitalists lost class power at some point in the past, and that now neoliberalism represents an effort to regain it. But the capitalist class has held state power consistently since the inception of capitalism, at least in the Western world. More accurately, neoliberalism represents an effort by capitalists to consolidate a radically new phase of unregulated capitalism.

6. Ibid., 59.

7. Ibid., 71.

8. Cox and Nilsen write that "between 1960 and 1997 . . . the ratio between the share of income received by the richest 20 per cent of the world's countries to that received by the poorest 20 per cent increased from 30:1 to 74:1; the richest 20 per cent of humanity received more than 85 per cent of the world's wealth, while the remaining 80 per cent had to make do with less than 15 per cent of the world's wealth" (ibid., 2).

9. "First Declaration of La Realidad for Humanity and against Neoliberalism," Zapatista Army of National Liberation, http://flag.blackened.net/revolt/mexico/ezln/ccri_1st_dec_real.html.

10. Mark Fisher, *Capitalist Realism: Is There No Alternative?* (Winchester, UK: Zero Books, 2009), 2.

11. Antonio Gramsci, *Selections from the Prison Notebooks*, ed. and trans. Quintin Hoare and Geoffrey Nowell Smith (New York: International, 1971), 175n75. The passage originally appeared in Antonio Gramsci, *Passato e presente*, vol. 6, *Quaderni del carcere* (Turin: Einaudi, 1951), 6. "Pessimism of the intellect" is sometimes translated as "Pessimism of the intelligence." Gramsci ascribes this passage to the novelist Romain Rolland.

12. See, e.g., Enrique D. Dussel, "From Critical Theory to the Philosophy of Liberation: Some Themes for Dialogue," *Transmodernity: Journal of Peripheral Cultural Production of the Luso-Hispanic World* 1, no. 2 (Fall 2011): 31. Dussel writes, "Communism is not some empirical future moment in history, but rather a postulate for practical orientation whose historical realization would be impossible." Here Dussel expresses a healthy dose of "pessimism of the intellect" but lacks any "optimism of the will."

13. Peter Hallward, "Communism of the Intellect, Communism of the Will," in *The Idea of Communism*, ed. Costas Douzinas and Slavoj Žižek (New York: Verso, 2010), 112.

14. Carlos Gallego, *Chicana/o Subjectivity and the Politics of Identity: Between Recognition and Revolution* (New York: Palgrave Macmillan, 2011), 202. Gallego argues that "radical universality . . . transcends artificially created boundaries like culture and nation," but "in fact resembles . . . classless socialism" (200).

15. Carl Freedman and Neil Lazarus, "The Mandarin Marxism of Theodor Adorno," *Rethinking Marxism* 1, no. 4 (Winter 1988): 95, 96.

16. Gramsci, *Notebooks*, 12. Louis Althusser's "Ideology and Ideological State Appara-

tuses (Notes towards an Investigation)," in *Lenin and Philosophy and Other Essays*, trans. Ben Brewster (New York: Monthly Review, 1971), 145, draws on Gramsci's theory of hegemony in theorizing Ideological State Apparatuses (ISAs) and Repressive State Apparatuses (RSAs). These two categories are based on the concepts of consent and coercion, respectively. Althusser explains that in practice ISAs and RSAs overlap in their functions, given that there is always a repressive aspect of the ISAs and an ideological aspect of the RSAs. "There is no such thing as a purely repressive apparatus," and similarly, "There is no such thing as a purely ideological apparatus." This implies that most people do not freely give their consent to be controlled; they do so with the tacit knowledge that their failure to grant consent would likely result in some form of coercion to force them into compliance. In other words, the stick is always hidden just behind the carrot.

17. Frederick Winslow Taylor, *The Principles of Scientific Management* (Mineola, NY: Dover, 1997), 63.

18. Gramsci, *Notebooks*, 309.

19. Wayne C. Booth, *The Rhetoric of Fiction*, 2nd ed. (Chicago: University of Chicago Press, 1983), 70. Originally published in 1961.

20. H. Porter Abbott, *The Cambridge Introduction to Narrative*, 2nd ed. (Cambridge: Cambridge University Press, 2008), 84–86.

21. For an analysis of metafiction in *The People of Paper*, see Saldívar, "Historical Fantasy." Saldívar argues that Plascencia's novel strives "to depict accurately the truth of which the text bears witness free of textual or historical coercions" (582). See also Alma Granado, "Rebordering the Borderlands: Writing Violence, (Im)migration, and Surveillance" (PhD diss., University of California, Berkeley, 2014), 51–75.

22. Although the topic of gender is beyond the scope of this essay, it is a central motif in *The People of Paper*. While some female characters, such as Little Merced and Sandra, are complex and assertive, others serve as the cause of sadness for male characters when they abandon their mates. Merced, Merced de Papel, Sandra, Liz, and Cameroon all abandon male characters for different reasons. The notion that women-induced sadness for male characters drives the novel could be read as problematic from a feminist perspective, and it deserves a full analysis. For a reading of Merced de Papel as a "gendered non-citizen," see Granado, "Rebordering the Borderlands," 64–69.

23. The novel's critique of the author and narrator also implicates, to a lesser degree, the readers because they form part of the implicit contract that determines the novel form. In thinking about her father's resentment toward Saturn for his pervasive vigilance of their lives, Little Merced begins to "feel her own resentment, not only toward Saturn, but also against those who stared down at the page, against those who followed sentences into her father's room and into his bed" (186).

24. Matthew Baker, "An Interview with Salvador Plascencia," *Nashville Review*, April 1, 2010, https://as.vanderbilt.edu/nashvillereview/archives/1084.

25. Raymond Williams, *Marxism and Literature* (Oxford: Oxford University Press, 1977), 78.

26. Ibid., 129.

27. Ibid., 121–27.

28. Ibid., 128–35.

29. Chris Harman, *Zombie Capitalism: Global Crisis and the Relevance of Marx* (Chicago: Haymarket Books, 2009), 292.

The Memoir in the Age of Neoliberal Individualism

DANIEL WORDEN

In his 1963 collection *The Presidential Papers,* Norman Mailer comments, "Once a newspaper touches a story, the facts are lost forever, even to the protagonists."[1] Mailer's critique of newspaper journalism uses the language of fiction to describe reality. Newspapers report "stories," not events, and those stories have "protagonists," not flesh-and-blood agents. Yet, Mailer's complaint seems to be less that newspapers willfully misrepresent facts than that newspapers can't tell good enough stories. In a draft of his 1968 book *The Armies of the Night,* Mailer writes, "Phenomenologically speaking, a newspaper is a dull social novel with a new draft put out daily by a factory of mediocre novelists."[2] By failing in literary terms, newspaper journalism also fails to convey any facts to the reader. Facts and fiction are not exclusive categories in Mailer's estimation; they are one and the same. If fiction is not factual, it's not a good story, and if facts are not arranged artfully, they lose their purchase on reality.

This understanding of fiction's claim on reality becomes dominant in the late twentieth century, especially in the works of the New Journalists, a disparate group of writers who turned to nonfiction prose as a profession and a literary form in the 1960s and 1970s and who would exert a tremendous influence on US literary and political culture. Perhaps because of the critique of representation associated with postmodernism in the 1980s and 1990s, the New Journalism remained largely a footnote to the major periodizing and conceptualizing works that established "postmodern literature." Even when texts like Mailer's *Armies of the Night* and Truman Capote's *In Cold Blood* are excerpted in the "fact meets fiction" section of the Norton anthology *Postmodern American Fiction,* they confirm the basic postmodernist thesis that reality becomes textual in the age of simulacrum.[3] The New Journalism, then, registers as a kind of minor tradition that mirrors postmodern metafiction, despite nonfiction's quite different representations of events, history, and reality as limitations to rather than licenses for literary imagination.

In recent years, though, literary nonfiction and the forms popularized by the New Journalists—Truman Capote's "non-fiction novel," Hunter S. Thompson's "gonzo journalism," Joan Didion's memoiristic approach to reportage, Tom Wolfe's intertwining of immersion and critical distance—have become unmistakably influential in literary culture. Especially in light of the "memoir boom" of the 1990s and 2000s, nonfiction prose forms have become both prominent in the literary marketplace and widely influential on contemporary writers who, even when they call their works "novels," write in the genre of the memoir. This turn to the memoir has occurred alongside a reevaluation of the legacy of postmodernism, as both critics and writers have increasingly turned to more explicitly economic categories like neoliberalism to periodize late twentieth and twenty-first-century literature. Accordingly, the focus on lived experience and material reality emphasized in the New Journalism, as opposed to the "history-as-text" play of the postmodern novel, is due a reevaluation as a major component of postwar literary history and the immediate context of the contemporary memoir boom.

In this essay, I will argue that the New Journalism articulates the affective structures of emergent neoliberalism, and in its propagation of the first-person voice and nonfiction form, memoir in our contemporary moment is uniquely outfitted to articulate the ways in which neoliberal reforms have isolated and limited, while championing and privileging, the individual. Using the stages of neoliberalism outlined in this book's introduction by Mitchum Huehls and Rachel Greenwald Smith, one could posit that the New Journalism, with its attention to political struggles (e.g., Joan Didion's coverage of the Black Panthers, Norman Mailer's reporting on the March on the Pentagon) and economics (e.g., the poverty-driven crime in Truman Capote's *In Cold Blood*, the Wall Street lives documented in *Money Game* by "Adam Smith"), captured the initial economic changes that occasioned neoliberalism. That is, the New Journalism documented the shift from an industrial economy to a finance economy and all of the attendant struggles that both occasioned and responded to that shift, or, as Joshua Clover has it, "capital's need for room to move beyond the industrial sector" in order to achieve "the average profit rate," a profit rate increasingly unavailable in industrial manufacturing in the United States by the 1970s.[4] The "memoir boom" and the literary uses of the memoir genre that occur in the 1990s and 2000s, then, reflect the cultural and ontological force of neoliberalism, as previous economic and political struggles recede, and the entrepreneurial idealism of free-market ideology is refracted as a solipsistic, isolated subject position, able to be reimagined and remade by a younger generation of writers for whom neoliberalism was not a series of reforms that happened during their young adulthood (as it was for the New Journalists), but a reality into which they were born.

Indeed, as Ben Yagoda remarks in his history of the genre's contemporary prominence, "memoir has become the central form of culture: not only the way stories are told, but the way arguments are put forth, products and properties marketed, ideas floated, acts justified, reputations constructed or salvaged."[5] As Yagoda notes, the "memoir boom" of the 1990s is exemplified by a handful of influential literary works, such as Tobias Wolff's *This Boy's Life: A Memoir* (1989), Mary Karr's *The Liar's Club: A Memoir* (1995), and Frank McCourt's *Angela's Ashes* (1996). The boom is also more notable for best sellers such as Susanna Kaysen's *Girl, Interrupted* (1993), Dave Pelzer's *A Child Called "It": One Child's Courage to Survive* (1993), Elizabeth Wurtzel's *Prozac Nation: Young and Depressed in America: A Memoir* (1994), and Frances Mayes's *Under the Tuscan Sun: At Home in Italy* (1996). These works from the twentieth century were followed in the twenty-first century by best sellers such as Augusten Burroughs's *Running with Scissors: A Memoir* (2002), Elizabeth Gilbert's *Eat Pray Love: One Woman's Search for Everything across Italy, India, and Indonesia* (2006), and James Frey's *A Million Little Pieces* (2003), initially sold as a memoir but relabeled a work of fiction after a prominent scandal and public dressing-down by Oprah Winfrey.[6]

The popular memoir has been an easy target for literary critics and cultural studies scholars, who view its vision of self-realization, its dramatization of suffering, and its emphasis on individual self-fashioning as evidence of memoir's privileging of the entrepreneurial individual. Along with reality television and "chick lit"—two other popular media forms that resonate as similarly invested in authenticity, suffering, and redemption, and that are also often associated with female readers and viewers—the memoir is typically viewed as a mere symptom of neoliberalism. For example, Walter Benn Michaels brands the memoir an "entirely Thatcherite genre," and Pamela Thoma has posited that the "culinary memoir," such as *Eat Pray Love* or Julie Powell's *Julie and Julia: 365 Days, 524 Recipes, 1 Tiny Apartment Kitchen* (2005), "is connected to the seemingly limitless demands for women's flexible labor in the marketplace and at home."[7] In her study of the memoir boom, Julie Rak argues that the memoir is a unique genre precisely because memoirs are "produced, and not just written. Memoir is a creative product . . . [it] can even be regarded as a brand produced by the publishing and book retailing industries."[8] Rak argues, too, that the memoir is an important site for the articulation of public values in our contemporary moment, and thus finds in the memoir a commodified and rigorously marketed iteration of the public discourse so central to Jürgen Habermas's or Michael Warner's accounts of the eighteenth century.[9] Despite their various approaches to the genre, all of the above critics seem to agree that the memoir matters not as literature but as a marker of something else: public ideals of citizenship in a fully commodified and branded literary marketplace, the privileging of moral character as a justification for economic inequality, or the promotion of neoliberal models of flexible labor and conventional gender roles. The memoir is a barometer of neoliberalism's idealization of entrepreneurial individualism, emphasis on constant production and consumption as markers of a good life, and erosion of the commons and public discourse. In short, the memoir is a neoliberal genre.

This account of the popular memoir is compelling, but the memoir's reach into literary culture is more diverse and complicated than an ever-growing number of best sellers adapted into Hollywood films or tell-all chronicles of B-list celebrities. In recent years, writers as diverse and varied in their forms, themes, and affiliations as Dave Eggers, Sheila Heti, Tao Lin, Maggie Nelson, Justin St. Germain, and Jesmyn Ward, to name but a celebrated few whom I will discuss in this essay, have turned to nonfiction forms and a more material orientation toward reality that emphasize economic and political limits. By viewing the contemporary memoir as an extension of the New Journalism, the memoir genre becomes visible as a literary mode that has, since neoliberalism's emergence and throughout its implementation, represented material necessities—the limits to economic growth, the narrowness of political engagement under neoliberalism, and the lack of upward mobility and individual wellness represented as widely available and desirable in venues like the *Oprah Winfrey Show*. From the New Journalism to the memoir boom, we can trace a cultural history of neoliberalism, from its uneven economic and political implementations to its establishment as an ontology that has also, by necessity, transformed literary culture.

Indeed, the New Journalism and neoliberalism's emergence (and dominance) coincide. Both emerge as movements in the 1970s and would be widely influential, if unevenly implemented in practice, from the 1980s through the 2000s. In this alternative literary history, one that links the New Journalism to emergent neoliberalism, rather than, say, postmodernism to globalization, the memoir boom is an outgrowth of the already-vibrant tradition of nonfiction prose in the late twentieth century, rather than a contemporary anomaly. If our immediate history is no longer postmodern but neoliberal, then the New Journalism matters as postwar literature in a way that it never has before. Indeed, literary works that employ tropes and tactics popularized by the New Journalism can stage the precarity and the devastations of life under neoliberalism. In this essay, I will argue that Joan Didion, a figure whose career bridges the New Journalism and the memoir boom, articulates a uniquely neoliberal subject position, one that captures the erosion of common meaning and the proliferation of the personal authorized by neoliberal reform. Extending yet also simplifying Didion's prose style, Dave Eggers makes explicit the political function of nonfiction prose and memoir under neoliberalism. Eggers's secondhand memoirs struggle with questions of authenticity and sincerity, while his recent novel *A Hologram for the King* figures Eggers's own memoiristic prose as a capitulation, rather than an alternative, to a neoliberal commitment to the promise of endless upward mobility and economic growth. In both Didion's and Eggers's prose, first-person voice, nonfiction form, and the memoir genre foreground both the disconnect between individuals and others and the ways in which the distance between individuals and others is a gap produced by impersonal structures. As I demonstrate in this essay, contemporary writers have represented these structures and their effects through memoiristic devices. These impersonal structures can be made visible in texts that trade in nonfiction forms and first-person voice.[10]

After all, if one of neoliberalism's cultural accomplishments has been the idealization and isolation of the entrepreneurial individual as the benchmark of success, then the first-person voice in literature might rise to ubiquity as a genre convention because it is simply how our culture thinks of itself. Insofar as this mode is widespread, writers might just as well strive to articulate alternative models of subjectivity as reinforce hegemonic subjectivity through the first-person voice. The memoir and its attendant conventions need not signal one relation to the neoliberal conditions that have occasioned their ubiquity. Charting the memoir's ties to the New Journalism of the 1960s and 1970s helps to make visible the political possibilities of the memoir, the ways in which nonfiction prose can represent central tensions of late capitalism rather than merely smooth out those tensions with an appeal to the palliative, authorial self.

Joan Didion and Fragmentation

For many New Journalists, such as Norman Mailer or Hunter S. Thompson, literary nonfiction fused aesthetic and political aspirations. This connection was a kind of survival mechanism, as both writer and reader witness the increasing failures of the New Left to produce the changes that it envisioned in the face of rising conservatism and increasing neoliberal reforms in the United States and internationally. Perhaps no New Journalist better exemplifies the fragmentation that these failures generate and the ties between the New Journalism and the memoir than Joan Didion. In his review of Didion's critically and popularly successful 2005 memoir *The Year of Magical Thinking*, John Leonard linked Didion's memoir, about her husband's death and her daughter's ultimately fatal illness, to her entire body of work, treating the book as a culmination of the style, affect, and relation to events that Didion had developed in her reportage and fiction. Along with that, Leonard concludes his review with a single-sentence paragraph: "I can't imagine dying without this book."[11] Both an astute prose stylist, known for her political detachment and cool reason, and an author of an essential guide to grief, life, and death, Didion's career itself demonstrates the stylistic, aesthetic, and social genealogy of the contemporary memoir in the New Journalism.

From her early essay collections to her recent grief memoirs, Didion's works explore the ways in which our political and social categories have become mere fictions within the shifting economic and political environments occasioned by neoliberal reforms, wherein categories like "citizen," "worker," "nation," and "union" have ceased to represent but instead offer a nostalgic vision of a past mode of capitalist accumulation. Didion's focus on the fragmentation between category and reality works in her prose in a number of ways. First of all, fragmentation operates at the level of content. Her work as a journalist includes essays about disparate topics, and her fiction—most notably *A Book of Common Prayer* (1977), *Democracy* (1984), and *Play It As It Lays* (1970)—draws on her journalism quite explicitly, be it in the descriptions of the renamed Salvadoran setting, Boca Grande, of *A Book of Common Prayer*, the dramatization of the CIA presence in Vietnam in *Democracy*, or the meditations on California highway and water systems in *Play It As It Lays*. In keeping with the first-person style of many New Journalists, Didion details her own life as a journalist in her nonfiction, and as she bounces from city to city and country to country on assignment, the only stable places in the United States and beyond become non-places such as hotel bars and airport lounges.

This first-person disorientation dominates Didion's journalism, and through that mode of focalization, Didion's prose dramatizes the experience of living under neoliberalism, living in a rapidly privatizing world. Similarly, her fiction is written in the first person, with a female narrator who is consciously writing the story being read, often troubled by her inability to make sense of the events and relationships that she is narrating. Both Didion's journalism and her fiction can then be read as experiential guides to US culture and US international entanglements in the late twentieth century, from San Francisco, Malibu, and Miami to Bogota, San Salvador, and Saigon. The interconnectedness of her fiction and nonfiction shatters any conventional literary taxonomy that would make a distinction between the real and the imaginative, the journalistic and the novelistic. Her literary style and the form that her prose takes use fragmentation as an organizing principle, bouncing from images and moments, denying the reader any singular or totalizing framework or explanation. This pastiche might produce a sense of totality within fragmentation, perhaps, but Didion leaves the resolution of the fragments to the reader. Moreover, her nonfiction prose circulated originally as single essays, published in glossy magazines or literary reviews, and was only later collected in book form. The unifying principle that underlies all of these varied types of fragmentation is literary style, the first-person voice that Didion adopts in both her journalism and fiction. This tension between style and fragmentation, between a unified, coherent narrative voice and that voice's dissolution as it articulates disparate and irresolute events, produces a literary form that captures key facets of neoliberalism: the privileging of entrepreneurial individualism, the privatization of public resources, and the proliferation of new, niche markets. Didion's prose registers the erosion of common meanings and the hyperindividualism fueled by neoliberal culture.

Upon the 2005 publication of her memoir *The Year of Magical Thinking*, Didion's career would reach a new height. Awarded the National Book Award for Nonfiction, named a finalist for the National Book Critics Circle Award and the Pulitzer Prize for Autobiography/Biography, and adapted into a stage play of the same name, in which Didion was played by Vanessa Redgrave, *The Year of Magical Thinking* documents the death of Didion's long-time husband John Gregory Dunne, the ultimately fatal illness of her daughter Quintana Roo Dunne Michael, and the author's process of grieving. In keeping with her earlier works' emphasis on narrative structures and their failures, Didion tries to make sense of her husband's death and her daughter's illness by reading books and analyzing life as one analyzes a work of literature, only to find no sense, no possible interpretation:

> I went to the UCLA Medical Center bookstore. I bought a book described on its cover as a "concise overview of neuroanatomy and of its function and clinical implications" . . . the book was by Stephen G. Waxman, M.D., chief of neurology at Yale–New Haven, and was called *Clinical Neuroanatomy*. I skimmed successfully through some of the appendices, for example "Appendix A: The Neurologic Examination," but when I began to read the text itself I could only think of a trip to Indonesia during which I had become disoriented by my inability to locate the grammar in

Bahasa Indonesia, the official language used on street signs and storefronts and billboards. . . . *Clinical Neuroanatomy* seemed to be one more case in which I would be unable to locate the grammar.[12]

What the memoir makes clear is that no amount of reading, no amount of research will make sense of what happened. Instead, the memoir concludes with a memory and an embrace of that memory's ephemerality, its detachment from any grand narrative or control:

> I think about swimming with him into the cave at Portuguese Bend, about the swell of clear water, the way it changed, the swiftness and power it gained as it narrowed through the rocks at the base of its point. The tide had to be just right. . . . Each time we did it I was afraid of missing the swell, hanging back, timing it wrong. John never was. You had to feel the swell change. You had to go with the change. He told me that. No eye is on the sparrow but he did tell me that.[13]

Didion's *The Year of Magical Thinking* and her follow-up memoir *Blue Nights* document fleeting moments that the author remembers, yet Didion refuses to give those moments significance. Instead, Didion presents them as mattering only to her, and as always at risk of being lost. As she writes at the end of *Blue Nights*, "the fear is for what is still to be lost."[14] Personal experience—the arbiter of truth in the age of neoliberalism—turns out to not document anything, to have no bearing on the events that determine a life, and to be in constant danger of being further eroded, further hollowed out. For all of the memoir's personality, the personal has no larger bearing, no larger meaning. The aesthetic function of memory in Didion's memoirs of loss is also a dramatization of memory's unimportance, of the personal's negligible status under a regime for which personal initiative is purportedly all.

Dave Eggers and Holograms

While Didion writes about the hollowness of the politics of the personal that authorize neoliberal reforms, Dave Eggers and his McSweeney's publishing ventures are dependent on valorizing the personal and the intimate, as the aesthetic category of the "New Sincerity" often invoked to discuss McSweeney's points out. A host of contemporary writers come to mind when one thinks of experimental riffs on the memoir—some of whom will be discussed in this essay—but Eggers has been centrally involved not just in the writing of but also in the publication of and activism surrounding contemporary literature that blurs memoir, novel, and nonfiction. After making a celebrated debut with the self-ironizing memoir

A Heartbreaking Work of Staggering Genius, Eggers has continued to use the tropes of the memoir even though he no longer writes about himself or his family. His two recent secondhand memoirs, *What Is the What* and *Zeitoun*, the former labeled a novel, the latter labeled a work of nonfiction, share a formal design that privileges the personal voice as the sole arbiter of experience, a design that conforms to the hyperindividualism of neoliberal culture, while trying to renew ethical bonds between reader, writer, and character.

What Is the What and *Zeitoun* both foreground their own constructedness, but *What Is the What* begins with a preface authored by Valentino Achak Deng, the only piece of the novel that purports to be his autobiography that is penned by him. In the preface, Deng describes the process by which the novel was researched and written:

> This book was born out of the desire on the part of myself and the author to reach out to others to help them understand the atrocities many successive governments of Sudan committed before and during the civil war. To that end, over the course of many years, I told my story orally to the author. He then concocted this novel, approximating my own voice and using the basic events of my life as the foundation. Because many of the passages are fictional, the result is called a novel. . . . This is simply one man's story, subjectively told.[15]

Deng and Eggers's shared desire to "reach out to others" forms the basis for the text, a text that is classified as a novel because of its subjectivity, the very quality that also, of course, registers as a kind of aesthetic, if not factual, truth and authenticity. The novelized memoir, then, serves as an overtly activist form, an incitement by the author and subject to make sure that, in Deng's words, the readers of the novel do something "to prevent the same horrors from repeating themselves."[16] The expansiveness of Deng and Eggers's desire renders the text a kind of broad, sincere hope and faith in the potential of life narrative to produce recognition and change. As Deng narrates at the closing of the novel, "Whatever I will do, I will find a way to live, I will tell these stories. I have spoken to every person I have encountered these last difficult days, and every person who has entered this club [the gym where he works] during these awful morning hours, because to do anything else would be something less than human. I speak to these people, and I speak to you because I cannot help it. It gives me strength, almost unbelievable strength, to know that you are there."[17] This ethical, mutually empowering relation among text, subject, and author marks the formal aspiration of *What Is the What* and, arguably, Eggers's work more generally—the aspiration to produce a text that will function as an intimate, ethical interface, a connection that then transforms moral obligation into the pleasure of labor for the collective good.

If *What Is the What* is the utopian, expansive version of the memoir, then *Zeitoun* moves in a more cynical direction. A book that is described not as a novel but as a work of nonfiction, *Zeitoun* is written in the third person, and while it has the same expansiveness of possibility as *What Is the What*, the narrative also undercuts its own faith in the aesthetic/ethical bond generated by nonfiction narrative. Beginning with epigraphs from Cormac McCarthy's *The Road* ("in the history of the world it might even be that there was more punishment than crime") and Mark Twain ("To a man with a hammer, everything looks like a nail"), *Zeitoun* foregrounds cynicism and violence.[18] The book is about Abdulrahman Zeitoun, a contractor who survives Hurricane Katrina in New Orleans. Zeitoun works to rebuild New Orleans in its aftermath, yet ultimately, and in keeping with the book's epigraphs, the narrator finds in Zeitoun's survival and commitment to work something tragic and sad. Strikingly, the text concludes much like *What Is the What*, with the articulation of a renewed ethical commitment:

> As he drives through the city by day and dreams of it at night, his mind vaults into glorious reveries—he envisions this city and this country not just as it was, but better, far better. It can be. . . . There is much work to do, and we all know what needs to be done. . . . So let us get up early and stay late, and, brick by brick and block by block, let us get that work done. If he can picture it, it can be. This has been the pattern of his life: ludicrous dreams followed by hours and days and years of work and then a reality surpassing his wildest hopes and expectations.[19]

Once again, the text concludes with an aspirational commitment to a better world. But, then, *Zeitoun*'s final sentence is a question: "And so why should this be any different?" This closing question does not affirm Zeitoun's faith in hard work but makes it clear that Zeitoun's optimism, however admirable, also entails an amnesia—that Katrina and its aftermath "diminished the humanity of them all."[20] Kathy, Zeitoun's wife, seems to cope with this through memory loss: "It's shredded, unreliable. The wiring in her mind has been snapped in vital places."[21] Eggers's narration of heroic, optimistic, ethical individuality falters in *Zeitoun*, as it becomes clear that the difference at the conclusion of the text is that Zeitoun's work ethic is misguided, clearly unsuited and insufficient to realize his dreams of upward mobility.

Like *What Is the What*, *Zeitoun* also begins with a caveat—that "this book does not attempt to be an all-encompassing book about New Orleans or Hurricane Katrina. It is only an account of one family's experiences before and after the storm."[22] Eggers's prefacing in both texts diffuses what Kenneth Goldsmith has described as the deeply uninteresting question of authenticity that plagues literature and, especially, the memoir today, mainly by making authenticity a function of form.[23] Eggers's memoirs call attention to their constructedness, thereby making clear that a text cannot conform to reality in an easy, mimetic relationship. Despite this careful prefacing, *Zeitoun*, like Eggers's *Heartbreaking Work of Staggering Genius* before it, became the subject of some controversy in 2012 when, contrary to Eggers's depiction of him as a loving husband, Abdulrahman Zeitoun was arrested for assaulting his wife (he was acquitted in 2013). Moreover, the formal caveats and explanations at the beginning of both texts serve to formalize the ethical commitment of the text. For that is, after all, what Eggers's texts hinge on—the incitement of ethical action on the part of the reader. This is, arguably, the goal of much "historiographical metafiction," but Eggers's difference lies in his laying bare the neoliberal impetus of such a formal imperative. Rather than provoking some vague sense of victimhood, historical tragedy, or imperative that human rights violations happen "never again," *What Is the What* and *Zeitoun* force the reader to exit through the gift shop, as it were. The final pages of each text contain information about charities to support, making the ethical cast of the memoir and witnessing overtly economic rather than merely emotional.

Eggers's two secondhand memoirs are compelling for the way that they lay bare the instrumentality of literature in the service of ethics, and thus they implicitly brand a wide swath of contemporary literature a kind of literature of bad faith, insofar as it elicits a similar ethical response but without a proper channel for individual investment or expenditure. His recent novel, *A Hologram for the King*, meditates on the question of what might be done to restore a sense of productivity, belonging, even dignity to white-collar workers increasingly downtrodden and exploited during the economic "downturn" of 2008. Pico Iyer, in the *New York Times Book Review*, celebrated Eggers's *Hologram* as a kind of " 'Death of a Globalized Salesman,' alight with all of Arthur Miller's compassion and humanism," and one can see how this is an easy position to take on a novel that is preoccupied with its central character.[24] The generically yet symbolically named "Alan Clay" signifies both middle-manager whiteness and the malleability that is expected in today's economy of any worker. The novel does indeed dwell on Alan Clay's failing prospects, as in this moment, when he is worrying about having enough money to pay his daughter's college tuition: "Had he planned better, had he not been so incompetent, he would have whatever she needed. He had twenty years to save $200k. How hard was that? It was ten thousand a year. Much less assuming any interest on the money. . . . He thought he could make the $200k at will, in any given year. How could he have predicted the world losing interest in people like him?"[25] What this passage points to, though, is less the novel's fixation on eulogizing or even romanticizing the corporate employee than the novel's insistence that the individual's voice, privileged by the literary form of the memoir and the regime of neoliberalism, no longer functions as a site of aspiration. The novel concludes with Alan Clay in the empty King Abdullah Economic City in Saudi Arabia, a pet project of the Arab nation's ruler, but one never fully realized. Alan is there, initially, to sell hologram technology to the king, but his US-based company loses out to a Chinese firm. Alan decides to stay in the built but unpopulated city, and the novel's titular technology, the hologram, functions both as a plot point and as a figure for the forms of spectral presence that the memoir and Eggers's literary aesthetic attempt to generate. At the novel's conclusion, Alan gambles on his future usefulness to the king, the king who has never appeared. "He had to hope for amnesia," the narrator remarks, both his own amnesia and that of his potential audience. Amnesia would mean that Clay's own failure to succeed in the global economy would result not in disillusionment, but in a renewed effort to become a properly entrepreneurial individual. Amnesia allows for the renewed production of personhood, a personhood that looks much more like a hologram than a flesh-and-blood agent. Clay's hologram serves as a figure for Eggers's own aesthetic project—the production of a spectral presence that promises a better world, a better world that, it turns out, cannot be articulated or even thought through the compromised, aspirationally neoliberal individual.

The Memoiristic and the Nonfictional in Contemporary Literature

Eggers's *A Hologram for the King* questions the sincere aesthetics and politics of his secondhand memoirs, and other contemporary writers employ the memoir to represent the often hidden reality of limits in our contemporary moment—limits to economic growth, limits to upward mobility, limits to individual desire and initiative. In many works of contemporary literature that either are explicitly memoirs or use the genre of the memoir while labeling themselves fiction, disconnection and irony become figures for thinking of literature's relationship to the reader and, more broadly, for individuals' connection to each other in the age of neoliberalism. Like Eggers in *What Is the What*, the great theorist of autobiography Philippe LeJeune and the great champion of literary identification Oprah Winfrey find in the memoir a marker of authenticity and the chance for the reader's self-realization through intimate contact with an other—that is, they offer an ethical account of the memoir. Contrary to this dominant understanding of the memoir, many contemporary writers seem to seize on the memoir to dramatize the inability to even formulate an ethical bond with others.[26] These works represent human relations—including relations between the reader and the writer—as impersonal and structural rather than as personal and ethical, and as limited by material realities often thought to be fluid by free-market ideology.

These contemporary, memoiristic works often stage human relations in repetitive, rule-bound, and ultimately irresolute scenes, dramatizing the lack of closure, the inability to realize something about the self, and the incapacity for subjects to identify with one another in our neoliberal era. Moreover, these scenes of disidentification and irresolution depend on descriptions of material limits, juxtaposing the fluidity and flexibility of the neoliberal subject to the structures of inequality that facilitate and constrict what counts as human action and thought.

For example, in the concluding chapter of Sheila Heti's *How Should a Person Be? A Novel from Life* (2012), the narrator, named Sheila, watches two of her friends play squash. The two friends, Margaux and Sholem, are both painters, and they have decided to let a squash game decide which one of them won the "Ugly Painting Competition" that the friends had decided to hold. Sheila is "really eager to know who would win," so she comes along.[27] At the squash court, the game begins:

> The game went very slowly at first, then grew more and more focused. Soon Margaux and Sholem were running back and forth, breathing very heavily. They smacked the ball against the wall, dodged into each other's part of the court, and slammed against the back wall, groaning. They nodded briefly when the other made a good move. They rubbed sweat from their brows and hit the ball too high. They ran forward and bent low, and at one point Sholem threw himself to the ground. Margaux followed the rolling ball, walking very slowly, and tossed it to Sholem to serve. He smacked it high in the air and ran to the edge of the court and missed.[28]

After this goes on for "about half an hour," Sheila and her friends realize that they don't know the score. They focus their attention on the game, "but none of us could hear anything from below except for explosions of laughter, moans, and cursing, and Sholem saying, 'Fuck! I hate this fucking game!' / We remained very still, and we watched. Then finally Jon said, in his sweetly caustic drawl, 'I don't think they even know the rules. I think they're just slamming the ball around.' / And so they were."[29] The semblance of a game that is merely the pained exertions of two artists is a fitting representation of the "New Sincerity" aesthetic often associated with the McSweeney's school and our memoir culture more broadly. Artists are expected to suffer for us. Yet, Heti's novel represents this game as a process—a game without rules that is nonetheless played as if it has rules comes to look more like art and less like competition. The circumscription of the scene—the court, the rackets, the ball, the walls, the players—frames the game, like a painting, photograph, or play, as an aesthetic pursuit. Concluding with this game still in progress, Heti's memoiristic novel arrives not at a unified self but instead at a recognition of how external forces determine the self.

A related sense of directionless action, of a structured activity that, in fact, has no meaning and no end point, occurs in the opening chapter of Tao Lin's 2013 novel *Taipei*, narrated by Paul, a New York–based, Taiwanese American writer who, at one point in the novel, gives a public reading where he reads one of Tao Lin's own poems, making the connection between author and narrator explicit. On an airplane going to Taipei, Paul thinks about Taipei as an alternative to life in America:

> On the plane, after a cup of black coffee, Paul thought of Taipei as a fifth season, or "otherworld," outside, or in equal contrast with, his increasingly familiar and self-consciously repetitive life in America, where it seemed like the seasons, connecting in right angles, for some misguided reason, had formed a square, sarcastically framing nothing—or been melded, Paul vaguely imagined, about an hour later, face-down on his arms on his dining tray, into a door-knocker, which a child, after twenty to thirty knocks, no longer expecting an answer, has continued using, in a kind of daze, distracted by the pointlessness of his activity, looking absently elsewhere, unaware when he will abruptly, idly stop.[30]

As with the squash match that closes Heti's *How Should a Person Be?*, Lin's image of a child at the door knocker finds in the self only repetition within confining limitations, limits that are recognized by the participant and the narrator but unable to be transcended. Here, the memoiristic allows for the recognition of a narrow frame, the way in which the effusive self is circumscribed by the promise of unlimited play.

In Maggie Nelson's 2009 book *Bluets*, a collection of 240 prose pieces about the color blue written in the first person, the color blue, as well as other colors, becomes shorthand, a way of describing complex structures that pull us away from the world rather than attaching our language to it: "Fifteen days after we are born, we begin to discriminate between colors. For the rest of our lives, barring blunted or blinded sight, we find ourselves face-to-face with all these phenomena at once, and we call the whole shimmering mess 'color.' You might even say it is the business of the eye to make colored forms out of what is essentially shimmering. This is how we 'get around' in the world. Some might call it the source of our suffering."[31] *Bluets* dwells on how, as Nelson articulates it in an essay, "the most seemingly immaterial forces are, in fact, material."[32] This material basis for our perceptions, for our livelihoods, for our literary and aesthetic pleasures, when acknowledged, places the reader in a new awareness of her surroundings, a new space to contemplate the stubborn materiality of our world, often characterized as fluid, networked, immaterial.

This emphasis on material limits—a squash court, a door knock never to be answered, the shimmering relations that we reduce to the idea of "blue"—is the political accomplishment of nonfiction prose under neoliberalism. The juxtaposition of idealism and the self with material limits functions as an aesthetically inflected ideology critique, a bringing back from the flows of the free market into the stubborn material realities of neoliberalism's actual effects on society and the limits neoliberal institutions and legislation place on individuals. The most striking example of how nonfiction can represent this, in a way that gestures back to the New Journalism, is in a work of nonfiction reportage. Adrian Nicole LeBlanc's *Random Family* is painstakingly researched narrative journalism about a poor family in the Bronx. At the end of *Random Family*, a mother and her daughters visit the daughters' father, Cesar, who is going to be in jail for a long time still:

> Toward the end of the visit, Nautica begged Cesar to give her a pony ride, as he had when she was little, where he bounced her like a piece of popcorn on his knees. He did—for a good ten minutes. Then he held her lengthwise like a barbell and pushed her into the air. Mercedes watched, her awe and longing clear. When Cesar began to spin Nautica around, Mercedes couldn't contain her desire. "Can you do that to me?" she asked breathlessly.
>
> She caught herself as quickly, and her expression turned stony. The hope became a dare. Since she was a baby, no one had been able, or willing, to carry her. She weighed 130 pounds now.
>
> Cesar placed Nautica down and squatted before Mercedes. Drawing out the moment, he rubbed his chin. Then, very seriously, he examined his big hands. He measured the width of his grip below Mercedes's knees. Mercedes had braced herself for rejection; then, the next thing she knew, she was up in the air. She went rigid with excitement and terror. "No, *Daddy!*" she shrieked giddily.
>
> He adjusted her on his shoulders. She clutched his hair and dug her legs into his armpits. Then he paraded his daughter around the honor room and into the regular visiting area, where they took another lap past the inmates, who smiled and nodded as Cesar introduced his oldest girl. He pushed out the door to the enclosed cement courtyard. An April wind had whipped up, and everything was flying, so he quickly ducked back inside, exaggerating the drop as they went over the threshold.

"*Daddyyy!*" Mercedes squealed, nearly losing her balance. She regained it as he steadied. He headed back to their table, where Nautica grinned and Coco gazed up at them, like a little girl in awe of a Christmas tree. Mercedes was trying not to smile but she couldn't help it. "I'm going to fall! Daddy! I'm too heavy!" she said urgently.

"Relax, I ain't going to drop you, don't worry," Cesar assured her. He's been lift-ing weights almost daily for the last five years. To himself, he said, "Listen, you light as a feather to me."[33]

The lyricism of the passage and its use of dialogue, free indirect discourse, and explication all contribute to a heart-warming effect. It is hard for a book to make me cry, but this one does it every time. My response, though, has less to do with what is on the page than the looming reality that the book sets up prior to this scene: Cesar is going to drop his daughter, figuratively. He is in prison, and even if he gets out, there is little for him in the world that awaits outside, a world of poverty, limited opportunities, and broken social services. The affective reach of this passage is not personal, but structural. I cry not for Cesar, but for the broken social world that Cesar has no choice but to inhabit, that we all have no choice but to inhabit in one way or another.

In a 2013 interview marking the ten-year anniversary of *Random Family*'s pub-lication, LeBlanc reflected on the book's reception: "I often felt disturbed that readers were surprised by the experiences of the people in the book. Many are shocked, I think, to discover that people in poverty have complicated, meaningful lives—in other words, that the people in the book are, in fact, human beings."[34] This humanity is a function not of identification and recognition, but of identi-fication's estrangement from the text. In Justin St. Germain's recent memoir *Son of a Gun*, about the murder of his mother by his stepfather, he writes about watch-ing his mother watch herself on television. A neighbor was murdered by her husband, and St. Germain's mother was interviewed by the local news. St. Ger-main remarks, "She'd never been on TV before, and she asked us if that was how she really looked, if that was her real voice. She didn't recognize herself."[35] This passage is a metatextual moment, a reference to St. Germain's own representa-tion of his mother's murder, and St. Germain's awareness that his mother might not find herself recognizable in the pages of this book about her. Articulating a similar idea in her recent memoir *Men We Reaped*, a chronicle and memorial of the many young African American men the author knew who died young, Jesmyn Ward writes, "There is a great darkness bearing down on our lives, and no one acknowledges it."[36] At once a reference to institutionalized racism, crime, and drug abuse stemming from a lack of opportunities and the erosion of public education and other services, Ward's sentence, like St. Germain's passage above, stages the major accomplishment of literary nonfiction—the representation of neoliberal structures and their reorganization of our everyday lives. The memoir and nonfiction prose at their best estrange us from ourselves and make visible the structures that produce our subjectivities, the rules that bind us to a way of life that is in constant crisis yet also shows no sign of ebbing.

NOTES

1. Norman Mailer, *The Presidential Papers* (New York: Berkley, 1970), 18.
2. Norman Mailer, "The Armies of the Night, Handwritten Draft," 1967–68, Folder 2, Box 77, Norman Mailer Papers, Harry Ransom Center, University of Texas at Austin.
3. See Paula Geyh, Fred G. Leebron, and Andrew Levy, eds., *Postmodern American Fiction: A Norton Anthology* (New York: Norton, 1997).
4. Joshua Clover, *Riot Strike Riot: The New Era of Uprisings* (New York: Verso, 2016), 132.
5. Ben Yagoda, *Memoir: A History* (New York: Riverhead, 2009), 28.
6. For a reading of the James Frey controversy, see Julie Rak, *Boom! Manufacturing Memoir for the Popular Market* (Waterloo, ON: Wilfrid Laurier University Press, 2013), 179–205.
7. See Walter Benn Michaels, "Going Boom," *Bookforum*, February/March 2009, www.bookforum.com; and Pamela Thoma, "What Julia Knew: Domestic Labor in the Recession-Era Chick Flick," in *Gendering the Recession: Media and Culture in an Age of Austerity*, ed. Diane Negra and Yvonne Tasker (Durham, NC: Duke University Press, 2014), 130. See also Leigh Gilmore, "American Neoconfessional: Memoir, Self-Help, and Redemption on Oprah's Couch," *Biography* 33, no. 4 (Fall 2010): 657–79; Ruth Williams, "*Eat, Pray, Love*: Producing the Female Neoliberal Spiritual Subject," *Journal of Popular Culture* 47, no. 3 (June 2014): 613–33; and, for a related take on reality television, Anna McCarthy, "Reality Television: A Neoliberal Theater of Suffering," *Social Text* 25, no. 4 (Winter 2007): 17–41.
8. Rak, *Boom!*, 44.
9. See Jürgen Habermas, *The Structural Transformation of the Public Sphere: An Inquiry into a Category of Bourgeois Society*, trans. Thomas Burger (Cambridge, MA: MIT Press, 1991); and Michael Warner, *The Letters of the Republic: Publication and the Public Sphere in Eighteenth-Century America* (Cambridge, MA: Harvard University Press, 1990).
10. Walter Benn Michaels's work on neoliberalism and aesthetics has been influential on my thinking, though Michaels's ultimate emphasis on the importance of unity and autonomy privileges abstract art, chiefly photography and experimental poetry. I am more interested in prose that more directly grapples with, rather than abstractly gestures to, the affective, cultural, economic, and social effects of neoliberalism. See Walter Benn Michaels, *The Beauty of a Social Problem: Photography, Autonomy, Economy* (Chicago: University of Chicago Press, 2015).
11. John Leonard, "The Black Album," *New York Review of Books*, October 20, 2005, www.nybooks.com/articles/2005/10/20/the-black-album/.
12. Joan Didion, *The Year of Magical Thinking* (New York: Knopf, 2005), 104.
13. Ibid., 227.

14. Joan Didion, *Blue Nights* (New York: Knopf, 2011), 188.

15. Dave Eggers, *What Is the What* (San Francisco: McSweeney's, 2006), 5.

16. Ibid.

17. Ibid., 474–75.

18. Dave Eggers, *Zeitoun* (San Francisco: McSweeney's, 2009), 7.

19. Ibid., 335.

20. Ibid., 246.

21. Ibid., 303.

22. Ibid., 9.

23. See Kenneth Goldsmith, *Uncreative Writing: Managing Language in the Digital Age* (New York: Columbia University Press, 2011), esp. 6–8.

24. Pico Iyer, "Desert Pitch: 'A Hologram for the King' by Dave Eggers," *New York Times Book Review*, July 19, 2012, www.nytimes.com/2012/07/22/books/review/a-hologram-for -the-king-by-dave-eggers.html.

25. Dave Eggers, *A Hologram for the King* (San Francisco: McSweeney's, 2012), 135.

26. See Philippe Lejeune, *On Autobiography*, ed. Paul John Eakin, trans. Katherine Leary (Minneapolis: University of Minnesota Press, 1989), esp. 3–30; on Oprah Winfrey, see Janice Peck, *The Age of Oprah: Cultural Icon for a Neoliberal Era* (Boulder, CO: Paradigm, 2008), esp. 175–210.

27. Sheila Heti, *How Should a Person Be? A Novel from Life* (New York: Henry Holt, 2012), 305.

28. Ibid., 305–6.

29. Ibid., 306.

30. Tao Lin, *Taipei* (New York: Vintage, 2013), 16.

31. Maggie Nelson, *Bluets* (Seattle: Wave, 2009), 20.

32. Maggie Nelson, "All That Is the Case: Some Thoughts on Fact in Nonfiction and Documentary Poetry," in *Lit from Within: Contemporary Masters on the Art and Craft of Writing*, ed. Kevin Haworth and Dinty W. Moore (Athens: Ohio University Press, 2011), 156.

33. Adrian Nicole LeBlanc, *Random Family: Love, Drugs, Trouble, and Coming of Age in the Bronx* (New York: Scribner, 2003), 403–4.

34. Anna Altman and Katia Bachko, "'Random Family' Ten Years On: An Interview with Adrian Nicole LeBlanc," *New Yorker*, July 26, 2013, www.newyorker.com/books/page -turner/random-family-ten-years-on-an-interview-with-adrian-nicole-leblanc.

35. Justin St. Germain, *Son of a Gun: A Memoir* (New York: Random House, 2013), 95.

36. Jesmyn Ward, *Men We Reaped: A Memoir* (New York: Bloomsbury, 2013), 250.

PART III

NEOLIBERALISM AND LITERARY REPRESENTATION

The Perpetual Fifties of American Fiction

MATTHEW WILKENS

If there's a core to the critical concept of neoliberalism, it must be that the market has come to define a horizon of possibility for contemporary thought. What's troubling about that fact then isn't really the triumph of the market as such, but the naturalization of market forces in ways that shut down nearly all avenues of resistance. Fighting the market has come to make about as much sense as fighting gravity. You can do it, in the sense that you can build an airplane to leave the ground, for a time. But what does that mean? Only that you can use the existing structure for ends it already provides. Airplanes don't defy gravity; they work with it. In the economic case, there's a market niche for antimarket goods and services, but that's hardly the same thing as a position outside of or antagonistic to the market itself.

That's the theory, anyway, one that fits with the last, "ontological" stage of neoliberalism, as Mitchum Huehls and Rachel Greenwald Smith define it in the introduction to this volume. If this model is true, it should have direct consequences for the form and content of contemporary cultural production, literature included. We know, for example, that the geography of economic output changed markedly over the course of the twentieth century as markets became much more globally integrated. Did literary geography globalize in similar ways and at similar times? I think it should have, if we take seriously the horizon-of-thought interpretation of neoliberalism. Not that the two should have moved in lockstep, of course, but we would expect to find some sort of positive correlation between them on relatively short timescales. If a large fraction of the world's economy moves to China and India, we should see literature pay more attention to those countries. This is true not so much because literature is driven by economic concerns—some of it is, but we don't need to assume that the economy per se is a central literary concern to see the same effect—but because the neoliberal situation from which contemporary fiction is produced takes the functions of the market as its structuring parameters. This is a long-winded way of saying that the neoliberal world looks like the market. If the market changes, say, by becoming more globally dispersed, then so does the world. We'd then expect literature to change along with it, assuming a basic commitment to representational realism.

The alternative is that the neoliberal order covers its tracks, so to speak, through ideology. But why would that be the case? It doesn't comport especially closely with either the theory or the experience of late capitalism. We know perfectly well that China and India are major economic powers, and there's no need for market forces to hide their prominence. In fact, the horizon-of-possibility interpretation assures us that an older version of ideological power, one in which the members of the base are unaware of the superstructure's machinations and of the true material conditions of their existence, has been replaced by an open and direct embrace of the fetishized market. Neoliberalism, then, necessarily works against statist or national politics as principles of organization, since such politics inter-rupt the frictionless necessity of the global market. It would thus be surprising to find that contemporary fiction failed to align, in one way or another, more closely with the current distribution of the global economy than did the literature of ear-lier generations.

So we have a relatively clear framework for contemplating the literary effects of neoliberalism. How would we set about evaluating it? The conventional an-swer would be to read a handful of books that, for one reason or another, we be-lieve are especially indicative of neoliberal thinking at work. That could take us a long way, as many of the other contributions to this volume demonstrate. But it doesn't malign such work to observe that there are a couple of reasons we might want additional methods in the present case. For one thing, we worry a bit about cherry-picking. There are a lot of books; most of them are unknown to us.[1] We wouldn't need an ounce of bad faith to find ourselves with a selection of texts that doesn't look much like the bulk of what's been written over the past century or so. For another, the market-normalizing or market-routinizing effects of neolib-eralism are the sort of thing we'd expect to find suffused throughout literary pro-duction as a whole. By this I mean that while any one book might or might not engage with some aspect of the global economy, the conception of neoliberalism as a horizon of thought means that the baseline of economic embodiment in fiction ought to have shifted in recent decades, perhaps by a small amount, but specifically across the whole of literary output—on average, as it were. That is to say that contemporary fiction, taken in sum, should be at least a bit more closely aligned with economic factors than it was fifty or a hundred years ago, since the economy has lately come to play a more central role in our perception of the world around us.

We're talking, then, about a method to assess economic alignment and to do so over a significant sample of twentieth-century fiction. There's no way to do this by traditional means, since there's no way to read a significant sample of twentieth-century fiction. Taking the second part first, we need to assemble a sizable body of fiction, one that's plausibly representative of post-1900 literature in general, and we need to identify features of those books that a computer can process. We need easily countable data not because it's objective or nonideological or somehow more true than features that are hard to count—it's none of those things, and ideology isn't the point anyway—but because things that are hard to count are also slow to count, meaning that they don't scale well. If the idea is to examine a large-scale phenomenon in a large-scale corpus, we need a method that doesn't require days to carry out for each book, nor days more per book to repeat when we decide to look for some other feature that we didn't examine the first time.

A lot of things are countable and computable about books these days: words, first and foremost, along with the contexts in which they appear and the linguistic company they keep. A computational approach could be as simple as searching for specific terms or as complex as finding statistically co-occurring topic clusters, but it makes sense, in the present case, to pursue a path between those extremes. Terms alone likely aren't enough, both because they require us to know in advance what we're looking for (indeed, what *are* the terms most indicative of the achieved expression of neoliberal thought in millions of texts we haven't read?) and because we have to worry about polysemy and linguistic drift over time. More statistically sophisticated approaches to content analysis don't require as much a priori knowledge, but it's still hard to know to what extent a cluster of terms related to getting and spending, say, indicates market engagement in the relevant and consistent sense across multiple decades.

What I propose instead is an approach based on the type of literary-geographic attention I mentioned above: identify the places that are used in twentieth-century fiction and examine how their distribution changes over time alongside geographic shifts in economic output. This approach certainly doesn't avoid all of the difficulties associated with term- and topic-based approaches, but it has the merit of using a symptomatic textual feature that's relatively easy to identify, that suffers fewer (although not zero, of course) obvious issues of polysemy than do some directly market-related terms, and about which it's possible to form an explicit expectation concerning its relationship to economic change.

This isn't to say that geography is uniquely telling in either the literary or the

economic case. What's ultimately of interest is the changing relationship between markets and culture. Geography just happens to be a useful feature linking shifts in economic output to changes in cultural representation, a feature that
we can assess more easily than some others. And that's no small thing! After all,
one of the ways we often justify literary study in general is to point out that books
allow us to see things about a society that would be hard to perceive otherwise,
even (or maybe especially) if they do it indirectly. The relationship between economic and literary geography works in the same way, just on a larger scale.

To be as clear as possible at the outset: the interpretation of neoliberalism that
I've offered has as a consequence the expectation that literary-geographic usage
will have become more closely aligned with economic geography over the course
of the twentieth century. It's the trend that's more important than the absolute
correlation between the two; it may be the case that literary geography doesn't
line up very well with economic geography overall, but we'd expect the two to
have come closer together as the market increasingly defined a horizon of possibility for understanding the world in the later part of the century. To preview the
result: this trend is only very weakly and inconsistently borne out in a corpus of
about ten thousand American novels published between 1880 and 1990, a finding that casts some (inconclusive, I hasten to add, but suggestive) doubt on the
horizon-of-possibility interpretation of the neoliberal hypothesis.

Assembling a Corpus and Methods

To build a more or less representative subset of twentieth-century American fiction, we queried WorldCat for the most widely held volumes of fiction published
in the United States between the late nineteenth century and the present day.[2]
From these, we sampled roughly the top ten thousand as ranked by the total number of libraries holding at least one copy. For reference, the most widely held title
was *Beloved* by Toni Morrison; toward the bottom of the list were long-forgotten
nonclassics like *42 Days for Murder* by Roger Torrey (Goodreads has heard of it;
Wikipedia and I have not), as well as minor works by better-known writers (Theodore Dreiser's *A Hoosier Holiday* is close to my own heart, if not, apparently, to
many others'). Biographical information was then assembled by hand for every
included author in order to assign national origin. The final working corpus contained 8,971 volumes authored by Americans and published between 1880 and
1990.[3] These texts amounted in sum to just shy of one billion words. Google
Ngram data were used to check results for the period 1991–2008 where appropriate. Figure 1 shows the distribution of words per year in the corpus; note in
particular the impact of copyright in suppressing library holdings after 1923.

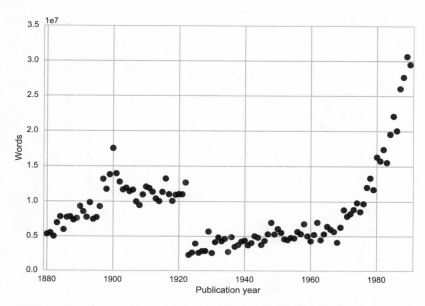

Figure 1. Words per year in the working corpus, from a representative subset of American fiction published between 1880 and 1990.

Location references were extracted from the texts and matched with geographic data via a process previously described.[4] Briefly, the Stanford named entity recognizer was used to identify strings of words used in each text as locations.[5] These strings were then processed through Google's geocoding interface, which returned structured information about each location, including its type, the political-administrative regions containing it, and its precise latitude and longitude coordinates. I reviewed the results of both processes by hand to the extent possible, though a total output of more than three million location occurrences precluded individual examination. Major locations were essentially always correct: "Boston" means the city in Massachusetts; "Japan" is a country in Asia. "Cambridge" and "Charlotte" are trickier, though for different reasons. In such potentially ambiguous cases, the pattern of other locations in each volume was used to select the proper referent, be it a place or an exclusion (in the case of mistakenly identified character names). The corrected results show an accuracy of about 90 percent against a human-coded test set. This is good, but not perfect; it's worth bearing in mind that some noise remains in the final data.

Figure 2 shows the number of occurrences aggregated by nation (that is, all mentions of the nation itself and of any locations within its borders) in the full

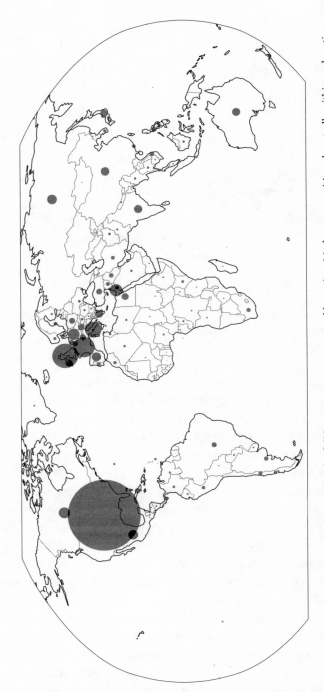

Figure 2. Geographical locations referenced in the full literary corpus, aggregated by nation. Markers are positioned centrally within each nation; marker area corresponds to total number of occurrences.

corpus. Note the extent to which the United States and Great Britain dominate the literary-geographic imagination. I'll have more to say about this below.

For economic data, I have relied on historical GDP (gross domestic product) figures as reported by the Maddison Project.[6] Historical economic data are harder to come by than you might imagine, and historical GDP numbers have all the problems of GDP calculations in general, plus those introduced by the mists of time. But it's hard to find an obviously better proxy for economic importance even today, especially if we want one that also covers the nineteenth and early twentieth centuries.[7] Modern economic statistics are largely a product of the post–World War II period, meaning that few continuously tabulated series extend back beyond about 1950. The Maddison Project collates and harmonizes disparate research in economic history to produce comparable, continuous, and inflation-adjusted GDP series based on purchasing power parity from 1800 through the present. So while we need to be clear that GDP isn't quite a holistic measure of economic production or a perfect stand-in for relative economic significance (to say nothing of cultural prominence or national well-being), it's about the best we can do, especially for the period before World War II. Like place-name mentions as a measure of literary attention, GDP share is an accessible if imperfect symptom of economic weight.[8] The Maddison GDP numbers are summarized in figure 3 for ten large nations (China, Germany, France, the United Kingdom, India, Italy, Japan, Mexico, Russia, and the United States) that appear often in the literary data and have significant contemporary total GDP.[9]

It's also possible to examine raw GDP, of course, but those figures are less useful, both because the numbers are comparatively very small before the last few decades of the twentieth century and, more importantly, because literary-geographic attention is a mostly fixed resource. By that I mean that the number of location references per million literary words is essentially flat over time, so we shouldn't expect to see far more references to, say, Italy just because Italian GDP grew by an inflation-adjusted factor of 17 between 1900 and 2000. The relevant economic measure is each nation's share of total GDP rather than the level of GDP itself.

A few things stand out in figure 3. One is that China had the largest economy in the world until the late nineteenth century, when the United States overtook it. India's GDP was similar to Britain's for much of the nineteenth and early twentieth centuries (although per capita numbers were another matter). World War II did bad things to Germany's economy, as did the collapse of the Soviet Union to Russia's. The US economy emerged from World War II in comparatively good shape, globally speaking, and maintained a historically elevated share of overall

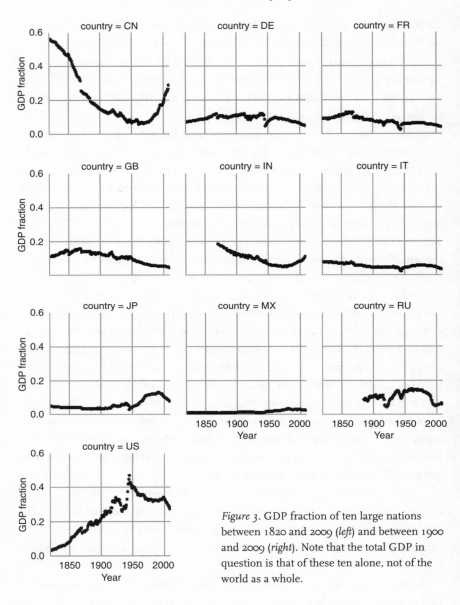

Figure 3. GDP fraction of ten large nations between 1820 and 2009 (*left*) and between 1900 and 2009 (*right*). Note that the total GDP in question is that of these ten alone, not of the world as a whole.

economic output through the fifties. US GDP share remained relatively steady—and very high—until 2000, when it began to drop sharply.

One of the points the data also make clear, however, is that before the firm entrenchment of the Industrial Revolution, it wasn't possible for people in one nation to be radically wealthier, on average, than those of any other. This isn't at

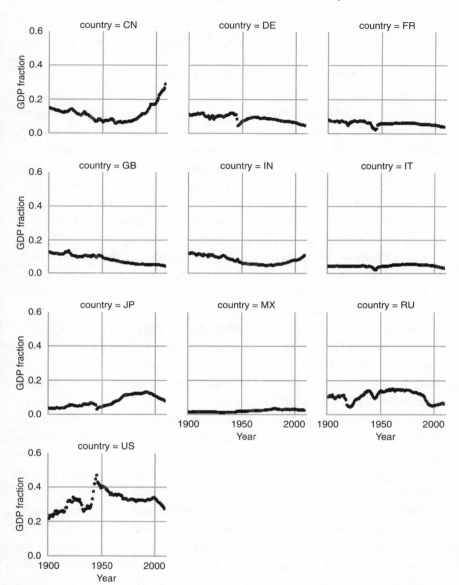

all the same thing as saying that there was notable equality of economic distribution in the preindustrial age. But it's hard to do subsistence agriculture or preindustrial trade all that much better than anyone else at the level of nations or cultures, and so GDP before about 1900 tends to be dominated by population size. The right panel of figure 3 shows GDP for the same ten nations, restricted to the era after 1900, which best reflects differences between modern economies. This is the subset of the economic data used in the analysis that follows.

American Fiction Is Interested in the United States

It comes as no particular surprise that US authors are more likely to write about places in the United States than are their non-American counterparts. Comparative information is limited, given the orientation of the literary corpus toward US authors, but a small sample of British fiction from the same period reveals a stark domestic bias in each case. US authors use US locations in preference to British ones by about 8:1, while British authors use nearly twice as many locations in the United Kingdom as they do American places. The magnitude of this skew is striking. Across the full period, US locations account for more than 60 percent of all country-identifiable place references (that is, excluding things like "Pacific Ocean" that cannot be associated with any single nation) in the corpus. The 60 percent figure is, moreover, very stable across the 110-year data set (see fig. 4), despite bouncing around from year to year; there's a slight apparent downward trend, but it's not statistically significant.

Already, then, it's clear that the extent to which places in the United States are used in American fiction doesn't track especially closely the much more distinctly marked changes in US GDP fraction over the same period. Compare the trend (or lack thereof) in figure 4 to the analogous GDP share data over a similar time span (1900–1990) as shown in figure 5.

In fact, US locations are so consistently dominant in American fiction that all of the other nations examined are underrepresented relative to their GDP share in most or all of the years of the twentieth century. This fact is visualized in figure 6, which plots the annual difference between literary location share and GDP share for the same ten large countries.

Perfect correlation between literary representation and economic output would follow the black line at zero in every case. There's not a lot of excess representation left after the United States absorbs most of it. France manages about par across the period, as does Italy. Britain's rising degree of representation is mostly about its shrinking share of GDP against flat literary numbers. Mexico starts to fall below par as its economy grows in the seventies and eighties.

To get a handle on how all of these degrees of over- and underrepresentation interact over time, we can measure the degree to which GDP share in a given year correlates with literary representation share across the century. To do that, we plot the fraction of literary occurrences as a function of GDP share for the ten nations over every possible combination of years (1900–1990 for literature, 1900–2009 for

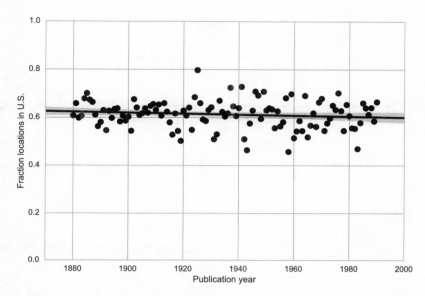

Figure 4. Fraction of location references to the United States and places within it in the literary corpus from 1880 to 1990.

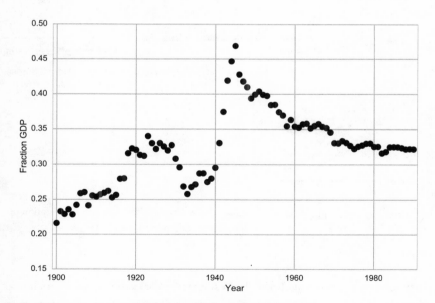

Figure 5. US fraction of GDP among ten large nations, 1900–1990.

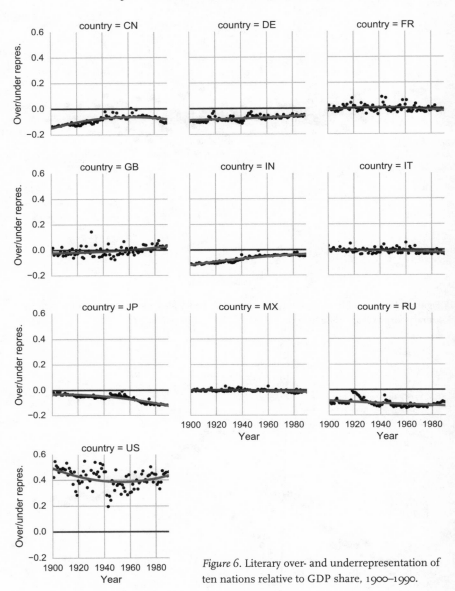

Figure 6. Literary over- and underrepresentation of ten nations relative to GDP share, 1900–1990.

GDP) and measure the quality of the best linear fit for each pair. So for each pair of possible years, we have something that looks like figure 7 (which happens to be for literature published in 1971 and GDP share in the same year). But don't get too hung up on figure 7; there are over ten thousand others of the same form.

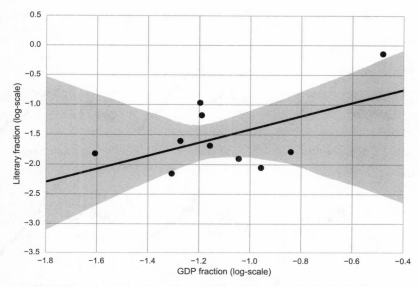

Figure 7. Literary location share (in 1971) as a function of GDP share (also 1971) for ten large nations. Both axes are log scaled.

From each of those ten thousand plots, we extract what's called the r^2 value, which estimates the fraction of variance in literary attention explained by variation in GDP share. The r^2 values are all over the place, from near zero (very poor correlation) to about 0.8 (perfect correlation is 1.0). The r^2 value for the data in figure 7 is 0.3, a pretty marginal fit. Figure 8 shows what these r^2 values look like for a few years of literary output in the late sixties and early seventies. Each dot in figure 8 corresponds to a single measurement of the type shown in figure 7. So in the top left of figure 8, we have the r^2 values for fiction published in 1967 measured against GDP shares in each of the 110 years between 1900 and 2009. The best fits—that is, the closest alignments between literary attention share and GDP share—are indicated by the highest points on that plot, which cluster around 1950–60. The next plot to the right (top middle) shows the same thing for fiction published in 1968, and so on. As you can see, literary-geographic usage in those years generally correlates most closely with the geographic distribution of GDP as it existed around 1950, which is where each plot peaks.

Ok, so it's tempting to conclude, looking at figure 8, that American fiction lagged economic changes by around twenty years, since books published in the late sixties and early seventies spread their geographic attention in patterns closest to the distribution of GDP circa 1950. That doesn't seem ridiculous, and while

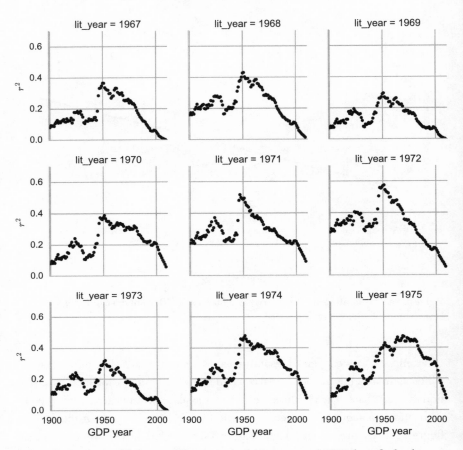

Figure 8. Goodness of fit between literary geographic usage and GDP share for books published between 1967 and 1975.

we might have imagined things otherwise—a more strongly presentist literary orientation, a longer historical lag, perhaps even some economic predictive power for literature—that time gap feels plausible. Except that the gap isn't constant. In fact, 1950 GDP share is nearly *always* the best predictor of American literary-geographic attention, as much for books published in 1900 as for those that appeared in 1990, as we can see in figure 9, which plots the year of closest GDP fit for each year of literary output.[10]

Figure 9 is unexpectedly and distressingly flat. The horizontal band of points around 1950 means that, as far as the geographic orientation of American fiction is concerned, it has always been the fifties. True, there's a very slight rise in the data, meaning that the average year of best fit increased by a few years over the

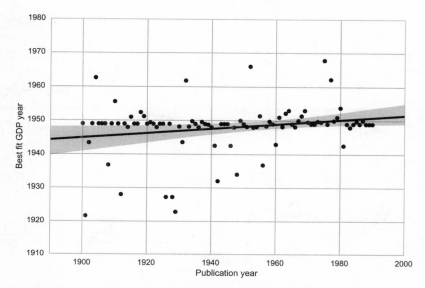

Figure 9. Average year of best GDP share fit as a function of text publication year, 1900–1990.

course of the century. But it's not much, especially considering the magnitude of the economic changes involved. Things aren't looking especially good for any presumptive link between economic and literary geography. The constancy of the fifties as the era of best fit also means that literary geography becomes in effect more conservative with every passing year, reflecting an increasingly distant and outmoded past simply by standing still.

Maybe We Should Focus Less on the United States

Focusing a bit less on the United States is always a good idea, and it makes particular sense in the present case. A large part of what's going on here is clear if we recall figures 5 and 6. The United States is always significantly overrepresented in American fiction relative to its share of global economic output. It just so happens that US GDP share peaked around 1950. A literary geography perpetually weighted heavily toward US locations therefore misses the economic mark by the smallest amount when that mark is highest, hence the stability of 1950 GDP share as the best correlate of US-centric fictional geography.

But what if we leave the United States out of the analysis, so that we're looking at the ways in which American authors treat only international locations? That approach removes the overwhelming prominence of the United States and might

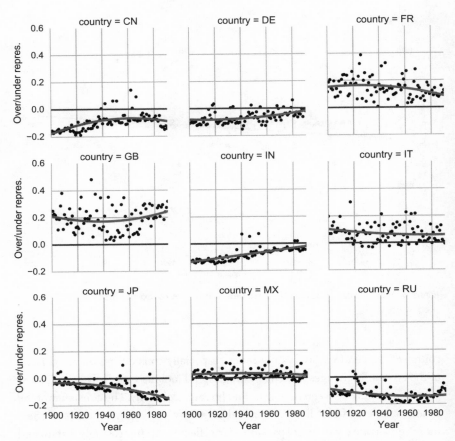

Figure 10. Literary over- and underrepresentation of nine nations relative to GDP share, 1900–1990.

allow us to see trends that aren't dependent on home-country chauvinism. Figure 10 is the analogue to figure 6, showing over- and underrepresentation relative to GDP share for nine nations (the same as above, minus the United States) between 1900 and 1990.

This view of the data makes much clearer the lingering geoconceptual dominance of western Europe in American fiction. Britain, France, and Italy—the traditional domains of the Americanized grand tour and still the sites of disproportionate cultural prestige through the late twentieth century—are all consistently overrepresented. Germany is well behind, although less so later in the century. No one cares about Russia unless there's a war on, nor, again apart from World War II, much about Japan, at least as sites of geographic reference.

More interesting, perhaps, are the three expanding economies of China, India, and Mexico. Mexico is almost always slightly overrepresented, most likely due to a combination of its comparatively small economy (especially early in the century)—meaning that even fairly light literary use is enough to reach parity—and neighbor effects in the American corpus. Still, this prominence is yet another piece of support, however modest, for the ongoing transnational and hemispheric reconception of American literature. China and India, while rarely overrepresented, come meaningfully closer to proportional representation over the course of the century, and while they're almost never overused relative to their economic share, there's a meaningful increase in their degree of representation as literature moves closer to the present day. India in particular is a surprise in this respect; there's a nontrivial upturn in Indian GDP share through the eighties, with which literary use of Indian locations appears to keep pace. This is one of the few cases in which such a close, sustained correspondence is visible.

On the whole, though, the degree of correlation between GDP share and literary-geographic attention isn't what we'd expect, even in the case of India and China. Figure 11 shows literary share as a function of GDP share over the period 1900–1990 for those two nations. In both cases, the data are noisy, but the trend is negative (more strongly so in the case of China), which means that higher GDP share tends to line up with lower literary usage. This is not at all what we expected at the outset.

The trends in these figures, however, are controlled in large part by the early years of the century, in which both countries had large GDP shares but drew little literary treatment from American authors. It would be more revealing to see how the non-American locations as a group track GDP share over time. We can do that with a plot of the year of closest GDP share fit for each year of literary output (see fig. 12 and compare fig. 9, which shows the same data with the United States included).

This looks promising, if a bit hard to explain in full. Recall that when the United States was included in the data, there was a dense band of points around 1950, indicating that American authors throughout the period used geographic references in a way that most closely resembled midcentury economic geography. With the United States removed from the picture, things shift forward dramatically. Most of the best fits are with economic geography as it existed from the eighties forward, and many of them are to the latest possible dates. The trend, moreover, is positive in time, if only modestly, indicating a closer alignment between economic and literary geography in contemporary American fiction than in early twentieth-century literature.

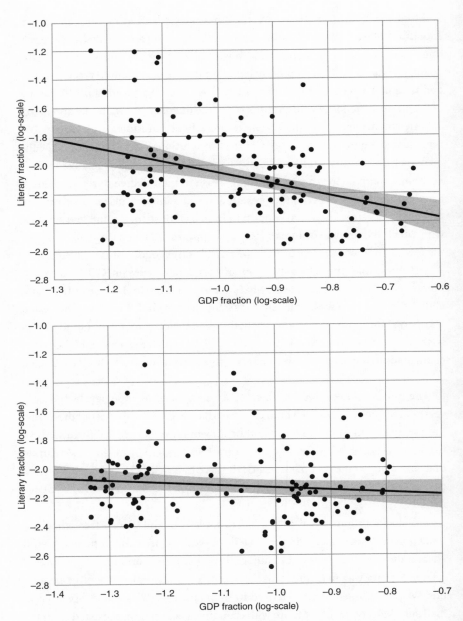

Figure 11. Share of literary geography as a function of GDP share, 1900–1990. Both values are log scaled. *Top*, China. *Bottom*, India.

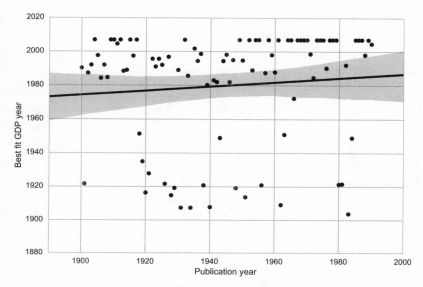

Figure 12. Average year of best GDP share fit as a function of text publication year, excluding US data.

But there are two problems with this conclusion, only one of which is visible in figure 12. The invisible problem is that the goodness of fit in nearly all of these cases is really poor, averaging only about 0.3 and fluctuating wildly from year to year (recall that a perfect linear fit is 1.0). What that means is that even though literary-geographic usage resembles turn-of-the-twenty-first-century economic output more closely than that of any other time, it doesn't resemble such output very closely at all. The US case also wasn't great, but the degree of fit was 50 to 100 percent better, enough to lend some credence to the observed trend (which, in that case, was essentially fixed in time and flat). Without the United States and its geographic dominance, there simply isn't much overall correlation between the geographic distribution of the global economy and usage rates of foreign locations in US fiction. And in any case (this is the second problem), even if the data in figure 12 reflected much better underlying fits, it's hard to imagine a plausible explanatory mechanism for a situation in which literary usage was routinely decades (or as much as a century) in front of economic change. Not that it would be impossible to do so, but really, how many believable ways can we complete the sentence, "American authors throughout the twentieth century devoted their attention to the world outside the US in ways that resembled the distribution of twenty-first century capital because . . . "?

Where does all of this leave us? The answer is, without much support for the interpretation of neoliberalism as a horizon of contemporary thought, in at least one place where we expected to find it. There's no compelling evidence of a shift toward closer alignment between literary-geographic attention and economic geography over the course of the twentieth century up to 1990. Given that fact, there's also, of course, no observed shift toward any shorter temporal span between changes in economic and literary output, since the two aren't well aligned in any case. There are, however, a couple of changes in twentieth-century literary-geographic usage worth noting. There appears to have been a very slight decrease in the amount of attention devoted to locations in the United States (and in "classical" belletristic western Europe) and a corresponding uptick in others, including Russia, China, India, and Mexico. These changes are small, and they don't track economic shifts very well, but they do show at least some small sensitivity in American fiction as a whole to developments beyond US borders.

Still, there are two overwhelming traits of literary-geographic attention in twentieth-century American fiction: (1) the United States is hugely overrepresented, and (2) this overrepresentation is extremely stable over time. This might mean that literary geography is a bad place to look for changes in fictional content. It's also possible that what changes over time is the set of associations attached to places rather than the usage rates of those places themselves. I find that claim implausible—could there really be an important, culture-wide reevaluation of geographic significance that just happened to have no impact on the distribution of locations used?—but it's an abstract possibility. Or it might be that all of the relevant literary action occurs in the period after 1990, which isn't included in the current corpus, despite more than a century of geographic near-stasis immediately preceding it. The explanation would fit with an understanding of ontological neoliberalism as an exclusive phenomenon of the post–Cold War period; to evaluate it, we require an expansion of the current research corpus, currently under way. These are all avenues to pursue in extension of the present work.

But recall the hypothesis from which we began, that neoliberalism represents a horizon of contemporary thought as binding on literature as on any other form of cultural production. There's little in the data I've presented here to support that claim. We should take seriously the possibility, in our future work on neoliberalism, that the ways in which the logic of the late capitalist market shapes the culture that embeds it are less usefully conceived as limits than as pressures or (exceedingly subtle) tendencies. I suspect that some readers will agree; of course, neoliberal logic isn't ironclad and isn't everywhere the same. But I don't think that this is a small concession, either. The claim was never, even in the strongest sense, that every book would look the same. The claim was that books in general would reflect the operations of the market because the market was the inescapable structuring principle of contemporary thought. If that's not so—and, again, I hasten to add that the present results certainly don't mean it *isn't* so, just that it looks a bit less likely—if books don't reflect the market especially well, then it seems to me that we have to at least entertain the possibility that the market is not *the* structuring principle of contemporary thought. This strikes me as a large point indeed.

NOTES

1. There have been millions of English-language novels published since 1900. Even if you've read a thousand of them (as I have not), that's less than 0.1% of the total.

2. WorldCat holdings are obviously an imperfect proxy for abstract importance, but they are perhaps no worse than any other conceivable measure. For an extensive treatment of the fundamental difficulties raised by the term *representative* with respect to contemporary literary corpora, see Mark Algee-Hewitt and Mark McGurl, *Between Canon and Corpus: Six Perspectives on 20th-Century Novels*, LitLab Pamphlet 8 (Stanford, CA: Stanford University, 2015).

3. A listing of the volumes in the corpus, as well as all other data related to this chapter, is available from mattwilkens.com/data.

4. See Matthew Wilkens, "The Geographic Imagination of Civil War–Era American Fiction," *American Literary History* 25, no. 4 (2013): 803–40.

5. For details of the Stanford named entity recognizer, see Jenny Rose Finkel, Trond Grenager, and Christopher Manning, "Incorporating Non-local Information into Information Extraction Systems by Gibbs Sampling," in *Proceedings of the 43nd Annual Meeting of the Association for Computational Linguistics* (Ann Arbor, MI, 2005), 363–70.

6. See Jutta Bolt and Jan Luiten van Zanden, "The Maddison Project: Collaborative Research on Historical National Accounts," *Economic History Review* 67, no. 3 (2014): 627–51; and Angus Maddison, *Contours of the World Economy 1–2030 AD: Essays in Macro-Economic History* (Oxford: Oxford University Press, 2007).

7. For an accessible and far-reaching consideration of issues related to GDP and other measures of national accounts, see Joseph E. Stiglitz, Amartya Sen, and Jean-Paul Fitoussi, *Report by the Commission on the Measurement of Economic Performance and Social Progress* (Paris: Commission on the Measurement of Economic Performance and Social Progress, 2010).

8. GDP per capita is an obviously unsatisfactory measure, since it overstates the significance of small, wealthy nations. Intermediate constructs that weigh both total and per capita economic output—such as squared GDP per capita—are an alternative under active investigation for future work.

9. Absent from current consideration among large economies are Brazil and Indonesia, neither of which appears sufficiently often in the literary corpus to support meaningful

annual statistics. This fact tells us something about the imaginative prominence of those countries in twentieth-century American fiction.

10. In order to avoid single-year outliers, the year of best fit in fig. 9 is an average of the five best-fitting GDP years for each year of literary publication. For reference, these years are the five highest points in each of the plots of the type presented in fig. 8.

The Neoliberal Novel of Migrancy

SHERI-MARIE HARRISON

In this essay, I describe Teju Cole's *Open City* (2011) and Chimamanda Ngozi Adichie's *Americanah* (2013) as neoliberal novels of migrancy, a category I propose not as a wholly novel one but rather as an acknowledgment of how neoliberalism has transformed the standard tropes of immigrant fiction and its varied preoccupations with identity, national assimilation, and cosmopolitanism.[1] Indeed, while the latter two preoccupations may seem contradictory as investments for immigrant fiction—national assimilation in its rootedness and cosmopolitanism in its unrootedness—both are unified in their opposition to the provincialism of the homeland left behind and of immigrant enclaves in the adopted cosmopolitan American home. As I hope to show, the neoliberal novel of migrancy splits these two imperatives, establishing a contradictory tension between cosmopolitanism's endorsement of unallied global mobility and the rootedness of national assimilation. This split breaks down the classic immigrant novel's standard trajectory from ethnic identity to national cosmopolitanism, replacing this simple, linear trajectory with a free-floating transnational cosmopolitanism more akin to that of capital itself than that of the assimilated citizen.

As this formulation suggests, these novels do not thus simply eschew economics for identity in the manner that Walter Benn Michaels imputes to the contemporary multicultural novel.[2] Rather, we might say, they formally position migrant subjects as analogues of capital. The nation remains important for them, but not as a fixed goal; rather, the immigrant novel's trajectory mirrors neoliberal capital's paradoxical reliance on the nation as an economic mechanism that can facilitate competitive conditions for the free flow of capital and increasing globalized wealth. This cuts against what otherwise threatens to become a problematic conflation of cosmopolitanism and the unfettered mobility of capital, enabling these books to function not only as symptoms but also as critiques of neoliberalism.

They mount their critique by depicting their subjects not as free-floating vessels for the accumulation of value but as subjects very immediately bound up in structures of global exploitation.

Throughout this essay, then, neoliberalism describes a contemporary economic ideology underwritten by the logic of free-market capitalism that informs governmental policies—like immigration and social welfare services—and shapes sociocultural paradigms in ways that influence the lived realities of populaces. The socioeconomic implications of free-market capitalism and its rationale of a deregulated global flow of capital not only facilitate the neoliberal logic of individual self-actualization unmoored from the welfare of a collective but also appear in immigrant and minority fiction about migration as a means through which systemic discrimination and inequity can be negotiated successfully.

It would be incorrect, then, to say that Cole's and Adichie's novels are unconcerned with identity. But they are not concerned with identity as something one moves either away from or toward. Rather, they treat it as something that shapes and is shaped by one's movement through a globalized world. In this way their work contradicts the false assumptions that, first, contemporary immigrant, minority, or multicultural fiction is too narrowly concerned with identity and, second (and more importantly), discourses of identity, as they appear in contemporary fiction, are separate from or unconcerned with conversations about capital and economic inequities.

Identity, Neoliberalism, and Novels

The latter point about identity is where the usefulness of a new taxonomic category —the neoliberal novel of migrancy—resides for contemporary immigrant fiction that is invested in animating how neoliberal habits and ideologies muddle the standard tropic expectations of the form. One could ask, why not just call these books neoliberal novels—a term already in circulation—rather than add another term into the mix? One reason for using differentiating terminology is the presence of competing critical claims about neoliberal novels. Critics like Michaels and Jeffrey Williams, for example, despite significant differences, juxtapose immigrant fiction's foregrounding of identitarian concerns to critiques of neoliberalism. Williams, on the one hand, suggests that novels that "foreground racial, ethnic, sexual, or other cultural identity and respond to the politics of status and recognition in contemporary American culture" should be considered "diversity" or "multicultural" novels.[3] As such, the term *neoliberal novel* should be reserved for those books that "foreground the economic and political consequences of the past thirty years."[4] Michaels, on the other hand, takes a less protective view of the neoliberal novel, reserving the term instead for immigrant fiction that "represents and enables" neoliberal inequality because of its distracting focus on identity politics.[5] As Michaels sees it, immigrant fiction in its focus on identity does more to bolster the economic inequalities produced by neoliberalism than it does to repudiate them. More specifically, immigrant fiction's "focus on identity functions not just to distract people from the increase in inequality but to legitimate it."[6] In this way, the neoliberal novel's increased appreciation of identity and diversity as societal values is not effective in combating hostility and discrimination against identitarian difference (racial, gendered, sexual, for example). For Michaels, our preoccupation with both poles—the appreciative and the hostile—amounts to an "indifference to the increasing economic inequality that has been a hallmark of American society since the mid-1970s (the beginning, according to economists, of American neoliberalism)."[7] I think that Michaels's argument has a core of truth but doesn't quite capture the complexity of contemporary immigrant or minority fiction's relationship to economic inequalities.

My argument thus necessarily parts ways with Michaels on the question of whether identitarian foci in immigrant fiction can only represent and enable neoliberalism. Though Adichie's and Cole's novels explore identitarian themes, this should not disqualify them from the conversations about economics and capital that they undoubtedly engage. Beyond proving that these novels' thematic exploration of identity does not disqualify them from conversations about economics, though, describing them as neoliberal novels, without appending migrancy, would not account for the revisionist work novels like Cole's and Adichie's accomplish in relation to immigrant fiction. It also would not account for the ways critical presumptions about identitarian foci continue to erroneously exclude immigrant fiction from conversations about neoliberal economic inequality. I thus use the term *neoliberal novel of migrancy* to signal how these novels elicit a merger between critical discourses about immigrant fiction and neoliberalism. I also use it to suggest that the identitarian focus of contemporary immigrant fiction does not, as Michaels contends, always function as a distraction from increasing economic inequality. Rather, it serves to simultaneously legitimate and critique neoliberalism.

Recognizing this simultaneity is important because even in its legitimating capacity the neoliberal novel may indeed convey more complexity about the immigrant subject's position vis-à-vis neoliberalism than Michaels's conceptualization of it allows. Paul Gilroy's consideration of the relationship between black and migrant communities and "the neoliberal thematics of uplift, self-responsibility and self-improvement" is useful in thinking about why narratives that appear to legitimize neoliberalism—in this case self-help books—should not necessarily be dismissed out of hand and/or relegated to other conversations entirely.[8] According to Gilroy, "The continuing effects of systematic racism on black life cannot be dismissed and there are instances where that very impact seems—perhaps even where racism is to be sacrificed in capital's interests—to have inclined people towards the solutions proffered by neoliberal styles of thought which can be taken over, possessed and made one's own. In other words, the history of being denied recognition as an individual has actually enhanced the appeal of particular varieties of extreme individualism."[9] In this way, even the narratives that legitimize neoliberalism have something to tell us about the realities of economic inequality under neoliberalism.

Returning to my suggestion that the neoliberal novel of migrancy serves to simultaneously legitimate and critique neoliberalism, in this essay I examine how *Open City* and *Americanah* critique neoliberal capital's transcendence of the nation, through their protagonists, and present the violent and embodied implications attendant upon this transcendence. The protagonists of both novels are transnational subjects—Nigerian immigrants—who are in many ways exemplars of national transcendence. Cole's protagonist, Julius, is a successful, newly graduated psychiatrist, and *Open City* is structured around his disconnected musings as he wanders around New York and Brussels—sites of contemporary capital concentration and capital's relationship to nation if there are any. Adichie's Ifemelu, meanwhile, is a self-made blogger who, after a rough start to her life in America, eventually makes enough money to sell her condo, close her successful blog, and move back to Nigeria, despite having become a naturalized American citizen. Both Julius and Ifemelu, as transnational subjects, interestingly parallel the circulation of capital. In this way, we might say that their stories offer allegories of unregulated and transnational neoliberal capital in the same way that stories of more traditional immigrants offered allegories of nation. Of course, one might note that in transcending the trajectory of national assimilation these novels only embrace cosmopolitanism all the more readily, rejecting not only the classic immigrant novel's rejection of the provincial home country but also the form of cosmopolitanism associated with America or other supposedly more enlightened nations. As these novels make clear, however, under neoliberalism the transcendence of nation associated with capital is anything but self-evidently positive. Cole's novel considers the consequences of this shift for cosmopolitanism by exploring the nuances of accountability, Adichie's by detailing the tenuous nature of safety and security for the impoverished transnational subject. In this way, both novels do not simply mimetically reproduce the global status of capital. In their hands, their characters' stories become ways of critiquing that status as well.

Cosmopolitanism, Capital, and Accountability in *Open City*

In *Open City*, Cole traces the connections between cosmopolitanism, transnational agency, and capital. Whereas in its original nineteenth-century iterations cosmopolitanism's valuation of national transcendence seemed self-evidently good in its capacity to form global ties that would counteract prejudice, discrimination, and ultimately inequality, under neoliberalism, cosmopolitan transcendence of the nation no longer bears out this certainty. *Open City*'s characterization of Julius offers a compelling disruption of the neoliberal logic that transcending the nation via cosmopolitan practice remains (or perhaps ever was) a viable route to good global politics.

As Pheng Cheah et al. work to convey in *Cosmopolitics: Thinking and Feeling beyond the Nation*, the meaning of cosmopolitanism is transitory and temporally contingent; the term refers to something different in our post-national contemporary world, in terms of both the practices it describes and who practices them, than it did in the nineteenth century.[10] Whereas in its earliest manifestations it applied to European wanderers (variously privileged or despised for their transience), today it expands to include migrants with all sorts of national or cultural moorings, irrespective of prior boundaries like class or gender. Of course, cosmopolitanism in practice has always aspired precisely to efface such differences. As Bruce Robbins explains, "understood as a fundamental devotion to the interests of humanity as a whole, cosmopolitanism has often seemed to claim universality by virtue of its independence, its detachment from bonds, commitments, and affiliations that constrain ordinary nation-bound lives."[11] Paradoxically, it is in this detachment from national bonds that the cosmopolitan immigrant wanderer becomes an idealized and trusted source for knowledge about migrant realities and thus becomes a central feature of immigrant fiction.

But as Cole's novel suggests, the parallels between the unfettered movement of the cosmopolitan immigrant wanderer and neoliberal capital bear out far less idealized implications. Cole's cautious approach to cosmopolitanism facilitates an inversion in the politics of reading immigrant fiction that resets the aesthetic stakes of the immigrant novel. Indeed, *Open City*'s critique of cosmopolitanism is also the vehicle for its critique of neoliberal capital's detachment from and transcendence of national rooting. In the contemporary neoliberal model of migrancy—the new immigrant model, if you will—the individual as cosmopolite models herself on capital committed to endless movement across borders and commits to personal enrichment in various spaces. As *Open City*'s protagonist makes clear, however, cosmopolitanism's viability as a more humanitarian and efficacious way of imagining a brand of global citizenship unrestrained by national lives is compromised under neoliberalism, because its politics of national transcendence resembles too closely capital's own policy of national transcendence for the purpose of protection from taxation and regulation. In this way, we can understand cosmopolitanism as complicit with the neoliberal global finance model that relies on offshore banking, for example, to avoid paying national taxes. What *Open City*'s portrayal of Julius makes apparent is that good global politics need more than the simple model of transcending the nation that cosmopolitanism provides. In particular, it needs some way of imagining a structure beyond the nation that would be able to control neoliberal capital.[12] The attendant imaginative and material challenges to such an endeavor are not exactly the subject of Cole's or Adichie's novels, yet in depicting their transnational wanderers, the books inevitably take these challenges up.

As the quintessential immigrant cosmopolite, Julius is defined in large part by his physical and economic mobility, as well as his appreciation and consumption of high aesthetic objects—classical music and visual art in particular. He is an enthusiastic classical music listener; he contemplatively peruses art galleries; he does not quite get all the hype about jazz. In his wanderings throughout the novel, both literally and imaginatively, across New York City, Brussels, and Nigeria, there are resonances of the nineteenth-century flaneur, a figure that Pieter Vermeulen notes "anticipates a cosmopolitan ethos that thrives on intercultural curiosity and the virtues of the aesthetic."[13] When he is not wandering through city streets, Julius contemplates visual art and music by artists that include Jan Van Eyck, John Brewster Jr., Paul Claudel, Diego Velázquez, and Gustav Mahler.

These scenes of contemplation nevertheless ironically highlight Julius's disconnection from the people and places around him. Much like neoliberal capital, his interests neither dwell locally nor serve national concerns. Moreover, his experiences of appreciating various high cultural aesthetic objects are entirely solitary exercises that repel rather than encourage contact with others. While listening to the classical music being played in a Tower Records store, Julius is unable to fully immerse himself in the experience of listening and enjoying because "it simply wasn't possible to enter the music fully, not in that public place." Amid the enjoyment of classical music—among fellow aficionados no less—the presence of others disrupts his ability to fully appreciate the final movement of Mahler's *Das Lied von der Erde* and essentially disrupts his "rapt" listening experience of being "swaddled in a private darkness."[14] Indeed, Julius seems like the converse of Robbins's notion of cosmopolitanism as "an ideal of detachment" in which "actually existing cosmopolitanism is a reality of (re)attachment, multiple attachment, or attachment at a distance."[15] For Julius, detachment is a constant, but unlike Robbins's cosmopolite, his detachment doesn't successfully facilitate connection and attachment. Moreover, Julius's inability to listen to music in public reveals the limitations of cosmopolitanism as a contemporary politics that can achieve detachment from nation and from the unregulated wanderings of capital. As *Open City* shows, Julius's cosmopolitanism does not offer a viable model for getting beyond not only the nation but also—crucially—capital.

Julius's curtailed experience of fully appreciating music publicly thus can be interpreted as representing the inability to get to the next stage of public organization made necessary by the global circulation of capital. Bruce Robbins responds to this particular critique of ineffectual cosmopolitan practice by offering the term "cosmopolitics." Robbins's term is "intended to underline the need to introduce intellectual order and accountability into this newly dynamic space of gushingly unrestrained sentiments, pieties, and urgencies for which no adequately discriminatory lexicon has had time to develop."[16] If, as Robbins suggests, "the time for cosmopolitics is now," Cole's characterization of Julius lays bare the limitations of cosmopolitanism in marshaling the accountability that is necessary for equality, largely because cosmopolitanism cannot shake off its neoliberal complicities.[17] Julius's insistence that the publicness of his immediate environment disrupts his ability "to enter the music fully," his ability to enjoy it freely without localized interferences, also lays bare the problem with cosmopolitanism's sense that the nation is the primary obstruction to good global politics, rather than globalized free-market logics of capital accumulation.

The narration of this failure through multiple instances of disconnection between Julius and other minor characters he encounters throughout the novel, despite what is supposed to be his unmoored cosmopolitan openness, forms the basis of what I argue is *Open City*'s commentary on the neoliberal ends cosmopolitanism sometimes serves. Through Julius, the novel tests the limits of cosmopolitan practice and ultimately challenges the notion that cosmopolitan achievement, aesthetically and culturally, exerts material influence on global power and politics. Moreover, perhaps even more damningly, cosmopolitanism hardly makes the individual a better global citizen.

An example of how the novel undermines the notion that aesthetic appreciation in itself is a vehicle for empathy and meaningful connection comes when Julius visits the post office to mail a copy of Kwame Anthony Appiah's *Cosmopol-*

itanism: Ethics in A World of Strangers to Farouq, a Moroccan immigrant whom he has met in Brussels. During the errand, Julius becomes annoyed by the prattling of an African American postal worker, Terry, who asks Julius, "Say, brother, where are you from?" While Terry's fraternal claim on Julius, based on race, is commonplace enough, Terry subsequently uses this to fetishize Julius's continental Africanness. At work here is a critique of universal diasporic filial relations. Terry says to Julius, "I could tell you were from the Motherland. And you brother have something that is vital, you understand me. You have something that is vital for the health of those of us raised on this side of the ocean."[18] In an earlier encounter with a fellow African cab driver, we are introduced to Julius's discomfort when strangers attempt to "lay claims on him."[19] His exchange with Terry proves all the more awkward because the postal worker attributes to Julius—by virtue of his Africanness alone—the titles of "visionary" and "journeyer," which in turn prompts an impromptu poetry recitation.

The scene's contrapuntal contrast between the comedy of Terry misrecognizing Julius as kin and the gift of Appiah's *Cosmopolitanism* for Farouq presents a dual criticism of identitarian discourses' essentializing tendencies and cosmopolitanism's tendency to efface meaningful connections. In its critique of both, the scene troubles racial collectivism and cosmopolitanism—each featuring variably in immigrant fiction—as strategies for combating prejudice, discrimination, and inequality. Indeed, while both appear throughout the novel as complicit with neoliberalism, in the distracting sense that Michaels suggests is rampant throughout minority fiction, they also function in the novel as vehicles for critiquing neoliberalism's focus on the individual that works to eschew collective responsibility and accountability. We can see this most obviously in the gift of *Cosmopolitanism.* I hesitate to describe Farouq as Julius's friend because their conversations do not reflect any more intimacy than the other conversations Julius has throughout the novel. But they do reflect less indifference and hostility on Julius's part than do his interactions with characters like the cab driver and Terry. In a conversation about Muslim extremism, Farouq's friend Khalil says he supports Hamas and Hezbollah as "doing the work of resistance."[20] In response, Julius only pretends to affect the outrage that he thinks he is expected to in this conversation. "I was meant to be the outraged American," he says, and subsequently asks Farouq, "Do you support Al-Qaeda too?" Farouq explains his position as follows: "King Solomon gave a teaching once about the snake and the bee. The snake, King Solomon said, defends itself by killing. But the bee defends itself by dying. . . . So, each creature has a method that is suitable to its strength. I don't agree with what Al-Qaeda did, they use a method I would not use, so I cannot say the word support. But I don't cast judgment on them . . . in my opinion, the Palestinian question is the central question of our time."[21] Though the reader is not told how Julius feels about any of this, Farouq is positioned as the obverse of Julius's cosmopolitan practice insofar as he poses a question about which people are entitled to an occupied territory as the "central question of our time." Indeed, the gift of Appiah's book conveys where Julius stands in such debates, literally embodying a version of individualized cosmopolitan diplomacy that Khalil in this scene resists and with which Farouq wrestles. It is an invitation of sorts for Khalil to consider citizenship in this world more globally, something that is enabled by receptiveness to art and literature from other places—that is, it is an encouragement to unfetter his allegiances from national geopolitical moorings and extend them to more global/transnational ones. It is presented in the context of the enduring territorial conflicts in the Middle East that have fostered the rise of religious extremism and terrorism. In a way, Julius proffers Appiah's book and the cosmopolitanism it espouses against the backdrop of this conversation as a solution to such geopolitical conflicts over territory. Aesthetic objects—in Appiah's argument—are the key to understanding and being open to the others with whom we share the planet. The irony here rests in Julius's own belief in this brand of cosmopolitan conviction and its complete detachment from the way he proceeds through life and interacts with others—as the incident with Terry attests. In other words, Julius's cosmopolitan conviction bars rather than enables meaningful connections with others, and as such holds no real power to effect material global change.

This irony is further compounded once we consider Julius's disturbing lack of familial allegiance and territorial encroachment, which are all the more alarming because of their associations with violence and exploitation. I am referring here to the character Moji's accusation of rape against Julius. Despite observing and relaying to the reader multiple histories of human rights abuses that continue to exist in real and phantasmal ways, Julius himself is no more humane at the beginning of the novel than he is at the end. The much-discussed rape accusation against Julius, leveled seemingly out of nowhere, is where we might begin to think about how the novel not only challenges literary cosmopolitanism as a vehicle for material change but also conveys its complicity with neoliberal discourses that cloak or perhaps even render mundane daily human rights abuses. By personalizing Moji's rape accusation (alongside histories of human rights violations) and Julius's dismissal of it, the novel thus narrates the embodied stakes of violence that attend the unaccountability of global capital.

The scene unfolds abruptly and jarringly not only because it seems to come out of nowhere (it only seems this way because of Julius's physical and mental wanderings) but also because of Julius's response to Moji when she confronts him, the break in the narrative's chronological progression, and finally the novel's resumption without resolution after this disturbing revelation. It is here, at the level of form, that the novel's critique of neoliberal cosmopolitanism meets a larger critique of universal male privilege, which in turn makes the violence attendant with neoliberal economic policies all the more real—corporeal perhaps. What becomes clear in the progression of this scene is that Julius, like global capital, cannot conceive of himself as having done wrong or as taking advantage of vulnerability and thus as being accountable to anyone beyond his own moral compass. The rape accusation then is also about transparency and about being accountable in ways that neoliberal logics of capital accumulation preclude.

Put another way, the indictment of male privilege in the form of Moji's rape accusation functions as a materializing vehicle for the novel's critique of the embodied violence that is attendant upon a lack of accountability and transparency in the movement and growth of capital globally. As Cole tells Aaron Bady in a recent interview, only a few critics, academic and nonacademic alike, "intuit a feminist commitment in the book."[22] Cole, in his conversation with Bady, points us to an online review of the novel by Alyssa Rosenberg as one of the discussions that seems to fully grasp the terrain of gender politics that the novel treads. Rosenberg suggests plainly, "Julius didn't forget assaulting Moji because he's a sociopath who can easily put a rape out of his mind—he forgot assaulting Moji because he doesn't understand himself to have assaulted her in the first place."[23] Moreover, as Rosenberg suggests, "this doesn't absolve him of moral responsibility, then or now. In fact, it shows him to be more globally detached and inconsiderate than we'd previously seen. It's a revelation that forces us, and Julius, to revisit everything we've come to understand about him."[24] In a novel that is also very much about geopolitical invasions and domination, introducing the long-ago rape into the narrative does not only convey how a lived cosmopolitanism renders Julius detached to the point of near sociopathy.[25] It is also, crucially, analogous to how capital's transcendence of national boundaries via deregulation, alternative investment strategies, and tax-free offshore banking breaks down channels of transparency and accountability. Moreover, this situation renders all the more vulnerable those who have neither access nor proximity to capital.

In the narrative, the reader receives Moji's revelation of the rape retrospectively, as an afterthought. Julius had already left Moji's boyfriend's house (where he spent the night after a party), stopped at a diner for coffee, and was making his way home. When she is finished speaking to him about the rape, she asks him,

"Will you say something now? Will you say something?"[26] If Julius has a response to Moji, he doesn't say it to her or to the reader. Instead, before we even learn that something happened between the two, Julius preemptively considers whose perspective is most valuable in accusations of villainy, the victim's or the villain's. The paragraph begins with what can be read as a neoliberal declaration of the individual's sovereignty: "each person must, on some level, take himself as the calibration for normalcy." He tells us, "From my own point of view, thinking about the story of my life, even without claiming any especially heightened sense of ethics, I am satisfied that I have hewed close to good."[27] It is perhaps his cosmopolitan practice that grants him this confidence in his own goodness, but he nonetheless has cause to doubt himself in this instance in light of Moji's certainty. He reflects, "She had said it as if, with all of her being, she was certain of its accuracy."[28] In this instance, the narrative dramatizes through Moji's and Julius's competing certainties—as imagined by Julius—the problems of opacity and unaccountability that attend neoliberal logics of unallied individuality. The closest Julius comes to an admission of wrongdoing comes from his knowledge as a practicing psychiatrist: "I know the tells of those who blame others, those who are unable to see that they themselves, and not the others, are the common thread in their bad relationships. These are character tics that reveal the essential falsehood of such narratives. But what Moji had said to me that morning, before I left John's place, and gone up the George Washington Bridge, and walked the few miles back home, had nothing in common with such stories."[29] In acknowledging that Moji did not tell her story with any of the usual tics that betray falsity, which he is familiar with from his professional life, Julius indirectly accepts what she says as truth, but he does not make the additional step toward acknowledging his role as perpetrator or even making amends. In a moment that is similar to his inability to fully enjoy music publicly in Tower Records, the ability to get to the next stage—a version of being in public that might involve collective responsibility beyond the regimes of both the nation and global capital—remains in the realm of the unimaginable. For all his erudition, Julius, in his inability to admit wrongdoing and be held accountable to Moji or himself, seems not admirable but morally questionable and ultimately dangerous.

Cole's novel also troubles the notion of "an ideal of detachment" as meaningful and efficacious to global citizenship through Julius's alienation not only from his mother but also from his mother's mother country, Germany. The novel's stymieing of this ideal of detachment is also evident in Julius's trip to Brussels, where he aims to find his maternal grandmother, so he can finally discover the reason for his estrangement from his mother. Despite this worthwhile goal of reconnection, Julius goes to Brussels and never actually tries to find his grandmother beyond a feeble phone book search. Ironically, Julius's multiple possibilities for habitation—racially or nationally—produce more confusion than they do opportunities for empathetic connections to others. It is in this framework that we must consider the novel's preoccupation with multiple literal territorial invasions and attendant human rights violations on which the manifestation of our modern reality was contingent. These include the United States' internment of its domestic Japanese population during World War II, the violent suppression of Native Americans by Dutch settlers, Idi Amin's repression of Ugandan Indians, the lingering legacies of slavery, and the struggles of Haitian and Liberian refugees. In the latter two cases, the detained Liberian whom Julius visits and the Haitian immigrant who shines his shoes both have stories of horrific economic and political strife that precipitate their flight from their homelands, stories that contrast sharply with the luxury that is Julius's ease of movement through the world. This contrast in the ease of movement that is facilitated by capital becomes visible when Julius is compared to other immigrants who are bereft of capital and have decreasing hope within neoliberal realities for gaining access to capital and its protections. In this way it parallels Ifemelu's ability to escape, with her American boyfriend's help, the struggles that other characters in Adichie's novel must undergo in the absence of significant capital.

Non-nationality, Safety, and Security in *Americanah*

In *Americanah*, it is Ifemelu's romantic relationship with a white and wealthy Baltimore heir, Curt, that enables her to get her first job out of college, and this in turn eventually supports the immigration filings necessary for her to work legally in the United States. In the novel, she reflects on what is often a period of trepidation for student visa holders: the end of a course of study. She recalls it as a time when job recruiters "all became noncommittal when they realized she was not an American citizen, that they would, if they hired her, have to descend into the dark tunnel of immigration paperwork." Curt's naive sense of the ease of obtaining immigrant status—he gets her an interview at an office in downtown Baltimore for a PR position and tells her, "all you need to do is ace the interview and it's yours . . . the good thing about this one is they'll get you a work visa *and* start your green card process"—is demystified by the novel's understanding of the would-be immigrant's circular quandary: she needs legal permission to work, but she needs a job to support the filing for immigrant status.

The novel tells us that the constantly editorializing Ifemelu accepts Curt's announcement as good news, and "yet a soberness wrapped itself around her."

Her soberness comes from her personal knowledge of other immigrants in similar positions who don't have Curt's capital and the access to employment and immigration opportunities it grants. Thus, "Wambui was working three jobs under
the table to raise the five thousand dollars she would need to pay an African-
American man for a green-card marriage, Mwombeki was desperately trying to
find a company that would hire him on his temporary visa." In these examples,
capital bridges the distances among legal status, economic stability, and enabling
opportunities for immigrants, via both illegal and legal channels. Ifemelu thus
finds herself feeling, "in the midst of her gratitude, a small resentment: that Curt
could with a few calls, rearrange the world, have things slide into the spaces that
he wanted them to."[30] Close proximity to capital both enables economic mobility
and offers protections within the nation not otherwise available to transnational
subjects, whose position as non-nationals implicitly and explicitly inhibits their
access to capital.

As we saw, Cole's novel explores the breakdown of cosmopolitan ideals under
neoliberalism by addressing the nuances of accountability; Adichie's novel does
so by detailing the tenuous nature of safety and security for the non-national
subject. Ifemelu's encounter with sex work in her very first semester at an American university portrays what happens to the vulnerable, capital-less transnational
subject under neoliberalism. Faced with the need to buy food and pay for school
and housing, Ifemelu tries to get work but is denied at every turn, largely because
of her immigration status and her ignorance of a variety of cultural codes that
require her to perform or sublimate her foreignness situationally. Thus, while
using the ID card of a woman named Ngozi (because she is not authorized to
work with her student visa), she mistakenly says her real name and ultimately
does not get the job. Later, her friend Ginika, a Nigerian herself but fully assimilated to American life because she migrated as a teenager, advises her, "you could
have just said Ngozi is your tribal name and Ifemelu is your jungle name and
throw in one more as your spiritual name. They'll believe all kinds of shit about
Africa."[31] Ifemelu's difficulties during her first fall semester arise largely as a result of her ignorance about the derisive and stereotypical ways in which Americans imagine her as a young black woman from an African country. She describes
this time as one of obstructed vision: "the world was wrapped in gauze; she could
see the shapes of things but not clearly enough."[32] When she ultimately resorts
to sex work, her unfamiliarity with an iconic Andy Warhol print reflects not only
her alienation from all things American but also the commodification of her
vulnerability. "Bare but for a bed and a large painting of a tomato soup can on the
wall"—this is how Ifemelu describes the bedroom of a man who will pay her to

help him "relax." This scene thus explicitly contrasts two objectified things—a non-American black woman's body and art—to suggest the ways both are rendered as commodities.

Ifemelu finds herself here because she has answered an advertisement in a local paper that reads, "Female personal assistant for busy sports coach in Ardmore, communication and interpersonal skills required." When she meets the man in person for the first time, she is told that of the two available positions, "one for office work and the other for help relaxing," only the latter remained available, the office work position having gone to a Bryn Mawr student.[33] The phrase Bryn Mawr here reflects a racialized and perhaps classed division of labor between the Nigerian immigrant and the women's liberal arts college attendee. Ultimately, her roommates' insistent demands for her share of the rent forces Ifemelu into the desperate position of accepting the tennis coach's offer. What this suggests is that without the protections afforded by nation and capital—here, the right combination of racial and national status to receive a legitimate job—the transnational subject's freedom to cross borders or assimilate are significantly curtailed. Ifemelu's status outside of the protections of national belonging thus pushes her into sex work. This contrasts sharply with the experience of Julius, whose cosmopolitanism is underwritten by such protections (and who is, in many ways, more like the tennis coach).

Ifemelu experiences her exchange with the tennis coach as humiliating and traumatizing, all the more so because she perceives herself as having freely consented to his offer. While it is happening, however, the novel's narrative perspective consists of a mixture of her present and past thoughts that indicates her confused processing of the dynamics of choice and consent as they relate to the bottom line of being paid:

> She did not want to be here, did not want his active fingers between her legs, did not want his sigh-moans in her ear, and yet she felt her body rousing to a sickening wetness. Afterwards, she lay still, coiled and deadened. He had not forced her. She had come here on her own. She had lain on his bed, and when he placed her hand between his legs, she had curled and moved her fingers. Now, even after she had washed her hands, holding the crisp slender hundred-dollar bill he had given her, her fingers still felt sticky; they no longer belonged to her.[34]

It is tempting here, contra Michaels's claim that the neoliberal novel avoids questions of class in favor of those of cultural difference, to point to the famous passage in Marx's first volume of *Capital* in which he exposes the idea that the worker and the capitalist approach each other as equal traders "constrained only by their own free will" who "exchange equivalent for equivalent" as in fact the primal scene of inequality under capital: "He, who before was the money-owner, now strides in front as capitalist; the possessor of labor power follows as his labourer. The one with an air of importance, smirking, intent on business; the other, timid and holding back, like one who is bringing his own hide to market and has nothing to expect but—a hiding."[35] In locating the nadir of Ifemelu's time in America in this exchange, the novel highlights the economic dimensions of her problems. At the same time, her economic status is explicitly imbricated with issues of identity, and these should thus not be either dismissed as distractions or exported to other conversations entirely. Indeed, by insisting on Ifemelu's understanding of this episode as a choice, the novel suggests the way in which a neoliberal language of individual economic agency is inevitably inflected by such factors as race, gender, and national status. Here we thus see how the neoliberal novel of migrancy offers narrative context as well as the imperative for thinking about economics and identity simultaneously. Moreover, the fact that Adichie's novel gives us this low point in Ifemelu's early days in the United States serves as an illuminating counterpoint for the terms through which she is able to escape the menial, servile, and sexualized locations of labor and remuneration to which she was originally confined within the United States as a transnational subject without capital. It makes clear the ways in which capital relies on the very existence of nations, and their unequal distribution of rights, for the exploitation of labor power, on which it depends for profit.

Conclusion

Ifemelu's decision to move back to Nigeria, after essentially achieving and then abandoning the American dream (home ownership *and* citizenship), and Julius's cosmopolitan detachment from humanity, which plays out in unsettling and perhaps violent ways, both work to confound the deterministic script that views immigrant assimilation into American society as the endgame of immigrant fiction. Both novels, in this way, trouble the normalized expectations of immigrant fiction in order to reset its aesthetic stakes and in turn launch critiques of neoliberal capitalism. Though this essay focuses on these two novels, it does so to offer a model for thinking about contemporary fiction by Marlon James, Junot Díaz, Zadie Smith, Helen Oyeyemi, and Kei Miller, among others, that troubles the normalized expectations of immigrant, national, multicultural, or minority fiction by animating the workings of neoliberal capitalism within localized contexts. If, as I have been arguing, the genre of neoliberal migrant fiction provides a framework for expressing the lived stakes of global economic inequality, then attending to it provides an important way of addressing the localized contexts of specific works of fiction (be they New York, New Jersey, Kingston, Lagos, London, or elsewhere) without being insular or inattentive to national or global frameworks.

In the cases of *Open City* and *Americanah*, drawing parallels between the transnational immigrant subject and neoliberal capital achieves this. The first thing one notices when one considers novels of migrancy like these is that unlike the earlier form of the immigrant novel—with its linear plot and definite endgame of becoming a member of the United States or some other wealthy nation—these novels foreground spaces outside the United States (not only Nigeria but also Belgium and England). This foregrounding does not serve as an endorsement of cosmopolitanism, but rather deploys cosmopolitanism critically, both as a medium for animating and understanding this geographical/formal nonlinearity and as an aesthetic analogue of the shift in capital that we refer to as neoliberalism. Whereas in the immigrant novel the individual models herself on the nation and commits to a process of development and modernization, in the neoliberal novel of migrancy the individual models herself on a form of capital committed to endless movement across borders and commits to enrichment in various spaces. Ultimately, however, both novelists suggest the ways in which such aspirations remain stymied by the global presence and operation of capital in conjunction with the nations that no longer contain it.

NOTES

1. Teju Cole, *Open City: A Novel* (New York: Random House, 2012); Chimamanda Ngozi Adichie, *Americanah: A Novel* (New York: Alfred A. Knopf, 2013).

2. Walter Benn Michaels, "Model Minorities and the Minority Model—the Neoliberal Novel," in *The Cambridge History of the American Novel*, ed. Leonard Cassuto, Clare Virginia Eby, and Benjamin Reiss (Cambridge: Cambridge University Press, 2011), 1016–30.

3. Jeffrey J. Williams, "The Plutocratic Imagination," *Dissent*, Winter 2013, www.dissentmagazine.org/article/the-plutocratic-imagination.

4. Ibid.

5. Michaels, "Model Minorities," 1029.

6. Ibid., 1027.

7. Ibid.

8. Paul Gilroy, " ' . . . We Got to Get Over Before We Go Under . . . ' Fragments for a History of Black Vernacular Neoliberalism," *New Formations*, 80/81 (December 2013): 23.

9. Ibid., 35.

10. Pheng Cheah and Bruce Robbins, eds., *Cosmopolitics: Thinking and Feeling beyond the Nation* (Minneapolis: University of Minnesota Press, 1998).

11. Bruce Robbins, "Actually Existing Cosmopolitanism," in *Cosmopolitics: Thinking and*

Feeling beyond the Nation, ed. Pheng Cheah and Bruce Robbins (Minneapolis: University of Minnesota Press, 1998), 1.

12. Thomas Piketty imagines this more tangibly as an entity that can impose a universal wealth tax. In economic terms, this would decrease the threat of divergence by curtailing the rates of return on capital. See Thomas Piketty, *Capital in the Twenty-First Century*, 1st ed., trans. Arthur Goldhammer (Cambridge, MA: Belknap, 2014).

13. Pieter Vermeulen, "Flights of Memory: Teju Cole's *Open City* and the Limits of Aesthetic Cosmopolitanism," *Journal of Modern Literature* 37, no. 1 (Fall 2013): 41.

14. Cole, *Open City*, 22.

15. Robbins, "Actually Existing Cosmopolitanism," 3.

16. Ibid., 19.

17. Ibid., 20.

18. Cole, *Open City*, 186.

19. Ibid., 40.

20. Ibid., 120.

21. Ibid., 121.

22. Aaron Bady, "Interview: Teju Cole," *Post45*, January 19, 2015, http://post45.research .yale.edu/2015/01/interview-teju-cole/.

23. Alyssa Rosenberg, "Rape and Memory in Teju Cole's *Open City*," *ThinkProgress*, March 28, 2012, http://thinkprogress.org/alyssa/2012/03/28/453078/rape-and-memory -in-teju-coles-open-city/.

24. Ibid.

25. For a more extended discussion of Julius's fugue states and the sociopathy they belie, see Pieter Vermuelen, "Flights of Memory: Teju Cole's *Open City* and the Limits of Aesthetic Cosmopolitanism," *Journal of Modern Literature* 37, no. 1 (2013): 40–57.

26. Cole, *Open City*, 245.

27. Ibid., 243.

28. Ibid., 244.

29. Ibid., 243–44.

30. Adichie, *Americanah*, 204.

31. Ibid., 133.

32. Ibid., 132.

33. Ibid., 155.

34. Ibid., 156.

35. Karl Marx, *Capital: An Abridged Edition*, ed. David McLellan (Oxford: Oxford University Press, 2008), 113.

Neoliberal Childhoods

The Orphan as Entrepreneur in Contemporary Anglophone Fiction

CAREN IRR

Since the 1980s, neoliberalism has emerged as a shorthand or slogan for a set of economic policies that includes deregulation of financial markets, privatization of national industries, and fiscal consolidation or austerity measures. Although long favored by the International Monetary Fund (IMF), these policies have also been roundly criticized for the economic inequality they foster. In 2016, these critiques came home to roost when two of the IMF's own leading economists argued that neoliberalism has been oversold and that the increased economic inequality attributable to neoliberal policy "hurts the level and sustainability of growth."[1] Concluding that "policymakers, and institutions like the IMF that advise them, must be guided not by faith, but by evidence of what has worked," these economists highlight the fact that between the 1980s and the 2010s neoliberalism had transformed from a policy into an article of "faith."[2] Neoliberalism shifted, in other words, from a policy to an ideology.

To understand the workings of ideology, Louis Althusser's formulation remains useful. Unlike literal-minded theorists who treat ideology as an unmediated expression of class interest, Althusser defines ideology as "an imaginary representation of individuals' imaginary relation to their real conditions of existence."[3] This doubly imaginary relationship involves both illusions about and allusions to real conditions. It is not mere illusion alone, though, and that is why ideology can be interpreted to "discover the reality of this world beneath the surface."[4] This Althusserian treatment of ideology provides starting points for understanding both sociocultural processes of subject formation and the manufacture of a dominant social consensus.

To interpret neoliberal ideology as it has shifted away from a narrow set of policies and saturated innumerable aspects of social life, becoming an ideological dominant, we can examine the effects it has had on conceptions of the social subject in formation—i.e., the child. This concern is prominent in recent Anglophone fiction about childhood. Novels about children written for adult audiences sort through a matrix of competing ideologies of the child. To isolate the most distinctive features of the dominant neoliberal sensibility in these works, it helps to take a few steps back to briefly examine the situation from which they emerged. We need to give neoliberal ideologies of childhood some history.

Since the 1930s, in advanced capitalist democracies, large swaths of childhood have fallen under the eye of the state. Child protection agencies intervene in homes where abuse or neglect are suspected, highly regulated public schools oversee children's education, and child labor laws define the limits of children's engagement in the workplace. These welfare state initiatives conceive of children as inherently innocent. Regardless of any possible moral failings of the parent, the welfare state seeks to cultivate the child's talents and support his or her growth. This approach authorizes state intervention in the name of the child's best interests and well-being and looks to "promote a healthy, 'well-adjusted' society by supporting the production of healthy, well-adjusted selves."[5] In an influential formulation in *Childhood*, the sociologist Chris Jenks describes this cluster of attitudes and projects as Apollonian; the Apollonian child, he asserts, "has natural virtues and dispositions which only require coaxing out into the open."[6] Thus, from Jenks's perspective, both antiabortion activism and progressive child-centered education might be understood as expressions of the ideals of the welfare state. Both protect the perimeter of the child's environment in order to allow the full flourishing of a uniquely individualistic sensibility within those bounds— ideally through free and open play rather than control and discipline.

The latter approach is more characteristic of a sensibility that Jenks labels Dionysian. Conceiving of the child as inherently demanding and pleasure driven, and thus susceptible to evil, the Dionysian account favors forms of parenting and institutional control that consist of "distant and strict moral guidance, through physical direction."[7] While literary historians might associate the Dionysian approach to childhood most immediately with the punitive Dickensian orphanage, Jenks points out that it persists as well in later Christian and psychoanalytic accounts of the child. He stresses the ongoing debate between Dionysian and Apollonian approaches that organized discussions of child welfare throughout the twentieth century.

Both sides of this dialogue about childhood rely heavily on institutional— usually state—oversight. Hence, both are markedly at odds with the antistatist tendencies that are central to twenty-first-century neoliberalism. In their efforts to strip down the state to its policing functions, ardent neoliberals relocate responsibility for cultivation of the self from state agencies to the child itself. Highly competent, a full participant in his or her own upbringing, largely autonomous, and fully capable of independent choice, the ideal neoliberal child engages in continuous self-care. From this angle, regardless of the parents' well-being, the ideal neoliberal child is functionally a social orphan, existing largely outside of the guardianship of both the family and the state. Building on Jenks's terminology, Karen Smith calls this figure the Athenian child. She describes how "neoliberal and advanced liberal rationalities of rule create the need for reflexive, adaptable, 'enterprising' subjects equipped with the capacity to actively work upon themselves."[8] The ideological project of inventing the Athenian child creates a new common sense for parenting. This common sense is most visible in its violations— which include both excessive applications of welfare state protections (e.g., the arrest of parents who allow school-age children to walk home or play in parks alone) and inappropriately disciplinary parents (e.g., the Tiger Mother). These residual practices violate the dominant neoliberal norm of the child who behaves as a largely independent, unparented, and entrepreneurial self defined by consumption habits and individual rights.

Over the past decade, scholars in childhood studies have identified a number of distinctively neoliberal institutions influencing the lives of contemporary children. They have documented ways that a child who is understood as a self-motivated and independent agent of choice is required to take on responsibility in areas as diverse as making appropriate consumer choices, avoiding screens, and preventing her own obesity.[9] The same child must also "own" his performance in school by taking responsibility for attendance, study time, grooming, and psychological well-being. Rather than parents or teachers governing the child, the child governs herself while adults retreat to the back seat; their primary role is to accept liability when or if the child fails to make the approved decisions. This is the reasoning adopted by neoliberals who advocate making teachers' salaries dependent on children's performance on standardized tests, for example, or punishing parents for a child's criminal activities.[10] Even responsibility for child abuse can be laid at the doorstep of neoliberal children, when they are exhorted to "stay safe" and "avoid stranger danger."[11] In innumerable situations, neoliberal ideology requires the child as entrepreneurial free agent to choose correctly (i.e., in accordance with neoliberal priorities) in order to merit reward and advancement or even to remain within the confines of the supposedly normal. To ensure that this cycle of normalization continues, an ever-expanding network of data collection, networked games, and finely tuned testing rubrics isolate particular skills and monitor the child's continuing capacity to choose. The neoliberal child, in other words, enjoys freedom from parental guidance in a context characterized by continuous surveillance that assesses whether or not she has made "good choices," as the saying goes. This entrepreneurial or Athenian child is socially orphaned and largely responsible for raising himself even when external support is tangibly available.

Research in childhood studies conclusively demonstrates that the neoliberal approach to childhood proves particularly difficult for poor children. When the standards for successful socialization require access to the expertise, autonomy, and individualistic behaviors most characteristic of and available to the upper middle classes in wealthy nations, then children from low-income families are judged as having been poorly socialized; seen through the lens of the dominant ideology, they fail to demonstrate themselves as sufficiently entrepreneurial.[12] Low-income children are most apt to be designated "at risk." Domestically in the United States, this leads to their subjection to a host of strategies designed not to alter an unequal distribution of resources but rather to instill normative middle-class values—strategies ranging from mentorship and social skills initiatives to enforced summer or after-school extensions of the environments most heavily controlled by dominant groups. To create security for the most domestically successful children, the United States then exports these neoliberal risk management strategies internationally.[13] This process both externalizes responsibility for the United States' own "failed" neoliberal subjects and describes poor children in the developing world as a danger to its own most protected youth population. The voluminous public discourse surrounding the "flood," "surge," or "invasion" of Central American child refugees reaching the border during summer 2014 provides innumerable examples of this logic; Honduran, Guatemalan, and Mexican children seeking refuge from violence or reunion with their US-based parents were described in the media as inherently threatening scam artists, criminals, and violence-prone gang members.[14] This "undisciplined" population of menacing children is crucial to neoliberal efforts to create "an escalating sense of panic and anxiety over 'children at risk' who are also understood to be 'risky children.' "[15] Neoliberals extend the same logic to many parts of the world; the increasingly young and mobile populations of the developing world are presented as an undisciplined and threatening horde, lacking proper oversight from family and home state alike. Where others might see refugees or young people caught in the crosshairs of geopolitical conflict, neoliberals see Dionysian orphans ungoverned by suitable parenting—dangerous figures who must be sealed off from the differently orphaned Athenian children who reside within the national fortress. Neoliberal discourse thus revives and exaggerates the figure of the Dionysian child in order to negate the welfare state's idealistic vision of the Apollonian child. Neo-liberals then install their ideal of the self-parenting entrepreneurial orphan as the future leader of a volatile global population.

In this respect, the neoliberal concept of the child echoes Max Weber's classic formulation of the entrepreneur in *The Protestant Ethic and the Spirit of Capitalism*. Weber's entrepreneur ascetically extracts himself from the networks of ca-maraderie and pleasure that preoccupy his contemporaries, setting in place the building blocks of self-control that ultimately allow him access to social control: "The ideal type of the capitalistic entrepreneur . . . avoids ostentation and unnec-essary expenditure, as well as conscious enjoyment of his power. . . . It is just that which seems to the pre-capitalistic man so incomprehensible and mysterious, so unworthy and contemptible."[16] The difference, however, is that while the Weber-ian entrepreneur rejects the temptation of the Dionysian comforts enjoyed by his perplexed peers, the late capitalist neoliberal entrepreneur revives a Diony-sian other in order to dismantle a social network mediated by the state. In so doing, the entrepreneurs of a neoliberal self-governing childhood atavistically re-turn to late nineteenth-century social scenes. In their promotion of orphanage care for the children of welfare recipients or their investment in the No Child Left Behind Act's continuous testing, the neoliberal account of childhood reveals itself as an internally contradictory matrix of views—i.e., as a syncretic ideology pre-mised on illusory class, national, and racial inequalities—rather than a coherent system of knowledge.[17] As an expression of this contradictory situation, the pop-ulations of children who are the objects of neoliberal initiatives thus find them-selves stripped of public resources such as food stamps, income supplements, or public investment in higher education even as they are simultaneously made the recipients of relentless scrutiny of their caloric intake, leisure activities, and cog-nitive functioning. Contemporary neoliberal childhood thus repeatedly restages the unresolved ideological conflicts within and among Apollonian, Dionysian, and Athenian sensibilities, and its representations expose the conflicted social situa-tions encoded within these sensibilities.

Perhaps because they include so many important contemporary concerns, scenes of neoliberal childhood—especially those that feature the "riveting image of the social orphan"—have proved extremely attractive to literary narratives directed at adult readers.[18] Orphan stories in particular allow adults to imagine the complex outcomes of neoliberal efforts to reshape the child's process of self-formation. They sort through the dilemmas intrinsic to the Athenian concept of the child while also staging that figure's dependence on and sometimes reversion to its Dionysian other.

Orphans have, of course, a long literary history. Orphaned children have served as exemplars of virtue in eighteenth-century didactic literature that aims to stamp out the child's Dionysian sinfulness, such as *Goody Two Shoes* (1765). They have provided sentimental reminders of the transformation of private life that occurs with market expansion in Dickens's more romantic and Apollonian narratives, and they test the boundaries between these two concepts of the child in the heroic adventure stories of Kipling and Twain. Thrust, as it were, naked into social life, apparently lacking the mediating protection of the family, orphans make the ideal protagonists for politically charged narratives addressing the most antisocial aspects of market economies. Periods of rapid reorganization and consolidation of social systems in the face of capitalist transformation have, to date, seen a proliferation of orphan narratives. The industrial 1850s, the rise of the post–World War II information economy, and the contemporary financial crisis all saw rising numbers of stories featuring orphans and orphanages.

Regardless of period, orphan stories normally use the figure of the orphan to assess the capacity of existing systems of social reproduction to sustain the human population during periods of massive economic reorganization. The orphan provides a figure of disturbance, contradiction, and possible failure for the reigning system of social reproduction, and the political tendencies of orphan narratives are generally most evident in the means the author uses to reincorporate that disruptive figure into the society at large. The orphan is the outlier whose exceptional situation allows the testing of reigning concepts of the child.

In contemporary fictions addressing neoliberal childhood, the crisis in question concerns the capacity of the orphan figure not only to survive but also to thrive in specifically entrepreneurial terms without institutional support. One important type of contemporary orphan story commits itself to describing the presumed superiority of private, usually faith-based care relative to the child welfare initiatives resulting from state-mediated intervention or state-funded institutions. This kind of narrative valorizes spontaneously organized communities of care while simultaneously expressing criticism of the state's inadequate efforts to prevent a Dionysian child from emerging. Maeve Binchy's best-selling *Minding Frankie* (2010) provides a particularly striking example of such a narrative. Set in twenty-first-century Dublin, Binchy's novel describes the solidarity of neighbors on a lower-middle-class cul-de-sac who join forces to care for an infant whose birth mother left her in the hands of a previously hapless resident who has been designated (wrongly, as it turns out) as the biological father. The neighbors pull together to keep the infant Frankie out of the clutches of a psychologically damaged social worker whose rigid requirements for care and supervision express her own needs rather than those of the child and, more to the point in the novel, the girl's nonbiological and nonadoptive caretakers. The novel depicts both the social worker and the deadbeat biological father (a much more elusive character) as inherently unsuitable guardians for Frankie after the death of the calculating birth mother. The birth family is thus imagined to be inherently dissolute and Dionysian. Instead of these equally undesirable state and biologically authorized forms of parenting, the novel prefers a kaleidoscope of informal but church-sanctioned care arrangements, situating the child among these in order to insist on the viability of social reproduction outside the state.

As Wendy Brown's observations on the consonance between neoconservatism and neoliberalism in the American context remind us, the latter continues to exploit social divisions (race, class, gender, nation, geography), remaining largely indifferent to claims for equality.[19] Thus, it should not surprise us to discover similar differentiations in the neoliberal literature of childhood. For instance, we note that the fundamental elements of Binchy's narrative recur most frequently in orphan stories featuring female protagonists. They are evident in Margot Livesey's *The Flight of Gemma Hardy* (2012), Frances Peebles's *The Seamstress* (2008), Lydia Millet's *My Happy Life* (2003), Leila Aboulela's *Minaret* (2005), Gail Tsukiyama's *The Language of Threads* (2000), and even somewhat differently Peter Carey's *His Illegal Self* (2008). These works wrestle with predecessor narratives that rescue the possibly illegitimate female orphan by integrating her into middle-class norms for social reproduction by way of marriage, often to a father figure. This reworking of Victorian norms is particularly clear in Livesey's novel, since it adapts the narrative situation of Charlotte Brontë's *Jane Eyre* (1847) to a contemporary Scottish setting. In Livesey's version, the Jane figure lives almost entirely outside the eye of the state; in a crucial scene, for instance, after fleeing the attentions of her Mr. Rochester, she loses her wallet and what little cash she has to a pickpocket on a bus and (in an image of extreme economic isolation that is almost a required scene in this body of literature) is reduced to wandering the countryside on foot. After collapsing at the side of a road, Livesey's Gemma is rescued, nursed, employed, and introduced to marriage opportunities by a local lesbian couple. Defined in the novel as necessarily operating outside of the state as a result of their sexuality, Gemma/Jane's lesbian surrogate parents offer their services to her purely voluntaristically and altruistically. Their generous care is systemically inexplicable yet vital to the Athenian child's imagined ultra-independence; the surrogate parents make no effort to connect Gemma to local authorities or her biological family. Only when Gemma independently decides to pursue knowledge of her long-dead birth mother's origins in exotic Iceland do her circumstances change. She travels on her own to her mother's village (where she is again aided by an older woman of inexplicable good will), and she rewrites her family narrative around a sense of a heroic, self-made iconoclasm forged in a remote fishing village. Refreshed with a new account of herself as a rugged individualist and fortified with a legacy helpfully preserved in an Icelandic bank, Livesey's twenty-first-century Jane Eyre is at last ready to reunite with her Rochester on the return flight. Her reentry into social reproduction, in other words, takes place by means of an entrepreneurial detour through geographical remoteness and a defining experience of isolation and self-reliance. Livesey's orphan heroine embraces the neoliberal ethic of the entrepreneurial self wholeheartedly.

In all of the other novels mentioned above, international mobility—or a collapsing of social distance accelerated by the so-called time–space compressions of neoliberalism—also features prominently in the female orphan's journey of self-discovery. A deep investigation into the local family is of little interest. Instead, orphaned heroines swerve outward, migrating, in Aboulela's case, from Khartoum to London or, in Peebles's novel, around northeastern Brazil and then to New York City. Peter Carey's male–female team of orphans flees New York City for rural Australia, while Millet's unnamed heroine recalls, from the confines of her condemned institution somewhere in the American heartland, her travels by boat and foot around the Americas. These mobile, wandering female orphans are released from local familial bonds that might embed them in a marital system of state-mediated responsibilities to others. Instead, they float dangerously free on the tidal wave of neoliberal economic change. The female orphan-heroes are presented in all of these works as having been liberated from containment in a dysfunctional nation-state by their mobility. Aboulela's heroine, for instance, flees a corrupt kleptocracy in which her father was implicated. After her mother's death and her brother's imprisonment, the heroine of *Minaret* is thus left bereft, lacking even the comforts of a community of expatriates in London, and after several missteps she successfully reinvents herself only by voluntarily joining a community of worshippers in a cosmopolitan London mosque.

The state in the person of the father also features in Peebles's novel of outlaws in 1930s Brazil. Peebles describes the world of *cangaceiros*, bandits who roamed the Brazilian countryside during a period of rapid capitalist reorganization of the economy and infrastructure. The titular seamstress is a young woman who detaches from residual and emergent state forms by joining the Dionysian bandits, while her Athenian sister marries the son of an elite family with ties to the state leaders who are pursuing the gang and attempts to leverage her influence. The orphaned sisters' relationship to one another and eventually to the next generation is thus controlled by a threatening father-in-law, and marriage once again fails to integrate the more compliant female orphan into social life. However, the more rebellious seamstress is also unable to escape containment within the increasingly systematized modern state, and her death ultimately triggers her sister's flight to North America. The necessity of flight also appears at the climactic conclusions to Tsukigawa's, Carey's, and Millet's novels, as intensive police scrutiny applied by the unsympathetic state threatens painful entrapment. In all of these novels, the orphan discovers herself only when she flees the state; periods of intense social isolation and wandering are required before she can reenter a largely voluntary extrastate community of care (whether Carey's Australian hippie commune or Tsukigawa's Chinese silk sisterhood) and participate in any project of social reproduction. The orphan as a mobile, independent entrepreneur of the self thus resolves the lingering traumas inflicted by the family of origin and the failure of the protective state by voluntarily choosing a new community of believers.

In an era when the mobility of orphaned children or young adults is in actuality quite limited, in part because of the absence of adult figures capable of navigating the complex architecture of passport controls and refugee citizenship, these novelistic accounts of the orphan's liberating migration are, of course, clearly imaginary.[20] These novels imagine the neoliberal child's exultant triumph over and release from state-maintained borders in an era when the rigidity of border controls has, if anything, intensified for child migrants, especially those from the developing world. The effect of this fantasy, then, is to propose an ideal impossible for the world's majority, an ideal that simply dispenses with older public modes of social reproduction without addressing the needs that created those forms. In novels played in the key of neoliberalism, the female orphan is precisely not the sentimental figure of impoverished need but rather that figure's phantasmatic inverse—a privileged, globally mobile recipient of Apollonian protection from the state.

Contemporary orphan stories with male protagonists take a somewhat different route through the same suite of issues—often veering even farther away from the institutions of family life. This drive toward extreme self-reliance develops the picaresque tendencies often evident in earlier male orphan stories such as Charles Dickens's *Oliver Twist* (1838), Mark Twain's *Huckleberry Finn* (1885), or Rudyard Kipling's *Kim* (1901). All of these titular orphaned boys are free to wander a society in transition because they mature outside the nuclear, parented family. Their dilemmas thus revolve around a quest to regulate their more anarchic and disruptively Dionysian tendencies (often homoerotic in nature). Toward that end, they are all incorporated into the labor market at a young age, and their plots turn on the relationships they develop with employers/exploiters from Oliver's Fagin to Huck's Duke and the spymaster in *Kim*. In contemporary fiction, however, the orphaned boy is already a self-regulating Athenian child; in fact, he is as likely to be an entrepreneurial organizer of other people's labor as he is to be an employee. This is one way the male orphan-hero manages some of the risk generated by neoliberal ideologies of childhood. As entrepreneurial employer, the non-white, developing-world orphan boy simultaneously figures the risk of a Dionysian "exterior" to neoliberalism and presents an imaginary resolution to that threat in the possibility of his identifying with the norms of the protected center. The fact that "risk" is more readily associated with male and nonwhite protagonists reflects, I would argue, the nightmarish but likely conjunctural affiliation of neoliberalism and neoconservatism rather than any inherent logic; it is an extremely potent association, nonetheless.

Embodying risk, then, the male orphan enters fiction by Amitav Ghosh, Aravind Adiga, Mohsin Hamid, Vikas Swarup, Nadifa Mohamed, Randy Boyagoda, and Tash Aw as an already self-disciplined ascetic subject, well prepared for the demands of the marketplace and eager to advance within it on the terms laid by the system itself. As the globally dominant American style of corporate capitalism in particular requires,[21] he seeks few comforts or holidays and rarely craves companionship. The prospect of intimacy continues to be figured as a dangerous queer menace in this fiction, but the child himself refuses this temptation rather than being governed by external authorities (such as the slave market in *Huck Finn*). In fact, in contemporary orphan stories, the male child rejects as abusive almost every invitation into intimacy, because he has internalized (although not without cost) extrinsic demands and defines himself primarily in terms provided by the market. Culture, language, religion, race, and the state are not major players in his narrative, except as regulatory functions to be evaded or outrun.

Beyond a quest for physical survival, the male orphan's motives in this fiction are imagined as the reemergence of a different sort of Dionysian drive—mainly vengeance.[22] In this respect, their literary predecessor is perhaps Heathcliff of *Wuthering Heights*, rather than the always already self-governing governess of *Jane Eyre*. Psychically wounded by familial or social abandonment, the contemporary male orphan/entrepreneur experiences a kind of loss that most readily expresses itself as calculated violence against the imagined source of pain. The orphan's Athenian labors are directed at collecting resources and social power that allow for the climactic expression of a lifetime's worth of resentment. There is no credible social institution or agency—police, courts, church, or state—to which the orphan turns for redress; he must take on the task of revenge himself. Contemporary stories of the vengeful orphan, in other words, propose a world in which the ideological incoherence of neoliberalism is phantasmatically resolved by a detour around social life altogether. Entrepreneurial strategies thus appear as the only available means for managing the dilemmas of a self organized around social failures; they allow the fantasy of a vengeful settling of scores to thrive and in so doing empty out or negate any drive to examine the host of complex factors that might create or worsen loss.

The use of entrepreneurial strategies to achieve the orphan's vengeance is especially evident in Swarup's 2005 *Q&A* (republished under the title *Slumdog Millionaire* after the release of the Oscar-winning film based on the novel). Swarup's novel uses the format of a high-stakes quiz show to examine the life story and desires of a male orphan in India. The conceit of the novel is that the orphan is being interviewed in order to ascertain that he actually knew the answers to the quiz questions himself; each chapter is organized around a question and provides narration of an incident that explains how the answer to the question embedded in the orphan's consciousness. This formal ploy initially suggests that the stakes of the novel involve the orphan's desire to prove himself a knowledgeable and legitimate game player, one whose access to the prize money was fairly acquired. The plot turns, however, on the revelation that the orphan's motives were actually personal, not purely financial. His performance in the game was organized strategically in order to facilitate his access to the host, a sleazy john who had abused the orphan's prostitute girlfriend. In seeking to avenge his girlfriend's abuse, the orphan solidifies his own earlier identification with her (she had herself been trafficked and socially orphaned by her family). He also acts out symbolically against the Fagin-like leader of a gang of street children who had tried to maim and sexually abuse him earlier in his childhood. The successful resolution of the climax of *Q&A*, then, hinges on the orphan's ability to discipline himself effectively in the tense competitive scene of the quiz show and the following investigation into its dynamics. He employs a doubly stressful form of self-control in order to have a brief encounter in a bathroom, a moment that promises an illusory means of control over the sources of his own social isolation.

Characterizations and plot constructions similar to Swarup's also appear in many other works. Tash Aw's *Five Star Billionaire* (2013), for instance, includes as one of its focal points in its exploration of the economic aspirations of Malaysian immigrants in Shanghai an angelic and lonely pop star isolated by his fame. Gary's agent has circulated a sentimental but false story of his being orphaned as a child and thus craving a kind of transcendent publicity. The real orphan of the novel, however, is the behind-the-scenes investor who lures a celibate businesswoman into a deal and an affair in order to ruin her. Very late in the novel the investor's personal motives are revealed: the woman's family had callously destroyed his father and left the boy adrift without social or monetary support. As in *Q&A*, then, an excessive drive toward vengeance serves as the orphan's primary psychological motive, and the revelation of this motive serves as the climax of the novel, while the bulk of the narrative's middle is devoted to entrepreneurial machinations and suggests a certain admiration for the many layers of cloaking and long-term deferral these involve. All the characters in Aw's Shanghai disguise or rename themselves in order to achieve status in the city's economy; regardless of position, they all employ some of the orphan's strategies, but only his motives are so directly presented. His desire for vengeance serves as a stand-in for the less crystalline motives of other figures.

Ghosh's *The Glass Palace* (2000) and *River of Smoke* (2011), Boyagoda's *Beggar's Feast* (2011), and (to a lesser extent) Mohamed's *Black Mamba Boy* (2009) all follow a similar pattern. An orphaned boy is set socially adrift and seeks out opportunities to establish himself financially in hopes of one day returning home to settle scores. Vengeful motives are not always expressed violently in these novels, but some kind of reckoning with the pointed failures of a father figure is always necessary, and the marketplace is the only sphere in which a self strong enough to meet this need is able to flourish. Ghosh's entrepreneurial heroes have already attracted some critical attention, so I won't belabor them here.[23] Boyagoda's and Mohamed's heroes are a little more complex. Set in Sri Lanka and Somalia, respectively, both novels trace the fortunes of a potentially Dickensian figure whose prospects are severely constrained by poverty and the failures of religious and aid organizations alike. They are not entrepreneurial in the most obvious sense (having ready access to capital and recognition as a manager of others' labor), but they do both clear the decks for the emergence of a neoliberal self by quickly dispensing with other options. Both narratives move the orphaned boy-hero through scenes devoted to exposing the limitations or hypocrisy of traditional culture—be it in the form of excess consumption in a monastery or sexual exploitation within the family clan. Both set the orphaned hero literally adrift on ocean voyages where his capacity for self-denial, silence, and absorption into a business enterprise is tested. Unlike the more open-ended destiny of Mohamed's hero, though, Boyagoda's Sam Kandy proves to be an unqualified success in business terms. At the end of the novel, observing a crowd of boys swarming around his van, he muses, "They weren't queued in a shipping agent's office waiting to go out into the world and take what they could of it. They were already taking from the world, and all the world they wanted was here and now." In contrast to this shortsighted rabble, "Sam Kandy had run enough, had taken and spent and broken and been given far more than enough to know what kind of races were run and won in vain. It was late, he was weary, yet he knew."[24] While Sam's role in "the races" does not always appear admirable in the novel, his competitive spirit and endless need to redress wrongs not of the "here and now" but rather of the past are its undeniable heart. Despite its ambiguity, Mohamed's narrative (based on her father's migration journey) similarly affirms the sacrifices of pleasure, comfort, intimate connections, and personal aspirations made by its hero. The entrepreneurial self who overcomes multiple betrayals and learns to rely on no one and nothing in a dangerously competitive life, figured as a race, is the destiny of the male orphan in these works.

To force the emergence of this orphan as entrepreneur, an evacuation of the social scene is usually necessary. The orphan tours available social institutions (the family, the orphanage, the religious institutions, and the like) in order to expose their failings, reject them, and take off on his own. Often this evacuating move is affirmed as a vital narrative premise, but sometimes it becomes a target of satire, especially in narratives that are more prone to an explicitly critical assessment of neoliberal assumptions. Mohsin Hamid's *How to Get Filthy Rich in Rising Asia* (2013) is probably the clearest example of the satirical approach to an entrepreneurial orphan story, but some of the same motifs are crucial to Aravind Adiga's *The White Tiger* (2008) as well. Hamid's novel invokes self-help slogans to tell the story of a personal and regional "rise" (though echoes of William Dean Howells's *Rise of Silas Lapham* [1885] appear, too). With chapter titles such as "Avoid Idealists," "Learn from a Master," "Work for Yourself," and "Be Prepared to Use Violence," Hamid clearly calls into question the origins of his protagonist's motivations and construction of self. As in the business self-help genre as a whole, Hamid's hero succeeds by internalizing marketplace imperatives and redefining himself not as the solitary adolescent orphan but rather as a budding entrepreneur. He "rises," as expected, and in so doing is able to make occasional contact with his fantasy love object, a model, but at the pinnacle of his ascension he experiences a medical crisis that is symbolically and narratologically entwined with the business plot. His "business [is] . . . quantified, digitized, and jacked in to a global network of finance" at the same moment in which the business owner has "become a kind of cyborg, part man part machine. Electrodes connect [his] chest to a beeping computer terminal mounted on a rack, and a pair of transparent tubes channel oxygen from a nearby metal tank to [his] nostrils and fluids from a plastic pouch into [his] bloodstream through a needle taped at [his] wrist."[25]

After this terrifying exchange, both the protagonist and his unnamed city enter a state of decline. Hamid, in brief, satirizes the extrinsic motivations of the orphan as entrepreneur and makes the effects of inhabiting that position hyperbolically terrible.

In Adiga's *The White Tiger*, we find a similar turn to direct address, since the novel is organized as a series of letters written by the orphaned protagonist to "His Excellency Wen Jiabao," the premier of China, on the occasion of a visit to India. Adiga's hero is also intent on rising, and his letters document not only his journey from village to city as a chauffeur but also his motives in turning toward vengeance against his wealthy employer. Rather than justifying the hero's violence with an abuse subplot that makes entrepreneurial ambition the resolution to anxieties resulting from deprivation, however, Adiga weds vengeance to the neoliberal sensibility. "HOW BIG CAN YOU THINK?" an advertisement challenges his hero in the novel's final pages; "I took my hands off the wheel and held them wider than an elephant's cock. '*That* big, sister-fucker!'" he responds.[26] His hero's inflated, aggressive mentality is invited and bolstered by his participation in an economy that fuses a desire for vengeance with a drive to succeed in economic terms.

In plotlines like those created by Hamid and Adiga, vengeance reproduces the deaths that created the orphan in the first place, creating cycles of excess and unmanaged antagonism that fuel neoliberal growth ideologies. The orphan who attempts to align himself fully with an entrepreneurial project thus becomes the parodic extreme not only of self-negating neoliberal asceticism but also of the evacuation of social knowledge characteristic of that discipline. The orphan as vengeful entrepreneur reveals the self-destructive core of neoliberal ideology when his character is reduced to an obsessive death drive. His status as human surplus leads to his being expelled from the cycles of social reproduction after the death of parents or guardians, and he subsequently attempts to make himself the hallmark of efficiency through total identification with market imperatives to grow ever bigger. This effort to recreate himself socially backfires, however, when the orphan-hero faces the prospect of being utterly eradicated, converted from human waste on the sidelines into an inhuman cyborg runner in a race with no end. Evacuation of the social system, in other words, morphs into an emptying out of the isolated protagonist who embodies the system's dilemmas. While the female orphan-hero accelerates into abstract mobility, the male implodes in negation, with both following the neoliberal logic to its absurd and inhuman consequences.

At this point, one might well ask whether contemporary fiction shows any signs of moving past this sort of reductio ad absurdum to provide alternative narratives of the entrepreneurial child's high-stakes process of self-making. Since contemporary orphan stories tend to downplay the value of a strictly liberal individualist model of the child's human rights by suggesting the complicity of that view with neoliberal idealizations of the orphan, do they envision any other possible futures for vulnerable children? What has been the fate, for instance, of the Eros-driven child who refuses the societies of control that Herbert Marcuse called the one-dimensional society?[27] Do orphaned narrators become parents themselves in a manner that suggests ways of connecting those populations that neoliberalism imagines as excessive or surplus to one another translocally, as it were? Can any autonomist account of social value that exists prior or exterior to capitalist circuits of accumulation and dispossession be located in this body of writing?

Some of these options postulated by critical theory begin to find narrative form in a minority strain of orphan stories. Lydia Millet's *My Happy Life*, for example, introduces a third vision of childhood. Elements of Millet's novella link the entrapped orphan's quest for her own lost child—one in whom she remains irrationally invested and for whom she willingly expends all of her available energy—to a fear of species extinction. Trapped in a condemned hospital, Millet's narrator recalls fleeting visions of her long-lost child at the horizon of her miserable world. As she rushes toward this vision of lost freedom, she revives her environmentalist ethic: "I knew that a child was not a possession. I never believed that Brother belonged to me, only that he *was* me."[28] This radical identification redirects a conventional reproductive futurism toward multispecies empathy. Millet's association of human isolation and extinction occurs at an even less allegorical level in her so-called extinction trilogy—*How the Dead Dream* (2008), *Ghost Lights* (2011), and *Magnificence* (2012). "She wants to know whether it's possible to live with death, to be endangered from the moment one is born. She's asking whether there's salvation to be found," a reviewer at the *Boston Globe* writes.[29] These questions launch Millet toward a radically anti-possessive relation to the disappearing and endangered beings of the world—human and animal alike. This seems to be the closest the new orphan stories come to presenting an alternative to neoliberalism's fixation on the human child as an independent economic actor, nurtured (if at all) by loose and unofficial community groups. In social welfare projects, however, if not in fiction, an even more forceful and elaborate account of options for orphans may be necessary if we are interested in contesting neoliberalism's consignment of the orphans of the developing world in particular to the margins of legitimate existence.

NOTES

1. Jonathan D. Ostry, Prakash Loungani, and Davide Furceri, "Neoliberalism: Oversold?," *Finance and Development*, June 2016, 39.

2. Ibid., 41.

3. Louis Althusser, *On the Reproduction of Capitalism*, trans. G. M. Goshgarian (London: Verso, 2014), 181.

4. Ibid.

5. Karen Smith, "Producing Governable Subjects: Images of Childhood Old and New," *Childhood* 19, no. 1 (2012): 28.

6. Chris Jenks, *Childhood* (New York: Routledge, 1996), 73.

7. Ibid., 71.

8. Smith, "Producing Governable Subjects," 33.

9. See Elisabeth Harrison, "The Body Economic: The Case of 'Childhood Obesity,'" *Feminism and Psychology* 22, no. 3 (August 2012): 324–43.

10. Deborah Albon and Rachel Rosen emphasize the influence of neoliberalism on schooling practices in *Negotiating Adult–Child Relationships in Early Childhood Research* (New York: Routledge, 2014), 25. Parental liability for student choices is a theme in Sarah L. Holloway and Helena Pimlott-Wilson, "Neoliberalism, Policy Localisation and Idealised Subjects: A Case Study on Educational Restructuring in England," *Transactions of the Institute of British Geographers* 37, no. 4 (October 2012): 639–54.

11. See Gillian Harkins, *Everybody's Family Romance: Reading Incest in Neoliberal America* (Minneapolis: University of Minnesota Press, 2009).

12. Income discrimination in child welfare policy is a central theme of Lynn M. Nybell, Jeffrey J. Shook, and Janet L. Finn's introduction to *Childhood, Youth, and Social Work in Transformation: Implications for Policy and Practice* (New York: Columbia University Press, 2009).

13. Erica Burman describes this process, linking the export of neoliberal self-management strategies, for instance, to microcredit schemes in "Deconstructing Neoliberal Childhood: Towards a Feminist Antipsychological Approach," *Childhood* 19, no. 4 (2012): 423–38.

14. For examples of coverage of the defensive and militaristic rhetoric used during child refugee crisis, see Gabriel Debenedetti, "In Town Halls, U.S. Lawmakers Hear Voter Anger over Illegal Migrants," *Reuters*, August 28, 2014, http://uk.reuters.com/article/us-usa-immigration-townhalls-idUKKBN0GS0AS20140828; Sarah Rumpf, "Texas Tea Party Leaders Release Plan to Secure Border, Criticize Perry," *Breitbart News*, September 5, 2014, www.breitbart.com/texas/2014/09/05/texas-tea-party-leaders-release-plan-to-secure-border-criticize-perry/; and Michael Martinez, Holly Yan, and Catherine E. Shoichet, "Growing Protests over Where to Shelter Immigrant Children Hits Arizona," *CNN*, July 16, 2014, www.cnn.com/2014/07/15/us/arizona-immigrant-children/.

15. Nybell, Shook, and Finn, *Children, Youth, and Social Work*, 14–15.

16. Max Weber, *The Protestant Ethic and the Spirit of Capitalism*, trans. Talcott Parsons (New York: Routledge, 1930), 33.

17. For a detailed account of neoliberal efforts to reestablish orphanages, see Richard B. McKenzie, ed., *Rethinking Orphanages for the 21st Century* (Thousand Oaks, CA: Sage, 1999),

esp. Ross D. London's essay "The 1994 Orphanage Debate: A Study in the Politics of Annihilation," 79–102.

18. Lisa Cartwright, "Images of 'Waiting Children': Spectatorship and Pity in the Representation of the Global Social Orphan in the 1990s," in *Cultures of Transnational Adoption*, ed. Toby Volkman (Durham, NC: Duke University Press, 2005), 185–212.

19. Wendy Brown, "American Nightmare: Neoliberalism, Neoconservatism, and De-democratization," *Political Theory* 34, no. 6 (2006): 690–714.

20. Majia Holmer Nadesan makes this point forcefully in *Governing Childhood into the 21st Century: Biopolitical Technologies of Childhood Management and Education* (New York: Palgrave, 2010), 165.

21. Tim Kasser et al., "Some Costs of American Corporate Capitalism: A Psychological Exploration of Value and Goal Conflicts," *Psychological Inquiry* 18, no. 1 (2007): 1–22.

22. My thinking on this subject has been greatly enhanced by the imaginative treatment of revenge fiction that appears in Kyle Wiggins's "Lethal Measures: The Politics of Revenge in 20th- and 21st-Century American Fiction" (PhD diss., Brandeis University, 2012). Wiggins describes a number of failed or impossible revenge schemes in revenge narratives that seek to redress systemic social ills.

23. Gaurav Desai, "Old World Orders: Amitav Ghosh and the Writing of Nostalgia," *Representations* 85, no. 1 (Winter 2004): 125–48.

24. Randy Boyagoda, *Beggar's Feast* (Toronto: Viking, 2011), 300.

25. Mohsin Hamid, *How to Get Filthy Rich in Rising Asia* (New York: Penguin, 2013), 183, 185.

26. Aravind Adiga, *The White Tiger* (New York: Free Press, 2008), 274.

27. Herbert Marcuse, *One-Dimensional Man* (Boston: Beacon, 1964).

28. Lydia Millet, *My Happy Life* (Brooklyn: Soft Skull, 2006), 90.

29. Jenny Hendrix, review of *Magnificence*, by Lydia Millet, *Boston Globe*, November 17, 2012, www.bostonglobe.com/arts/books/2012/11/17/review-magnificence-lydia-millet/ohuaqMGGfo1CfgGjHgF1LK/story.html.

Post-recession Realism

ANDREW HOBEREK

This essay makes two wagers: first, that the 2008 banking collapse and the recession that followed will ultimately prove the most significant events in early twenty-first-century literary history; and second, that at some point in the future critics will come to recognize Gillian Flynn's 2012 *Gone Girl* as the defining realist novel of this period. Of course, it might seem strange to label Flynn's popular crime thriller a work of realism. In making this claim, however, I am thinking of realism not as a technique for representing some preexisting reality, but as a practice of *inventing* new social logics, particularly in times of transition. *Gone Girl* does so, in ways that more obvious works of realism remain too mired in existing conventions to do.

As Mitchum Huehls and Rachel Greenwald Smith note in the introduction to this volume, in the twenty-first century neoliberalism—having earlier expanded from the economic into the political and sociocultural spheres—enters into a new ontological phase. In this ontological phase, the market saturates all spheres of life: it "does not require specific economic pursuits, political commitments, or ideological beliefs; it only requires our presence, our being in and of it." While I agree with Huehls and Smith's historical taxonomy of neoliberalism, as well as with their assertion that in this final phase it increasingly seems like "the world has become post-ideological and post-political," reading Flynn's novel complicates their account on two important fronts. First, and most basically, it suggests the way that literature in general can be out of synch with seemingly dominant cultural logics, for reasons that may have as much to do with its inherent conservatism as its ability to envision vanguard social logics. I begin by comparing *Gone Girl* with the work of Jonathan Franzen in order to suggest that the mainstream realist novel took time to acknowledge our world's saturation with neoliberalism precisely because it was committed to its own deeply ingrained account of middle-class subjectivity. Second, and relatedly, *Gone Girl* suggests that neoliberalism's ontological phase may not be as totalizing as we think, but may in fact be a particular worldview: that of the middle class, whose vehicle has historically been the novel and whose very existence is now threatened by the economic changes that neoliberalism has helped advance.

Flynn's novel announces its status as a middle-class fable in many ways, a number of which I discuss below. But the most obvious may be its reproduction of what is perhaps the ur-middle-class narrative since the eighteenth century, the story of a decadent aristocrat (in this case, the wealthy St. Louisan Desi Collings) who seeks to force himself on a middle-class woman. While *Gone Girl's* Amy Dunne may seem far from a Pamela-like paragon of virtue, and while she enacts her own baroquely violent vengeance on Collings, I argue below that she and her husband, Nick, serve as something like aspirational figures at a moment not of middle-class ascendance but of the class's seemingly imminent extinction. In this way, *Gone Girl* demonstrates how a seemingly ontological neoliberalism is in fact continuously constructing itself in the pores of culture.

Jonathan Franzen's novels, sometimes cited as the chief realist fiction of the new century, demonstrate the novel's belated relationship to neoliberalism. While *The Corrections* (2001) and *Freedom* (2010) acknowledge particular elements of the neoliberal economy—the rise of unregulated pharmaceuticals, the globalizing effects of the Internet, the growth of disaster capitalism—they remain unable to tie these isolated phenomena together into some larger picture of the contemporary social whole. In large part this is the case because they approach contemporary reality within the framework of an outmoded liberal subjectivity that predates the post-1980 triumph of market logic and social disinvestment that we call neoliberalism. Jeff Williams is, in this respect, not quite correct to say that the political liberalism espoused by *Freedom's* Walter Berglund is belied by his neoliberal economic beliefs, which include the notions that "government is cumbersome and inefficient, social problems can be more effectively handled through private means than public ones, the super-rich are not only entitled to political power but also make the best political choices, their interest serves the public interest, and those not rich are naturally supplicants to those who are."[1] In fact, as his job running the coal miner Vin Haven's Cerulean Mountain Trust demonstrates, Walter believes in neither the priority of private solutions nor the ability of the rich to make choices on society's behalf. Franzen's novel makes it clear that Haven does not fund the environmental trust out of idealism, but only as a way of whitewashing his participation in mountaintop removal. Walter believes that he can, however, bend Haven's self-interested motives in the service of enlightened public interest. Walter is, in this regard, a classic Kennedy liberal as defined by Sean McCann: a figure suspicious of both government bureaucracy and interest group politics (whether of the rich or of working people), who seeks instead to build social movements of disinterested citizens acting in the interests of the nation as a whole.[2] When he fails to make good on this goal, Walter, as Franzen's characters so often do, retreats from the disappointing terrain of public engagement back into private life—literally, to an old vacation cabin, and figuratively, into renewed domesticity with his formerly estranged wife Patty and the most limited, middle-class form of environmental protectionism (the creation of a private bird sanctuary) imaginable. If, as Rachel Greenwald Smith has convincingly argued, Franzen sees novel reading as a fundamentally neoliberal form of investment in one's own construction as an entrepreneurial subject,[3] the content of his novels continues to register a kind of shocked befuddlement at, and retreat from, a world that doesn't work in the terms of the late twentieth-century political liberalism that was displaced by the Reagan and Thatcher revolutions.

Williams is thus closer to the mark when he writes, "It is not that Franzen advocates neoliberalism, and in fact he exposes some of its dubious values, but, adhering to the conventions of literary realism, he cannot imagine any other possibility."[4] We can fine-tune this point even further, though, if we understand the conventions in question not as those of literary realism per se, but of a specific form of literary realism that has arguably lost its ability to describe contemporary reality. If Franzen's politics date back to the pre-1980 United States, a significant component of his aesthetic dates back about a hundred years earlier, to the Jamesian realism that, as Carrie Tirado Bramen puts it, "emerges from an understanding of the world as fundamentally hostile, constituted by limits and constraints of all kinds, beginning with those established by our own mortality."[5] If this version of subjectivity has always been, by definition, constituted in and through its mismatch with the existing social world, it is *fundamentally* at odds with the version of subjectivity central to neoliberalism. As Wendy Brown argues, neoliberalism is defined by the expansion of economic rationality to every sphere of life, including politics and subjectivity itself, with the result that we come to understand "the state as the manager of a firm and the subject as a unit of entrepreneurial and self-investing capital."[6] Neoliberalism promises to free the individual from the constraints imposed by the state and other nonmarket actors, but in fact, "as the province and meaning of liberty and equality are recalibrated from political to economic, political power comes to be figured as their enemy," and the individual is left subject to an inherently unequal "market formulation of winners and losers."[7] This subsumption of the political by the economic undermines

not only popular democratic sovereignty but also the forms of subjectivity associated with it:

> With the vanquishing of *homo politicus*, the creature who rules itself and rules as
> part of the demos, no longer is there an open question of how to craft the self or
> what paths to travel in life. . . . In the neoliberal *political* imaginary . . . we are no
> longer creatures of moral autonomy, freedom, or equality. We no longer choose our
> ends or the means to them. We are no longer even creatures of interest relentlessly
> seeking to satisfy ourselves. In this respect, the construal of *homo oeconomicus* as
> human capital leaves behind not only *homo politicus*, but humanism itself.[8]

If we accept Brown's account, then the everyday construction of subjectivity has
outstripped the aesthetic technologies that the realist novel has relied on to represent it. In other words, the drama of the individual's struggle with moral and
other limits that has been central to realism from James through Franzen no
longer provides an adequate representation of what people are like.

This problem goes beyond just the novel's representation of people, however,
and affects its ability to represent a social totality more generally. György Lukács
has famously argued that the modernists' fascination with subjectivity left them
"emotionally and intellectually . . . frozen in their own immediacy" and unable
"to pierce the surface to discover the underlying essence, i.e. the real factors that
relate their experiences to the hidden social forces that produce them."[9] But an
outmoded version of subjectivity arguably provides just as poor an instrument for
constructing a vision of social totality as an estranged one, approaching (as I have
suggested Franzen does) the features of neoliberalism as so many disconnected
social facts unconnected by any underlying logic. Contra Lukács, then, we might
understand the history of modernist innovation from James forward as a primary
resource for recalibrating our accounts of subjectivity, albeit one often unconcerned with reconnecting subjectivity to a larger social whole and—crucially in
the present context—now seemingly unable to keep up with the neoliberal remaking of subjectivity. Neoliberalism's transformation of the person into a form of
human capital is, to put it succinctly, unconcerned with the inner life as we have
traditionally understood—as the novel has traditionally taught us to understand—
it: "Human capital's constant and ubiquitous aim, whether studying, interning,
working, planning retirement, or reinventing itself in a new life, is to entrepreneurialize its endeavors, appreciate its value, and increase its rating or ranking.
In this, it mirrors the mandate for contemporary firms, countries, academic departments or journals, universities, media or websites: entrepreneurialize, enhance competitive positioning and value, maximize ratings or rankings."[10] This

is, in fact, not too bad a description of the main characters and narrators of *Gone Girl*, the troubled husband-and-wife pair of Nick and Amy Dunne.

Crucially, though, Flynn arrives at her novel's reconfiguration of subjectivity not through a commitment to literary experimentation, but rather through an investment in a particular tradition of noir fiction. This tradition, whose past exemplars include Patricia Highsmith and Jim Thompson, focuses on criminals rather than detectives and is committed to exploring extreme (rather than typical) forms of human behavior from the inside. And indeed, Flynn sees Nick and Amy as, for the most part, idiosyncratic figures different from those around them. Ironically, however, she presents through them what may be the normative form of subjectivity under neoliberalism.

This is the case at least partly because *Gone Girl* remains tied to another aspect of the noir tradition, its (distinctly realist) concern with the everyday details of social life. Fredric Jameson provides perhaps the best account of this element of noir in his 1970 essay "On Raymond Chandler." Jameson initially describes Chandler, in distinctly Lukácsian terms, as "primarily a stylist," a writer whose "sentences are collages of heterogeneous materials, of odd linguistic scraps, figures of speech, colloquialisms, place names, and local sayings, all laboriously pasted together in an illusion of continuous discourse."[11] But Jameson then goes on to note how Chandler's detective Philip Marlowe serves a realist function: "As an involuntary explorer of the society, Marlowe visits either those places you don't look at or those you can't look at: the anonymous or the wealthy and secretive."[12] In this way, Jameson contends, the detective provides the "external force" necessary to overcome the "initial American separation of people from each other."[13] This formal aspect of detective fiction has traditionally been insistently local in its orientation, from Chandler's Los Angeles through Dennis Lehane's Boston and *The Wire*'s Baltimore, for reasons that Jameson describes. But *Gone Girl* pushes beyond the local, yoking two locations—New York City and the Mississippi River towns of northeastern Missouri—in a general picture of the post-2008 United States.

On a first reading, it is easy to miss how obsessed *Gone Girl* is with the post-2008 recession. This is in large part because the novel's plot seems to be a distinctively private one focused on Nick and Amy Dunne's disastrously rocky marriage. Flynn has stressed this element of the book in interviews, declaring in one, for instance, "I just wanted to write about the darkest side of marriage that I could. I think I was a recent newlywed when I started writing it. I wanted to look at the ways marriage influences people and what it does when it goes wrong. I liked the idea of a he said, she said tug-of-war between Nick and Amy."[14] The book begins on the day of Amy's disappearance from their home in the fictional Missouri town of North Carthage, where Nick grew up and to which he and Amy have moved from New York City. The first part of the book alternates between Nick's chapters, narrated from some point in the future, about the aftermath of Amy's disappearance and his transformation into the prime suspect, and a series of diary entries written by Amy detailing the unraveling of their marriage. As those who've read the book (or watched David Fincher's 2014 movie adaptation) know, however, about midway through it is revealed that Amy faked her own death (as well as the diary entries) in order to punish Nick for the decline of their marriage and his affair with a young local woman. The chapters continue to alternate, but now both in retrospective narration, detailing Nick's participation in the investigation and Amy's experiences following her disappearance.

But if Flynn's intentional plans for the novel focused on this "he said, she said" structure and the content of marital strife, the story was colored by the time of its composition in ways that Flynn also notes in the same interview. Asked about the fact that Nick and Amy have lost their jobs in New York City prior to the move, and about a group of jobless men who figure in the plot, Flynn replies, "I started writing the book at the height of the recession, and I had been laid off from *Entertainment Weekly*. The job situation for journalists has recovered a bit, but at the time everyone was just getting fired. It made me feel that we were heading into a new era. How do you reinvent yourself? As Nick says in the book, journalists are sort of like buggy-whip makers and women's glove makers—their time has come to an end."[15] Hence, Flynn's own experience of economic precarity colored her portrayal of Nick, who, like her, worked as a magazine writer in New York until he lost his job in a layoff.

Although Nick, as Flynn notes, describes this event in terms of technological obsolescence produced by the Internet, he also makes clear that it was overdetermined by the post-2008 recession: "I had a job for eleven years and then I didn't, it was that fast. All around the country, magazines began shuttering, succumbing to a sudden infection brought on by the busted economy."[16] Indeed, *Gone Girl* is supersaturated with physical reminders of the recession. Almost the first thing Nick tells us—well before the news of Amy's disappearance—is that the couple lives in an outsized suburban McMansion that is evidence not of prosperity but of the opposite: they can only find houses to rent in "a miniature ghost-town of bank-owned, recession-busted, price-reduced mansions, a neighborhood that closed before it ever opened" (4). This "failed development" (4) is nearly empty; four months after the couple move in, one of the neighbors who first greeted them "lost her mortgage battle and disappeared in the night with three kids" (31). When a police officer tells Nick, early on, that they are looking into break-ins and squatters in the complex, Nick replies, "This whole town is overrun with pissed-off, unemployed people" (96). And indeed, North Carthage has lost its two main employers: a mall, built in 1985, "that once employed . . . one-fifth the population" (96) but then went out of business "store by store" when "the recession hit" (97); and a plant called River Valley Printworks that made the blue books used, as one of Nick's former schoolmates tells him, "for essays and shit in college" until it too was driven out of business by "computers, whatnot" (126).[17] Nick's mother and her friends regularly sell plasma to earn spending money, and the women who work at the facility where his father, who is suffering from dementia, lives are "underpaid, gruelingly underpaid, which was probably why they never smiled or comforted" (44).

Nor is this precarity simply a local phenomenon; the New York that Nick and Amy leave also registers the effects of the 2008 downturn. Nick loses his job in a second round of layoffs at his magazine (113); Amy is laid off from her own job as a magazine quiz writer (115); and Nick's sister Margo ("Go"), having already participated in the dotcom bubble of 2000, loses her second job as an investment banker "with the 2008 financial meltdown" (23). Moreover, Amy finds herself having to return the money—proceeds from a children's book series loosely based on her life—that her parents had earlier given her after they too go broke. Amy's parents lose their money not only because book sales have tapered off but also, more tellingly, because they have invested poorly and are now "underwater" on both their own house and the one in which Nick and Amy live (118). As Amy's mother tells her daughter, invoking the financial instrument responsible for the banking collapse that set off the 2008 recession, "We should write a book: *Amazing Amy and the Adjustable Rate Mortgage*" (118).

Gone Girl's persistent references to the 2008 collapse and its aftereffects lay the groundwork for its realism, but they do not provide—any more than Franzen's invocations of big pharma and mountaintop removal do—what Lukács calls "the real factors that relate [characters'] experiences to the hidden social forces that produce them." Indeed, *Gone Girl* suggests the inadequacy of existing realisms to comprehend these phenomena by having Nick and Amy turn to genre tropes to describe them. When Nick enters the now derelict Riverway Mall in search of information about Amy, for instance, he describes the scene as "suburbia, post-comet, post-zombie, post-humanity" (154). And Amy's diary entry about visiting the plasma bank with Nick's mother and her friends, a trip designed to provide evidence of Amy's (fictional) fear of blood, expresses horror at "the people being, what, being *farmed*" (212; italics in the original).

Here, however, *Gone Girl* departs from the noir tradition as Jameson describes it, insofar as it does not base its realism on the detective's (or anyone else's) ability to move through and describe otherwise discontinuous social spaces. The novel features a pair of detectives working Amy's disappearance, but they do not actually solve anything. Nor do Nick, as a returned former resident of North Carthage, and Amy, as an outsider viewing it for the first time, serve any sort of ethnographic function. On the contrary, their descriptions are most often characterized by misreadings. Early on, for instance, Nick tells a story about the bar he and Go purchase with the last of Amy's money and name "The Bar": "Yes, we thought we were being clever New Yorkers—that the name was a joke no one else would really get, not get like we did. Not *meta*-get. We pictured the locals scrunching their noses: Why'd you name it *The Bar*? But our first customer, a gray-haired woman in bifocals and a pink jogging suit, said, 'I like the name. Like in *Breakfast at Tiffany's* and Audrey Hepburn's cat was named Cat'" (10–11; italics in the original). Nick notes, "We felt much less superior after that, which was a good thing" (11), but there's not much evidence that he learns a lasting lesson. For instance, he only realizes five days into the investigation of Amy's disappearance that he did not get, as he expected, "dumb cops, cops from the movies, local rubes aiming to please, trusting the local guy" (238). Similarly, one of Amy's diary entries describes a housewarming party at which the local women greet her with stereotypes of New York City. But although she characterizes herself at the start of the entry as "the Margaret Mead of the goddamn Mississip" (161), her own descriptions of the women trade almost exclusively in stereotypes about Midwestern hairstyles, Midwestern recipes—"casserole[s] made from canned soup, butter, and a snack chip" (164)—and Midwestern niceness.

In what is perhaps Amy's most puzzling episode of misreading, she loses the large pile of cash she is carrying around with her by failing to exercise proper caution around a pair of fellow lodgers, Greta and Jeff, at the rundown Ozarks resort where she is hiding out. This almost seems like an authorial mistake, given Amy's repeated assertions of pride in the "patience, planning, and ingenuity" (318) that were required to fake her death and her skill at manipulating Nick, the police investigating the case, and others. In fact, Flynn calls attention to this incongruity: after the pair rob Amy, Greta tells her, "Next place you go, be more careful, okay? You gotta not look like a girl traveling by herself, hiding out" (411–12). Greta and Jeff may, in fact, be the best readers in the novel: they read Amy's situation very accurately and profit from their skill by $8,769 (407).

But this isn't actually very much money by the standard of other figures cited in *Gone Girl*. For instance, Nick and Go pay almost ten times that for The Bar (9);

one way in which Amy frames Nick is by running up charges in the amount of $212,000 on credit cards in his name (244); the celebrity lawyer, Tanner Bolt, whom Nick hires to defend him, requires a $100,000 retainer (282), which Go funds by double-mortgaging her house (475). When Greta takes Amy's money and estimates it (incorrectly) at "more'n a thousand, two or three," she asks Amy, "Damn, girl! You rob a bank?" (411). The clear implication is that a few thousand dollars transcends the boundaries of what Greta understands as realistic, and that she is no better at apprehending the social totality than anyone else in the novel.

Gone Girl thus leaves it up to readers, without the aid of character surrogates, to grasp "the real factors that relate [characters'] experiences to the hidden social forces that produce them." In this regard it is telling that so many of the book's big-ticket transactions involve real estate, not only because of the role that the bursting of the housing bubble played in the 2008 collapse but also because of the "fictitious" nature of the capital involved in this bubble. This word is used by David Harvey, who describes the bubble as follows: "Easy credit meant rising housing prices and high rates of turnover meant a plethora of opportunities to earn exorbitant fees and commissions on housing transactions. The bundling together of the mortgages (a form of fictitious capital) into collateralized debt obligations created a debt instrument (an even more fictitious form of capital) that could be marketed worldwide. These instruments of fictitious capital, many of which turned out to be worthless, were marketed to unsuspecting investors around the world as if they were investments certified by the rating agencies to be 'as safe as houses.' This was fictitious capital run wild."[18] While on the one hand Harvey contrasts this "fictitious" realm to the real world of productive capital and use values (houses as sources of shelter), on the other we can see it as a description of "the hidden social forces" responsible for such observable social phenomena as the empty houses in the Dunnes' subdivision. It is not the houses per se that constitute the novel's realism, but its efforts to limn these forces.

Here we can return to Nick and Amy's tendency to see the world in terms of clichés or mass cultural tropes and argue that *Gone Girl* seeks to construct a social totality at the level of characters' subjectivity. It does so by imagining the neoliberal subject as someone engaged with social fictions not as a reader but as a writer, in the broadest sense. To begin to see how this works, we can note the clever and seemingly throwaway fact that Amy becomes Facebook friends with her husband's mistress by using a fake name and a profile picture "stolen from a popup ad for mortgages (blond, smiling, benefitting from historically low interest rates)" (333). The syntax of the parenthetical series is an example of Flynn's care as a writer: the people who benefited from low interest rates during the 2007–8 bubble were in fact not homebuyers but realtors and others engaged in the market. This fake profile stands metonymically for all the personas Amy takes on throughout her life: "Amazing Amy. Preppy '80s Girl. Ultimate-Frisbee Granola and Blushing Ingenue and Witty Hepburnian Sophisticate. Brainy Ironic Girl and Boho Babe (the latest version of Frisbee Granola). Cool Girl and Loved Wife and Unloved Wife and Vengeful Scorned Wife. Diary Amy" (319). Amy's greatest skill is in fact adopting these personae: "The way some women change fashion regularly," she notes, "I change personalities" (299). She uses this skill for vengeance against Nick until she realizes that it can provide her with an even more expansive, and more figuratively and literally profitable, way of being in the world.

Of course, *Gone Girl* makes its most explicit connection between writing and profit via the *Amazing Amy* book series, written by Amy's parents, which provides their daughter with a trust fund worth $785,404 (116) before they reclaim most of it. When Amy first mentions the series in her diary, she expresses a predictable resentment at the way her parents used these books to passive-aggressively chide their real child for her failures—making the fictional character persevere in pursuits the real Amy had let languish, for instance (36). But as the diary and then Amy's retrospectively narrated sections progress, she expresses a very different sort of economically based resentment: "they plagiarized my childhood for the books" (117); "Until Nick, I'd never really felt like a person, because I was always a product" (302); "They never, ever fully appreciated the fact that they were earning money from my existence, that I should have been getting royalties" (321). The ambiguity here between Amy's life as a form of intellectual property robbed by her parents and Amy as herself a form of property—elsewhere Nick too describes her as "literally [her parents'] work product" (365) in their capacity as parents—suggests the crucial distinction between agency and objecthood at stake in the question of who controls Amy's story. Such control, as we have seen, has nothing to do with authenticity and everything to do with authorship and who profits from it.

Foregrounding this question of self-authorship helps us to see the subtle transition that Amy undergoes during her time hiding out in the Ozarks, and to reframe the theft of her money by Greta and Jeff. Near the start of the chapter in which we first learn that Amy is alive, having faked both her death and the diary entries we were reading, she notes, "I can tell you more about how I did everything, but I'd like you to know me first. Not Diary Amy, who is a work of fiction (and Nick said I wasn't really a writer, and why did I ever listen to him?), but me, Actual Amy. What kind of woman would do such a thing? Let me tell you a story, a *true* story, so you can begin to understand" (297; italics in the original). Here Amy expresses pride in authoring her diary persona, "a work of fiction," claiming her role as an author in the shadow of not only her parents but also her journalist husband. She seems to promise a return to authenticity, however, suggesting that the story she will now tell us is true. But in fact, this claim functions as an ironic joke about the form of the narrative itself, insofar as our understanding of the diary was driven by our expectations about the form (private, written in more or less real time, etc.) and its corresponding truthfulness: part of Amy's skill as an author was manipulating this form to give the illusion of veracity. Moreover, she undermines her own assertion of authenticity by capitalizing "Actual Amy" as she does the names of all her other personae. And the story she tells is doubly undermining, insofar as it relates how she first, as the one survivor of her mother's string of miscarriages, spent thirty-one years having to be "perfect"; and second, escaped from that "exhausting" performance by meeting Nick and wooing him in the guise of "the Cool Girl": "Nick loved a girl who doesn't exist. I was pretending, the way I often did, pretending to have a personality" (299).

But if it's personae all the way down here, and always has been for Amy, she still hasn't learned to turn this into a profitable way of being in the world. Nick's infidelities have revealed to her, she tells us, that she was not yet in control of her performances: "I had a new persona, not of my own choosing. I was Average Dumb Woman Married to Average Shitty Man. He had single-handedly de-amazed Amazing Amy" (315). Having utilized her skills to get revenge for this situation, she is now, she tells us, going to watch Nick's downfall while her money runs out and then—taking the performance to the hilt—do away with herself in order to provide the evidence of homicide that will send Nick to the death chamber (332). It is while watching the tabloid style *Ellen Abbott* show on daytime cable news that she begins to see another option, one exemplified by the show's host. Anxious for the show to begin, she thinks, "Hurry up, Ellen. Or: Hurry up, *Ellen*. We have that in common: We are both people and entities. Amy and *Amy*, Ellen and *Ellen*" (329; italics in the original). In marked counterpoint not only to Amy herself but also to the figures in the commercials that appear during the show—"You'd think all women do is clean and bleed" (329), Amy notes—Ellen Abbott is in control of the work product that bears her name. And unlike the *Amazing Amy* books, fixed in childhood and declining in sales, *Ellen Abbott* is ongoing. Amy still hasn't quite gotten the point, however: even after she decides, "I'm not going to die," she thinks, "The problem now though is money" (375). In this respect, Greta and Jeff's theft of her remaining cash serves a key plot point by forcing her to realize the potential not of money but of capital—in particular, the human capital represented by her gift for role-playing. The theft functions, that is, not as layoffs have done previously in the novel—making people spend their savings and become poor—but as layoffs function in neoliberal accounts of people freed from dead-end jobs to recognize their potential as self-entrepreneurs.[19]

Nick, meanwhile, is learning a similar lesson. Nick is vulnerable to Amy's plot in large part because, as she knows, he is bad at playacting. An early press conference provides just one instance of many in which he comes off poorly because he fails to convey the appropriate responses of a husband whose wife has disappeared in seemingly violent circumstances:

> I had worried about my voice wavering, so I overcorrected and the words came out clipped, like I was reading a stock report. . . . Utterly unconvincing, disconnected. I might as well have been reading numbers at random. . . .
>
> The news reports would show Nick Dunne, husband of the missing woman, standing metallically next to his father-in-law, arms crossed, eyes glazed, looking almost bored as Amy's parents wept. And then worse. My longtime response, the need to remind people I wasn't a dick, I was a nice guy despite the affectless stare, the haughty, douchebag face.
>
> So there it came, out of nowhere, as Rand begged for his daughter's return: a killer smile. (87)

Nick's roboticness and the Pavlovian manner in which he produces his utterly-inappropriate-under-the-circumstances smile serve, like the references to Amy as a "product," to cast him as an object rather than an agent. Here too the agency that is at stake is the agency of crafting one's own story. If Amy has the skill at role-playing without the profit, Nick has the profit without the skill at role-playing: as a result of media fascination with the crime, he tells us, "The Bar's business was booming," albeit with people who wish to drink "at the place owned by Lance Nicholas Dunne, the maybe-killer" (257).[20] Nick turns this around in two ways. First, he gives an impromptu camera-phone interview with a blogger that goes viral, impressing Amy as "heartfelt" (405) and shifting public opinion in his favor (413–14). Second, with coaching from Tanner Bolt and his ex–news anchor wife (who pelts Nick with jelly beans whenever he "tense[s] up" or lets his face look like "an undertaker's mask" [423]), he does a successful television interview. Here Nick, the laid-off print journalist, learns to manipulate precisely the media responsible for his obsolescence, in the process "taking control" by playing a new role: "I was no longer going to settle for being the possibly guilty husband or the emotionally removed husband or the heartlessly cheating husband. I was the guy everyone knew—the guy many men (and women) have been: *I cheated, I feel like shit, I will do what needs to be done to fix the situation because I am a real man"* (447; italics in the original).

Two things continue to distinguish Nick's transformation from Amy's, however. First, it arguably remains acting rather than the form of writing or authorship that is—as I will discuss in a moment—what is truly at stake. And second, it remains personal. As he tells Go when new revelations once again damage the public persona he has carefully rebuilt, "it doesn't matter what anyone else thinks. . . . What matters right now is what Amy is thinking. If *she's* softening toward me" (474; italics in the original). And indeed, on this front, he is successful: Amy, watching the television interview, thinks, "Nick is saying exactly what I want to hear. *Finally"* (470; italics in the original). As this phrasing makes clear, neither authenticity nor skill at reading is at stake here. Nick tells Go that "Amy was never a person with any sort of bullshit detector. If you said she looked beautiful, she knew that was a fact" (475). Nick is, as he knows, successfully manipulating his wife into returning home and saving him from the death penalty.

But what if we understand Amy's lack of a bullshit detector, at this point in the novel, not as a lack of skill at reading people's interiority, but as a recognition that such reading is irrelevant since performance is everything? Seeing this interview, Amy decides she wants to go home again, both because *Amazing Amy* sales "have skyrocketed" and her "greedy, stupid, irresponsible parents can finally pay back [her] trust fund. With interest" (471) and because she wants to return to her "old life" with a husband who's now "learned his lesson" and will play the role she wants: "my New Nick. Love-Honor-and-Obey Nick" (471). In the novel's third and final act, Amy does return home, where she spins her disappearance as an abduction by Desi Collings and seeks to construct a story of reconciliation with her now chastened husband. Nick, for his part, finds himself drawn to Amy— "I'd detect a nib of admiration, and more than that, fondness for my wife, right in the middle of me, right in the gut" (517)—and occasionally even finds himself accepting parts of her cover story because "She was that good a storyteller" (521). Still he resists, pretending to go along with Amy's plans while working with Go and the female detective who investigated him to try and catch his wife out. And when Amy begins writing a memoir about her experiences, Nick starts to author his own competing account.

These competing memoirs lay the groundwork for the novel's final vision of Amy's triumph as the author of her own story—and not just hers. "I have a book deal," she writes, "I am officially in control of our story" (544). In a pointed jab at her parents, who have accepted "a lovely fat sum" (536) to write a new *Amazing Amy* book, she notes, "I'm calling the book simply: *Amazing"* (544). But the book is not only a triumph over her parents, an exorcism of the identity in which they cast her. It is also, as the "our" indicates, a triumph over her husband, whose journalistic experience might seem to give him the advantage in the competition, but whose book project *Psycho Bitch* she forces him to delete by becoming pregnant (550–51). The final words of Nick's final chapter in the novel, "We are one long frightening climax" (553), express both his recognition of and discomfort with the story that Amy is authoring. He returns to speak, however, in the final paragraphs of the concluding chapter, which is narrated by Amy. In these paragraphs she expresses her dislike of his response to a question about why he treats her so well when she is pregnant: "He was supposed to say: *You deserve it, I love you*. But instead he said, 'Because I feel sorry for you.' 'Why?' 'Because every morning you have to wake up and be you' " (555; italics in the original). We might, as readers, feel inclined to cheer Nick on here for not only contesting Amy's wish to "ha[ve] the last word" (555) but also stubbornly maintaining his real self against the narrative she constructs.

Yet in the end, they are both still constructing narratives. And perhaps we shouldn't be so quick to dismiss Nick's feelings of admiration for Amy, or his grudging recognition that he really "couldn't return to an average life" with "a regular woman" (532). Maybe the book's ending *is* romantic. Maybe the book isn't even really, or primarily, about a marriage, but rather is the story of two people who lose their livelihoods thanks to the events of 2008 and in response learn to remake themselves—doing so in ways that not only restore their income but also put them more firmly in charge of it, because they are no longer employees but entrepreneurs leveraging their own human capital. Maybe *Gone Girl*, that is, is the story of the kind of subjectivity it takes to not only thrive but also take pleasure in the current capitalist era.

In one sense, this is a deeply ideological project, naturalizing the idea of the subject as human capital that is, according to Brown, best fitted to serve capital's interests. Yet precisely by grounding this form of subjectivity so insistently in a narrative of threatened middle-class existence, *Gone Girl* simultaneously denaturalizes it. One way of reading Flynn's novel, therefore, might be to say that in order to thrive within neoliberalism one has to be a bit—maybe more than a bit—of a sociopath. But even this reading is limited. Franzen's *Freedom* presents a case in which neither character nor author is able to assemble the various symptomatic phenomena of contemporary life into some workable whole, and in which the former, as a result, retreats into a form of privatized selfhood. *Gone Girl*, by contrast, shows that such retreat is unnecessary, since privatized selfhood is the structural logic of a world characterized by empty housing developments and health care workers too tired to perform intimate labor. Joshua Clover, writing about the decline of industrial labor struggles in the present era, asserts that "this outcome is not the consequence of political wiles, of some nefarious policy deployment under the heading of 'neoliberalism.' It is capital's own self-transformation from the perspective of labor—labor forced now to affirm capital in the same gesture through which it affirms its own being. . . . In its twilit lassitude, the working class is reduced to reproducing little beyond the conditions of its own immiseration."[21] Clover's scare quotes make clear his skepticism about the validity of the category of neoliberalism, but I take the force of this passage to be that if neoliberalism exists, it is no top-down conspiracy of capital, but rather a series of partial, local, uneven adaptations to it that nonetheless exhibit a clear tendency. *Gone Girl*, I would argue, makes much the same point. It is for this reason that it is the great realist novel of the early twenty-first century.

NOTES

1. Jeffrey J. Williams, "The Plutocratic Imagination," *Dissent*, Winter 2003, www.dissent magazine.org/article/the-plutocratic-imagination.

2. Sean McCann, "'Investing in Persons': The Political Culture of Kennedy Liberalism," in *The Cambridge Companion to John F. Kennedy*, ed. Andrew Hoberek (New York: Cambridge University Press, 2015), 59–74.

3. Rachel Greenwald Smith, *Affect and American Literature in the Age of Neoliberalism* (New York: Cambridge University Press, 2015), 33–37.

4. Williams, "Plutocratic Imagination."

5. Carrie Tirado Bramen, "James, Pragmatism, and the Realist Ideal," in *The Cambridge History of the American Novel*, ed. Leonard Cassuto, Claire Virginia Eby, and Benjamin Reiss (New York: Cambridge University Press, 2011), 304.

6. Wendy Brown, *Undoing the Demos: Neoliberalism's Stealth Revolution* (New York: Zone Books, 2015), 41.

7. Ibid., 42, 41.

8. Ibid., 41–42; italics in the original.

9. György Lukács, "Realism in the Balance," in *Aesthetics and Politics: The Key Texts of the Classic Debate within German Marxism* (1977; repr., New York: Verso, 1980), 36–37.

10. Brown, *Undoing the Demos*, 36.

11. F. R. Jameson, "On Raymond Chandler" (1970), in *The Poetics of Murder: Detective Fiction and Literary Theory*, ed. Glenn W. Most and William W. Stowe (New York: Harcourt Brace Jovanovich, 1983), 123–24.

12. Ibid., 128.

13. Ibid., 131.

14. Keith Lewis, "'Gone Girl' Author Talks about Her Missouri Roots,'" *Southeast Missourian*, October 20, 2013, www.semissourian.com/story/2015590.html.

15. Ibid.

16. Gillian Flynn, *Gone Girl* (New York: Broadway Books, 2012), 5. Hereafter cited in the text.

17. In a telling mistake, the reporter who interviewed Flynn in 2013 for the newspaper located in Cape Girardeau, the southeast (rather than northeast) Missouri town where Fincher filmed his adaptation, assumes that Blue Book refers to the annual state manual of Missouri that several years earlier had been shifted to online-only publication as a cost-savings measure by the state legislature. See Lewis, " 'Gone Girl' Author Talks"; Tim O'Neil, "Missouri's 'Blue Books' Made Extinct by Legislature," *St. Louis Post-Dispatch*, May 14, 2010, www.stltoday.com/news/local/govt-and-politics/missouri-s-blue-books-made-extinct -by-legislature/article_0b96664f-0b1f-5c4f-9265-0f93275bdf08.html.

18. David Harvey, *Seventeen Contradictions and the End of Capitalism* (New York: Oxford University Press, 2014), 32–33.

19. I owe this reading of the theft to the students in my Spring 2015 seminar "After the Crash: Capitalism and Fiction since 2008," who generally proved terrific interlocutors about Flynn's novels and were the first audience for some of the ideas I rehearse here.

20. Nick has just told us that his first name, which he fought to discard in school, has been resurrected by the media as "the dreaded three-name judgment reserved for serial killers and assassins" (256).

21. Joshua Clover, *Riot. Strike. Riot: The New Era of Uprisings* (New York: Verso, 2016), 149–50.

PART IV

NEOLIBERALISM AND LITERARY INSTITUTIONS

The Author as Executive Producer

MICHAEL SZALAY

In 1990, David Foster Wallace announced that US fiction had become, in effect, a subsidiary of commercial television. "American fiction remains deeply informed by television," he declared. Much of that fiction is "less a 'response to' televisual culture than a kind of abiding-in-TV." Speaking for his generation of novelists, he declares that "television has formed and trained us." Television, Wallace argues, has taught writers a self-conscious voyeurism different from the kind found in classical Hollywood cinema (in TV "espial," actors tacitly acknowledge the existence of the audience), and it has led them to embrace a species of irony derived from advertising. But the influence he tracks is not a matter of simple cause and effect. "Television," he writes, "even the mundane little businesses of its production, have become my—our—own interior."[1] How to understand that business as both within and encompassing the writer's person? For that matter, what does it mean for US fiction to "abide in TV"? Wallace's novella "The Suffering Channel" provides one answer, insofar as it points toward two kinds of channels (an intestine and a TV outlet) and two kinds of incorporation (as ingestion into alternately human and corporate bodies).

The business in question is neither mundane nor so little. Set in 2001, and published in *Oblivion* (2004) by Little, Brown, which was at the time owned by AOL–Time Warner, "The Suffering Channel" describes an AOL–Time Warner in "Wall Street freefall" (290), obliquely refering to the conditions that would lead to the sale of the imprint. Formed in 2000 in the largest merger in US history, even as the dot.com bubble was beginning to burst, by 2004 the media transnational was an object lesson in the follies of the new economy and had begun selling off many of its far-flung assets. The disintegration of the conglomerate, Wallace suggests, provides a glimmer of hope for the novelists once published by its subsidiaries. For Thomas Hobbes, corporations were "like many lesser commonwealths, in the bowels of a greater, like worms in the entrails of a natural man."[2] For Wallace, authors are worms in the entrails of the greater entity that is their corporate employer. The objet d'art–shaped shit that issues from Brint Moltke's alimentary canal (captured live on TV) represents the literary commodity produced under such conditions: when writers live within corporations and when the business of television production lives within them—TV channels in their digestive channels—those writers produce crap. The breaking apart of the corporate body might therefore promise the voiding of the corporate entrails and the passing of the incorporated writer—and the concomitant voiding of corporate business from the writer's insides. Thus does Wallace link the possibility of literary integrity with the corporeal integrity of persons on the one hand and corporations on the other.

Jennifer Egan's *Look at Me* (2001) and Colson Whitehead's *John Henry Days* (2001) also feature brief but telling references to Time Warner, but to different effect. For Wallace, AOL–Time Warner is in freefall; for Egan and Whitehead, writing in the lead-up to the big merger, Time Warner represents the apotheosis of the information economy. The two use the company as a synecdoche for an encompassing network of digitally mediated, post-Fordist relations that seem to have replaced the industrial labor relations with which the novel came of age. Anticipating the turn below to Walter Benjamin, we might say that, for them, the media corporation oversees "a mighty recasting of literary forms" that collapses "the distinction between author and reader" to reflect what these writers take to be a more general collapse between consumers and producers.[3] For Egan, the subject of this essay, that project leads, in her 2010 *A Visit from the Goon Squad*, to an elaboration of the conditions under which novelists now work within Time Warner's HBO. *The Sopranos* inspired her novel, Egan says, which makes sense given David Chase's claim that he first conceived of Tony Soprano as a TV producer. Optioned by HBO, *Goon Squad* develops the allegory about television production already implicit in the drama. But Egan's implied creator is less self-possessed and authoritative than Chase's, and less an abject victim of corporate concentration than Wallace's. Egan reconciles prestige novelists to managerial authority within the TV industry even as she casts the author as a late-arriving back-formation created by executives on the one hand and readers on the other.

"The Suffering Channel" divides what we might call its author function, its implied novelist, between Moltke and the equally hapless journalist Skip Atwater, an atavistic "salary man" who answers to the unpaid interns running the fashion magazine at which he works. The two make up the corporate body of the implied author as he labors within companies like Time Warner. Egan's author function is no less corporate—and, in fact, is more encompassing. The creative workers in *Look at Me* and *A Visit from the Goon Squad*—fashion models, ghostwriters, publicists, agents, journalists, photographers, musicians, and record producers— are related aspects of the transmedia novelist as she assumes different roles in the media industry and becomes in turn a kind of corporation unto herself, one among many worms within the entrails of the greater corporate commonwealth. Egan's incorporated author—always potentially a corporate employee—also supervises the production company within.

That supervisory role bears significant resemblance to the role performed by celebrity TV "showrunners" like David Chase, and for good reason. Lauded as a new kind of auteur, and yet beholden to network and studio executives while overseeing collaborative productions in which he has no strong copyright, the showrunner has become for novelists like Egan an unavoidable measure not simply of their success within the media industry, but of their struggle to reconcile the contradictory aspirations and affordances that characterize contemporary authorship.[4] The breaking apart of AOL–Time Warner is an important part of this story: it coincided with the rising influence of the showrunner and suggested corresponding opportunities for novelists, who might now imagine themselves working (once again) not within a vertically integrated transnational (as Wallace did when Time Warner owned Little, Brown), but between loosely coordinated units within a more dispersed and distributed production process. Under these auspices, the author as executive producer is as much brand as middle management: she provides the template that coordinates otherwise far-flung media. Real agency and control nevertheless elude her. With her managerial responsibilities comes the corresponding sense that she is a conduit or channel, her body a vessel rather than a point of origin.

My aim is not to accuse Egan or her peers of compromising some sacrosanct standard of aesthetic integrity essential to the creation of legitimate fiction. Nor do I mean to suggest, in the words of Dana Spiotta's *Eat the Document* (2006), that serious fiction should make us feel "as if we didn't have AOL Time Warner or Viacom tattooed on our asses."[5] Rather, I ask how and toward what end novels written in the image of "quality" TV revise the criteria by which literary integrity and autonomy are judged. I thus read Egan's fiction as a version of 1990s management literature, which, according to Luc Boltanski and Eve Chiapello, demonstrates not simply why a given administrative vision is propitious for a specific firm and the cadres there employed, but how that vision modifies inherited aesthetic and ethical standards for a larger group as well. That ideological project no doubt reflects many of the neoliberal imperatives outlined in this collection. Put more narrowly, Egan struggles to resolve contradictions inherent in the opportunities now afforded novelists by the rise of a newly prestigious and ostensibly literary television format.

Look at Me and the HBO Novel

In Whitehead's *John Henry Days*, the journalist "J." focuses "on the industrialinformation age angle" when reporting on a festival held in honor of the legendary pile driver from whom the novel borrows its name. J. considers the relation of his labor to Henry's. He and the other journalists, he thinks, "were like day workers who crowded the farmer's truck every morning for penny-work." But in his case, the farmer is a Time Warner website, which needs from him "not stories, not articles, but content. Like a mineral."[6] *Look at Me* pursues its "industrialinformation age angle" by cutting back and forth between its protagonist Charlotte Swenson, a one-time model, and, among others, a psychotic history professor (based on Wallace), Moose, who "worked feverishly" to discover *"what had gone wrong"* and "what, precisely, had been lost in the ineluctable transformation from industry to information." He "sensed that a terrible reversal was in progress whereby the genius of the Industrial Revolution would be turned on people themselves; whereby human beings would be assembled from parts just as guns and boots and bicycles had been once."[7]

Charlotte embodies that reversal; her face has been reconstructed in the wake of a devastating car accident. No longer recognizable, and thus out of work, she sells her story to an Internet startup, Ordinary People—funded by Time Warner and Microsoft—that "turn[s] people into cottage industries" (202) by making their day-to-day lives available over live web feeds to subscription-paying consumers. "Don't they own just about everything?" (203), she wonders, while considering this "frightening sponsorship" (204). So why shouldn't they own her life as well? It seems, at first, that they won't: the terms of her agreement do not require that she sell her IP outright; the startup rather takes a 50 percent commission on any royalties she receives from the sale of products associated with the transmedia franchise that her life will become (such as books, TV shows, movies, video games, and Barbie dolls). Nevertheless, in the end, she sells all of her "identity rights" to Ordinary People, and thus to Time Warner and Microsoft.

Most of those with whom the company contracts are what it considers "ordinary," which tends to mean associated with either precarious or industrial labor. As Thomas Keene, the CEO, explains, readers of the *New York Times* don't have to wonder, "Hey, what would it be like to be a coal miner?" They can "answer that question in a totally frictionless way" and "go straight inside a coal miner's life"

(198). Coal miners and other ordinaries get the extra income that they need: "Joe Shmoe gets rich for being Joe Shmoe," says Charlotte. And those fortunate enough not to work in factories get access to the ordinaries from whom they are alienated. "We work in offices, dealing with intangibles," says Keene; "we go to lunch and talk to other people surrounded by intangibles. No one actually makes anything anymore" (200). The startup would break through the surround by "wearing down that weird divide between folks like us, who deal in intangibles, and folks that're out there in the trenches, getting their hands dirty" (204). Egan's skepticism is palpable. All the same, and even granting the distance she places between herself and Moose and Keene, *Look at Me* romances the disappearing industrial working class, perversely, the better to motivate Charlotte's ultimate decision to sell to the company "exclusive rights to any and all property both tangible and intangible relating to the creation and maintenance of Subject's Identity, including but not limited to her name, image, possessions, domicile, personal history, photographs, private correspondence, diaries, travelogues, financial records, medical records, and any and all additional data pertaining to Subject's Identity." Liberated by this dispossession, and no longer burdened by ownership even of herself, Charlotte "wriggled from inside my life like a sheep shorn of too many winders' wool, pink skin tingling in the brusque, immediate air" (414).

The windfall from the sale is bountiful, even if "not nearly what she was worth" (414). The very privileged Charlotte will remain "folks like us." She remains, we might say, a woman of "quality," where that word denotes both a class of persons and a class of television. One of Keene's off-the-cuff remarks about why lives like hers qualify for coverage at all explains the novel's enigmatic ending, in which a creative worker gains her freedom by accepting (a lot of) money and giving up rights in her labors (in this case, her life itself). She is paid for her story, Keene explains, because his company has "created an offshoot of Ordinary People that he likened to Premium Pay cable: 'Extraordinary People'" (201). Charlotte is HBO, rather than, say, ABC. And it would be premium cable, and not just the Internet—and by extension, old media Time Warner rather than new media Microsoft or AOL—that would subsequently supply Egan and her peers with a robust account of what it meant to write "quality" fiction while expecting no rights.

Charlotte's story is thus extraordinary, we might say, in the way that Egan's own story would become after the publication of *Goon Squad*, which won the 2010 National Book Critics Circle Award and the 2011 Pulitzer Prize and, more importantly here, promised to be one of the first prestige novels influenced by an HBO drama to be adapted as an HBO drama. The genre-bending novel, organized as a series of songs on an LP, follows a punk band and its groupies from the 1970s into the not-too-distant future. But its fascination with the musical underground notwithstanding, Egan situated the work at the intersection of nineteenth-century autonomous literature and one of Time Warner's most lucrative properties. She claimed that Marcel Proust's *Remembrance of Things Past* and HBO's *The Sopranos* had each shaped *Goon Squad* in basic ways.[8] The debt was repaid in full: days after receiving her Pulitzer, Egan announced she would executive produce HBO's adaptation of the novel.

It is not surprising that Egan should have singled out *The Sopranos* as a yardstick for cultural prestige, even if her debt to the novel is hard at first to glimpse. The *New York Times* compared the mob drama to the films of Erich Von Stroheim and Rainer Werner Fassbinder and called it "the greatest work of American popular culture of the last quarter century."[9] Celebrated in countless similar accolades, *The Sopranos* made possible a generation of so-called "quality" drama and inaugurated a new "golden age of television." That drama spoke powerfully to novelists. No less a prophet of innovation than William Gibson declared, "Television has—particularly at the HBO level in the United States—become a completely new genre. Something like *Deadwood* or *The Wire* is a whole new thing—there was no equivalent to that medium before. It's like a new way of telling stories."[10]

At the same time, and along with almost every critic in the country, novelists declared the HBO drama a return to the nineteenth-century novel (while typically saying little about that novel's oft-invoked "realism"). As Michael Chabon put it, for instance, "There can't be a novelist in America who watched *The Wire* and didn't think, 'Oh my God, I want to do something like that.' . . . The tapestry is so broad, it's like a 19th-century novel."[11] Production companies took note. "At some point in the last year," said Michael London in 2011, the producer whose Groundswell Films brought *Goon Squad* to HBO, "everyone in the business had an epiphany that the DNA of cable television has much more in common with novels than movies do." He added, "It's not just that novels make good adaptations. It's that novelists make good adapters."[12] Showtime and HBO agreed: the premium channels recruited a raft of lauded novelists to adapt their work or create directly for TV: Egan, Salman Rushdie, Jonathan Franzen, Jonathan Lethem, Michael Chabon, Gary Shteyngart, Jeffrey Eugenides, Karen Russell, Chad Harbach, Sam Lipsyte, and Jonathan Safran Foer, to name a few. "What's next?" the *Washington Post* asked Shteyngart in 2012. "I've given up on fiction," he quipped. "And like every other writer in America, I'm working on an HBO series."[13]

The relationship between prestige writers and the culture industry was by then already a long one. Hollywood studios paid the likes of Faulkner, Fitzgerald, and Hemingway substantial sums for the rights to their work. But those novelists had no real status within production and did not influence the adaptation of their material. Hence, Hemingway's claim that "the best way for a writer to deal with Hollywood [is] to arrange a rendezvous with the movie men at the California state line: 'you throw them your book, they throw you the money, then you jump into your car and drive like hell back to where you came from.'"[14] The major studios have tended in turn to be as indifferent to industry writers as to novelists: because of the long-standing importance of the director to film production, even the most well-paid screenwriters have little to do with actual film production.

Not so in the television industry: long described as a "producer's medium," TV has tended since the 1980s to elevate staff writers (of whom there are around eight, give or take, serving on most shows) to the position of "showrunner," a figure who typically leads the writers' room while supervising all of those involved in the making and marketing of that show. Showrunners are management, endowed by studios with the power to hire and fire—even if many prominent showrunners assumed top negotiating positions on behalf of labor during the 2007–8 WGA Writers Strike. Prestige novelists rarely cite these managerial functions; they usually romance the showrunner's authorial sovereignty. Rushdie thus remarks that, "In television, the 60-minute series, *The Wire* and *Mad Men* and so on, the writer is the primary creative artist. You have control in the way that you never have in the cinema. *The Sopranos* was David Chase, *West Wing* was Aaron Sorkin. Matthew Weiner is *Mad Men*."[15] True enough as far as it goes, but being the "primary creative artist" means more than being the writer whose typed words matter most, as Shteyngart seemed to recognize. "HBO has made the writer king," he said. "It's a fabulous time for us. . . . You create the tune and others play the instruments."[16] In this account, the author is composer, conductor, and musical director: the cultural field to which many of our most feted novelists have committed fosters fantasies of managerial omnipotence.

The reality is that showrunners are middle management. To be sure, the most prominent among them have enjoyed unprecedented freedoms while pursuing "their" visions. But TV production is inherently collaborative, and, moreover, showrunners answer to their employers while coordinating the various creative inputs of their workforces. By the terms of the Minimum Basic Agreement set out between the Writers Guild and the studios and networks, showrunners are subject to the power of the network or studio "to direct the performance of personal services in writing . . . or in making revisions, modifications, or changes" to what they write (MBA Art. 1.C.1.a.(a)). And finally, despite whatever acclaim an adoring public heaps on them, or however generous their compensation, they are subject to the work-for-hire doctrine and hold only "separated rights" in the products of their labor.[17] In short, a showrunner does not own the show that he or she oversees, any more than he or she controls what is done with it after it is made.

That prestige novelists are not so easily reconciled to these conditions might explain why, as of this writing, not one series created by any of those named above has yet aired. Conversely, it might be that studios need literary prestige more than they do actual literary labor: better to show the world Jonathan Franzen desperate for an HBO series and then reject the pilot he helped produce than to employ him—potentially for years. Furthermore, it is not clear that all or even a significant portion of the novelists listed above want to become showrunners, rather than, say, executive producers with a far less active role in the day-to-day running of a given production (the showrunner is one among a number of executive producers typically attached to a show). But Rushdie sounds as if he did— as did Franzen, during his failed bid to bring *The Corrections* to HBO. (He's now listed as an executive producer of Showtime's adaptation of *Purity*, which is how Shteyngart is listed on Showtime's upcoming adaptation of *Super Sad True Love Story*.) Egan, for her part, was upfront from the start that she wanted others to oversee the adaptation of *Goon Squad*. "I don't envy them the job," she said. "But then again, that's partly because I have no idea how to do it."[18]

Benjamin, Brecht, Virno

In his 1934 essay "The Author as Producer," Walter Benjamin offers criteria for evaluating a writer's politics. Rather than asking, "What is the attitude of a work *to* the relations of production of its time?" he writes, "I would like to ask, 'What is its position *in* them?'" "This question," he goes on, "directly concerns the function the work has within the literary relations of production of its time. It is concerned, in other words, directly with the literary *technique* of works" (81). As Miriam Hansen explains, "the German word *Technik* far exceeds the [English] term *technique*; it refers to both artistic and extra-artistic, industrial and preindustrial practices."[19] Accordingly, for Benjamin, the author who develops a given technique "will never merely work on products but always, at the same time, work on the means of production" (89). This, in turn, requires a self-conscious relation to the material and human inputs required by the production and circulation of writing. A writer who is self-conscious about technique is self-conscious about his place in the division of labor. An author who transcends "the barrier between writing and image" by learning to integrate photography into his writing, for example, is one who transcends "the specialization in the process of intellectual production" and thus "discovers his solidarity with the proletariat—his solidarity with certain other producers who earlier seemed scarcely to concern him" (87).

Benjamin draws from Bertolt Brecht's 1931 essay "The *Threepenny* Lawsuit," which argues that, "like the manual laborer, the intellectual worker has only his naked labor power to offer," before adding that the intellectual worker "is his labor power and nothing more than that. And, just like the manual laborer, he needs these means of production more and more to exploit his labor power."[20] Implicit here, and crucial to Benjamin's sense of "the literary relations of production," was Brecht's account of how writers engaged a productive "apparatus," a term that has enjoyed sustained critical attention, from Louis Althusser and Michel Foucault to Jean-Louis Baudry and Giorgio Agamben. The term serves Brecht in much the way that "technique" does Benjamin.

Brecht's essay recounts his rationale for suing the producers of the film *The 3 Penny Opera*, based on his play. He had contracted with a production company to supply the script, but the company declined to use the script as offered, and he took them to court in a much-publicized suit, which he lost. His essay reopens the case, as it were, by justifying the impulses that led him to film in the first place. He aspired to work with word and image, as Benjamin would later recommend. Writers have no choice but to do so: "No longer is a cognitive act possible outside the general production process," Brecht maintains; "production means to be in the production process" (190). Those who urge writers to refrain from working with film companies would

> deprive us of the apparatuses which we need in order to produce, because more and more this kind of producing will supersede the present one. We will be forced to speak through increasingly complex media. . . . The old forms of transmission are not unaffected by the newly emergent ones nor do they survive alongside them. The film viewer reads stories differently. But the storywriter views films too. The technological advance in literary production is irreversible. The use of technological instruments compels even the novelist who makes no use of them to wish that he could do what the instruments can, to include what they show (or could show) as part of the reality that constitutes his subject matter, but above all to lend to his writing the character of using instruments. (161)

Brecht moves from insisting that artists depend financially on the film industry, and must "speak through increasingly complex media," to asking how those complex media speak through them. That ventriloquism is both intentional and symptomatic, and it encompasses industrial relations as well as technical media:

writers strive to show what films show, but in so doing, their work becomes an expression of, or the form of appearance assumed by, "the commercial organization [of the film industry]" (188), which includes newspapers, investment banks, and promotion agencies, as well as copyright law and a "machinery of justice [that] works as one component in the general machinery of production" (191).[21] Writing that assumes "the character of using instruments," then, also assumes the character of the apparatus on which the novelist is dependent.

The technical affordance most famously reproduced in *Goon Squad* is the PowerPoint presentation, that most emblematic of corporate management tools. Egan's tour-de-force appropriation follows in the footsteps of David Byrne, who had been working with PowerPoint for years, and lends her writing "the character of using [managerial] instruments." But we learn little about the apparatus in question when we focus only on Egan's relation to this or that technical format. The twelve-year-old who produces the PowerPoint presentation contrasts it to her mother's found art, assembled from more obdurate "junk" (264). Egan seems keen to demonstrate a corresponding digital mastery. Yet her characters lionize analog formats over and against the "*digitization*" of music, which results in an "*aesthetic holocaust*" (23). As a whole, *Goon Squad* celebrates the analog in just the way that HBO dramas typically do (as in the credit sequence of *Vinyl*, the HBO drama most obviously indebted to *Goon Squad*).

In the end, when considered on their own, particular technical media, formats, and affordances reveal only so much. Better to consider them in conjunction with the sectoral and corporate exigencies that make up the media apparatus writ large. In the context of television, those sectoral tendencies might include the abolition of the Financial Interest and Syndication (fin-syn) rules and the proliferation of cable channels in the early 1990s, the bursting of the dot.com bubble and the subsequent importance of pay cable television as a hedge against unpredictable blockbuster gate receipts, the consolidation of and specialization within agent firms, the breaking of the 2007–8 Writers Guild of America strike, the emergence of direct-to-consumer digital distribution technologies and the proliferation of nonindustry television producers, and the advent of shareholder activism. Such trends organize creative workers' relations to the medium and, in turn, inflect how particular corporate exigencies take more seemingly technical and even aesthetic shape: HBO's now long-standing love letter to the analog, for instance, first codified in its 1993 "static" intro and discernible in the content of most of its flagship dramas ever since, would become during the new millennium inextricable from the network's repudiation of the digital synergy that had motivated Time Warner's merger with AOL. HBO CEO Jeffery Bewkes led the in-house charge against AOL soon after the merger—and later became Time Warner's CEO—by championing old-school analog virtues (synergy is "bullshit," he would claim) and embracing the shareholder activism foisted on Time Warner as a result of the debt it assumed from the merger.

We need not stop while making claims like these at the single media transnational. The fortunes of these transnationals wax and wane as a function of systemic capitalist dynamics—so, for example, declining rates of profit in US industrial production during the 1980s and 1990s precipitated capital's flight into finance, whence it was lent, in part, to consolidating media transnationals prepared to assume large amounts of debt. But at the very least we must linger with the media corporation. This is an entity just as inclined to allegorize itself as to delineate its place and function in the economy as a whole—such that a television drama about the underground mob economy of New Jersey can seem, in addition to much else, a story about HBO and the writers there employed. Reading corporate artifacts requires taking measure of how fundamentally they are formed and deformed by corporate exigencies. Of course, media texts also bear the imprint of the dynamics that define the media sector as a whole, and there is no more unabashed justification of the conflation of those dynamics with those governing the economy as a whole than the one offered by Paolo Virno, a post-Fordist enthusiast who reframes many of the issues adumbrated by Benjamin.

Benjamin says nothing about Fordism per se (Antonio Gramsci elaborates the concept the year that Benjamin publishes "The Author as Producer") and, in fact, analogizes readers to industrial workers in a manner that anticipates post-Fordist celebrations of the consumer's role in production. For him, "a mighty recasting of literary forms" (82) was revising "the distinction between author and reader" (83). In the "Work of Art" essay, he claims that "the distinction between author and public is about to lose its axiomatic character." Benjamin thinks that "the reader is ready to become a writer," and thereby "gain access to authorship," because "literary competence" had become "a common property" (47). Still, in "The Author as Producer," authors become producers (and avoid being hack writers) only to the extent that they are able, "first, to induce other producers to produce, and, second, to put an improved apparatus at their disposal." "And this apparatus is better," he thinks, "the more consumers it is able to turn into producers—that is, readers or spectators into collaborators" (89).[22] For Virno, on the other hand, the transformation of consumers into producers represents not the socialization of Fordist production, but a core feature of post-Fordist production, in which all work becomes "a supervisory and regulatory activity" that requires a "changing and intensifying of social cooperation" between producers and consumers.[23] The cooperation between a performer and her audience is here emblematic; he turns to "the activity of virtuosos [and] of performing artists" (52), especially, because he thinks that "productive labor, in its totality, appropriates the special characteristics of the performing artist" (54–55).

Virno's ultimate aim is to show that industrial production, far from having been outsourced to the global periphery—or, indeed, having suffered a globally systemic decline in profitability—has escaped the factory, to now encompass cultural consumption. Indeed, for Virno, culture is more than simply emblematic, since the culture industry is more than one industry among many others. He locates "the matrix of post-Fordism" in that sector of the economy "in which there is 'production of communication by means of communication'; hence, in the culture industry" (56). For Max Horkheimer and Theodor Adorno, the culture industry was "weak and dependent" on "the most powerful [industrial] sectors of industry: steel, petroleum, electricity, chemicals."[24] For Virno, the culture industry has long functioned as R&D for the postindustrial economy writ large: "it fine-tuned the paradigm of post-Fordist production on the whole" and then "became, from a certain point on, exemplary and pervasive" (58), as the language and story factory that made everything else possible. The culture industry "plays the role of *industry of the means of production.* . . . The culture industry produces (regenerates, experiments with) communicative procedures, which are then destined to function also as means of production in the more traditional sectors of our contemporary economy" (61). These means of production are widely available to all, Virno thinks, which is why he considers post-Fordism incipiently communist. Brecht and Benjamin render cultural production collaborative in the name of returning it to workers. They would socialize the means of cultural production. Giddier about capitalism, Virno romanticizes the joys of distributed creativity and mystifies ownership. Property rights don't matter when language belongs to everyone. So too he mystifies corporate hierarchy, by echoing the management literature critiqued by Luc Boltanski and Eve Chiapello, in which "*managers* do not seek to supervise or give orders. They do not await instructions from management before applying them. They have understood that such roles are outmoded. They become 'team leaders,' 'catalysts,' 'visionaries,' 'coaches,' 'sources of inspiration.' "[25]

That account nicely describes the self-conception of more than a few "quality" TV showrunners, who tend to distance themselves from network and studio executives even as they cast themselves as one among a company of equals within the writing room.[26] But TV production is hardly the only relevant context in which to explore Virno's mystifications. Marketing and brand management texts frequently declare the brand an impersonal algorithm able to coordinate both producers and consumers. Borrowing from the likes of Virno, Adam Arvidsson considers brands "a kind of medium in themselves"—"not so much a means of communication as . . . a framework, or a 'place' where we can have experiences."[27] The brand is a sui generis creation that renders production, marketing, and consumption indistinguishable. It thus produces in the realm of circulation the illusion of the collaboration production to which Brecht and Benjamin committed, but shorn of its radical promise. The brand is for Arvidsson "a commercially managed context of action," a "hyper socialized, de-territorialized factory."[28]

Egan understands the novel as a "commercially managed context of action," a "framework or place" overseen by an implied author who must seem both more and less than the sum of her parts: more, because she must anticipate and manage collaborative circuits between her text and its readers, within and beyond the media industry, and less, because those circuits threaten her superannuation and risk transforming her into an atavism no longer required by the downsizing agencies of her own brand. The advent of Web 2.0 and the host of accompanying declarations that consumers are the producers that matter most no doubt heightened that tension, already latent in a range of postmodernist fiction.[29] But so too have the opportunities available to prestige novelists within "quality" TV production exacerbated contradictions latent in contemporary authorship. Novels with one eye on "quality" TV know themselves to be both essential blueprints and superfluous, the first and yet one among many possible incarnations of a single story. The author implied in these novels is correspondingly schizophrenic—both origin and back-formation, both manager and managed, both possessed and dispossessed of rights.

Brecht describes a version of this schizophrenia when he declares that capitalism renders "the whole of literature, such as it is produced by individuals . . . more and more questionable" (149). The illusion that authors matter is essential to the film apparatus that he describes (as it is now for HBO). But that apparatus celebrates authors even as it wants little more than their names and reputations. "To reach the market," he writes, "an art-work, which is in terms of bourgeois ideology the adequate expression of a personality, must be subjected to a very specific operation that splits it into its components." Brecht demonstrates this operation with a "Chart of the Dismantling Process" that details "the disintegration of the literary product, of the unity of the creator and work, meaning and story, etc. The work can be given a new or several new authors (who are personalities) without eliminating the original author for the purpose of market exploitation" (177). Brecht insists that this "dismantling," which he also calls "demontage" (179), is less a betrayal of the labor necessary to the creation of a literary product than its condition: "The dismantling process is, in other words, a production process" (180). Brecht's screenwriter writes from within this process, which dismantles him as much as his work, into a name capable of marketing a brand, in which he has no rights, derived from but not reducible to his original creation.

A post-Fordist version of that dismantling is implicit in *Look at Me*, which splits its implied author along multiple lines (between two "Charlottes," for instance, and between the older Charlotte, a fashion model, and the ghostwriter who produces her story). But what might otherwise seem a broadly postmodernist multiplication of authors takes on a more industrially pointed cast: Charlotte can sell her life's Identity Rights, finally, because her branded persona no longer needs her attached to it. Along these lines, *Goon Squad* concludes with the music producer Bennie Salazar and his assistant Alex discussing Sasha Grady, Bennie's ex-assistant turned maker of found junk art who leaves the industry after Bennie discovers her kleptomania. If, on the one hand, her art harkens back to Duchamp's "ready-mades"—the name borrowed from standardized rather than bespoke textile production—on the other it suggests the contemporary novelist's ability to elevate cultural materials not of her own making, simply by signing her name to them. Sasha's thievery must be disavowed, then, because it bespeaks not simply the general thievery of music producers (a notoriously perfidious class of creative workers), but that aspect of contemporary literary production that seems most like theft. But if, as we will see in the next section, Egan seems particularly conscious of how novelists channel materials not their own, she also captures the theft to which they must themselves submit. Sasha has been vital to Bennie's success, and in this respect she is, like Charlotte, a version of the recusant novelist forced to walk away from her own creation, and thus dispossessed of her moral and legal rights. Seen both ways, Sasha presides over the end of the novel in her absence, as the necessary and unnecessary condition of *Goon Squad*'s post-Fordist assembly. So too will the one-time punk Scotty Hausmann, another authorial fragment, seem at novel's end both essential and superfluous.

The Gold Record Standard

"Honestly, I can't figure out why my book has won so many prizes," Egan declared. "Why does a book like this become such a big deal?" Of course, *Goon Squad* is explicitly about what it means to make art a big deal. From first to last, it describes the transformative effects of good publicity. One of its publicists so changes the conversation surrounding a murderous dictator that he transitions his coun-

try to democracy. More centrally, the novel culminates in the marketing of a con-
cert headlined by Scotty Hausmann. The event is unmistakably reflexive. "I see
everyone out there hustling," Egan said of novelists, "we're all really trying. I'm
certainly not against marketing. This is the world we live in, we have to do it. I've
certainly become much more comfortable with it. . . . Now it feels pretty natural."[30] It becomes so naturalized that it suffuses her novel. "You're a natural, I'm
telling you," says Bennie to Alex.[31] The two will manufacture Scotty's success out
of digital whole cloth, lifting him from total obscurity and overnight making him
a period-defining celebrity. This triumph of a novel ends, in other words, with a
triumph of marketing.

Ethical and aesthetic questions are unavoidable. "A natural what?" (337), wonders Alex. He's paid to bribe a team of putatively independent bloggers into celebrating Scotty's music. Uneasy with the job, Alex thinks to himself, "He was
owned . . . having sold himself unthinkingly at the very point in his life when
he'd felt most subversive" (316). And so he muses that "people's opinions weren't
really their own" (315), and he frets about *"being bought"* and *"selling out"* (319).
By and large, Egan wants us to think Alex too severe in his self-censure. Why
worry about corporate overlords when all creative expression is, in effect, a surfing of the zeitgeist? Scotty turns out to be as good as advertised. He's spent years
"underground" (335), "forgotten and full of rage" (336). Alex worries he's lost that
rage and is not up to the big event. Scotty seems an empty vessel, "a shell whose
essence had vanished" (332). He looks "gutted" (332), Alex thinks, a "quavering
husk" (335). But that emptiness turns out to be essential to Scotty's success. Hollow, he is, to borrow the name of one of the novel's bands, the perfect "conduit"
of the crowd's energies. Throughout *Goon Squad*, characters struggle to manufacture moment-defining culture: a publicist, for example, "had conceived of an
event crystallizing an era that had already passed. For a publicist, there could be
no greater failure" (143). But Bennie and Alex succeed precisely by making Scotty
a vessel for the collective expression of the crowd. "And it may be," Egan writes,
"that a crowd at a particular moment in history creates the object to justify its
gathering, as it did at the first Human Be-In and Monterey Pop and Woodstock"
(335). After his momentous performance, Scotty "entered the realm of myth,
everyone wants to own him. And maybe they should," Egan writes. "Doesn't a
myth belong to everyone?" (336).

That rhetorical question issues in part from the "postpiracy generation" whose
ascendance *Goon Squad* chronicles, "for whom things like 'copyright' and 'creative ownership' do not exist" (26). But it also bespeaks the qualified relation to
copyright and creative ownership that Egan imagines on behalf of prestige nov-

elists interested in the media industry. In part, the novelist is a pirate who borrows and can never own what is not hers. Dispossessed and marginal, Scotty believes ardently in the digital, which he thinks provides him access to realms of experience otherwise denied him: "if we human beings are information processing machines, reading X's and O's and translating that information into what people refer to as 'experience,' and if I had access to all that same information via cable TV . . . then, technically speaking, was I not having all the same experiences those other people were having?" (96–97). This logic allows Scotty to think himself equal parts TV producer and consumer: surfing cable TV, "I created my own show out of all those other shows, which I suspected was actually better than the shows themselves" (96). Egan will disabuse Scotty of his rationalizations—in one instance, with echoes of Daisy Buchanan, he is overcome by one of Bennie's very expensive shirts; the digital image cannot reproduce the aura of wealth—but the larger point is simply that, in making a better TV show out of those that he consumes, Scotty is a figure for the novelist who, with money in her voice, channels, is a conduit for, material not her own. His dispossession, moreover, captures the dispossession of rights required of the novelist when she *actually* makes TV (in Egan's case, executive producing the adaptation of a novel that was itself her own version of *The Sopranos*).

US novelists remain in firm possession of both their moral and legal rights, and this sets them apart from most workers in the creative industries, wherein, according to Nicholas Garnham, "labor is exploited not, as in the classical Marxist analysis of surplus value, through the wage bargain, but through contracts determining the distribution of profits to various rights holders negotiated between parties with highly unequal power."[32] Published novelists like Egan have leverage in these negotiations: if on the one hand even substantial advances amount to relatively low wages when amortized over the time it takes to write a novel, on the other, novelists face no structural compulsion to give up their copyrights in their negotiations with publishers—unlike TV writers, who cannot work outside of a corporate context, and who must agree in advance to give up the rights to their work.[33] Moreover, the vogue for transmedia storytelling, of which *Goon Squad* is itself a strong expression, augments rather than lessens an author's leverage. Simone Murray, for instance, describes "the phenomenon of twin-track authorship, whereby a writer works simultaneously on a book and screenplay version of a story with the intention of pursuing whichever is contracted first, and then converting the cultural and financial capital secured in one industry into enhanced bargaining power in the other." This captures how "story" now precedes any one format, and the equally fluid manner with which "novelists" now broker a story's conversions between formats. Witness Tom Perrotta—one of two showrunners on HBO's *The Leftovers*, based on his novel of the same name—who leveraged a movie deal for his unpublished manuscript *Election*, previously rejected by the publishing houses to which he sent it, into a book deal.[34]

But possessing either cultural or financial capital is not quite the same as possessing ownership. However lucrative, selling material to HBO, say, means having only separated rights in that material—henceforth, and at best, the novelist shares ownership with a producing studio and cedes creative control over subsequent versions of that material to the studio. That fact goes far in explaining the sense of belatedness common to contemporary fiction that turns reflexively to the media industry—by the likes of Egan, Wallace, Whitehead, Spiotta, and Jonathan Lethem—in which authors are, like Scotty, "quavering husks" through which sectoral and corporate relations speak.

Thomas Whiteside delineated those relations as early as *The Blockbuster Complex* (1980), published at the start of what would prove to be a long cycle of concentration in the media industry. He anatomizes a "merchandizing program in which books, movies, and television programs based on a single work—and all associated promotion—are fused into a coordinated whole, as a packaged 'property.'" In this way, "actual authorship often becomes an ancillary consideration in what I have heard called in Los Angeles 'the spontaneous generation of a literary property.' This 'generation' does not have to take place in the mind of a writer; it can occur around a conference table in the office of a producer or an agent, who may then add to it 'elements,' including the writer, who is 'acquired' sooner or later in the packaging process." One year later, Raymond Williams noted a similar phenomenon, when describing "the corporate professional stage" of cultural patronage. For writers in an increasingly capitalized publishing industry, he writes, "the most available social relations are those of employment . . . with the ideas for books coming from new professional intermediaries (publishers' editors) within the market structure, and authors being employed to execute them."[35]

Claims like these no doubt strike many as according corporate media too dire a sway over those who are still at bottom independent artists. But contemporary novelists working in multiple formats within the media industry frequently describe "the spontaneous generation of literary property" and express a corresponding suspicion about their own claims to originality and property. Jonathan Lethem, for instance, in addition to writing voluminously about popular music, comics, and film, produced *Omega the Unknown* for Marvel Comics. When I asked him about working for Marvel, he reiterated ideas central to "The Ecstasy of Influence," in which he celebrates the commons while insisting on the always already borrowed nature of all cultural materials. He agreed to work for Marvel "to do work for hire, which I did, and to be enmeshed in the deeply impure operation that seems, to me, its glory." The glory in question was a branded property. Lethem wanted not ownership but "the communal participation": working for hire, he said, "is like being in a gigantic rock band." But he was drawn specifically to Marvel because, under "the particular Marvel brand of creativity . . . the ostensible authorial voice is a back formation, because the best creators, Kirby and Ditko, were drawing the entire story and then handing it to someone like Stan Lee, who would just fill in the word balloons. Then it would say, 'Written by Stan Lee, drawn by Jack Kirby.' But the storytelling, the deeper meaning. . . . It's like, don't look where the voice is. You might be fooled about who actually made the thing. And the voice may only be a kind of a late-arriving decoration."[36] Lethem often casts his own voice as a back-formation of Marvel and, ultimately, the Disney Company, which functions in his fiction analogously to how, I am arguing, Time Warner functions in Egan's. The paradigms of creativity espoused by the two companies are different: still invested in the trappings of literary culture, Time Warner pays lip service to its original creators in ways that Disney does not. Even so, in Lethem's *You Don't Love Me Yet* and *Chronic City*, as in *Look at Me* and *Goon Squad*, the "death of the author" is less a theoretical fact than an industrially propitious one.

Propitious for the industry, which gets to assemble and disassemble its authors as needs dictate, and propitious for the novelist, who gets to join whatever rock band he dreamed about when young. But there are deeper undercurrents belying that fantasy. The author as executive producer is also the author as pawn and stooge. "Television is a deep, indirect subject of *Chronic City*," Lethem said, before adding, "I've thought for a long time that if you saw it the right way, *Chronic City* was a great HBO-type show."[37] (He tried to sell HBO that novel before contracting to create an entirely new story for it.) The novel describes a retired TV actor who agrees to play a public part in an elaborate conspiracy and then forgets that his persona is made up, rather than actually his life. "Lots and lots of people," said Lethem, "at other levels and in other frameworks, invest in bogus moral landscapes and take them into their bodies." The language recalls Wallace's writer— "the mundane little businesses of television production" having become "his own interior." It might also recall Benjamin, whose writing on film, Miriam Hansen reminds us, describes the ingestion or "innervation" of the film apparatus into the collective body of the film audience.[38] But ultimately, *Chronic City* suggests, its protagonist figures the novelist who takes into his body the moral landscapes and economic interests of Manhattan's elite. That novelist is a channel (or conduit) not simply for TV producers, but for the city's financial class.

In a similar if slightly less melancholic key, *Goon Squad*'s musician-cum-novelist takes into his body more than just the crowd's energies. A back-formation created by the likes of Bennie and Alex, Scotty also recalls the urban reorganization of Paris at capital's behest (his last name is Hausmann, after all). Neither fans nor producers are finally the authors that most matter here. Just as the Conduits are the favorite rock band of one of the novel's hedge-fund managers (129), so too Scotty is a conduit for finance as it colludes with military force. He performs at Ground Zero, the footprint of the absent World Trade Center, with police helicopters flying overhead. We glimpse here an apparatus far more extensive than the media industry's alone. But it is only a glimpse, finally, because Scotty's body is not simply a conduit for capital but a screen, behind which Egan secrets all that she cannot acknowledge, to paraphrase Benjamin, about the place of literary relations of production within relations of production generally.

"He's absolutely pure," says Bennie, "Untouched" (313). These qualities might seem to make Scotty the perfect representative of the antiestablishment punk scene that brings together this novel's characters. But he is, at the same time, pure in the way that the event's chief marketer, Lulu, thinks language is "pure," when it contains "no philosophy, no metaphors, [and] no judgments" (321). She advises Alex to embrace pure language in an effort to move him past qualms about manipulating social media to publicize Scotty. Alex replies, "if your reasons [for promoting a concert] are cash, that's not belief. It's bullshit." But for Lulu, belief *is* cash. She thinks, "If I believe, I believe." Reasons are irrelevant; things are what they are. This formulation solves a problem in Alex's long-standing crisis of self-belief, which Egan traces to an evening he spent years ago with Sasha, Bennie's assistant. While in therapy for kleptomania, Sasha stole from Alex's wallet not money, but a slip of paper on which somebody had written, "I BELIEVE IN YOU" (19).

We might take the slip of paper as a kind of psychic reserve, one that guarantees the integrity of the punk generation whose fortunes *Goon Squad* chronicles. It is in this respect a substitute for money: believing in themselves, and believed in by others, Egan's punks do not need financial success, even if, as adults, they seek it. Or we might take the theft to represent the theft of a collective belief in art, perpetrated by old and new adherents to the doctrine of the readymade. But given the novel's preoccupation with gold, it is also tempting to read the stolen slip of paper as a representation not just of Alex's lost self-confidence, or Egan's confidence in art, but also of a more general loss of faith in the value to which money refers, one exacerbated by Nixon's formal uncoupling of the dollar from gold. Lulu would solve both problems with little more than the snap of a finger. For her, and one suspects for Egan as well, language can no more exist in tension with belief than cash paper or profits can exist in tension with what Slavoj Žižek calls, in an effort to figure value, "the body within the body" of gold—the "*sublime material*" of money, "that 'indestructible and immutable' body which persists beyond the corruption of the body physical."[39] Seen from Virno's perspective on the culture industry, this analogy between language and money is very much the point. For him, and for Egan, language and communicative action are endlessly and renewably productive. This specious New Economy fantasy—at the heart of mergers like the one between AOL and Time Warner—clarifies what it is that moves through Scotty's empty body during his performance. Where Colson White-head thinks of story as a raw mineral akin to iron ore, Egan thinks of the crowd's energies, as they find expression in Scotty's music, as musical gold: those energies are themselves the sublime material of money. Call this the gold record standard, in which consumption is production, the one activity identical to the other.

Another substance might better capture what it is that moves through this felicitous, self-confirming circuit. The hollow Scotty is not the only character in either this novel or recent fiction whose body channels some kind of gold. Published the same year as *Goon Squad*, Jonathan Franzen's *Freedom* compares its narrative structure to the therapy sessions in *The Sopranos* (*Goon Squad* also begins with a scene of therapy). Both channeling *The Sopranos*, the novels also share what might otherwise pass as a narrative coincidence: a central character who swallows and then presumably defecates gold. In *Freedom*, one of the protagonists swallows and then struggles to pass a wedding ring. But when finally he does, he must dig the ring out of his own shit. In *Goon Squad*, Bennie routinely swallows gold flakes, because he thinks they will enhance his sexual potency, and because they remind him of the gold records he's lost the ability to produce. Gold captures his nostalgia for the staying power of analog artistry. Real gold doesn't "tarnish" (34), Bennie thinks, unlike the overproduced digital "shit" (echoes of both Wallace and Jeffrey Bewkes) that he has been making "to satisfy the multinational crude-oil extractors he's sold his label to" (23). Only time will tell which substance Egan's novels will be said to channel.

NOTES

1. David Foster Wallace, "E Unibus Pluram: Television and U.S. Fiction," in *A Supposedly Fun Thing I'll Never Do Again* (Boston: Back Bay Books, 1998), 34, 44, 32.

2. Thomas Hobbes, *Leviathan* (New York: Simon & Schuster, 2008), 245.

3. Walter Benjamin, "The Author as Producer," in *The Work of Art in the Age of Its Technological Reproducibility* (Cambridge, MA: Harvard University Press), 82, 83. Hereafter cited in the text.

4. See Catherine Fisk and Michael Szalay, "Story Work: 'Non-Proprietary Autonomy' and Contemporary Television Writing," *Television and New Media*, June 2016, http://tvn.sagepub.com/content/early/2016/06/08/1527476416652693.abstract.

5. Dana Spiotta, *Eat the Document* (New York: Scribners, 2006), 144.

6. Colson Whitehead, *John Henry Days* (New York: Doubleday, 2001), 297, 21.

7. Jennifer Egan, *Look at Me* (New York: Anchor, 2001), 53. Hereafter cited in the text.

8. Boris Kachka, "*A Visit from the Goon Squad* Author Jennifer Egan on Reaping Awards and Dodging Literary Feuds," *Vulture*, May 11, 2011, *www.vulture.com/2011/05/jennifer_egan_goon_squad_inter.html*.

9. Vincent Canby, "From the Humble Mini-Series Comes the Magnificent Megamovie," *New York Times*, October 31, 1999; Stephen Holden, "TELEVISION / RADIO; Sympathetic Brutes in a Pop Masterpiece," *New York Times*, June 6, 1999.

10. William Gibson, interview by Zack Handlen, *AV Club*, September 7, 2010, www.avclub.com/article/william-gibson-44836.

11. Alexandra Alter, "TV's Novel Challenge: Literature and the Screen," *Wall Street Journal*, February 22, 2013, www.wsj.com/articles/SB10001424127887323478004578306400682079518.

12. Quoted in Craig Fehrman, "The Channeling of the Novel," *New York Times*, December 18, 2001, www.nytimes.com/2011/12/18/books/review/the-channeling-of-the-novel.html.

13. Ron Charles, "Gary Shteyngart's Super, Sad, True Comedy," *Washington Post*, April 21, 2012, www.washingtonpost.com/blogs/arts-post/post/gary-shteyngarts-super-sad-true-comedy/2012/04/21/gIQAQ8FmXT_blog.html.

14. Simone Murray, *The Adaptation Industry* (New York: Routledge, 2012), 26.

15. Vanessa Thorpe, "Salman Rushdie Says TV Dramas Comparable to Novels," *Guardian*, June 11, 2011, www.theguardian.com/books/2011/jun/12/salman-rushdie-write-tv-drama.

16. Gary Shteyngart, interview by Robert Birnbaum, *Morning News*, December 16, 2010, www.themorningnews.org/article/gary-shteyngart.

17. See Catherine Fisk, "The Role of Private Intellectual Property Rights in Markets for Labor and Ideas: Screen Credit and the Writers Guild of America, 1938–2000," *Berkeley Journal of Employment and Labor Law* 32, no. 2 (2011): 258–62.

18. David Itzkoff, "Jennifer Egan Discusses TV Plans for 'A Visit from the Goon Squad,'" *New York Times*, April 21, 2011, http://artsbeat.blogs.nytimes.com/2011/04/21/jennifer-egan-talks-tv-plans-for-a-visit-from-the-goon-squad/.

19. Miriam Hansen, *Cinema and Experience: Siegfried Kracauer, Walter Benjamin, and Theodor Adorno* (Berkeley: University of California Press, 2011), 211.

20. Bertolt Brecht, "The *Threepenny* Lawsuit," in *Brecht on Film and Radio*, ed. Marc Silberman (Slingsby, UK: Methuen, 2016), 162. Hereafter cited in the text.

21. And, as Brecht puts it elsewhere, "the products of writers, composers, and critics take on the character of raw materials: the finished product is turned out by the apparatus." Quoted in Roswitha Mueller, *Bertolt Brecht and the Theory of Media* (Lincoln: University of Nebraska Press, 1989), 17.

22. Brecht's enthusiasm for audience participation shaped his passion for radio. "Brecht had in mind a huge network of channels that would not only send but also receive program material," writes Meuller; "it would make the audience not only listen but also speak, and instead of isolating the listeners it would locate them in relation to each other. By changing the radio from an apparatus for distribution to an apparatus for communication, it would represent a truly democratic—as Brecht put it—utilization of the media" (Mueller, *Bertol Brecht*, 26).

23. Paolo Virno, *A Grammar of the Multitude* (Los Angeles: Semiotext(e), 2004), 62. Hereafter cited in the text.

24. Max Horkheimer and Theodor Adorno, *The Dialectic of Englightenment* (Palo Alto: Stanford University Press, 2007), 96.

25. Luc Boltanski and Eve Chiapello, *The New Spirit of Capitalism* (London: Verso, 2007), 77.

26. See Fisk and Szalay, "Story Work."

27. Adam Arvidsson, *Brands: Meaning and Value in Media Culture* (New York: Routledge, 2006), 77, 13.

28. Ibid., 76.

29. See Maria Bose, "Branding Counterculture in Pynchon's *The Crying of Lot 49*," *Studies in American Fiction* 43 (2016): 73–96.

30. Kachka, "*Visit from the Goon Squad* Author Jennifer Egan."

31. Jennifer Egan, *A Visit from the Goon Squad* (New York: Anchor, 2011), 337. Hereafter cited in the text.

32. Nicholas Garnham, "Cultural to Creative Industries," *International Journal of Cultural Policy* 11, no. 1 (2005): 20.

33. The Bureau of Labor and Statistics, which garners its data from an occupational employment survey, tells us that the average salary of a novelist in 2010 was $56,420, which it bases on an assumed hourly wage of $26.24 (this assumes roughly 270 days of work at eight hours per day). See www.bls.gov/ooh/media-and-communication/writers-and-authors.htm.

34. Murray, *Adaptation Industry*, 43.

35. Thomas Whitehead, *The Blockbuster Complex* (Middletown, CT: Wesleyan University Press, 1981), 72; Raymond Williams, *The Sociology of Culture* (Chicago: University of Chicago Press, 1995), 52.

36. Jonathan Lethem, interview by Michael Szalay, Pomona College, November 17, 2013.

37. Ibid.

38. Hansen, *Cinema and Experience*, 80.

39. Slavov Žižek, *The Sublime Object of Ideology* (New York: Verso, 1989), 18.

Neoliberalism and the Demise of the Literary

SARAH BROUILLETTE

On Some Tendencies in Critiques of Neoliberalism

Christian Garland and Stephen Harper have recently observed that a significant portion of the scholarship that treats neoliberalism is interested in defending democratic institutions against neoliberal market conditions. The research that they take issue with tends to suggest (and is built on a view of capitalism that allows it to suggest) that reform of the current system—pushing for "good jobs" and a robust social safety net for all, for instance—continues to be a viable terrain of struggle.[1] In setting up a critique of the marketization and economization of things that were once ostensibly nonmarket, what is too often ignored—and I will point to exceptions—is the total global picture in its dynamic historical emergence.

Just to begin, one might point out that the expansive welfare state was built on the foundation of America's postwar hegemony, when its industrial capacity set the standard for the ratcheting up of global competition that characterized capitalism in its expansive phase. We cannot ignore the relationship between this expansive capitalism and relatively full employment and the days of government largesse; nor can we in good conscience overlook the environmental and social effects of the growth and expansion of industry and the catastrophes attendant upon American efforts to hold on to its precarious hegemonic status in the decades that followed. Furthermore, when there were in the relatively advanced postwar economies protections against incursions of "market logic" into some domains, there were people elsewhere who were just being brought into circumstances of waged labor, and their exploitation was the grounds for others' prosperity. These realities make it difficult to accept claims, like Wendy Brown's, that neoliberalism is "the rationality through which capitalism finally swallows humanity."[2] "*Finally?*" one wonders.

In fact, at times, perhaps especially in accounts of conditions in higher education, it is as though the word *neoliberal* simply signals the introduction into one's relatively elite enclave of conditions from which one might have thought a certain level of education and privilege served as protection. It can seem like neoliberal reforms are such a focus of interest because forms of work whose relation to economic rationality had been characteristically more indirect—the professoriate —have been reshaped in ways that threaten their distinction. We find thus some fairly pastoral views of the more immediate postwar period, as though before the neoliberal era the university was a broad church free from injustice, disconnected from the reproduction of classed, gendered, raced relations and from the formation of a particular employment strata, that is, the technocratic and professional-managerial elite. Terry Eagleton claims, for instance, that "since Margaret Thatcher, the role of academia has been to service the status quo, not challenge it in the name of justice, tradition, imagination, human welfare, the free play of the mind or alternative visions of the future,"[3] and Wendy Brown praises pre-neoliberal higher education for "developing intelligent, thoughtful elites" and "enacting a principle of equal opportunity and cultivating a broadly educated citizenry."[4] While acknowledging that access to higher education used to extend more deeply into the middle and lower classes than it does now, it is nevertheless important to emphasize that "cultivating a broadly educated citizenry" was never separable from preparing people for the labor market, nor can it be disentangled from the development of liberal, democratic, capitalist citizenship. Just to be clear, I am not impugning all of the people fighting for public higher education. I think it is important, though, to have clear eyes about what the university has been and can be, and it is important also to keep in view the necessity of total transformation, given the ways in which university structures can preserve divisions that are dangerous rather than enabling (mental versus manual labor, elite versus service work, and so on).

Attending the more pastoral approaches I have in mind is a damning neglect of how exceptional the post–World War II situation was, along with a fairly sanguine view of "full" Fordist employment and its accompaniments, such as a robust welfare system and affordable higher education. It is as though, as I have said, elite conditions for some workers somewhere were not premised on exclusions and inequities in other places; as though there is nothing really important to note about the environmental effects of the economy of overconsumption on which it was all built; and as though there is also nothing worth noting about the role of social welfare as a supplement to waged work that sustains class relations

rather than posing the sort of threat to them that would really do away with capitalist economic rationality.

I could certainly proliferate examples of this kind of thinking. Just for example, though, in a piece published in *PMLA*, commenting on the dearth of jobs in
literary studies, Walter Benn Michaels makes the point that we are unwise to try
to secure—in the neoliberal fashion—"the monetary value of a degree in literature." He argues that it is not advanced degrees but rather a "living wage" and a
"union card" that are the "plausible" means of giving the most people the best
chance of "equality." We should thus be less interested in jobs in literary studies
and more interested in fighting for a "living wage" via trade unionism. Training
in literature can then be a supplement to one's quality of life rather than a career
path.[5] Needless to say, this argument presumes that there is nothing integrally
wrong with waged labor, and that it is in fact possible under capitalism for everyone to receive enough pay to live relatively well. But isn't capital always, as Angela
Mitropoulos argues, precarious for most people most places, as "stability here
has always entailed formalising relative advantages between workers"?[6]

Refusal to treat seriously key features of the historical geography and dynamic
development of capitalism results in oversights that ultimately undermine the
political insight of too much neoliberalism research. What is more, the tendency
in analyses of neoliberalism to downplay the complicities and compromises of the
more immediate postwar decades reflects a refusal to think seriously about the
reproduction of social relations postcapitalism. So as analyses of neoliberalism
evince a reluctance to reckon with some of the realities of postwar capitalism, they
also express some desire to hold on to the idea that a wholesale transformation
in how we reproduce ourselves as social beings is not necessary. Instead, they
appeal to democratic institutions that need only be strengthened in such a way as
to protect from the depredations of "markets" those crucial nonmarket goods like
water, nature, and health. Necessarily outside of the frame of analysis is the fact
that distributionist or welfarist policies may no longer be viable, given the economic stagnation and massive government debts to which the policies dubbed
neoliberal have responded, and given how broad the push has been to give an
ever-greater share of what remains to an ever-smaller and more powerful portion
of the population.

There are remarkable exceptions, of course. In David Harvey's, David Mc-
Nally's, and Silvia Federici's work there is a close relationship between developments in governance, human experience or subjective expressions, and capitalism's driving logic and causal role. We can consider, for instance, what Harvey

calls accumulation by dispossession,[7] Federici names "the new enclosures,"[8] and McNally discusses as a dramatic quadrupling of the world's global labor force between 1980 and 2005, in which hundreds and millions of peasants fled poverty and dispossession, looking for waged work, having had their land seized—just for example—under mandate of International Monetary Fund structural adjustment programs. McNally notes that as a result, for the first time in history the "majority of the world's inhabitants now live in urban spaces."[9] This swelling of the global working class and of the reserve army of labor has clearly had dramatic effects on the world capitalist system.

This kind of scholarship, which will insist on looking at neoliberal policy shifts in relation to foundational restructurings of the world capitalist economy, in its cycles of growth and contraction, has the greatest purchase on contemporary social relations. In the terms recently offered by Garland and Harper, this is work that manages to "move beyond the critique of 'excessive,' 'financial,' 'de-regulated' or 'neoliberal' capitalism" to incorporate a critique of the labor–capital relation in general, and of the dominance of the accumulative capitalist value form over the collective determination of collective needs and how to meet them.[10] These takes are most propitious owing to their wide view of the history and totality of the world system; hence, following this logic, work that does this foundational analysis and yet does not use the term *neoliberalism* at all—and indeed McNally doesn't use it often, and nothing really rests on it when he does—is still doing more to capture the social reality of our world than studies that attribute some agency to a governing rationality or normative reason/logic that somehow becomes committed without real engine or cause to telling people they need to develop their human capital and become little hothouses of self-managed entrepreneurial zeal.

Neoliberalism and Literature

Needless to say, there are writers who are interested in a topical way in the phenomena associated with neoliberalism and incorporate that interest into their work. Literature is, additionally, part of the world of thought that helps to build and shape the self-managing neoliberal subject, and there are writers involved, with various levels of self-scrutiny, in institutions that have been described as having a neoliberalizing effect or component (the rise of the creative writing program in university English departments, for example). What concerns me here is something different, as befits my broader wariness about some of the emphases apparent in standard critiques of neoliberalism.

Literary study of neoliberalism has been most nuanced in its treatment of literature's accordance with and dissent from neoliberal affects and dispositions (the neoliberal mind-set, neoliberal ideologies, the neoliberal imaginary, neoliberal thought, etc.). What I want to advance instead is a grounding claim about the way in which global capital's dynamic expansion and contraction structure the literary field. My basic premise, which I will try to defend below, is that the literary field's tendencies and capacities are tied to the fate of the real economy; indeed, the real economy has an absolutely foundational structuring role in transformations in the fate of the literary as a set of affects and dispositions.

The broad post-1960s trend of economic stagnation and contraction has meant that fewer people have access to reliable wages; fewer people are positioned to engage in the forms of learning and self-cultivation (such as literary studies) that are the least *apparently* instrumental; more people are in precarious work; more people are living with stress, mental illness, addictions, and other kinds of anguish; and more people are threatened with superfluity and by the policing, imprisonment, and repression that attend it. The things that are necessary to the development of the specifically literary disposition, which were always relatively distinguishing and elite, are now decreasingly available in this context. These include the leisure and focus to read for relatively long periods of time, exposure to the kind of education that inculcates the value of the literary and other aesthetic experiences, available and relatively welcoming public institutions of expressive art and culture, and so on.

The aesthetic field of cultural production and experience is as a result being de-developed, along with secure employment, the English department and other traditional university humanities courses, the nuclear family, the capacity to make a living only writing literary books, the belief that the state should provide support to individual writers for their solo-authored creative projects, and so on. This decline occasions a variety of reactions. A recent turn to trying to save literature by diversifying access to its creation, dissemination, and readership is one form of response. Academic interest in propping up the autonomy of the aesthetic—with the literary only one variety of this aesthetic, of course—is another. I understand both as symptomatic responses to a marked decline in the status and the economic foundation of a particular, unique, historically contingent and currently residual sociolect.

We can start with recent expressions of concern about the whiteness and exclusivity of the literary field, including audiences, executives, editors, authors, prizes, and the literary academy. Not without exception, of course, and not without conflict, controversy, and moments of significant possibility, the literary industries are very white. I recently attended a talk that Viet Nguyen gave on this topic at the University of California, Irvine, in which he cited statistics indicating that 89 percent of what gets published in the United States is by white authors. He discussed feeling pressured to represent a delimited racialized community in order to succeed.[11] Motivated by his presentation, I spent some time looking at statistics about diversity in the British, American, and Canadian literary industries. I will focus here especially on the British case, because I already know that context somewhat well.

Some ten years ago now Arts Council England sponsored a report called *In Full Colour*, which was the first study to look at black, Asian, and minority ethnic (or BAME) people in the books trades. The report uncovered institutional bias in the trades, and some initiatives were put forward as redress: these included paid internships for BAME graduates at Faber, Random House, and Penguin and prizes designed to support BAME writers.[12] A follow-up report released last year states that these initiatives basically had no effect.[13] Instead, the book industry has been in decline, and changes to it have actually negatively affected diversity. Publishers have, in the report's words, "retrenched and become more conservative in their editorial and employment choices" (4). The supported pathways into the field that the 2005 publishing industry study resulted in were entry level. People from BAME backgrounds working in publishing continue to stay "at relatively junior levels" and continue to tend not to be involved in decision-making around manuscripts and overall lists (5).

The foundation of the follow-up 2015 report is a survey of 203 UK-based published novelists, of which 30 percent put themselves in the BAME category. It reveals that BAME writers are less likely to have agents for their first or subsequent novels, and that they are more likely to feel as though their work is not commercially viable. When asked to explain this situation, they are inclined to note assumptions within publishing houses about what white readers are likely to want to read. Most BAME novelists said ethnicity was the main focus of their publicity campaign. There is a "BAME angle" that they understand as an imposed focus on ethnicity betraying and sidelining the "more universal" aspects of their work (8).

Risk management plays a part here. Historically, literary publishing has rarely been a very lucrative trade. Once literary fiction became somewhat commercially viable, publishers were for a while (maybe for sixty to eighty years from the late nineteenth into the mid-twentieth century) accustomed to very small profits; they were forced to try for something bigger, but with the backing of hugely increased marketing budgets, when they were subsumed by media corporations and conglomerates beginning in the 1960s. The risk associated with a product that is definitively "creative," that is, not produced by a machine or formula but rather by an individual whose unique expressive subjective life is what the product *is* in some respect, has to be managed in several ways. A key technique has been intensive marketing of writers' most apparent biographies. This marketing tendency both reflects and advances the literary's particular identity: as the expression and manifestation of the individual psychic life, the product of expressive genius, the close articulation of the liberal person, basically, including all its anxiety and self-consciousness and self-doubt about its place in the world and attendant horrors.

Thus, an important way to understand the struggles of BAME writers with their own racialization is in relation to the tendencies of cultural commodification and the nature of the specifically literary commodity. Among the facets of this commodity are the marketing focus on individual biographical authors, reflected of course in the strictures of copyright; the dependence on journalistic capital accrued from circulating works with compelling stories attached to them; and the debt to a humanist liberalist particularism that makes the individual the privileged pathway onto anything like the universal.

The 2015 survey found that "42 per cent of respondents from a BAME background wrote literary fiction, making it by far the biggest genre for BAME writers in the poll." The next biggest genre was young adult fiction, at 26 percent, with women's commercial fiction (including romance) at 8 percent of respondents. Of the biggest-selling genres, crime accounted for only 4 percent of BAME novelists' output. "Science fiction and fantasy was written by eight per cent of respondents and horror by 10 per cent." There thus seems to be a marked "propensity of the industry to publish writers of colour under the 'literary' banner" (9). It is, of course, possible that people who are not white are not writing as many manuscripts in other genres; these statistics are not available. What the report claims is that BAME writers are effectively confined within the literary niche, and the possibility of making a decent living as writers is stymied because they cannot get at the mass-market book. In other words, a BAME writer setting out to work as a full-time novelist is at a disadvantage in being somewhat restricted to the least remunerative market niche.

According to Nielsen Bookscan information cited in the 2015 publishing report, "Crime, romance and YA books make up almost half of the adult fiction market in the UK," while, as we know, books that are more deliberately literary are "witnessing a decline in market share" (9). An earlier moment, characterized by the commercial success of figures such as Zadie Smith, Salman Rushdie, and Monica Ali, all writing about contemporary multicultural Britain, was what one contributor to the report calls a "false dawn" (13). As is the case in prize culture, there is a certain industry self-fashioning as open, liberal, cosmopolitan, and elite, such that works are deliberately chosen for inclusion in a literary list because the list cannot be entirely or "too white" (26). What gets obscured in this self-fashioning of the literary as "diverse," and in the highlighting and prizing of particular BAME figures, is precisely the "hugely disproportionate" whiteness of the industry as a whole and the number of publishing industry people "drawn from the English upper middle classes." There remains a remarkable "level of independent wealth" within the publishing industry (15). Of the 2015 survey respondents, 89 percent agreed that personal contacts and recommendations were a "significant source of new clients," and 80 percent of industry staff "hold a post-graduate diploma, higher degree or industry-specific accredited qualification." The report suggests that "novelists able to finance a creative writing degree, will be better placed to meet literary agents whom they may approach at a later date with a finished manuscript." Also, given "post-graduate university fees at £9,000 a year and entry-level salaries in publishing very low," accumulated debt may discourage those from less elite backgrounds from considering publishing as a viable career (22).

A survey of the Society of Young Publishers was another part of the background to the report. It revealed that "19 per cent of respondents achieved their first job in publishing through an unpaid internship," and another 19 percent through paid internships. "A further 13 per cent achieved their first job through a personal contact, such as a family member or friend." So some of the primary routes into the publishing business are barriers "to those outside the affluent professional classes, [which] explains why the industry remains dominated by White, public school educated, 'Oxbridge' graduates, even though this group represent a tiny fragment of the overall UK population." Only 11 percent of the survey respondents had ties with non-Oxbridge universities or more market-facing colleges (22–23).

It is crucial to note now that the motivation behind the collection of this data is the effort to keep the industry viable by making the business case for diversity. The 2015 report's opening states that "in an industry that operates increasingly on a global level, the absence in most publishing houses of staff at a senior level with Indian or Chinese heritage—especially in international sales—risks putting the UK trade at a disadvantage for working in these significant and growing markets." More importantly, it states that by 2051 "one in five people in the UK is predicted to be from an ethnic minority; a rise from 14 per cent in 2011 to at least 30 per cent. In London, the proportion of BAME people is already 40 per cent. Those with a mixed heritage are in the fastest growing ethnic group in the UK: over one million people (two per cent) of the population are of mixed race and this is expected to more than double over the next 30 years." In this light, the book industry "risks becoming a 20th century throwback increasingly out of touch with a 21st century world" (2–3).

We can compare a second 2015 survey, tellingly titled *Panic!*, this time extended to the whole British cultural field. It began from the assumption that the cultural sector, which represents 5 percent of the British economy and has been valued at nearly 77 billion pounds, "seems to be losing its maverick sparkle." It then sought to explore the impact of "housing costs, benefits changes, higher education fees, reduced arts provision in schools, unpaid internships and low salaries" on creative professionals. The aim was to "encourage government, cultural institutions and businesses to reflect on their part in a situation where just 18.1% of Britain's cultural workforce were brought up by parents who did traditionally working-class jobs, as compared to 34.7% in the country as a whole."[14]

In a report that galvanized the work of the *Panic!* survey, Vikki Heywood, chairman of the Warwick Commission on the Future of Cultural Value, which includes many powerful art-world figures, claims, "There are barriers and inequalities in Britain today that prevent [living 'a rich cultural life'] from being a universal human right. This is bad for business and bad for society."[15] The interests of business and interests of society are assumed to be thoroughly inseparable here; this is a common feature of all government-based or government-supported commentary on the cultural fields. Echoing Heywood's worries, the *Panic!* survey's aim then is to "galvanize support" across the cultural sector for the "young, future heroes of art," given the production of "hard evidence for the common impression that the arts sector is a closed shop where most people are middle class."[16]

Here are some relevant details from the *Panic!* report, which I am citing directly or paraphrasing:

- the majority of white people in the arts don't acknowledge the barriers facing BAME people trying to find a foothold in the sector;
- women are more likely than men to have worked in the arts sector for free, and when they are paid, they are paid less;
- 88 percent of respondents working in the cultural industries have worked for free at some point;
- 38 percent of respondents working in the cultural industries do not have a contract;
- 30 percent of BAME people think that ethnicity is very important to getting ahead, but only 10 percent of white people believe that ethnicity is very important to their chances of getting ahead;

- 76 percent of respondents working in the arts had at least one parent working in a managerial or professional job, and over half had at least one parent with a degree.

When added to the fact that "nearly 90% of respondents had worked for free at some point in their career," we get a clear sense that it is very difficult for most people to establish viable creative careers.[17]

These reports and suggested measures are clearly efforts to respond to industry contraction. They do not disguise this fact. It may be that the moment of growth of the cultural workforce is behind us; it is probably too soon to say for certain. But certainly in the immediate moment it is clear that stagnation in the real economy is manifesting in austerity-climate decreases in public support for culture, in people having less money to spend on culture, and in high rents that come with the ballooning FIRE sector (finance, insurance, and real estate, aka "the city of London"). All this is bad news for the creative class. In these reports nonwhiteness is basically a code for "hopefully newly commercial viable" and "without another pathway into this tried industry." The situation for the Anglo-British literary book appears to be particularly dire. The "literary" as we have known it—the B-format trade paperback publishing under an imprint like Vintage or Farrar, Straus & Giroux, reviewed in the major culture papers, added to university syllabi—is being treated as an area of relative nondynamism vis-à-vis the cultural economy in general.

Before returning to this point about nondynamism, we should turn now, all too briefly, to consideration of recent interest in art's autonomy—meaning its irreducibility to commodity status or its ability to function both within the marketplace and outside of its dominant logic. In his recent article "What We Worry about When We Worry about Commodification," Nicholas Brown argues that "the work of art is a commodity that is unlike any other in that it must, in order to make the claim to be an artwork, almost make the claim that its material existence as a commodity has no bearing on its being as an artwork."[18] The answer to the question in his title, "what do we worry about when we worry about commodification," is precisely this: we worry about the "subtraction of normativity." What concerns him is the dominance within the marketplace of preferences—like I prefer double-stuffed to regular Oreos—over "normative force" judgments backed up by reasoned analysis and argument.

In his analysis meanings are normative; they can only be understood or misunderstood. Commodities, in contrast, elicit or fail to elicit our preferences. Works of art by definition fear being reduced to this status. The threat of "real subsumption under capital" is precisely here: the work's normative force will be eroded. It will have no meaning, nothing subject to aesthetic judgment. Paraphrasing Kant, Brown writes that in an aesthetic judgment "we find something 'beautiful' . . . but we are indifferent to its existence. The work of art is, in its being as an artwork, exempted from use value, which is the only way it can be exempted from the economic." He adds, paraphrasing Adorno, that artworks confront their "potential commodity-being," and he argues that the work's intention is "analytically identical with its meaning." A work of art is "saturated with intention"; "a work is a thing that calls for close reading, a self-legislating artifact."[19]

I have no space here to give full voice to my response to this approach, and probably not enough language from the philosophy of art. Suffice it to say that I do not think that art has more normative force than anything else, and I would want to emphasize that art's self-conception in this regard is a highly interested and positional one. I think that the aesthetic exists in a variety of historically shifting forms of relation to capital, and the nature of what it can do for people, including what it can mean, is entirely dependent on their own position within the wider world of capitalist social relations: education, work, family, and so on, all the things integral to inculcation in certain modes of aesthetic apprehension and all the things that make culture useful to us in a given moment or galvanizing or affirmative or what have you. Nor do I think that there is a synoptic vantage from which an aesthetic object's intention can be adduced, which makes me wonder what the point is in insisting that aesthetic objects are distinct from ordinary things because they imagine themselves as intentional (that is, are bearing intentions no one need ever glean). There are instead, I would say, a series of prosaic factors that underpin the autonomous aesthetic and determine our allegiance to it today—and I mean truly prosaic, like the existence of tenure and other kinds of secure employment, relative stability in one's employment, family life and home-ownership, and education in certain cultural codes. I do not see what we gain from an insistence on art's intentionality—as compared, say, to a model in which all meaning is a matter of shifting correspondence and divergence in some set of relations: among a given text (from commercial advertisement to literary work), a consumer or reader or user (instructed by a given history of education in whatever relevant modes of perception), and a determining situation of consumption or apprehension (loud or quiet, busy or still, surrounded by related works and influential paratexts or not).

I admit that the argument for the political importance of aesthetic autonomy does not appear to have any immediate relation to the concerns about industry diversity I have been describing. Yet being tied to a particular market niche is a form of determination that writers will oppose to an autonomy they desire but cannot achieve due to racialized marketing and audience demographics. Also, both have to do with a sense that literature as a category of expression is being threatened and needs protection. Diversity is the language of marketing departments and autonomy the language of the intelligentsia, but it seems like neither can name the truth that the literary is historically particular and now residual. Perhaps the nature of the bourgeois sociolect is clarified here in the relation between these two modes, that is, between the mode of wanting more diversity for cultural commerce and the mode of wanting literature and/or the aesthetic to be anticommerce. Pierre Bourdieu diagnosed this as the desire to avoid being debased by heteronomous determinations. In *Distinction* he showed that the cultural elite justifies its status by preferring to consume culture that appears to be relatively free of any use at all. It claims to transcend the realm of grubby politics and struggle by emphasizing that the objects it enjoys are superior to those emphases while also in their very indifference providing a heightened insight into them and lens onto them.

Whiteness is in part precisely about privileged access to the bourgeois sociolect —to what Bourdieu would call its unique symbolic capital: its power to ordain those with high levels of it the people who get to determine what counts as literary culture. The history of Anglo-English literary production cannot be conceived separately from this whiteness. Literature's development has depended on the discretionary income of consumers and on middle-class literacy pitting itself against mass culture (or, more recently, acting as a discerning connoisseur of mass culture), and that literacy itself results from a particular path of urbanization and industrialization (themselves dependent on imperializing unevenness), and so on. In other work I have described how the recomposition of labor at a lower standard of living and the exacerbation of wealth disparities have shrunken and retrenched the literate elite and "reading class" in their positions; people who are not in a relatively elite social position are simply unlikely to become writers and readers of what scholars of literature tend to regard as specifically literary writing. The qualities of expression valued in the literary—complexity, depth, individuality, inwardness—are available elsewhere (in "quality television," say) or are being rethought. The things distinct to the literary, that is, instruction in the bourgeois sociolect as an individually distinguishing sensitivity to the capacity of language to humanize, elevate, individualize, interiorize, enliven, and so on, have become occasions for debate and struggle. So many writers have been embroiled in fights about the legitimacy and authenticity of their access to the experiences they write about. This reflects the sense of the literary as an elite profession that is startlingly unattainable for most people and that disguises the social dynamics of authorship in celebration of the singular writer protected by copyright and thrown into the limelight as the work's origin and occasion.

The foreboding sense of unfolding catastrophe (remember the title: *Panic!*), which we know so well from university employment, reflects how abysmal and vertiginous it can feel to lose one's economic footing. But the underlying causes of this vertiginous feeling are very real and are not really being reckoned with sufficiently. Let us consider, in this light, Brown's claim that faith in aesthetic autonomy against market rationality is crucial to opposing capitalism today. He argues that a "plausible claim to autonomy" is "the precondition for any politics at all," and that to make this claim we need to "return to immanent critique, to the notion of self-legislating form; in other words, to the conception of literature formulated by the German Romantics at the turn of the 19th century."[20] What I want to study, instead—and what I have sought to present in snippet view here— is the deep implication of capitalist unevenness, division, and contradiction in the entirety of what Etienne Balibar and Pierre Macherey once called "the literary effect."[21]

NOTES

I wish to thank Annie McClanahan, Dessa Bayrock, Emilio Sauri, Michael Szalay, David Thomas, John Coleman, and Joshua Clover for helping me to think about and write this piece.

1. Christian Garland and Stephen Harper, "Did Somebody Say Neoliberalism? On the Uses and Limitations of a Critical Concept in Media and Communication Studies," *tripleC* 10, no. 2 (2012): 413–14.

2. Wendy Brown, *Undoing the Demos: Neoliberalism's Stealth Revolution* (New York: Zone Books, 2015), 44.

3. Terry Eagleton, "The Death of Universities," *Guardian*, December 17, 2010, www .theguardian.com/commentisfree/2010/dec/17/death-universities-malaise-tuition-fees.

4. Brown, *Undoing the Demos*, 24.

5. Walter Benn Michaels, "Dude, Where's My Job?," *PMLA* 127, no. 4 (October 2012): 1009.

6. Angela Mitropoulos, "Precari-Us?," *Transversal*, March 2005, http://eipcp.net/trans versal/0704/mitropoulos/en.

7. David Harvey, *A Brief History of Neoliberalism* (Oxford: Oxford University Press, 2005).

8. Silvia Federici, "The Debt Crisis, Africa and the New Enclosures," *Midnight Notes* 10 (1992).

9. David McNally, "From Financial Crisis to World-Slump: Accumulation, Financiali-

sation, and the Global Slowdown," *Historical Materialism* 17 (2009): 52. See also Aaron Benanav and John Clegg, "Misery and Debt," in *Contemporary Marxist Theory*, ed. Andrew Pendakis et al. (New York: Bloomsbury, 2014), who argue that "the story of the post-war period is that of the tendential abolition of the remaining global peasantry, first as self-sufficient, and second as peasants at all, owning the land on which they work" (587).

10. Garland and Harper, "Did Somebody Say Neoliberalism?," 421.

11. Viet Thanh Nyugen, "Postwar Asia under Empire" (lecture, University of California, Irvine, May 26, 2016).

12. Danuta Kean, ed., "In Full Colour: Cultural Diversity in Book Publishing Today," *The Bookseller*, March 12, 2004, supplement.

13. Danuta Kean, "Writing the Future: Black and Asian Authors and Publishers in the UK Market Place," *Spread the Word*, May 2015. Hereafter cited in the text.

14. "Survey Results," *Panic!* report (London: Create London, 2015), www.createlondon.org/panic/survey.

15. Vikki Heywood, *Enriching Britain: Culture, Creativity, and Growth* (Warwick Commission on the Future of Cultural Value, 2015).

16. "About," *Panic!* report (London: Create London, 2015), www.createlondon.org/panic/about.

17. Ibid.

18. Nicholas Brown, "What We Worry about When We Worry about Commodification: Reflections on Dave Beech, Julian Stallabrass, and Jeff Wall," *nonsite.org*, April 5, 2016, http://nonsite.org/editorial/what-we-worry-about-when-we-worry-about-commodification.

19. Nicholas Brown, "The Work of Art in the Age of Its Real Subsumption under Capital," *nonsite.org*, March 13, 2012, http://nonsite.org/editorial/the-work-of-art-in-the-age-of-its-real-subsumption-under-capital.

20. Ibid.

21. Pierre Macherey and Etienne Balibar, "Literature as an Ideological Form: Some Marxist Propositions," in *Marxist Literary Theory: A Reader*, ed. Terry Eagleton and Drew Milne (London: Wiley-Blackwell, 1996), xx.

The Humanist Fix

How the Campus Novel Sustains the Neoliberal University

LEIGH CLAIRE LA BERGE

A Gargantuan Fall? Literature on the Precipice

In Sam Lipsyte's 2010 novel *The Ask*, Milo Burke, an artist turned institutional development officer at a mediocre arts school—the school is actually called Mediocre University—listens to his superior, Vargina, describe the precarity of their professional lives. "This whole game is poised for a gargantuan fall," she explains. "What game?" Milo asks. "Higher education," she responds. "Of the liberal arts variety. Fine arts in particular. When times get tough, people want the practical. Even the rich start to find us superfluous . . . worse is the pain of tuition payers. They . . . start to resent the price we charge to fool their children into thinking they can have a lucrative career in, say, kinetic sculpture."[1]

Lipsyte's novel is a rich, comedic account of a story we all know: the humanities are in a tenuous position, and those of us still employed in its ambit are lucky, but the nature of luck itself is fleeting and uncertain. Do you have research money for trips? Are you teaching a conceptual poetry survey? Then let us "enjoy these aimless days while we can," to quote fictional academic Jack Gladney, because they won't last long.[2] Gladney's laconic assessment offers two hints crucial to my study: first, that the scene of the humanities is an aimless one, and second, that the scene itself is soon to expire. The narrative that locates the humanities as the most vulnerable and expendable nodal point within the university precisely because it is nonpractical is one that most humanities scholars will know well. How that long, even foundational, discourse of the humanities as nonpractical has been transformed since the 1980s and why the campus novel is a site to begin to understand the structure, symptomatic valence, and profitable potential of this discourse today will be the subject of this article, as I move among work in literary studies, political economy, and a new field that some have begun calling critical university studies.[3] I hope to coordinate the political economy of the university with some newer issues of the genre that Mark McGurl has so convincingly delimited as "the campus novel" in order to demonstrate what rhetorical and structural work the humanities accomplishes in what I delimit as the financial or neoliberal university.[4] My focus on the campus novel is central both because this genre results from the same changing university structure that I track and because it constitutes one of the university's genuinely self-reflexive forms.[5]

In order to organize the co-constitutive relationship between university form and literary form, I articulate together three historical processes as they adhere to a collection of millennial campus novels that includes Lipsyte's *The Ask*, Francine Prose's 2000 *Blue Angel*, and Jonathan Franzen's 2001 *The Corrections*.[6] The first process I isolate is the institutional coherence of the campus novel itself. In McGurl's explication, the campus novel is one of two genres that result from the postwar rise of the master of fine arts (MFA), of university-based, credentialed creativity, itself an index of what McGurl calls the largest patronage system of the arts the world has known. If you want to train as a writer, get an MFA. And if you are a writer and you want a stable income to support your writing, get hired to teach in an MFA program. In 1945 there were eight MFA-granting institutions in the United States; by 2005 there were over 300. The campus novel, I will argue, offers a lesson in not only what writers are doing in the university but also, synecdochally, what the humanities are doing in the university. "Write what you know," the old adage goes, and authors in the university and their fictional protagonists in the millennial campus novel know two things: (1) they are aware of the precarious position of the humanities—departments are overstaffed and budget cuts loom; and (2) they know that a new institutional code called "political correctness" has reorganized humanities professors' careers, as well as their ability to write, research, and teach.

The historical reorganization and subsequent logic that make universities as fine arts patrons sensible, that both give us the campus novel as an institutional discourse and make us no longer take note of the fact that poets, nuclear scientists, and MBAs in finance all run next to each other on the treadmill at the campus gym, or that the campus even has a gym with treadmills, introduce my second process. If this is a sensible depiction of a university, then what is a university? A utopian site of democratic possibility? A corporate research park? A payday loan lender? Each description could be accurate, but I will focus here on the university as a peculiar configuration of value production defined in large part by its nonprofit status, originally a postwar designation that is still with us today.[7] This

nonprofit status might eventually be jeopardized by the rise of for-profit education, but, for the moment, the designation confers on universities certain tax
privileges that have become foundational to how the university sustains itself.[8]
These benefits include being able to receive gifts tax-free, the ability to accumulate interest on investments tax-free, and the ability to avoid real estate taxes. Indeed, the benefits of the nonprofit structure seem to impel wealthier universities
to accumulate.[9] Universities maintain their nonprofit designation because they
serve "a public good," primarily but not exclusively through activities such as
"basic scientific research," and because they lack a shareholding structure. One
cannot buy stock in a university. But one can purchase a university bond, a fact
that serves as the gateway to the third process I discuss, namely, the imbrication
of universities into the organization of capital accumulation now understood as
financial.[10]

We often hear adjectives such as *financial* or *neoliberal* used to mark our contemporary mode of accumulation, but these terms have a range of connotations.
By *financial* I invoke the work of Robert Meister to stress the tendency of capital
to create "vehicles of capital accumulation that are not necessarily investments in
expanded production," through technologies like the Black–Scholes–Merton formula that enable the pricing of risk to be separated from the commodity to which
that risk is attached. Once so priced, risk can be bought and sold.[11] By *neoliberal*
I mean the private capture of public wealth.[12] Finance may be a risk-dependent
regime, but for some assets to be traded for their risk, other assets must be guaranteed as safe, a job that falls to the federal government. Universities have become
crucial in the production of safe assets as they generate two low-risk holdings:
university bonds and government-guaranteed student debt.[13]

The cumulative effect generated by this financial, neoliberal infrastructure is
that, improbably, it seems that almost everybody in the university loses money,
from the students, who must go into debt; to humanities departments, which
always seem to be approaching a fiscal precipice; to the state, which now, under
austerity conditions, cannot fund public universities. That lack of funds, in turn,
increases student debt, places the humanities, again, on the chopping block, and
so on. But this narrative may be deconstructed on several levels, starting with the
fact that the humanities are among the most profitable sites in the university; it
is the sciences that are the most costly.[14] Nonetheless, that empirical observation
will turn out to be less important than the discourse of valuelessness that remains
stubbornly attached to the humanities. Indeed, in being perceived as valueless,
the humanities bring tremendous value to the university. This ability of the hu-

manities to lock in value conceptually and produce profit materially from ongoing forms of real and imagined debts within the university will guide my reading of these novels.

Moving among the genre of the campus novel, the discourse of political correctness that circulates through it in its millennial instantiation, and the institution of the nonprofit university, I show how the organization of financial accumulation that I have tentatively sketched here reconfigures our understanding of the institutional support for literature and, somewhat reflexively, reconfigures our understanding of what kind of literature institutional support produces. I argue that campus novels internalize and reproduce an institutional tension that articulates together the structuring role of the humanities' perceived valuelessness —purposelessness in a Kantian parlance; "aimless" in Jack Gladney's words; "[im]practical" in Vargina's—and the accumulative possibilities of that lack in the contemporary financial or neoliberal university. The humanities are valued because they organize a discourse of lack of value within the university, and this contradiction ultimately becomes a site of profit. Finally, I suggest that the campus novel not only represents the work of the humanities in the financial or neoliberal university but also accomplishes that work—what I have called elsewhere the potential liquidity of fiction.[15]

Purposelessness with Purpose:
Literary Aesthetics in the Neoliberal University[16]

The campus novel has a storied history. On Vladimir Nabokov's campuses, poetic but pathetic men cultivate their non-normative desires; the more recent and recognizable characters of Don DeLillo's *White Noise* include professors who decode cereal boxes and inflate their foreign language–speaking abilities; Richard Russo's *Straight Man* includes an English professor who will do anything, including urinating on himself, to avoid certain departmental colleagues. As these vignettes suggest, the college campus has long been a location for satirical elaboration, a tradition the three novels I read here continue. In this section, I critique *Blue Angel*, *The Ask*, and *The Corrections* as metonymically enframing a new discourse of the humanities' traditional purposelessness through their satirical emplotment of what the novels understand as "political correctness," a historical if revanchist idea that marginalized subjects have destroyed campus culture through their assumption of institutional power.

Discourse about the humanities' valuelessness or purposelessness is as old as the humanities itself, but the narratives through which that discourse is delivered are updated by age. In the 1890s university patron and TIAA-CREF founder Andrew Carnegie criticized the humanities for propagating "dead languages" and "petty squabbles." In the late 1990s and 2000s, the humanities' valuelessness finds a home in the novel-based discourse of "political correctness." These novels understand not only that racial and sexual minorities have succeeded in restructuring the university to their own ends, but also that this restructuring is particularly apparent in and destructive of the humanities. The sciences might have to abide by political correctness, but only the humanities have allowed the content of their intellectual output to become "politically correct," and, in these novels, it is this discourse of humanities-based political correctness that renders campus an effete, otiose, and valueless place. Political correctness is not exclusive to the novel, of course, nor to the humanities. Nonetheless, my locating of purposelessness in its millennial form is important because it is the presence of purposelessness that, in part, distinguishes universities from corporations; purposelessness buttresses universities' nonprofit status and thus their ability to accumulate.

Francine Prose's *Blue Angel* continues the campus novel's generic tradition of making the protagonist a writer. In the novel's content, the fictionalized writer will record the changing political atmosphere of campus, while the text's form, a campus novel, is, as McGurl suggests, a direct result of federally backed, postwar expansion of fine arts and writing into the university.[17] Campus novels are older than the postwar era, of course, but with the incorporation of writers into university faculty, campus novels cease to be about the student experience and instead become about the faculty experience.[18] *Blue Angel's* Ted Swenson holds small workshops on a private New England campus in a classroom so picturesque that the alumni magazine has selected it to be photographed with his class in it for its upcoming publication, no doubt for fundraising purposes. Swenson was once a New York City–based novelist, but he moved to eponymous Euston College in Euston, Vermont, for its ease, simplicity, and communal intimacy. His wife works at the college infirmary, and they attend campus-wide convocations together. Campus for them is more than a profession; it is a life structure, as colleagues and friends become a singular category, as professional problems become marital problems, and so on. Jonathan Franzen's *The Corrections*, while partially set on the same sort of private, paradigmatic campus, the unnamed "D—— College" in Connecticut, may be harder to characterize as a campus novel in toto. Yet the plot strand that follows critical theorist Chip Lambert narrates precisely—if compactly—the scope of the postmillennial campus novel. *The Ask*, the most adventurous of these texts, radically renarrates campus life in terms similar to what Jeffrey Williams has called the microgenre of "the adjunct novel." In Williams's telling, the new campus novel is narrated by those who never achieve professorial status.[19]

In *The Ask*, campus is limned by the world of "Toosh-Dev," or Institutional Development, and while other campus novels note the circulation of money as a continual mise-en-scène, *The Ask* takes as its setting the office charged with raising it.

Different as they are, *The Corrections*, *Blue Angel*, and *The Ask* cohere, and they do so as millennial campus texts. Much as one of the residual, signature moves of modernism is that of medial self-reflexivity, the campus novel considers not only the limits of prose and novelistic narrative form but also the limits of the university itself. These texts explore how campus is bounded ideologically and experientially. We may never have had a "classic campus novel," but in this newer issue of the genre there exists a rather consistent series of amended thematic concerns. The sexual politics of campus, for example, while always present, as David Lodge's *Nice Work* attests to, have here been updated and more importantly institutionalized. In each of these novels the protagonist is fired for sexual harassment or hate speech, both derivatives of the codes of what is understood pejoratively as "political correctness." In these novels, political correctness is figured as a set of institutional codes that govern the university, both formally through codification and informally though an environment of suspicion, anxiety, and inducement. The notion of professors sleeping with their underlings hardly marks a new plot development—remember the case of John Williams's *Stoner*—but being fired for doing so does indicate a historical shift.

Sometimes the protagonist's infraction against the codes of political correctness is the result of having been seduced by an ingenue, as in *Blue Angel*; sometimes it's the result of a hapless comment gone wrong, as in *The Ask*; and sometimes it is without a structurally sound plot provocation, as in *The Corrections*. Sexual harassment/hate speech as political correctness is important because it places the plot within the structures of campus governance and its associated tropes of regulation and compliance, of institutional histories and memories. And while American literature's fictional campuses have always been populated by petty incompetents and striving buffoons, on these contemporary campuses the lunatics are running the asylum, and the lunatics are women, gay men, and people of color—the *others*.[20] One of these novels' concerns with political correctness is that it regulates different campus populations differently. Political correctness might be redefined in these texts as the unsatisfactory compromise formation that results in the wake of the *others'* reactionary claim to power. The more minoritized the subject, the more latitude she has to disregard even the most basic institutional codes and still prosper: in *The Corrections*, Cali Lopez, the "Filipina lesbian" who lied about having a certain degree, gets promoted from assistant to full professor (and ultimately becomes provost); in *Blue Angel*, one of the witnesses before the campus sexual harassment board is a gay man who openly sleeps with his students with no recrimination; the cutthroat head of institutional development in *The Ask* is a black woman and "crack-baby" named Vargina, perhaps a less noteworthy name if this were a Thomas Pynchon novel, but it's not, and given this character's actions, *vagina dentata* seems the intended reference.

The consequence of their infractions against political correctness is that our protagonists are cast out of the humanities—we have a painter, a novelist, and a critical theorist. They are then forced to plot an unsuccessful return to the real world, otherwise known as the private sector. We are, oddly, not accustomed to thinking of private universities as participating in "the private sector," and these novels ironically and helpfully challenge that assumption. Millennial campus novels as a rule are set on private campuses, but what exactly is the difference between a public or private university and the private sector anyway? In this case, perhaps the most important difference is that a university has English and fine arts departments, a fact that is crucial to our protagonists and, I will suggest, is crucial to the mode of capital accumulation in which these texts are imbricated. No matter how supposedly "corporate" universities become, they do support pursuits such as belles lettres and fine arts, which, by definition, are not profit oriented within universities. A comparison to an actual "corporation" reveals the depth of the difference. Regardless of how many resources any corporation puts into the charitable funding of arts, culture, or even universities, it does so with the assumption that its recognized largesse will at some undefined point in the future become fungible.

Another difference between college and corporation that is important to these protagonists is the almost complete acceptance in academic conversation of talk about how fruitless, disorganized, morally bankrupt, and perhaps even obsolete one's own department, if not university, is. Freud included education on his tripartite list of "impossible professions" in which one may "be sure beforehand of achieving unsatisfying results," and for these characters that sentiment functions as a kind of ethos.[21] This latitude to understand and express the possibility of one's own or one's institution's failure not as a threat but as a necessity produces a certain freedom that provides some of the satiric content in these novels. Yet one needs to remain within the university to appreciate this situation; failure as a teacher or researcher will not necessarily lead to exile, but breaching the codes of "political correctness" will.

Indeed, these novels may be tentatively conceived of as satirical on the basis of their relationship to that tangled scene of institutional and economic transformation that they include under the rubric of political correctness. Political correctness encompasses a set of contradictory institutional arrangements that each of our protagonists initially supports. Chip coauthors the campus code of conduct at D—— College in hopes of bolstering the service portion of his pre-tenure vitae in *The Corrections*. *Blue Angel* begins with the foreshadowing scene of a campus-wide meeting that outlines for faculty the heightened vigilance Euston College will be assuming vis-à-vis professor/student interactions, a meeting convened by the eagerly named character, Dean Bentham. *The Ask* opens with a passage that attempts not to satirize but to ironize how one can support the knot of arrangements and discourses grouped under the "political correctness" rubric. As Milo sits at his turkey wrap wrapper–strewn desk in Institutional Development, this conversation transpires between Milo and his colleague, "the office temp," Horace. Horace begins:

> "We're the bitches of the First World."
>
> "Horace," I said. "That's a pretty sexist way to frame a discussion of America's decline, don't you think? Not to mention racist."
>
> "I didn't mention anybody's race," said Horace.
>
> "You didn't have to."
>
> "PC Robot" [said Horace].
>
> "Fascist Dupe" [returned Milo].[22]

Horace "didn't have to" mention the co-constitution and thus, necessarily, the co-articulation of nationality, gender, and race because this logic has been accepted and indeed is understood in these novels to structure institutional university culture. *Social Text*'s 1997 special issue, "Queer Transexions of Race, Nation, and Gender," was once radical, but now it has become clerical common knowledge and can be brought into office squabbles far away from the editorial desk.[23] It will be Horace, in fact, who has Milo dismissed for "hate speech." Horace and Milo, the office's straight white men, jokingly accuse each other of enforcing "PC" codes, but the larger irony is that within the plot structure of the novel, both the reader and Milo are unaware of the "hate speech" when it occurs. When Chip and Swenson, by contrast, sleep with their female undergraduates, both the reader and the protagonist know that disciplinary action will soon follow, and it does. In *The Ask*, the transgression itself is nondescript, and the reader and protagonist will not understand its import until later, when Vargina informs Milo of his termination.

The satirical object of these novels remains ambiguous—is it political correctness, the humanities, or the university itself?—because all three work together: political correctness, as we will see, is a humanities-based enterprise, and the humanities metonymize the university as such. My own understanding of conventional satire derives from Steven Weisenburger, and it maintains that satire is a comparatively conservative genre whose aim is to maintain rather than undermine sites of institutional power and coherence.[24] In mocking and exaggerating regulative norms, conventional satire insists on the flexibility of precisely such norms and thus marshals support for them. But exactly what norm is being satirized in these novels? Professors should not sleep with their students. That much we know. Yet what used to be accepted as a fringe benefit of male professorial life has become, under the rule of administrators like *Blue Angel*'s Dean Bentham, a site of disciplinary surveillance and punishment. Thus, Swenson is described early in the novel as "the only sucker at Euston who never slept with his students."[25] Yet it is unclear whether he's a sucker because he hasn't availed himself of the privilege or because he will soon do so.

Should he or shouldn't he? These novels attempt to satirize both the supposedly convent-like campus atmosphere that now prevails under the dictates of political correctness and the extracurricular libidinal desires of their protagonists. Thus, their route to arriving at that hoped-for criticism of political correctness relies on establishing characterological hypocrisy through the indexing of truth to individual sexuality. As Foucault would have predicted, this indexing constitutes the limit, even structural weakness, of each text. To say that one desires sexually what is forbidden is to say only what is tautological about the recursive structure of desire itself. Chip Lambert is described as "more in favor of queer theory than queer practice" during one sexual liaison with his student Melissa. "Yes, he was contradicting himself," the novel explains in another scene as he flips through a Sunday *Times* looking for lingerie advertisements instead of locating the book review. Ted Swenson cannot complete any sexual act with his student Angela, to say nothing of completing his novel. And Milo Burke's wife is having an affair with a gay man.

These novels offer a somewhat ambivalent critique, then. They do not make a demand for professorial access to the student body, in singular or as a demographic, nor do they accept that punishment by dismissal in the case of a trespass is justified. In that sense, political correctness constitutes the discursive limit and possibility of each text. A look through 1990s university print culture, from the now-folded *Lingua Franca* to the *Chronicle of Higher Education* and more popular news publications such as *Time* and the *New York Times*, explains why this would be the case. Such a history reveals that one of the central sites of translation from university-based humanities to the popular imaginary of them was indeed "political correctness." For example, one *New York Times* article, "The Rising Hegemony of the Politically Correct," included a description of political correctness as a form of "Stalinist orthodoxy" in which English students would be graded on "politics" not "literature."[26] This period also witnessed the initial circulation of Roger Kimball's idea of the "tenured radical" who uses her institutional safety to excoriate the institutional culture that provides her pulpit, a figure Franzen refers to in 1996 as an "academic Che Guevara" who "lectures on the patriarchal evil *du jour* while their TIAA-CREF accounts grow fat on Wall Street."[27]

These novels, then, employ political correctness as it was employed throughout the 1990s in journalism and academic print culture, as a kind of institutional narration of the humanities that also reveals changes in university structure. Nonetheless, the fact of the humanities is crucial. The science professor might be forced to implement affirmative action policies in staffing his lab, but the lab will still be regarded as legitimate. Conversely, the business professor might sleep with his undergraduate student, but his rational choice theory won't seem less plausible for his doing so. As it affects the content of intellectual production, political correctness is a drama private to the humanities. While the rest of the university writes patents and applies for grants, in these novels and in print culture, the humanities are now understood and narrated through the discourse of political correctness, a drama in which nothing of substance happens, but one that humanities departments and university administrators nonetheless devote much energy to managing.

Formally, this novelistic use of political correctness generates multiple plot provocations and resolutions, many based on a balance of individual versus institutional contradictions as they manifest in the white, male, heterosexual experience of the humanities. Can the colleague who teaches "Text Studies in Gender Warfare" be trusted? It is a class based on "the dominant male patriarchy sticking it to women, which I guess is kind of true," reports Swenson's informant on this particular colleague's pedagogy.[28] Does the fact that "the Woman's Student-Faculty Alliance" hasn't yet "camped out on Swenson's doorstep" mean that it won't? Do Chip's repeated critiques of "phallologocentrism" do anything for him? Milo is the one who advises Horace not to refer to America as a "bitch of the first world," and yet it is Milo himself who is fired for "hate speech." These novels ask us to question whether anyone actually believes in political correctness or whether it is simply a code of humanities-based careerism used to excise a certain constituency and ground the rise of others. Chip's assistant professor colleague at D—— College, Vendla O'Fallon, has just published a memoir whose title, *Daddy's Girl*, itself suggests some of these concerns. O'Fallon, as a woman, is in a better position than Chip to receive tenure in their textual artifacts department. And yet her book's title implies that she is firmly in the ideological grip of an older era. Meanwhile her name reveals similar problems: a "fallon" is a sexy woman, while a "vendla" is a wanderer. Perhaps she is a roving seductress, and if so, surely she cannot be tenured over Chip on a campus that ostensibly demands nonpatriarchal pedagogies, right? And yet it is the anxious fear that she will surpass him that sends Chip into the career-ending young arms of his student Melissa.

Finally, these novels use political correctness to insist that the proper place for the humanist is within the confines of the university, which I read as an argument that the humanities themselves belong in the university. These protagonists *may* falter within universities—after all, each was fired—but they will *certainly* falter outside of them. In much the same way, because the humanities have become so indulgent and absurd within the university, it is impossible for them to exist outside of it. Where else can one find an English department? Indeed, what were these humanities practitioners actually doing before their dalliances, in the case of Chip and Swenson, and before his off-color remark, in the case of Milo? Swenson led writing workshops in which undergraduates produced short story after short story of bestiality encounters. Chip's "Consuming Narratives" course was filled with students who were, by its end, in no way equipped to deconstruct how "socially conscious" advertising possesses the same capitalist logic as socially indifferent advertising, and he fails to turn his dissertation, "Doubtful It Stood: Anxieties of the Phallus in Tudor Drama," into a monograph. Milo was not particularly gifted at soliciting or managing donations—"asks" in the parlance of Toosh Dev—but he also wasn't successful as a student painter when he attended the same art school at which he now works as an administrator. Where else could these men work? They were doing little of value, as were their students, a population composed of, in Milo's words, "fat middle children in baseball caps who write derivative screenplays and charge around coffee shops."[29]

But then again, the freedom of the humanities comes from that freedom to engage in what is valueless, impractical, existential. Think of W. H. Auden's famous claim of his craft: "poetry does nothing." The humanities' lack of translatability from the ideal to the practical is definitional to the exercise of its faculties. Christopher Newfield notes that the longer tradition of humanistic inquiry is based on the nineteenth-century, Kantian-informed intention that it "[does] not claim to reveal a real beyond laws and contingencies or deny determination in ordinary life [but] instead offer[s] . . . the experience of oneself as free." He explains that in the humanities of the early university "the aesthetic functioned for many devotees as a principle of freedom, of free development, and free agency."[30] Its value was found in its valuelessness, its purpose found in its purposelessness.

Yet, if we know anything of capitalist cycles of accumulation, it is that capital metabolizes sites of uselessness into those of exchangeability. As the rise of finance changes the coordinates of the possibility of value capture within the nonprofit university, the purposelessness of the humanities, as we will now see, becomes newly purposeful.

Our protagonists do, if dimly, cognize these economic changes. They worry that their humanist careers, oriented as they are toward universities, are expiring. Their complaints about universities are dominated by two themes: (1) the pervasiveness of political correctness, which, as we have seen, is crucial to the setting, the plot, and the discourse of these novels; and (2) these protagonists are concerned about what appears to them as the "corporatization" of the university— the proliferation of brand names, the concern with fund-raising, the willingness to accommodate whichever student or donor promises more money. Whatever their own politically incorrect behavior, and they themselves don't make excuses, for these protagonists universities too engage in some troubling actions that, like their own, seemingly contradict their values. It's not just Chip and the sorry fate of his "Consuming Narratives" course that's of concern. As Milo's Toosh-Dev colleague Vargina explains while discussing a potential "ask" for the dance program from the wife of a "successful military caterer," "We can't wash the bad off anybody's money, now, can we? But we can make something good out of all the misery." Milo, in response, levels a critique: "Blood sausage, anyone?"[31] Euston College tries to offset its wealth of money with a wealth of diversity, the hoped-for effect of political correctness, but that doesn't work either. When Swenson's one African American student, Makeesha, speaks in their workshop of the failures of verisimilitude in another student's "ghetto"-based story, he notes to himself that she doesn't hail from an urban environment, but from Dartmouth, New Hampshire. For Swenson, political correctness produces a veneer of racial diversity, not a substance of economic equality.

Nonetheless, for all the criticism of the corporate culture of the university, we must return to the signal difference between the corporation and the university: the latter still do maintain and fund English and fine arts departments. And the protagonists cannot be critical of the fact that universities are still willing to employ people like them, authors of texts like the unpublishable "Doubtful It Stood," novelists who can't finish their novels, or painters-cum-fund-raisers who can't paint or raise funds. The fact that universities retain the humanities no matter how corporate they become is crucial to the campus novel, which is a humanities-based enterprise in more ways than one. As the genre of "the program era," the campus novel is a result of the professionalized, credentialized arts and humanities institutionalization that went hand in hand with the postwar expansion (1945–73) of universities. The campus novel is restructured into the faculty-based campus novel when universities incorporate writers into English departments. But as the postwar expansion inevitably fades and universities transform from sites of the production of skilled workers to sites of surplus-money absorption through debt encumbrance in a post-1970s era of finance, institutionalized literature turns against institutional literary and cultural studies. Within these novels, it is those same professionalized arts and humanities that employ our protagonists and that they now criticize.

The fictional universities of campus novels can use the discourse of political correctness to get rid of our protagonists, but they cannot get rid of the humanities in part because of the same corporatization about which these characters complain. These protagonists need their fictional universities as patrons of the humanities, but actual universities need the humanities to define themselves as nonprofit. In showing how little is done, how little value is contained, how expendable the humanities are, these novels show that the humanities remain valueless or purposeless and only suitable for a place not concerned with accumulation. Thus, their hosts, universities, are nonprofit institutions. As we saw in the first section and will now consider more fully in the next section, universities need their nonprofit status to accumulate and produce value in the manner they do. They must remain corporate, soon to be figured as financial, and nonprofit simultaneously, and the humanities provide that possibility through their perceived valuelessness. If the biggest remaining difference between a university and a corporation is that the former have English and fine arts departments, then the university needs to maintain the humanities no matter how hysterical or absurd they are perceived to be because the university needs to maintain itself.

Everything That Rises Must Converge: Debts, Dollars, and Development

Today, the dominant idiom for understanding the relationship between universities and the economy revolves around "privatization." Private universities are already private, of course, and public universities, under the strain of austerity management, are "becoming privatized."[32] Yet as a conceptual orientation, the public/private division of universities conflates more than it reveals. Public universities, as has been well documented, obtain much of their funding from private sources: the University of Michigan and the University of Virginia, for example, now receive under 8 percent of their funding from the state. Meanwhile, on a dollar-to-dollar, per-student basis, wealthy private universities receive more federal funds than public ones.[33] Harvard University, the nation's wealthiest nonprofit, receives the most federal support for its students. The more important distinction, then, is one of scale, and the term of measurement is money. Universities' revenue typically arrives through three major streams: (1) tuition; (2) return on endowment; and (3) research, which makes money through government grants and public–private partnerships, and development, which makes money through securing monopoly rents. In each case, universities' ability to sustain themselves and to grow economically depends on their state sponsorship through their nonprofit status. Thus the *New York Times* recently played on the phrase "going public" with a headline that claimed "Some Owners of Private Colleges Turn a Tidy Profit by Going Nonprofit."[34]

A nonprofit status offers a college or university a different set of profit-making opportunities than a for-profit status. The logic that undergirds this distinction has been explored by Dan Nemser and Brian Whitener, who argue that universities allow for "a cycle of wealth transfer that moves federal dollars directly into corporate and bank coffers."[35] That process does not constitute a historical novelty, of course. Rather, their claim of "circulation in the new university" highlights how universities' role in facilitating the basic structural project of any mode of capitalism—namely, the privatization of profit and the socialization of loss—has been transformed in a financial era. Nemser and Whitener argue that universities offer a site to absorb and stabilize the overproduction of money capital, itself traceable to the mid-1970s. "Banks, hedge funds, and institutional investors have begun investing heavily in and through universities, buying up construction and other bonds as well as student loans. . . . Some of the money that once was put into the faltering credit and mortgage markets has found a new home in the student loan and secondary student loan markets."[36] Indeed, for them, universities now constitute a recognizable and repeatable structure of accumulation. In this section, I want to trace briefly how a surplus of money circulates through the universities' three revenue streams, tuition, endowment return, and research and development, on its path from public to private. In each case, we may observe how the university functions as a site of value production unable to be replicated in a for-profit corporation. My point is qualitative, not quantitative, and it is one that will ground our return to the novels with a sense as to the economic specificity of the work they accomplish.

Tuition

No observer of universities has failed to notice that college tuition has risen faster than any other consumer good in the past forty years, far outpacing inflation, housing, health care, and so on. Unsurprisingly, tuition began its now-meteoric rise with the institution of government loans for students, in a manner similar to the rise of housing prices that followed the institution of the mortgage-interest tax deduction. The trajectory of nonprofit profit that may be traced through student loans is both structuring for and symptomatic of my argument. A many-headed hydra, in 1972 government-sponsored student loans were added to Pell Grants, a form of federal financial aid that did not need to be repaid. But when standout public education systems such as the California system and the City University of New York began to impose tuition on their once-free education, loans became available so working- and middle-class children could continue to afford college.[37] And when tuition then outpaced the amount and availability of government-sponsored loans, private lenders stepped in to fill the gap. In 1996 the Clinton administration instituted FFELP (Federal Family Education Loan Program), in which the federal government would back not only government-sponsored but also private student loans.[38] With ever more money available, universities knew that ever-rising tuition would be paid, and with government guarantees virtually eliminating risk, lenders knew that student loans constituted a safe, steady return on investment.

The importance of steadily rising tuition goes beyond a profit/loss calculus, however. Student loans do double duty: First, they both function as a safe asset and help to produce liquidity, and it is liquidity that enables the myriad transactions of which financialization is composed. Meister explains this cycle with US Treasuries generally: "the Fed must create enough debt to satisfy the demand of global financial markets for safe assets while controlling inflation through limits on public spending."[39] In other words, in producing safe assets, the university perversely assists the structure of financialization, which then demands austerity, and it is austerity that requires student loans in the first place. Second, rising tuition offers a site for the university to exercise its pro bono credentials: it will discount its tuition for those who need it through financial aid. Thus, "giving away" parts of this now-inflated tuition, the university doubles down to assure its status as a nonprofit charity. For the public good, it "gives away" millions of dollars a year in tuition credits to students through financial aid, an action befitting a charity. The liberal arts add a further credential to this disposition: students are willing to undertake debt for a liberal arts education that will give them no marketable skills. The professors, too, are there "not for the money"—workers with their level of education could obviously make more, as lawyers, medical doctors, business people, and so on.

Endowment

I mention endowment here only because it has become a popular trope through which to debate how profitable a nonprofit institution can or should be. For any particular institution, the nonprofit designation makes returns made off the endowment tax-free: the bigger the endowment, the grander the subsidy. Thus, it is schools such as Harvard, Yale, and Princeton that now have begun a conversation about whether universities' nonprofit status should be terminated. The *American Conservative*, in its article "Paying Tuition to a Giant Hedge Fund," claims that Harvard's "great scholars and teachers receive aggregate total pay of around $85 million. But in fiscal 2004, just the five top managers of the Harvard endowment fund shared total compensation of $78 million, an amount which was also roughly 100 times the salary of Harvard's own president." The magazine goes on to claim that these figures "demonstrate the relative importance accorded to the financial and academic sides of Harvard's activities."[40] Such articles point out that Harvard's state of financial affairs would not be a problem were it not, along with other wealthy universities, given tax exemptions and thus government sponsorship that comes with their nonprofit status. Nonetheless, while a popular trope, investment return from endowment applies only to a relatively small number of schools.

Research and Development

The year 1980 is when something called "political correctness" begins to circulate in print culture; it is also the year of the Bayh–Dole Act, which initiated a legal structure that specifically provides for the privatization via patent of publically funded, university-based research.[41] Bayh–Dole will transform the university as a whole, but its local possibilities will resonate most strongly in the sciences, where patents are pursued. Indeed, when commentators like Rodrigo Alves Teixeira and Tomas Nielsen Rotta suggest that financialization should be understood as the search for monopoly rents, they have in mind patents as an example par excellence.[42] But while Bayh–Dole initiates a structure of the private capture of wealth at nonprofit universities, the extent of patent-based profit must not be overstated. Most patents will never make money, and most research grants will cost the university more money than they will generate because the university must provide "matching costs." To Chris Newfield's claim that the humanities do the work of making universities profitable, we can now add: the humanities also do the rhetorical work of rendering universities nonprofit.

What the sciences and engineering can do is produce "basic scientific research." This nonprofit and nonpatentable research transpires in universities through federal government sponsorship. Such research is needed for patentable, profitable work, but any for-profit body would have little interest in undertaking it. Not only do universities undertake such "basic" research, but their nonprofit status also enables them to flaunt industry standards, and in some cases minimum wage, in their payment to researchers. In the sciences, Newfield estimates that universities pay ten cents on the dollar for scientific labor in the form of graduate student work.[43]

We also must include college sports under the research and development rubric, since they too function under the sign of monopoly rents. Their umbrella organization, the nonprofit National Collegiate Athletic Association (NCAA), provides a particularly clear depiction of this structure, and it may also be seen as a metonym for the larger labor politics and economic policies of the university.[44] The state supplies the sporting infrastructure; the players play for free; merchandise is sold; television contracts are signed: impressive revenues are generated through monopoly rents. Indeed, the nonprofit designation exemplifies precisely Panitch and Konings' understanding of "neoliberalism" as state delimitation of and support for a market dedicated to private extraction and appropriation.[45]

The university, then, is a market, a spatially and temporally delimited site of value capture that has its nonprofit status as both its regulatory device and its regulative idea. We now seem far afield, however, from political correctness, the campus novel, or the humanities themselves. It is true that in industry and foundation reports such as "Finances of Public Research Universities" and "Diminishing Funding, Rising Expectations," the humanities are hardly mentioned.[46] Yet, like the strange ontology of Edgar Allan Poe's purloined letter, they are a visible and structuring presence in the university as it navigates its nonprofit yet profitable structure, as it veers ever closer to its institutional double: the for-profit corporation. And, in our current moment, let me suggest that it is the humanities that stand between universities and the fate that befell health insurance companies in the 1970s, when courts ruled that nonprofit and for-profit concerns could not be clearly differentiated in terms of mission, which caused health insurance companies to lose many of the tax breaks associated with their nonprofit status.[47]

But for now, productions like the campus novel both constitute and represent this ongoing process of differentiation between the corporation, whose goal is money for its shareholders, and the nonprofit, whose goal is social betterment not indexed to money returned back to the institution. This division reveals the long inheritance of capital and its converse, the aesthetic. Indeed, as many a critic has noted, the rise of capitalist teleology coincides with the rise of the aesthetic itself.[48] When everything becomes directed toward the teleological end of profit, the aesthetic emerges as a nonteleological category. It is "final without end" in Kant's famous words. While capital seeks to generate profit without limit, the aesthetic provides "a finite experience of the infinite," again from Kant.[49] Education as commodity and education as noncommodity is one of the most faithful inheritors of this, modernity's most fundamental contradiction: what is most valued from a capitalist vantage point, making money, is also what is most devalued. And what is most devalued, making money, is also what is most valued.

It's not that this contradiction is particularly apparent in the humanities; rather, it's that the humanities are the result of this contradiction and they have as their twenty-first-century framing device the nonprofit university. On the one hand, universities must defund the humanities in order to render themselves corporate, qualitative, and ends-oriented places, and "political correctness" is part of that strategy. Newfield excoriates the leftist commentators who claim that culture is a distraction from economics by claiming that "the cultural wars were economic wars."[50] This attack on the humanities through their proliferation into cultural and ethnic studies is what the new circulation of capital demands, and this is what our protagonists in these campus novels complain about. When Vargina prophesies that "this whole game is poised for a gargantuan fall," she is quite correct in her assessment, at least at the level of affect. Who working in the humanities hasn't shared her concern?

Yet universities must and will maintain the humanities in order to render universities themselves fundamentally different from their corporate peers; in order to be nonprofit, they must be, in Kant's words, nonpurposive, and the humanities provide this. Perhaps, then, the "gargantuan fall" remains true to its etymology: even if one falls precipitously, one remains in the humanistic world, in this case that of Rabelais. And it is here that we may return to the question of the generic form of these campus novels and the work that such form accomplishes in the financial or neoliberal university.

McGurl's point is this: put writers in a university, and not only will they repeat to students the mantra "write what you know," but they will in fact live by that mantra themselves. They will write what they know.[51] That is, they will write what it is like to teach students to write what one knows—the basic conceit of the faculty-centered campus novel, whether or not the protagonist is a "writer." In this increasingly self-referential loop, these novels and their authors sustain an institutional discourse about the humanities through a literary form that derives from and critiques the humanities' codification and professionalization in the university. By using the theme of political correctness to represent the humanities as still yet newly purposeless, these novels testify to the valueless foundation that defines the university, gives it its nonprofit status, and allows it to become the profitable institution we now know it to be.

It did not "have to be" the discourse of political correctness that accompanied this new organization of accumulation. Capitalism does not demand this or that reactionary ideology. However, for this accumulation to be university based, its discourse had to be purposeless in order to sustain a conception of valuelessness. Yet political correctness does not simply coincide with the financialization of the university in these novels; it both historicizes a change in university funding and population and challenges whether these novels should be read as satirical. By suggesting not only that the humanities are useless but also that *the others* are in control, these novels continue a discourse of post-1970s conservative retrenchment that has enabled public universities to be defunded and partly privatized while private universities are, in part, publically funded.[52]

Newfield offers this history. Throughout the 1960s and 1970s, as universities were opened up to larger segments of the population through federal subsidies such as Pell Grants and the GI Bill, conservatives began to seek some form of economic realignment as a way to limit higher education. The "Culture Wars" offered a way to use universities' new minority subjects and their disciplines— Latino studies, experimental art, women's studies, queer studies, ethnic studies— to defund the university by claiming that such research was no longer generally humanist, but politically particular.[53] That defunding went through the humanities, targeting women, queers, people of color, and working-class students and scholars, their academic and artistic work, and their ability to thrive in a university setting.

That story we may already know. I am interested in how its rhetorical effects continue to reverberate in a manner that both diminishes and obfuscates the humanities' role in the university. Once so defunded, university-based sciences can, in theory, make up the difference from private sources. The gutting of funding was coincident with the Bayh–Dole Act for a reason. But the humanities will not be able to make up the difference through patents, through research, or through development.[54] If this inference seems sensible—What company wants to form a public–private partnership with the Victorianists? How will the modernists ever help garner a patent?—then we must pause to remember that the humanities enable research and development to proceed, not the reverse. This process, whereby it seems as though the humanities will be the ones to take the fall, is why McGurl says university writing programs are "custodians of the obsolete." "It is easier to see creative writing as one of the forms of obsolescence conserved by the university than as part of its R&D wing," he explains.[55] But it is here that we may also disagree with McGurl and return to the campus novel as the genre of "the program era" that he has so insightfully delimited. These novels, as well as the humanities, stabilize and make possible the university's research and development.

But we must also modify our reading of these novels as satirical in the context of Newfield's history. For Newfield, the culture wars provided the ideological justification necessary to begin "unmaking the public university." What I have read as political correctness is a white, upper-middle-class social retrenchment that arrives via the humanities: it begins by attacking, for example, Latino studies, and then restructures the political economy of the university. In the novels, by contrast, the humanities use this restructuring as a moment to reshuffle themselves in a manner that benefits minority subjects and confers on them institutional power. Thus, these novels have been read as satirical: who knew how ridiculous the humanities really were? Bestiality! Consuming Narratives! Kinetic sculpture! In fact, these novels must be read as reactionary. As has been repeatedly proven, the university still hires, promotes, and tenures predominantly white men.[56] In the novels, minorities can do no wrong, and white men can do no right. Milo ends up unwed and unemployed. Chip fairs slightly better with a wife, twins, and a job as a high school teacher. And Swenson is left to await a new profession, and possibly a new spouse. But satire as a mode presumes equality or better between its origin and its object, and usually the satirical object occupies in actuality a position of power. One cannot satirize from a position of greater to lesser power. As with their wedding of social contradiction to sexual hypocrisy, their choice of satirical object is a structural weakness of these novels. They tend more toward mockery. In the campus novel of yore, white male academics could attack, betray, supplant, seduce, and disorganize each other's careers and mistresses in the name of satire. In the contemporary campus novel, this tradition is threatened by a kind of derision and hatred of the *others'* perceived rise.

The Humanist Fix: Locating Accumulation in the Humanities

We can now trace a certain chain of contingent events and aesthetic forms that accompany them, each updated for its age. As the university expands in the postwar era, it professionalizes and codifies the arts and literary humanities, what McGurl calls "the program era." Novelists, now university based, write what they know, and the campus novel is reborn. With federal dollars, with civil rights demands and immigrant-based momentum, the university expands in both discipline and population throughout the 1960s. And yet already, by the mid-1970s, the expansion is threatened with the first stirrings of financialization. Think of the old Marxist notion of the tendency of the rate of profit to fall: all expansions must eventually become contractions. The university both benefits from and is compromised by this new constriction. It becomes newly available for a certain kind of profit and the production of safe assets, but only on the condition that it remains a nonprofit body.

These novels are both the result and the symptom of the process of circulation in the financial or neoliberal university. Universities will fund and maintain humanities departments, but only under the seemingly constant threat that they will not be able to do so much longer since they are now under the dictates of finance capital's austerity. But that can be subsumed under Marx's tendential law too: the end will never come for the humanities, but the end is always near. Humanities departments absorb and recycle a purposelessness that, against Kant, now has a purpose—to David Harvey's "spatial fix" that capital seeks in the built environment we can now add a "humanist fix" that it seeks in the university.[57] Thus, the discourse of disparaging the humanities is the discourse that helps to sustain them institutionally. In placing the humanities on an ongoing precipice, these novels contribute to a certain idea of the university that does differentiate it from a corporate structure. What the humanities give the university, then, is similar to the process of phantasmatic reciprocity that, as Lauren Berlant reminds us, Lacan claims constitutes the exchange of love.[58] Lacan says that love is "giving what you don't have to someone who doesn't want it." What the humanities have to give is precisely this "not having"; they offer a kind of nondirectional reason that is understood as purposeless and valueless. That becomes the basis for them to give another gift: they absorb and recycle the charge of their own futility as an institutional discourse. And that is ultimately what these novels are about. But it is also what these novels *are*. The publishing and circulation of the campus novel must be taken as evidence of and infrastructure for the new circulation of capital in universities: the campus novel does more than represent or generically delimit this new university form; it *is* the self-reflexive issue of this style of nonprofit accumulation. Not only do the humanities make money, but they quite profitably sustain the discourse of losing it.

NOTES

The genesis of this paper was a series of conversations with philosopher of science and aesthetics Dehlia Hannah. Two colleagues subsequently read this article and gave generative and generous comments that substantially helped me with revisions: I thank Ted

Martin and Ulrich Plass. Mark McGurl graciously helped me to understand better the substance and novelty of his, and my, arguments.

1. Sam Lipsyte, *The Ask* (New York: Picador, 2010), 136.

2. Don DeLillo, *White Noise* (New York: Penguin, 1984), 18.

3. For a map of this nascent field, see Jeffrey Williams, "Deconstructing Academe: The Birth of Critical University Studies," *Chronicle*, February 19, 2012, http://chronicle.com /article/An-Emerging-Field-Deconstructs/130791/.

4. Mark McGurl, *The Program Era: Postwar Fiction and the Rise of Creative Writing* (Cambridge, MA: Harvard University Press, 2009).

5. One could make a similar argument, I think, with fine arts using Howard Singerman's *Art Subjects* (Berkeley: University of California Press, 1999), which tracks the incorporation of the fine arts into the university and the institutional modes of art production that result, namely, institutional critique.

6. Jonathan Franzen, *The Corrections* (New York: Farrar, Strauss & Giroux, 2001); Francine Prose, *Blue Angel* (New York: Penguin, 2000).

7. Here begins my departure from McGurl's conception of the circulation of value within the university as engaged by the novel form. He borrows from Dean MacCannell's idea of an "experience economy," to locate creative writing as possessing a kind of value not reducible to labor time (McGurl, *Program Era*, 14). I will suggest that we do not need to engage the labor theory of value here.

8. For more on the rise of for-profit education as a logical result of changes in state funding to nonprofit education, see Robert Meister, "Debt and Taxes: Can the Financial Industry Save Public Universities?," *Representations* 116, no. 1 (2011): 128–55.

9. See Henry Hansmann, "Why Do Universities Have Endowments?," *Journal of Legal Studies* 19, no. 1 (1990): 3–42. Hansmann argues that universities' nonprofit status tempts wealthier universities to not "spend down" their endowments as long as the rate of return on the endowment is higher than the not easily compared rate of return on giving it away.

10. For a brief overview, see "An Education in Finance," *Economist*, May 18, 2006, www .economist.com/node/6958688. Note the particular dating, coincident with these novels: "Lehman Brothers reckons that the overall market for higher-education debt has tripled since 2000, to $33 billion, and there are abundant reasons besides the recent trend to believe that the market will grow much bigger yet."

11. See Dick Bryan and Michael Rafferty, *Capitalism with Derivatives* (London: Palgrave, 2005), on the rise of options pricing and a suggestion of how derivatives modify and complement age-old structural features of capitalism.

12. By *neoliberal* I also mean state intervention in the delimiting of certain markets to allow for the private capture of public money. Here I follow the crucial intervention in Leo Panitch and Martijn Konings, "Myths of Neoliberal Deregulation," *New Left Review* 57 (2009): 67–83, which claims, and it is worth stressing, that neoliberalism requires substantial intervention and regulation.

13. See Robert Meister, "They Pledged Your Tuition," http://cucfa.org/news/2009 _oct11.php.

14. Chris Newfield has argued this tirelessly for years: "It appears that the humanities and social sciences are major donors to science and engineering budgets, while being told that they are actually living off those budgets. . . . Science and engineering cost money and the humanities and social science teaching subsidize it." See Christopher Newfield, *Unmak-

ing the Public University: The Forty-Year Assault on the Middle Class (Cambridge, MA: Harvard University Press, 2008), 217.

15. See my "Fiction Is Liquid: States of Money in *The Sopranos* and *Breaking Bad*," *Journal of American Studies* 49, no. 4 (2015): 755–74.

16. *Valueless* and *purposeless* are similar terms in this archive, and, as in capitalism, purpose is equated with value. I will alternate between them, however, and when discussing texts and aesthetics I use *purposeless*; to make a claim on how that purposelessness reverberates in a wider social field, I use *valueless*.

17. This increase of funds for universities transpired through the National Defense Education Act of 1958. See the congressional reporting of that act at www.senate.gov/art andhistory/history/minute/Sputnik_Spurs_Passage_of_National_Defense_Education _Act.htm.

18. See Elaine Showalter, *Faculty Towers: The Campus Novel and Its Discontents* (Philadelphia: University of Pennsylvania Press, 2009).

19. See Jeffrey Williams, "Unlucky Jim: The Rise of the Adjunct Novel," *Chronicle*, November 12, 2012, http://chronicle.com/article/Unlucky-Jim-the-Rise-of-the/135606/.

20. I look at American campus novels, but of course England has its own fine tradition as seen in writers including Kingsley Amis and David Lodge; more recently, Zadie Smith has produced a transatlantic campus novel of sorts in her 2005 *On Beauty*, which also thematizes the culture wars and political correctness.

21. Sigmund Freud, in "Analysis Terminable and Interminable," claims that the other two impossible professions are psychoanalysis and government. Quoted in Janet Malcolm, *Psychoanalysis: The Impossible Profession* (New York: Knopf, 1981), front matter.

22. Lipsyte, *Ask*, 3.

23. Anne McClintock, Phillip Brian Harper, Jose Esteban Munoz, and Trish Rosen, eds., "Queer Transexions of Race, Nation, and Gender," special issue, *Social Text* 52/53 (1997).

24. Steven Weisenburger, *Fables of Subversion: Satire and the American Novel* (Athens: University of Georgia Press, 1995). Weisenburger helpfully distinguishes between conventional (think Jonathan Swift) and "degenerative" (more radical; think Pynchon's *Gravity's Rainbow*) satirical organizations.

25. Prose, *Blue Angel*, 77.

26. Richard Bernstein, "The Rising Hegemony of the Politically Correct," *New York Times*, October 20, 1990, www.nytimes.com/1990/10/28/weekinreview/ideas-trends-the -rising-hegemony-of-the-politically-correct.html.

27. See Roger Kimball, *Tenured Radicals: How Politics Has Corrupted Our Higher Education* (New York: Harper & Row, 1990); see also Jonathan Franzen, "Perchance to Dream: In the Age of Images, A Reason to Write Novels," *Harper's*, April 1996, 47.

28. Prose, *Blue Angel*, 35.

29. Lipsyte, *Ask*, 128.

30. See Christopher Newfield, *Ivy and Industry* (Durham, NC: Duke University Press, 2004), 66–69, although the entire third chapter, "The Humanist Outcry," is of great interest.

31. Lipsyte, *Ask*, 22.

32. See, e.g., Thomas Mortenson, "State Funding: A Race to the Bottom," *American Council on Education*, Winter 2012, www.acenet.edu/the-presidency/columns-and-features/Pages /state-funding-a-race-to-the-bottom.aspx. Mortenson reports, "Despite steadily growing student demand for higher education since the mid-1970s, state fiscal investment in higher

education has been in retreat in the states since about 1980. . . . The 2011 funding effort was down by 40.2 percent compared with fiscal 1980."

33. "10 Universities That Receive the Most Government Money: 24/7 Wall St.," *Huffington Post*, April 27, 2013, www.huffingtonpost.com/2013/04/27/universities-government -money_n_3165186.html.

34. See Patricia Cohen, "Some Owners of Private Colleges Turn a Tidy Profit by Going Nonprofit," *New York Times*, March 2, 2015, www.nytimes.com/2015/03/03/business/some -private-colleges-turn-a-tidy-profit-by-going-nonprofit.html?_r=0.

35. Dan Nemser and Brian Whitener, "Circulation and the New University," *Reclamations Blog*, June 8, 2012, www.reclamationsjournal.org/blog/?p=596.

36. Ibid.

37. For the California case, see Meister, "Debt and Taxes"; for the New York case, see William K. Tabb, *The Long Default* (New York: Monthly Review, 1984).

38. The program was ended in 2010 after the discovery of what Nemser and Whitener describe as "rampant fraud" ("Circulation and the New University").

39. Robert Meister, "Liquidity," conference paper at the University of Sydney, November 2013, cited with permission and forthcoming as a book from the University of Chicago Press.

40. Ron Unz, "Paying Tuition to a Giant Hedge Fund," *American Conservative*, December 4, 2012, www.theamericanconservative.com/articles/paying-tuition-to-a-giant-hedge -fund/.

41. "Bayh–Dole Act," *Wikipedia*, https://en.wikipedia.org/wiki/Bayh%E2%80%93Dole _Act.

42. For monopoly rents, see Rodrigo Alves Teixeira and Tomas Nielsen Rotta, "Valueless Knowledge-Commodities and Financialization: Productive and Financial Dimensions of Capital Autonomization," *Review of Radical Political Economics* 44 (2012): 448. For financialization as a mode of accumulation, see Greta R. Krippner, "The Financialization of the American Economy," *Socio-Economic Review* 3, no. 2 (May 2005): 173–208.

43. Newfield, *Unmaking the Public University*, 221.

44. Dave Zirin has done wonderful reporting about the NCAA both in his *Edge of Sports* radio show and in his regular contributions to the *Nation*.

45. Panitch and Konings, "Myths of Neoliberal Deregulation."

46. Council of Governmental Relations, *Finances of Research Universities* (Council of Governmental Relations, 2014), http://cogr.edu/COGR/files/ccLibraryFiles/Filename /000000000267/Finances%20of%20Research%20Universities_June%202014.pdf; National Science Foundation, *Diminishing Funding and Rising Expectations: Trends and Challenges for Public Research Universities* (National Science Foundation, 2012), www.nsf.gov/nsb/publi cations/2012/nsb1245.pdf.

47. See Hansmann, "Why Do Universities Have Endowments?": "The hospital industry is already further along down that path than is higher education, and there has been increasing pressure in recent years to eliminate tax exemptions for nonprofit hospitals— just as it was eliminated 25 years ago for nonprofit health-insurance companies—on the grounds that the services offered by nonprofit hospitals are not meaningfully different from those offered by for-profit hospitals" (11).

48. See Terry Eagleton, *The Ideology of the Aesthetic* (London: Blackwell, 1979).

49. The full text from Kant: "Pleasure in aesthetic judgement . . . is merely contempla-

tive. . . . The very consciousness of a merely formal purposiveness in the play of the subject's cognitive powers, accompanying a presentation by which an object is given, is that pleasure. For this consciousness in an aesthetic judgement contains a basis for determining the subject's activity regarding the quickening of his cognitive powers, and hence an inner causality (which is purposive) concerning cognition in general, which however is not restricted to a determinate cognition. Hence it contains a mere form of the subjective purposiveness of a presentation." Immanuel Kant, *Critique of Judgment*, trans. Werner S. Pluhar (Indianapolis: Hackett, 1987), 68.

50. Newfield, *Unmaking the Public University*, 6.

51. McGurl labels this "autopoesis" and connects it to Anthony Giddens and Ulrich Beck's concept of "reflexive accumulation" (*Program Era*, 12). But all accumulation in capital is reflexive; this term could be better scaled to the value production found in these novels and enjoined to the university form.

52. Newfield, *Unmaking the Public University*, 218.

53. This is a long and well-known history, and I won't rehearse it here. But see, e.g., the US Intellectual History blog maintained by American intellectual historian Andrew Hartman for an excellent emerging historiography: http://s-usih.org/2013/01/an-emerging -historiography-of-the-culture-wars.html.

54. Again, Newfield is key: these huge federal grants *cost* the university more than they offer, another widely misunderstood phenomenon. See all of chap. 12, "The Failure of Market Measures," in *Unmaking the Public University*.

55. McGurl, *Program Era*, 22.

56. According to various university websites, the ratio of male to female tenured faculty is about 3:1 at Research I universities.

57. David Harvey, *The Limits to Capital* (New York: Verso, 1982).

58. Lauren Berlant, *The Female Complaint* (Durham, NC: Duke University Press, 2008), 8.

MITCHUM HUEHLS is an associate professor of English at the University of California, Los Angeles. He is the author of *Qualified Hope: A Postmodern Politics of Time* (Ohio State University Press, 2007) and *After Critique: Twenty-First-Century Fiction in a Neoliberal Age* (Oxford University Press, 2016).

RACHEL GREENWALD SMITH is an associate professor of English at Saint Louis University. She is the author of *Affect and American Literature in the Age of Neoliberalism* (Cambridge University Press, 2015) and editor of *American Literature in Transition: 2000–2010*, forthcoming from Cambridge University Press.

JENNIFER ASHTON is an associate professor of English at the University of Illinois at Chicago. She is the author of *From Modernism to Postmodernism: American Poetry in the Twentieth Century* (Cambridge University Press, 2008) and the editor of *The Cambridge Companion to American Poetry since 1945* (Cambridge University Press, 2014). She is a founding board member of the online arts and political journal *nonsite.org*.

JASON M. BASKIN is an assistant professor of English at the University of Wyoming. His book *Embodying Experience: Modernism beyond the Avant-Garde* is forthcoming from Cambridge University Press. His writing has appeared in *Cultural Critique, Postmodern Culture, Mediations: Journal of the Marxist Literary Group,* and the volume *Understanding Merleau-Ponty, Understanding Modernism* (Bloomsbury, 2017).

SARAH BROUILLETTE is a professor in the Department of English at Carleton University. She is the author of *Postcolonial Writers in the Global Literary Marketplace* (Palgrave Macmillan, 2007) and *Literature and the Creative Economy* (Stanford University Press, 2014).

JANE ELLIOTT is a senior lecturer in English at King's College London. She is the author of *Popular Fiction as American Allegory: Representing National Time* (Palgrave Macmillan, 2008) and coeditor of "Genres of Neoliberalism," a special issue of *Social Text* (2013), and *Theory after 'Theory'* (Routledge, 2011). Her book *The Microeconomic Mode: Reimagining Political Subjectivity in the 21st Century* is forthcoming from Columbia University Press.

MARCIAL GONZÁLEZ is an associate professor of English at the University of California, Berkeley. He is the author of *Chicano Novels and the Politics of Form: Race, Class, and Reification* (University of Michigan Press, 2009).

SHERI-MARIE HARRISON is an associate professor of English at the University of Missouri–Columbia. She is the author of *Jamaica's Difficult Subjects: Negotiating Sovereignty in Anglophone Caribbean Literature and Criticism* (Ohio State University Press, 2014).

ANDREW HOBEREK is a professor of English at the University of Missouri–Columbia. He is the author of *The Twilight of the Middle Class: Post–World War II American Fiction and White-Collar Work* (Princeton University Press, 2005) and *Considering Watchmen: Poetics, Property, Politics* (Rutgers University Press, 2014).

CAREN IRR is a professor of English at Brandeis University. She is the author, most recently, of *Toward the Geopolitical Novel: U.S. Fiction in the 21st Century* (Columbia University Press, 2013), and she has published and coedited four other volumes as well as more than thirty articles and book chapters on social theory and contemporary American literature and culture.

LEIGH CLAIRE LA BERGE is an assistant professor of English at Borough of Manhattan Community College and a Faculty Fellow at the Grad Center, both at the City University of New York. She is the author of *Scandals and Abstraction: Financial Fiction of the Long 1980s* (Oxford University Press, 2015) and the coeditor of *Reading Capitalist Realism* (University of Iowa Press, 2014).

WALTER BENN MICHAELS is a professor of English at the University of Illinois at Chicago. His recent publications include *The Shape of the Signifier* (Princeton University Press, 2004), *The Trouble with Diversity* (Metropolitan, 2006), and *The Beauty of a Social Problem* (University of Chicago Press, 2015).

JEFFREY T. NEALON is the Edwin Erle Sparks Professor of English and Philosophy at Penn State University. His most recent books are *Foucault beyond Foucault: Power and Its Intensifications since 1984* (Stanford University Press, 2008), *Post-postmodernism; or, The Cultural Logic of Just-in-Time*

Capitalism (Stanford University Press, 2012), and *Plant Theory: Biopower and Vegetable Life* (Stanford University Press, 2016).

MATHIAS NILGES is an associate professor of English at St. Francis Xavier University, Canada. His essays have appeared in collected editions and journals such as *Callaloo, American Literary History,* and *Textual Practice.* He is the coeditor of *Literary Materialisms* (Palgrave Macmillan, 2013), *Marxism and the Critique of Value* (MCM', 2014), and *The Contemporaneity of Modernism* (Routledge, 2016).

MIN HYOUNG SONG is a professor of English at Boston College. He is the author of *Strange Future: Pessimism and the 1992 Los Angeles Riots* (Duke University Press, 2005) and *The Children of 1965: On Writing, and Not Writing, as an Asian American* (Duke University Press, 2013).

MICHAEL SZALAY is a professor of English at the University of California, Irvine, where he directs the Culture, Law, and Capital Center and chairs the English department. He is the author of *New Deal Modernism: American Literature and the Invention of the Welfare State* (Duke University Press, 2000) and *Hip Figures: A Literary History of the Democratic Party* (Stanford University Press, 2012).

MATTHEW WILKENS is an assistant professor of English and concurrent assistant professor of American Studies at the University of Notre Dame. He is the author of *Revolution: The Event in Postwar Fiction* (Johns Hopkins University Press, 2016).

DANIEL WORDEN teaches in the School of Individualized Study at the Rochester Institute of Technology. He is the author of the award-winning book *Masculine Style: The American West and Literary Modernism* (Palgrave Macmillan, 2011), the coeditor of *Oil Culture* (University of Minnesota Press, 2014) and *Postmodern/Postwar—and After* (University of Iowa Press, 2016), and the editor of *The Comics of Joe Sacco: Journalism in a Visual World* (University Press of Mississippi, 2015).